Constanza Cordoni
Seder Eliyahu

Studia Judaica

―

Forschungen zur Wissenschaft des Judentums

Begründet von
Ernst Ludwig Ehrlich

Herausgegeben von
Günter Stemberger, Charlotte Fonrobert,
Alexander Samely und Irene Zwiep

Band 100

Constanza Cordoni
Seder Eliyahu

A Narratological Reading

DE GRUYTER

ISBN 978-3-11-071047-2
e-ISBN (PDF) 978-3-11-053187-9
e-ISBN (EPUB) 978-3-11-053130-5
ISSN 0585-5306

Library of Congress Control Number: 2018941307

Bibliografic information published by the Deutsche Nationalbibliothek
The Deutsche Nationalbibliothek lists this publication in the Deutsche Nationalbibliografie;
detailed bibliografic data are available on the Internet at http://dnb.dnb.de.

© 2020 Walter de Gruyter GmbH, Berlin/Boston
This volume is text- and page-identical with the hardback published in 2018.
Printing and binding: CPI books GmbH, Leck

www.degruyter.com

Para Joseph – mi pequeño emperador

Contents

Preface —— XI

Abbreviations of Ancient Sources —— XIII

1	**Introduction —— 1**	
1.1	*Seder Eliyahu* and Scholarship —— 1	
1.1.1	What Is *Seder Eliyahu*? —— 1	
1.1.2	Textual Transmission —— 4	
1.1.3	The Problem of Dating and Locating *Seder Eliyahu* —— 7	
1.1.4	Language, Hermeneutics, Topical Agenda, Narrativity, and Medievality —— 15	
1.2	Narratological Readings of *Seder Eliyahu* —— 22	
2	**The Voices of *Seder Eliyahu* —— 27**	
2.1	The Title —— 29	
2.1.1	Paratext 1: bKet 105b–106a —— 29	
2.1.2	Paratext 2: Codex Vat. ebr. 31. —— 31	
2.1.3	Paratext 3: Talmudic Passages —— 32	
2.2	The "Metaleptic" Governing Voice —— 33	
2.3	The Biblical Character of Elijah in *Seder Eliyahu* —— 43	
2.4	Abba Eliyahu, Elijah, Anonymous I —— 49	
2.4.1	Appendix 1: Talmud Passages Introduced with the Formula *tanna debe eliyahu* —— 55	
2.4.2	Appendix 2: Passages in *Seder Eliyahu Zuta* Introduced with the Formula *meshum debe eliyahu hanavi amru* —— 58	
3	**A Typology of Narrative Forms of *Seder Eliyahu* —— 60**	
3.1	Non-narrative Texts —— 63	
3.1.1	Reports of Single Events —— 67	
3.1.2	Speech Acts, Mishnah Quotations, and *mikan amru* Statements —— 69	
3.2	Narrative in *Seder Eliyahu*: Preliminary Considerations —— 72	
3.3	Simple Forms —— 78	
3.3.1	Narrative *Meshalim* —— 78	
3.3.2	*Ma'asim* —— 88	
3.3.3	Pseudo-historical Narratives —— 93	
3.4	Composite Forms —— 95	

3.4.1	Homiletical-exegetical Narratives —— 95	
3.4.2	First-Person Narratives —— 117	
3.5	Conclusions: Homiletical Narration —— 126	

4 Parabolical Passages on the Disciples of the Wise —— 131
- 4.1 Preliminary Considerations —— 131
- 4.2 The Exegetical *Mashal*'s New Clothes —— 135
- 4.3 Narrative-Recapitulative Parables —— 146
- 4.4 Meta-Exegetical Parables —— 155
- 4.5 Rhetorical Questions and the Parables That (Do Not Always) Answer Them —— 164
- 4.6 Concluding Remarks —— 171

5 Men with Scripture but No Mishnah —— 175
- 5.1 *Seder Eliyahu Zuta*, Chapter 2 —— 177
- 5.2 *Seder Eliyahu Rabbah*, Chapter (14) 15 —— 187
- 5.3 *Seder Eliyahu Rabbah*, Chapter (15) 16 —— 194
- 5.4 *Seder Eliyahu Rabbah*, Chapter (13) 14 —— 209
- 5.5 Conversational Narratives —— 211
- 5.6 Conclusion —— 216

6 Late-Midrashic Stories of Women —— 220
- 6.1 Halakhic Contexts I: The Daughter's Rival —— 221
- 6.2 The Story of the White Days —— 226
- 6.2.1 Parallel I: bShab 13a–b —— 228
- 6.2.2 Parallel II: ARN A, Chapter 2 —— 230
- 6.2.3 The Scriptural Roots of the Rabbinic *Niddah* Laws —— 232
- 6.2.4 The Allegorization of *Niddah* —— 234
- 6.2.5 The Emergence of the White Days —— 236
- 6.3 Exegetical Contexts I: The Street of the Harlots —— 239
- 6.4 Exegetical Contexts II: Deborah —— 242
- 6.5 Exegetical Contexts III: Rachel —— 255
- 6.5.1 Parallel: *Ekhah Rabbah*, Proem 24 —— 258
- 6.6 Exegetical Contexts IV: Suicidal Women —— 262
- 6.6.1 "The joyous mother of children" (Ps 113:9) —— 262
- 6.6.2 "Let me die the death of the upright" (Num 23:10) —— 272
- 6.7 Exegetical Contexts V: *It Is Not Good that the Man Should Be Alone* —— 274
- 6.8 Conclusion —— 276

7 **Conclusion** —— 280

Bibliography —— 283

Indices —— 295
Index of Subjects —— 295
Index of Persons —— 298
Index of Rabbinic Authorities —— 299
Index of Karaite Authorities —— 300

Preface

I first came across the title *Seder Eliyahu* in a Sondierungsgespräch (an exploratory talk) with Prof. Günter Stemberger about potential research topics for a dissertation project. The idea of examining the narrative material of this post-classical rabbinic document goes back to his mention of the first-person narratives in *Seder Eliyahu*.

I thank Prof. Stemberger, Prof. Gerhard Langer, Prof. Alexander Samely, Prof. Olga Ruiz, and Prof. Florian Kragl for their suggestions after reading earlier versions of the chapters of this book. Alissa Jones-Nelson I thank for improving my English, without being finally responsible for it, and Nancy Christ at De Gruyter for her wonderful support and guidance as to the typesetting the manuscript in LaTeX. I also want to express my thanks to Dr. Sophie Wagenhofer at De Gruyter for her supervision of my book project.

Preliminary versions of chapter 2 and section 6.2 were published as articles titled as "The Emergence of the Individual Author(-image) in Late Rabbinic Literature," in *Narratology, Hermeneutics, and Midrash: Jewish, Christian, and Muslim Narratives from the Late Antiquity through to Modern Times*, ed. Constanza Cordoni and Gerhard Langer (Göttingen: V&R unipress, 2014), 225–250; and "Die weißen Tage oder warum die Frau immer noch als 'unrein' gilt, nachdem ihre Unreinheit aufgehört hat," *Protokolle zur Bibel* 21 (2012): 1–17, respectively.

Note on translations and style conventions: Scriptural passages are quoted primarily from the *New Revised Standard English Version*, occasionally from the *King James Bible*. The text of the translations has been modified where this was required by the rabbinic context of the quotation.

With minor modifications, the English text of the Mishnah is quoted following Herbert Danby, trans., *The Mishnah: Translated from the Hebrew with Introduction and Brief Explanatory Notes* (London: Soncino, 1933). For the translation of passages of *Seder Eliyahu*, I used the standard edition by Meir Friedmann, *Seder Eliahu Rabba und Seder Eliahu Zuta (Tanna D'be Eliahu)* (Vienna: Israelitisch-Theologische Lehranstalt, 1902; reprint, Jerusalem: Bamberger & Wahrmann, 1960), and *Pseudo-Seder Eliahu Zuta (Derech Ereç und Pirkê R. Eliezer nach Editio princeps des Seder Eliahu und einem Manuskripte, hierzu drei Abschnitte der Pirkê d'Rabbi Eliezer Kap. 39–41 nach demselben Manuskripte)* (Vienna: Israelitisch-Theologische Lehranstalt, 1904; reprint, Jerusalem: Bamberger & Wahrmann, 1960), and consulted the manuscript transcription of the Vatican Codex Ebr. 31 on the Maʾagarim Database of The Academy of the Hebrew Language as well as the English text of *Tanna děbe Eliyyahu = The Lore of the School of Elijah*, translated by William G. Braude and Israel J. Kapstein (Philadelphia, PA: Jewish Publication Society, 1981), whose introduction and notes I quote throughout this book.

Scriptural passages and rabbinic documents are quoted throughout the book in abbreviated form. Passages from the three parts of Friedmann's edition are quoted using the abbreviations "ER" for *Seder Eliyahu Rabbah*, "EZ" for *Seder Eliyahu Zuta*, and "PsEZ" for *Pseudo-Seder Eliyahu Zuta* before page and line numbers ("l."). Words and phrases which are in square brackets [ ] in Friedmann's text, with which he signals emendations to the MS readings, are put in the text of my translation in angular brackets < >. Wording I have added to facilitate the comprehension of either an elliptical phrase or sentence in the rabbinic wording or the scriptural co-text of a quoted verse is placed between square brackets [ ]. Round brackets ( ) are reserved for a) literal translations (preceded by the abbreviation "lit.") in cases in which I opted for a clearly non-literal rendering; b) translations of text set in Hebrew (text in double inverted commas); and c) transliterated expressions from Hebrew (set in italics); d) as well as the original Hebrew wording of certain words or phrases.

Abbreviations of Ancient Sources

Hebrew Bible

Gen	Genesis
Exod	Exodus
Lev	Leviticus
Num	Numbers
Deut	Deuteronomy
Josh	Joshua
Judg	Judges
1 Sam	1 Samuel
2 Sam	2 Samuel
1 Kgs	1 Kings
2 Kgs	2 Kings
1 Chr	1 Chronicles
Job	Job
Ps	Psalms
Prov	Proverbs
Eccl	Ecclesiastes
Song	Song of Songs
Isa	Isaiah
Jer	Jeremiah
Lam	Lamentations
Ezek	Ezekiel
Dan	Daniel
Hos	Hosea
Joel	Joel
Amos	Amos
Mic	Micah
Hab	Habakkuk
Zech	Zechariah
Mal	Malachi

New Testament

Matt	Matthew
Mark	Mark
Luke	Luke
Acts	Acts

Rabbinic Sources

Av	Avot
ARN	Avot de Rabbi Natan
AZ	Avodah Zarah
b	Babylonian Talmud
BB	Bava Batra
BM	Bava Metsia
BemR	Bemidbar Rabbah
BerR	Bereshit Rabbah
Ed	ʿEduyot
EkhR	Ekhah Rabbah
EkhZ	Ekhah Zuta
ER	Seder Eliyahu Rabbah
Er	ʿEruvin
EZ	Seder Eliyahu Zuta
Hul	Chullin
Ker	Keritot
Ket	Ketubbot
LeqT	Leqach Tov
m	Mishnah
Mak	Makkot
Meg	Megillah
MekhY	Mekhilta de-Rabbi Yishmaʾel
MekhSh	Mekhilta de-Rabbi Shimʿon b. Yochai
Men	Menachot
MidTeh	Midrash Tehillim
Miq	Miqwaʾot
Nid	Niddah
Pes	Pesachim
PesRab	Pesiqta Rabbati

PRE	Pirqe Rabbi Eliezer
PsEZ	Pseudo-Seder Eliyahu
Qid	Qiddushin
San	Sanhedrin
Shab	Shabbat
ShirR	Shir ha-Shirim Rabbah
SifBem	Sifre Bemidbar
SifDev	Sifre Devarim
SOR	Seder ʿOlam Rabbah
Sot	Sotah
Suk	Sukkah
t	Tosefta
Tam	Tamid
Tan	Tanchuma
Ter	Terumah
TPsJ	Targum Pseudo-Jonathan
WayR	Wayiqra Rabbah
y	Yerushalmi
YalqShim	Yalqut Shimoni
Yev	Yevamot
Yom	Yoma

1 Introduction

1.1 *Seder Eliyahu* and Scholarship: A *Forschungsbericht*

Seder Eliyahu has been quite heterogeneously appreciated in scholarly literature: It is described as a "uniform work stamped with a character of its own,"[1] as "wahres Juwel innerhalb der rabbinischen Literatur,"[2] but also as "one of the most baffling and intractable midrashim in our possession."[3] In the following pages, I will briefly discuss what appear to have been the main interests of research with respect to this work.

Among the aspects of the work that have received most scholarly attention, none has been as central as that concerning its date and place of composition. Myron Lerner even mentions *Seder Eliyahu* as prime example of how scholarship has passionately tried to fix the date of composition of a midrashic work:

> Among the midrashic works dealt with by Zunz, special attention should be focused on *Seder Eliyahu Rabba*. An allusion to "more than 700 years" that have transpired since the fourth millennium (= 240 CE) in chapter two prompted Zunz to assign the composition of the work to a Babylonian rabbi c. 974 CE. Nevertheless, almost one dozen scholars of the nineteenth and twentieth century contested these conclusions and have consequently offered multiple conflicting solutions to the date and the provenance of this enigmatic aggadic work.[4]

1.1.1 What Is *Seder Eliyahu*?

The question to which R. Natronai Gaon responded in the ninth century could have read more or less like this: What is *Seder Eliyahu*? The description cited above – the work consists of two parts, the former has three parts and thirty chapters, and the latter twelve chapters – targeted at a contemporary reader, is rather unsatisfactory for literary scholars of the present day.

---

[1] Jacob Elbaum, "Tanna De-vei Eliyahu," in *Encyclopaedia Judaica*, ed. Michael Berenbaum and Fred Skolnik, vol. 19 (Detroit: MacMillan Reference, 2007), 508.
[2] Günter Stemberger, *Midrasch: Vom Umgang der Rabbinen mit der Bibel* (Munich: C. H. Beck, 1989), 52.
[3] R. J. Zvi Werblowsky, "A Note on the Text of Seder Eliyahu," *The Journal of Jewish Studies* 6 (1955): 201.
[4] Myron B. Lerner, "The Works of Aggadic Midrash and the Esther Midrashim," in *The Literature of the Sages: Second Part*, ed. Shmuel Safrai et al. (Assen, Minneapolis, MN: Van Gorcum, Fortress, 2006), 147.

Over the course of the twentieth century, there have been many attempts at defining *Seder Eliyahu* by giving it (or denying it) a generic name. The fact that it does not appear to fit into the traditional genre categories of Rabbinic literature is evidenced by the broad range of terms used to refer to it in scholarly literature: ethical aggadah;[5] ethical midrash;[6] something *between* midrash and ethical treatise;[7] aggadic midrash work;[8] *semi*-midrashic work;[9] aggadic work, though in no way a midrash;[10] "genuine midrash";[11] "exoterically moralistic treatise";[12] and "a puzzling and fascinating tradition of hybrid character,"[13] to name but a few of the designations.

Instead of giving it a name, some scholars have attempted to describe it. It has been claimed that we are dealing with a text that is "admittedly faulty and corrupt, often beyond restoration."[14] A rather negative judgement of what others perceive as a coherent text, and one that reminds us of Werblowsky's description of the work as a "baffling midrash," is that given by Myron Lerner:

> The literary structure of *Seder Eliyahu* is most enigmatic and prima facie defies a logical presentation of the midrashic material. One receives the impression that the author has pre-

---

[5] See Leopold Zunz, *Die gottesdienstlichen Vorträge der Juden, historisch entwickelt*, 2nd ed. (Frankfurt am Main: J. Kauffmann, 1892), ch. 7, in which he discusses *Seder Eliyahu*, bears the title "Ethische Hagada."

[6] See Günter Stemberger, *Einleitung in Talmud und Midrasch*, 9th ed. (Munich: C. H. Beck, 2011), 378–381. Chapter 7 of the "Midraschim" part of the book is dedicated to "other aggadic works," among which are the so-called "ethical midrashim."

[7] Jacob Elbaum, "Tanna de-Vei Eliyahu: bein midrash le-sefer musar; iyunim bi-ferakim aleph-vav be-Tanna de-Vei Eliyahu [Tanna de-Vei Eliyahu: Between a Midrash and an Ethical Treatise: Analyses of Chapters 1–6 of Tanna de-Vei Eliyahu]," *Jerusalem Studies in Hebrew Literature* 1 (1981): 144–154.

[8] See Lerner, "Works of Aggadic Midrash," 151–153.

[9] Moshe Lavee, "Seder Eliyahu," in *Encyclopedia of Jews in the Islamic World*, ed. Norbert Stillman (Brill Online, 2010), emphasis added.

[10] According to Moshe David Herr, "Midrash," in *Encyclopaedia Judaica*, ed. Michael Berenbaum and Fred Skolnik, vol. 14 (Detroit: Macmillan Reference, 2007), 185, *Seder Eliyahu* is one of those aggadic works "which does not belong to the genre of Midrash at all."

[11] Werblowsky, "A Note," 201.

[12] David Stern, *Parables in Midrash: Narrative and Exegesis in Rabbinic Literature* (Cambridge, MA: Harvard University Press, 1991), 222.

[13] Lennart Lehmhaus, "Between Tradition and Innovation: Seder Eliyahu's Strategies in the Context of Late Midrash," in *Approaches to Literary Readings of Ancient Jewish Writings*, ed. Klaas A. D. Smelik and Karolien Vermeulen (Leiden: Brill, 2014), 216.

[14] Werblowsky, "A Note," 201.

served his ethical teachings in the form of a continuous monologue on what may be termed: "a midrashic stream of consciousness."[15]

Seder Eliyahu is neither an anthology of homilies, such as those found in homiletical midrashim, nor an anthology of exegetical midrashim on a biblical book; even if it contains passages that have been seen as somehow resembling the genre of rewritten Bible,[16] the work itself is not a typical example of this genre. In his book *Parables*, David Stern dedicates a section to the use of parables in *Seder Eliyahu*, describing the work itself in the following terms:

> Its author appears to have wished to compose a book that would be more unified and self-contained than a conventional midrashic collection, but he also seems to have wanted to preserve the traditional exegetical frame of midrash. The result is a kind of transitional work: an exposition of themes and ideas, but one whose coherent presentation is always being sidetracked by the lure of exegesis.[17]

Another general appreciation of the work, one which emphasises its coherence and consistency, is provided by Braude and Kapstein, the translators of the work into English. They remark:

> *Tanna debe Eliyyahu* has a unity of thought and feeling, of style and structure, that makes it seem the work of a single individual. Even if it be considered the product of a school, it is still likely that the text as we have it came from the head of the school, possibly a school named for him. In any event, he was a man of so strong a spirit as to impress it deeply upon the work, no matter how many of his disciples may have participated in its composition.[18]

Both parts, *Seder Eliyahu Rabbah* and *Seder Eliyahu Zuta*, seem to have been conceived as distinct parts (or cognate texts[19]) that transmit an ethical discourse consisting of religious teachings, passages of retold Bible, exegesis, and parables. Partly due to its textual coherence, *Seder Eliyahu* tends to be viewed as the literary product of a transitional time in the history of Rabbinic literature, between the time of the classical, collectively authored documents and the literature of single authors who use their names *as authors*, in the modern sense of the word.[20] There is a clear continuation from *Seder Eliyahu Rabbah* to *Seder Eliyahu Zuta*,

---

15 Lerner, "Works of Aggadic Midrash," 140n28.
16 See Stemberger, *Midrasch: Vom Umgang der Rabbinen mit der Bibel*, 191–198.
17 Stern, *Parables*, 211.
18 William G. Braude and Israel J. Kapstein, eds. and trans., *Tanna děbe Eliyyahu: The Lore of the School of Elijah* (Philadelphia, PA: Jewish Publication Society, 1981), Introduction, 3.
19 See Lehmhaus, "Between Tradition and Innovation," 216.
20 See chapter 2.

which can be grasped in their common topics, but above all in the phraseology used and in the characteristic first-person narratives. Each of the three sections that constitute the so-called *Pseudo-Seder Eliyahu Zuta* – as edited by Friedmann in 1904 according to the *editio princeps* Venice 1598 and the MS Parma 3111 (de Rossi 1240)[21] – has characteristic features of its own, which suggests that these are not related to the main body of *Seder Eliyahu* in the same way that its two parts are related to form a whole. Probably the most salient of the distinguishing traits of this *Pseudo-Seder Eliyahu Zuta*-conglomerate is the fact that the sages are quoted profusely in all three parts. The governing voice[22] of these parts conveys its message by letting named sages speak. Their voices open the three chapters of *Pirqe Derekh Erets* in the manner of a *petichah*, with the formula "R. X says/said" (אמר רבי ... / רבי ... אומר). In the case of *Pirqe R. Eliezer*, the chapters open with a question posed by R. Eliezer's disciples and the sage's subsequent answer, introduced with the formula פתח ואומר, or אמר להם. Finally, *Pirqe ha-Yeridot*, which offers an exposition on the fourth, fifth, and sixth descents of God, also quotes traditions in the name of several sages.

1.1.2 Textual Transmission

The complete *Seder Eliyahu* – that is, its *Rabbah* and *Zuta* parts – is transmitted in only one manuscript, the Codex Vat. ebr. 31,[23] as well as in the *editio princeps* Venice 1598, printed by Daniel Zanetti on the basis of a manuscript from the year

---

21 Meir Friedmann, ed., *Pseudo-Seder Eliahu Zuta (Derech Ereç und Pirkê R. Eliezer nach Editio princeps des Seder Eliahu und einem Manuscripte* (Vienna: Israelitisch-Theologische Lehranstalt, 1904). In *The Theology* and *Organic Thinking*, Max Kadushin refers to these thirteen chapters as the "Additions." The first three chapters of *Pseudo-Seder Eliyahu Zuta* are designated in Friedmann's edition as *Pirqe Derekh Eretz* (*Seder Eliyahu Zuta*, ch. 16–18), the seven chapters that follow as *Pirke R. Eliezer* (*Seder Eliyahu Zutta*, ch. 19–25), and the last three chapters as *Pirqe ha-Yeridot* (ch. 1–3). The latter offer a parallel to chapters 39–41 of *Pirqe deRabbi Eliezer*. Max Kadushin, *Organic Thinking: A Study in Rabbinic Thought* (New York: The Jewish Theological Seminary of America, 1938), observes that the first ten chapters of *Pseudo-Seder Eliyahu Zuta*, "without doubt written at a late period" (5), constitute a unit which makes use "of practically all of the concepts in the complex a configuration in which the concepts of Redemption, Paradise and Gehenna form the chief features." (199)
22 For the concept of the governing voice see Alexander Samely, *Profiling Jewish Literature in Antiquity: An Inventory, from Second Temple Texts to the Talmuds* (Oxford: Oxford University Press, 2013), ch. 2.
23 For a description of the manuscript, see Umberto Cassuto, *Codices Vaticani Hebraici: Codices 1–115; Bybliothecae Apostolicae Vaticanae Codices Manu Scripti Recensiti Iussu Pii XII Pontificis Maximi* (The Vatican: Biblioteca Apostolica Vaticana, 1956), 38–41; Malachi Beit-Arié, Colette

1186, which has not been preserved.²⁴ Codex Vat. ebr. 31, which also transmits the tannaitic midrash *Sifra*, was published in a facsimile edition as *Torath Cohanim (Sifra) · Seder Eliyahu Rabba and Zutta*.²⁵ Ulrich Berzbach, who studied the transmission of *Seder Eliyahu Zuta*, lists the following five manuscripts as independent textual witnesses to this part of the work: MS Parma 2785 (de Rossi 327); MS Parma 2342 (de Rossi 541); MS Oxford, Bodl. Libr., Mich. 910; MS Parma 3111 (de Rossi 1240); and MS Firkovitch Evr. IIa 157/1.²⁶ The character of *Seder Eliyahu Zuta*'s transmission in manuscripts, the print edition, and the *Yalqut* version has led scholars to assume several redactions.²⁷ Moshe Lavee reminds us that, although the manuscript transmission is almost exclusively European, "there is evidence for the cultural presence of the book in the Cairo Geniza" – for example, in the fragments discussed by Louis Ginzberg in chapters 22 and 23 of his *Genizah Studies*.²⁸ Certain manuscripts as well as the *editio princeps* of *Wayiqra Rabbah* preserve passages from the seventh chapter (i.e. Friedmann's chapter [6] 7) of *Seder Eliyahu*, annexed as concluding sections to the first three pericopes.²⁹

Depending on the textual witness, the *Rabbah* part consists of 29 (MS) or 31 (*editio princeps*) chapters, whereas the *Zuta* oscillates between 15 (MS) and 25 (*editio princeps*) chapters. As mentioned above, Natronai's responsum and the *Arukh* both describe the *Rabbah* part as consisting of 30 chapters, divided into three "gates" (parts), and the *Zuta* as comprising 12 chapters.³⁰ Friedmann attempted

---

Sirat, and Mordechai Glatzer, *Codices Hebraicis Litteris Exarati Quo Tempore Scripti Fuerint Exhibentes: De 1021 à 1079* (Turnhout: Brepols, 1999), nr. 38; Benjamin Richler and Malachi Beit-Arié, *Hebrew Manuscripts in the Vatican Library: Catalogue* (The Vatican: Biblioteca Apostolica Vaticana, 2008), 20–21.
24 Meir Friedmann, ed., *Seder Eliahu Rabba and Seder Eliahu Zuta (Tanna D'be Eliahu)* (Vienna: Israelitisch-Theologische Lehranstalt, 1902), Vorwort, v: "Der Herausgeber bezeugt, dass bis zu jener Zeit das Buch nur durch Citate bekannt gewesen sei, keiner aber kenne das ganze Buch."
25 The fact that the work is copied in the same manuscript as *Sifra* does not necessarily indicate that the copyist regarded *Seder Eliyahu* as a tannaitic work, as Braude and Kapstein, *Tanna děbe Eliyyahu*, introduction, 4n4 and 35n56, argue.
26 See Ulrich Berzbach, "The Textual Witnesses of the Midrash Seder Eliyahu Zuta: An Initial Survey," *Frankfurter Judaistische Beiträge* 31 (2004): 63–74.
27 See Stemberger, *Einleitung*, 379.
28 See above, p. 14. See also Lavee, "Seder Eliyahu."
29 See Lerner, "Works of Aggadic Midrash," 164; and Mordechai Margulies, ed., *Midrash Wayyikra Rabbah: A Critical Edition based on Manuscripts and Genizah Fragments with Variants and Notes*, 3 vols. (Jerusalem: Ministry of Education and Culture of Israel, 1953), vol. 1, 32–34 (WayR 1:15) = ER 33–34; 46–54 (WayR 2:12) = ER 36, 72–75 (WayR 3:7) = ER 37.
30 Natan ben Yechiel, *Aruch completum*, ed. Alexander Kohut, vol. 6 (Vienna: Brög, 1890), 27. On Natan's description, Friedmann, *Seder Eliahu*, Vorwort, iv, points out: "Ähnliches findet man im Aruch nicht zum zweitenmale; sah er sich etwa genöthigt, פרקי דר' אליעזר oder ילמדנו so zu be-

to adapt the text of the manuscript, distributing it so as to arrive at the number of chapters mentioned in the *Arukh*: This is the reason why certain chapter numbers in Friedmann's edition appear in parenthesis. The last ten chapters of the *Zuta* part, as transmitted in the Venice printing were published together with three chapters preserved in Codex Parma 1240 under the name *Pseudo-Seder Eliyahu Zuta*.

A more recent chapter in the history of the transmission or rather reception of the work takes us to Prague, where in the seventeenth century, the printer Samuel Haida prepared a new text edition based on the Venice print and a commentary, זקוקין דנורא ובעורין דאשא.[31] Haida's 1677 edition contains the text of the Venice edition, where it is designated as נוסחא ישנה, followed by Haida's version, נוסחא חדשה, and a commentary, זקוקין דנורא ובעורין דאשא (each chapter of Haida's reworked text is preceded by the corresponding chapter of the Venice edition). Subsequent reprints preserved only the revised text.[32] In his introductory chapters and foreword, Haida explains that he was moved to prepare a new edition of the text because of the many mistakes in the old version. Haida claims to have prayed and fasted until the prophet Elijah himself appeared to him and dictated the text he had dictated centuries before, whereby he alludes to a passage in bKet 105b–106a (see below). Haida's version was long considered the standard version of the work and was reprinted numerous times.[33]

---

schreiben? Man kann dies nur begreiflich finden in der Annahme, dass das Buch zur Zeit wenig bekannt war." The expression "gates" (שערים), used by the *Arukh* to refer to the parts of a work, may be – as Robert Brody, *The Geonim of Babylonia and the Shaping of Medieval Jewish Literature* (New Haven, CT: Yale University Press, 1998), 257, points out with respect to the structure of Seʿadyah's *Kitab al-Mawarith* – a translation of the usual Arabic term for chapters: أبواب.

31 Ulrich Berzbach refers to the fact that, even if Haida included the original text of the Venice printing next to his own corrected text, he modified it, evidence of which is the fact that he changed the expression בן דוד, found in the Venice edition, to משיח. On the reasons for this change, see Friedmann, *Seder Eliahu*, Vorwort, vii.

32 See Friedmann, *Seder Eliahu*, Vorwort, vii.

33 Haida's work appeared in the following editions, generally accompanied by a commentary: Hrubieszów, 1817; Jerusalem, 1869, 1870, 1900, 1906, 1907 (with commentaries by Aqiba Joseph b. Jechiel and Jacob b. Naphtali Hirz), 1954, 1956 (with an abridged translation in Yiddish by Judah Reuben Tsinkes and his son, Abba Saul), 1959 (with commentaries by Jacob Meir Schechter and Jacob b. Naphtali Hirz), 1960, 1967 (with a commentary by Chayyim Isaiah ha-Kohen and Jacob b. Naphtali Hirz), 1970 (synoptic edition with the text of the Venice edition), 1972 (with a commentary by Abraham Schick); Józefów, 1838, 1852; Königsberg, 1857, s.a. (ca. 1863, with a commentary by Jacob b. Naphtali Hirz); Lviv, 1799, 1826, 1849, 1850, 1859, 1861, 1862, 1863, 1864, 1865, 1867, 1869, 1870; Lublin, 1896, 1907, 1911, 1924 (synoptic edition with the text of the Venice edition), 1927; Minkowce, 1798; New York, 1956, 1960; Ostrog, 1838; Polonnoye, 1818; Prague, 1814; Przemyśl, 1887 (with a commentary of Joshua Alexander); Sudzilkow, 1826, 1833, 1834; Vilnius,

1.1.3 The Problem of Dating and Locating *Seder Eliyahu*

The question of the work's date of composition was first dealt with by Solomon Rapoport,[34] who regarded the text that has come down to us – which consists of two parts, with 31 and 25 chapters respectively – as having been composed in Babylonia in the middle or latter part of the tenth century, and therefore not identical with the one the *Arukh* describes, which is said to consist of three parts, of which the *Rabbah* part is said to comprise 30 chapters, while the *Zuta* part contains 12 chapters. It is not only the conflicting length and structure of the *Arukh*'s description with respect to the conserved text, but also the relative chronology of two passages – ER 6–7 and ER 163 – that led Rapoport to conclude that the text we know dates from the second half of the tenth century, from the time of Rav Sherira Gaon. The passages read as follows:

> For the world as we know it was intended to exist for six thousand years. Two thousand years in desolation, two thousand years with Torah, and two thousand years of the Messiah's reign. Because of our many sins enslavement has come upon us during the two thousand years which God had intended to be the Messiah's. Indeed, more than seven hundred of his years have already passed. (ER 6, l. 30–ER 7, l. 1)

> From the time the Second Temple was built until it was destroyed four hundred and twenty years elapsed, His hand being stretched out over them against every adversary and foe. From the time the Second Temple was destroyed until now nine hundred years have elapsed, during which time how often did He take them into His arms, hold them close, and kiss them! (ER 163, l. 25–27)

These chronological notes can be interpreted by adducing a talmudic passage (bAZ 9a, par. bSan 97a–b), according to which the two thousand years of the Messiah's reign begin 172 years after the destruction of the Second Temple (in the year

---

1839 (with two commentaries by Isaac Landau), 1880, 1900 (with a commentary by Jacob b. Naphtali Hirz), 1905; Warsaw 1850, 1857, 1863, 1870, 1873, 1874 (repr. Bergen-Belsen, ca. 1946), 1876, 1880 (synoptic edition with the text of the Venice edition), 1881, 1883, 1893, 1911, 1912 (with commentaries by Aaron Simhah of Gumbin and Jacob b. Naphtali Hirz); Zolkiew, 1753, 1796, 1798, 1799, 1805, 1807, 1808. Furthermore, two commentaries which partially quote the text of *Seder Eliyahu* should be mentioned: 1) *Luach Erez*, a commentary by Chaim Palagi (1788–1869), Smyrna, 1881; and 2) *Ramatayim Sofim*, a chasidic commentary by Samuel Shinwa, Warsaw, 1881, 1882, 1901, 1908, 1920; Jerusalem, 1937, 1954, 1959, 1966; Shanghai, 1946. The latter does not comment upon the text of *Seder Eliyahu*, but rather uses it for homiletical purposes. See Institute for Hebrew Bibliography, *The Bibliography of the Hebrew Book 1470–1960*, available online at http://www.hebrew-bibliography.com/. See Braude and Kapstein, *Tanna děbe Eliyyahu*, introduction, 11–12.
34 See Solomon Rapoport, "*Toledot R. Nathan*," in *Bikkure ha-ʿittim* (1829), 43n43.

242 CE. Thus, while the first note would refer to some time after the year 942 CE, the second would point to 968 CE. A third passage can be understood on its own as referring to the year 4744 AM or 984 CE:

> Thus from the time the world was created until the present time ninety-four fifty-year periods and forty-four single years have gone by. (ER 37, l. 19–20)

Leopold Zunz considered these three chronological passages as evidence of the work's date of composition in the year 974. As to its place of composition, he agreed with Rapoport that it originated in Babylonia.[35] Wilhelm Bacher also dated the work to the second half of the tenth century, around the year 970.[36]

Heinrich Graetz was the first to suggest that the work was written by an Italian, probably from Rome, in the tenth century. The references to Babel are nothing but an allegory for Rome, and the mention of the punishment of Gog and Magog in ER 15 and ER 24 are explained as allusions to the Hungarian invasions in Europe (889–955), during which Italy suffered especially. The work's European origins are also attested by the use of a chronology based on the years since creation instead of the Seleucid chronology, which was usual in Babylonia.[37] Moritz Güdemann agreed with Graetz as to both the time of composition in the tenth century and the work having been written by an European living in Italy.[38] He quotes several passages of *Seder Eliyahu* which lead him to conclude that the work belongs to the first period of the history of the Jews in Italy, during which only the beginnings of a scientific activity are identifiable.[39] He assumed that only someone who regarded the places named by the first-person narrator (Jerusalem, Babylonia, etc.)

---

[35] See Zunz, *Die gottesdienstlichen Vorträge*, 119.
[36] Wilhelm Bacher, "Antikaräisches in einem jüngeren Midrasch," *Monatsschrift für Geschichte und Wissenschaft des Judentums* 23 (1874): 266.
[37] Heinrich Graetz, *Geschichte der Juden vom Abschluss des Talmuds (500) bis zum Aufblühen der jüdisch-spanischen Kultur (1027)*, vol. 5 of *Geschichte der Juden: Von den ältesten Zeiten bis auf die Gegenwart*, 3rd ed. (Leipzig: Leiner, 1895), 294–295.
[38] See Moritz Güdemann, *Geschichte des Erziehungswesens und der Cultur der abendländischen Juden während des Mittelalters und der neueren Zeit*, vol. 2 of *Geschichte des Erziehungswesens und der Cultur der Juden in Italien während der Mittelalters, nebst bisher ungedruckten Beilagen* (Vienna: Hölder, 1884), 52–55 and 300–303.
[39] Güdemann, *Geschichte des Erziehungswesens*, 55: "Diese Auszüge mögen genügen, um einen Begriff von dem Buche zu geben, dem sie entnommen sind. Es bildet den Schlussstein der ersten Periode der Geschichte der Juden in Italien, in welcher zwar schon Anfänge wissenschaftlicher Bethätigung zu Tage treten, ohne jedoch zu weiterer Entfaltung und Ausbildung zu gelangen."

as exotic would name them at all.⁴⁰ Simon Eppenstein identifies the purity of the work's Hebrew as evidence for Italy as the place of composition, and he also locates *Pesiqta Rabbati* – a work that, in his view, stands close to *Seder Eliyahu*. The warning against doing business with a non-Jew in chapter 8 and the designation of the latter as גוי excludes the possibility of a Muslim environment.⁴¹

Gottlieb Klein describes the original conception of the work – its "Urform" – as "ein Missionsprogramm an die Heiden,"⁴² which was rescued from oblivion by an unknown rabbi and adapted to suit his own purposes and audience at the time of the Crusades. In spite of this medieval teacher's additions, Klein is persuaded that the original plan of the work can be recognised and described as a type of catechism:

> In katechetischer Form erteilt der Prophet Elias, der Vorläufer des Messias, seinen Jüngern Weisheitslehren, allgemeine Normen der Sittlichkeit, nicht Thora, sondern Derech erez verkündet er, denn er will die Heiden für das Reich Gottes gewinnen. Mit diesen Lehren ausgerüstet, sollen Elias' Schüler als Missionäre durch die Welt reisen und die Wege Gottes der Welt verkünden. Kurz und bündig wird das Missionsprogram entwickelt.⁴³

According to other scholars, *Seder Eliyahu* was composed much earlier. Meir Friedmann, whose introduction to his edition of the work is still the most comprehensive study we have,⁴⁴ regarded *Seder Eliyahu* as the authentic product of talmudic times – as having emerged sometime between the composition of the Mishnah and the close of the Talmud. Friedmann was persuaded that the work was authored by the prophet Elijah (or by an Elijah), to whom re refers as "Abba Eliahu" and with whom he identifies the first-person narrator of several narrative passages. The work as it has come down to us could have existed in some other form before it was eventually dictated to Rav Anan in the third century, as the Talmud passage bKet 105b–106a, an etiological narrative, reports. Friedmann interprets several passages as allusions to Persia and its religion of fire-worship and

---

40 Güdemann, *Geschichte des Erziehungswesens*, 301: "Ein weitgereister Mann spricht mit Vorliebe von den fernen Gegenden, die er gesehen, er wird nicht müde, von den äussersten Zielen seiner Wanderungen zu berichten."
41 See Simon Eppenstein, *Beiträge zur Geschichte und Literatur im Geonäischen Zeitalter* (Breslau: Koebner, 1913), 182–183.
42 Gottlieb Klein, *Der älteste christliche Katechismus und die jüdische Propaganda-Literature* (Berlin: Reimer, 1909), 68.
43 Klein, *Der älteste christliche Katechismus*, 79.
44 Friedmann's edition of *Seder Eliyahu Rabbah* first appeared in 1900 as a "Beiheft" (supplement) of the *7. Jahresbericht der Israelitisch-theologischen Lehranstalt*. In 1902 he published it with his edition of *Seder Eliyahu Zuta* and a commentary on both parts, מאיר עין. This edition was reprinted in Jerusalem in 1960, 1967, and 1969.

finds that several passages in midrashim undoubtedly quote passages from *Seder Eliahu*; thus he concludes that the text must have been written between the third and the sixth centuries.⁴⁵ He dismisses the dates in ER 6–7, ER 37, and ER 163 that point to the tenth century as later interpolations.⁴⁶ As regards the parallel traditions in *Seder Eliahu* and the Babylonian Talmud, Friedmann argues that neither borrowed from the other, but that these traditions both go back to earlier sources.⁴⁷ As regards the place of composition, Friedmann argues that the reference to tithes and the seventh year (ER 59) is evidence of the Palestinian origin of the work, where these practices were still observed during the time at which Friedmann assumes the work was composed.⁴⁸ Friedmann's theory concerning *Seder Eliyahu*'s early date of composition⁴⁹ was supported half a century later by Mordechai Margulies, who regarded the work as having been authored by a certain Abba Eliyyahu, who is mentioned in EZ 197 and speaks of his own life experiences in several other first-person narratives, in the first half of the third century, during the persecutions of the Jews by Yezdegerd I.⁵⁰

Jacob Mann also dated the work early, though his arguments do not involve the chronological precedence of *Seder Eliyahu* as compared to the Talmud. In the first section of his article on the modifications in the Jewish liturgy brought about by religious persecutions, Mann discusses examples of post-talmudic liturgical literature that provide evidence for the insertion of the first verse of the Shema in different sections of the service, apart from its daily recital with the Tefillah of Shacharit and Maʿarib. In the Babylonian rite, for example, this verse is introduced in the section known as לעולם יהא אדם. Mann argues that this section must have been known to the author of *Seder Eliyahu*, where it is introduced with the formula *mikan amru* as an "anonymous composition" of the sages and cited "in a greatly shortened form due to the copyists."⁵¹

---

45 See Friedmann, *Seder Eliahu*, introduction, esp. 77 and 82.
46 See Friedmann, *Seder Eliahu*, 37n52, 163n52.
47 See Friedmann, *Seder Eliahu*, introduction, 48.
48 See Friedmann, *Seder Eliahu*, introduction, 83.
49 See Friedmann, *Seder Eliahu*, introduction, 77–83.
50 See Mordechai Margulies, "Li-beayat qadmuto shel sefer Seder Eliyahu [The Problem of the Beginning of the Book Seder Eliyahu]," in *Sefer Asaf*, ed. Umberto Casutto (Jerusalem: Mossad ha-Rav Kuk, 1953), 370–390. William G. Braude, "Conjecture and Interpolation in Translating Rabbinic Texts: Illustrated by a Chapter from Tanna Debe Eliyyahu," in *Christianity, Judaism and Other Greco-Roman Cults: Studies for Morton Smith at Sixty*, ed. Jacob Neusner, IV: *Judaism after 70; other Greco-Roman Cults; Bibliography* (Leiden: Brill, 1975), 79, agrees with this dating.
51 Jacob Mann, "Changes in the Divine Service of the Synagogue due to Religious Persecutions," *Hebrew Union College Annual* 4 (1927): 247.

According to Mann, "[t]he whole setting of this section suggests a time of religious tribulation and trial when the declaration of the unity of God could only be made in secret (בסתר)."⁵² Mann's interpretation is partly based on that of R. Benjamin b. Abraham ʿAnav (thirteenth century), who suggests that the expression "in secret" alludes to a generation affected by persecution.⁵³ Benjamin appears to have had before him a text of *Seder Eliyahu* with passages that were omitted by the copyist of MS Vat ebr. 31 – among others, the very expression בסתר, which, curiously enough, is missing from the text of *Seder Eliyahu* that has come down to us.⁵⁴ The phrase is also used in chapter 18, though in a narrative rather than a liturgical context, as part of the characterisation of a priest: מעשה בכהן שהיה ירא שמים בסתר. Mann sees the Babylonian origin of the work also evidenced in its contents, which he argues clearly show "that the author lived for a considerable time in Babylon and that in a good deal of his work he depicted conditions of Jewish life in that country."⁵⁵ So Mann takes the first-person narrative in the first chapter, an account of the anonymous rabbi getting arrested and being subsequently confronted by a priest, as a factual account of events in the author's life in Babylonia. This episode demonstrates the power of the Zoroastrian priests, who were usually referred to as Magians.⁵⁶ Both the allusion to the private prayer in the phrase בסתר and the account of the dispute with a חבר, the religious title with which a Zoroastrian priest is referred to in the text,⁵⁷ point to a redaction of *Seder Eliyahu*

---

52 Mann, "Changes in the Divine Service," 247.
53 R. Benjamin b. Abraham ʿAnav is quoted by his brother Zedekiah in his liturgical treatise *Shibboleth ha-leket*: ור״ב אחי נר״ו כתב שראוי לומר בסתר שלא אמרו אבא אליהו אלא כנגד דורו של שמד שגזרו שלא לקרוא את שמע ולא היו יכולין להיות יראין בגלוי, ע״כ הזהירם וזרם לקבל עליהם עול מלכות שמים בסתר. See Friedmann, *Seder Eliahu*, 118n28.
54 See Albert Ringer, "A Persecution was Decreed: Persecution as a Rhetorical Device in the Literature of the Geʾonim and Rishonim; Part 1," *European Journal of Jewish Studies* 6, no. 2 (2012): 186–188, for a critical appraisal of Mann's methodology. Ringer argues that persecution as a stimulus for a change in liturgy can be understood in *Seder Eliyahu* as a part of a literary topos, instead of as a reference to a historical reality.
55 Mann, "Changes in the Divine Service," 249.
56 Mann, "Changes in the Divine Service," 306, argues as follows: "The priest promised the captive his freedom, if he answered his questions, which indicates the political influence the Magians had on the government officials, whose raid probably was the result of the former's instigation. Such a situation obtained in Babylon and in Persia under the Sassanids, especially under Yezdejerd II and Perōz, who were dominated by the powerful Magian priests, but certainly not under the rule of Islām, not to speak of Italy where such a situation does not apply at all." See also Friedmann, *Seder Eliahu*, introduction, 82.
57 Shai Secunda, *The Iranian Talmud: Reading the Bavli in its Sasanian Context* (Philadelphia, PA: University of Pennsylvania Press, 2014), 39, argues that the depiction of rabbis conversing with Persians in the Babylonian Talmud is the greatest proof we have that language could not

"not long after 455" – that is, after the persecutions of Jews in the Sasanian Empire under the rule of Yazdegerd II (454–455) and his son Perōz.[58]

In an appendix to his article, Mann addresses the question of the date and place of redaction of *Seder Eliyahu*, observing:

> All scholars, who have assigned the redaction of this Midrash to the 10th century by reason of the late dates …, have overlooked the significant fact that nowhere is there mentioned the rule of Islām extending, as it did then, from Persia and the eastern provinces to Babylon, Syria, Palestine, Egypt and whole of North-Africa and reaching out to Europe by the occupation of Spain and also of Sicily.[59]

The only reference to Ishmael's children (ER 65), he points out, "evidently alludes to the more or less independent Arab tribes extending from the Arabian peninsula proper right to the confines of Babylon at the lower Euphrates."[60] In recent times, Norman Roth has pointed to two further passages in *Seder Eliyahu*[61] that he regards as "clear anti-Muslim references." According to PsEZ 32, Abraham will refuse to say grace, arguing that out of him "came seed which provoked the Holy One, blessed be He" – that is, the seed of Ishmael. In the context of a homily on the hidden light of creation in PsEZ 36, God explains to Israel that whereas the light

---

have constituted a communication barrier between rabbis and Zoroastrians. "Nowhere does the Bavli emphasize or even mention any linguistic difficulties inherent in these encounters – for example by describing misunderstandings or by ascribing a role to translators. Evidently, whether they used Aramaic, Persian, or a mixture of both, some rabbis were able to converse with Persians without great difficulty." *Seder Eliyahu* does not mention linguistic difficulties either, even though the language used, Hebrew, is one not assumed to have been a vernacular in Sasanian Mesopotamia, where such an encounter could have taken place.

58 Mann, "Changes in the Divine Service," 250 and 305.
59 Mann, "Changes in the Divine Service," 303.
60 Mann, "Changes in the Divine Service," 303–304. Jacob N. Epstein, *Mavo le-nusaḥ ha-mishnah [Introduction to the Text of the Mishnah]* (Jerusalem: Magnes Press, 1948), 762–767 and 1302–1303, agrees with Mann's suggested date of composition, but puts forward a double authorship theory: R. Anan is seen as the compiler of a first version, which was amplified in the course of the fifth century, during the times of the persecutions under King Perōz. Other defenders of the early date of composition include Eliezer Atlas, *Ha-Kerem* (1888): 100; and Isaac Dov Ber Markon, מספרותנו העתיקה : שלשה מאמרים in "לתולדות המדרש תנא דבי אליהו" (Vilna: Piroshnikov, 1910), 4,2 who suggested the third century, under Jezdegerd I, or the first half of the fourth century under Constantine the Great, respectively; Samuel Klein, "דברים אחרים על סדר אליהו," *Ha-Hed* 7 5692/1932: 18, considered the second half of the fourth century under Emperor Julian as probable date of composition; Zeev Jawitz, כנסת ישראל I, (London, 5647/1887): 382–386, and תולדות ישראל, vol. 9, מראשית רבנן סבוראי עד סוף ימי הגאונים: המחצית הראשונה (London: Narodizqi, 5682/1922), 225–228, dates the work to the seventh century, under Emperor Heraclius, and locates its composition in Palestine.
61 These are actually in the so-called *Pseudo-Seder Eliyahu Zuta*; see below.

is intended for them, darkness is meant for the children of Esau and the children of Ishmael.[62]

A third position, which is currently accepted as the correct one, dates the work to the ninth century. Avigdor Aptowitzer proposes the first half of the ninth century as the date of composition for the text we know, which he assumes to have superseded an older version from the talmudic period.[63] Among the arguments he adduces for such a dating are the recurrent warnings against close relations with non-Jews, which he reads as emerging out of the same Sitz im Leben as the warnings against close relations between Christians and Jews by the Christian Patriarch Jeshu bar Nun, who lived in the first quarter of the ninth century.[64] Furthermore, the depiction of Babylonia in exalted terms in ER 98, as the place where the messianic times will begin, is a notion Aptowitzer sees as reminiscent of *Pirqoi Ben Baboi* (end of the eighth century).[65] Regarding the place of redaction, he argues that this is undoubtedly Babylonia: This can be read in the work's attitude towards conversion,[66] the liturgical formulas[67] used, as well as the depiction of certain customs (pertaining to weddings, for example) as practised in Babylonia.[68] The author himself, however, is seen as Byzantine.[69] To my knowledge, Aptowitzer is the only scholar who has addressed the question of the multiple, diverse geographical references (to Yavne, Jerusalem, Babylonia, etc.) in the first-person narratives, arguing that it is not possible to infer from them the work's place of composition.[70]

Moshe Zucker suggests the middle of the ninth century as *Seder Eliyahu*'s time of composition due to its apparent polemics against the heretical writings of Chiwi al-Balkhi (ninth century), against the Karaites in general and Daniel al-Qumisi (mid-ninth century) in particular. Zucker proposes the years between 850 and 860

---

[62] See Norman Roth, *Jews, Visigoths and Muslims in Medieval Spain: Cooperation and Conflict* (Leiden: Brill, 1994), 209–210.
[63] See Avigdor Aptowitzer, "Seder Elia," in *Jewish Studies: In Memory of George A. Kohut, 1874–1933*, ed. Salo W. Baron and Alexander Marx (New York: The Alexander Kohut Memorial Foundation, 1935), 23–24.
[64] See Aptowitzer, "Seder Elia," 17.
[65] See Aptowitzer, "Seder Elia," 20–23.
[66] See Aptowitzer, "Seder Elia," 6.
[67] See Aptowitzer, "Seder Elia," 6. For example, the phrase אהבת עולם is part of the Babylonian rite.
[68] See Aptowitzer, "Seder Elia," 8. Whereas in Palestine the Tefillah was uttered aloud, in *Seder Eliyahu* we read: "A man who says the Tefillah loud enough so that he hears himself, [is praying as though God were hard of hearing, and hence] is bearing false witness against Him."
[69] See Aptowitzer, "Seder Elia," 13.
[70] See Aptowitzer, "Seder Elia," 32–33.

as *terminus ante quem* for the composition of the work, because it is mentioned in the *Responsa* of R. Natronai b. Hilai, who was Gaon of Sura during the mid-ninth century.[71] Incidentally, Natronai is the first to claim that the work consists of a *Rabbah* and a *Zuta* part, that the former has three gates or parts, and thirty chapters, and the latter only twelve chapters – a description that would appear again in the *Arukh*.[72] The tone of the work's polemics was deliberately neutralised to allow the reader to regard the work as an ancient one.[73] In an article dedicated to the language of *Seder Eliyahu*, Ephraim Urbach also came to the conclusion that the work was composed in the ninth century.[74]

Finally, Louis Ginzberg, came up with a theory that seeks to explain why some passages in *Seder Eliyahu* can be dated to a time shortly after the close of the Mishnah, while others appear to have originated only after the close of the Babylonian Talmud, and – if the chronological notes are not to be considered as interpolations – why a final redaction could have taken place only in the tenth century. In his introduction to chapters 22 and 23 ("Fragments on Repentance and Gehenna") of his *Genizah Studies*, he argues that *Seder Eliyahu* once consisted of a *baraita* and a talmud attached to it, as is the case with the tractate *Kallah*.[75] This claim is based on rubrics in certain Genizah fragments which appear to allude to a "talmud" of *Seder Eliyahu*.[76] The text which has come down to us is a combination of *baraita* and commentary or "talmud"[77] and is on the whole a much shorter text than the original. Ginzberg further argues against Friedmann's treatment of the last ten chapters of *Seder Eliyahu Zuta* as "additions," arguing that it is likely they once constituted a section of the original "talmud" of *Seder Eliyahu Zuta*. In his

---

71 See Moshe Zucker, *Al targum Saadya ben Gaon la-Tora: parshanut, halakha, u-polemiqa [Rav Saadya Gaon's Translation of the Torah]* (New York: Feldheim, 1959), 117–127 and 205–219.
72 [וששאלתם] מהו סדר איליהו רבה וסדר אליהו זוטא (כתובות קו ע״א) ה[ללו משניות חיצוניות הן, וסדר אליהו רבא האוי ג׳ באבי] תלתין פירקי, סדר אליהו זוטא תרי עשר פי[רקי, ודאמרינן בגמרא תני דבי אליהו, כלהון בגווייהו]. The quotation follows [Natronai bar Hilai, Gaon], *Teshuvot Rav Natronai bar Hilai Gaon [The Responsa of Rav Natronai bar Hilai Gaon]*, 2nd ed., ed. Robert Brody (Jerusalem: Ofeq, 1994), 651, (§ 553).
73 See Zucker, *Rav Saadya Gaon's Translation*, 205n797.
74 See Ephraim Urbach, "Le-sheelat leshono u-meqorotaw shel Sefer Seder Elijahu [On the language and the sources of Seder Eliyahu]," *Leshonenu* 21 (1956–1957): 183–197.
75 See Louis Ginzberg, *Midrash and Haggadah*, vol. 1 of *Genizah Studies in Memory of Solomon Schechter* (New York: Jewish Theological Seminary, 1928), 189–191.
76 See Ginzberg, *Midrash and Haggadah*, 194 and 198. This theory was contested by Mann in "Genizah Studies," *The American Journal of Semitic Languages* 46 (1930): 263–283.
77 See Ginzberg, *Midrash and Haggadah*, 190. See also Max Kadushin, *The Theology of Seder Eliahu* (New York: Bloch Publishing Company, 1932), 15n46; Kadushin, *Organic Thinking*, 48; and Cordoni, "Emergence of the Individual Author," 242–244.

book *Organic Thinking*, Max Kadushin supports Louis Ginzberg's theory, according to which trying to fix the time of *Seder Eliyahu*'s composition to the fourth or the tenth century is a fruitless task, since "our text was written or compiled during the entire Rabbinic period; and it can be taken, therefore, to be representative of that period."[78] Such an approach to the problem of the time and place of composition of *Seder Eliyahu* is not necessarily incompatible with the idea of a single redactional authorship at the end of the period.[79] It is precisely the combination of the unity of conception and the effacement of any hint of place or time of composition in late midrashim – such as *Seder Eliyahu* or *Pirqe de Rabbi Eliezer* – that Dina Stein sees as characteristic of the poetology of these post-talmudic texts.[80]

The question of the geographic provenance of the work is seldom addressed nowadays. Amos Geula, in papers presented at the Tenth EAJS Congress in Paris (2014) and the BAJS Conference in Edinburgh (2017), pleads for Byzantium as a plausible place of composition, basing this argument on the trips of the first-person narrator. Regarding the origins of the author himself, it can be argued that he need not have been residing in Babylonia when he composed the work, but he might have been a Babylonian emigrant who had fled from Abbasid rule.[81]

1.1.4 Language, Hermeneutics, Topical Agenda, Narrativity, and Medievality

Apart from the passionately discussed issue of when and where the work was composed, a number of other aspects of *Seder Eliyahu* have been studied. The most comprehensive pieces of research literature are Friedmann's introduction to his edition and Max Kadushin's books *The Theology* and *Organic Thinking*. Friedmann's detailed introductory study of *Seder Eliyahu* is concerned with demonstrating that the work was written down by pupils of the prophet Elijah – that it was ultimately authored by the prophet himself. For this purpose, he discusses the biblical Elijah cycle and the Rabbinic passages that deal with the prophet's

---

78 See Kadushin, *Organic Thinking*, 12.
79 See chapter 2 on the problem of *Seder Eliyahu*'s authorship.
80 See Dina Stein, "Pirqe deRabbi Eliezer ve-Seder Eliyahu: heʿarot maqdimot ʿal poʾetiqa u-mercharv be-midrash ha-meʾuchar [Pirkei deRabbi Eliezer and Seder Eliyahu: Preliminary Notes on Poetics and Imaginary Landscapes]," *Jerusalem Studies in Hebrew Literature* 24 (2011): 5–6.
81 Commenting on the consequences of the breakdown of the Abbasid Empire, Marina Rustow, "Jews and the Islamic World: Transitions from Rabbinic to Medieval Contexts," in *The Bloomsbury Companion to Jewish Studies*, ed. Dean Phillip Bell (London: Bloomsbury Academic, 2013), 102, points out that "[s]tarting in the late ninth century, generation upon generation of migrants left Iraq and Iran for the West – not just Jews but everyone. Babylonian Rabbinic loyalists spread all over the mediterranean basin."

apparitions,[82] the nine talmudic baraitot that are introduced with the phrase תנא
דבי אליהו, as well as other baraitot which have parallels in *Seder Eliyahu*.[83] Friedmann sees the antiquity of the work as attested by the fact that several midrashim and prayer books borrowed material from it.[84] He also provides an exhaustive list of the scriptural verses quoted,[85] pointing out which among them receive special midrashic attention.[86] In both *The Theology* and *Organic Thinking*, Max Kadushin discusses the statements or teachings of the work – not differentiating between *Seder Eliyahu Rabbah* and *Seder Eliyahu Zuta* – as constituting a coherent system, a "theology," or an "organic complex." The complex is understood as comprising several Rabbinic concepts, which are built in their turn on the four so-called fundamental concepts of Rabbinic theology – God's loving-kindness, God's justice, Torah, and Israel.[87]

Other contributions have focused on aspects that can be interpreted as evidence of the work's cultural context. Jacob Elbaum, for example, analyses passages of *Seder Eliyahu* that allow him to view it as having certain traits of esoteric literature;[88] Adiel Kadari analyses selected passages of *Seder Eliyahu* and other works in terms of an idealisation of Torah study: in the passages of *Seder Eliyahu* he discusses, the importance of academies in small towns is emphasised, and the study of Torah is described in terms of mystical experience, with the divine Beit Midrash in the time to come as its spatio-temporal setting, whereby Kadari points to the possible presence of motifs from Hechalot literature.[89] In another article, Kadari discusses *Seder Eliyahu*'s ideology as placing the study of Torah above everything else – a study that can take place anywhere, thus opposing the centralisation of knowledge in Babylonian academies.[90]

---

[82] See Friedmann, *Seder Eliahu*, introduction, 2–44.
[83] See Friedmann, *Seder Eliahu*, introduction, 44–76.
[84] See Friedmann, *Seder Eliahu*, introduction, 77–83.
[85] See Friedmann, *Seder Eliahu*, introduction, 133–139.
[86] Friedmann, *Seder Eliahu*, introduction, 132: המקראות שעליהם הדרושים סבבים הם.
[87] For a critical appraisal of Kadushin's approach, see Lehmhaus, "Between Tradition and Innovation," 217n14.
[88] Jacob Elbaum, "Tanna deve Eliyahu ve-sifrut ha-sod ha-qedumah [The Midrash Tana Devei Eliyahu and Ancient Esoteric Literature]," *Jerusalem Studies in Jewish Thought* 6, nos. 1–2 (1987): 139–150.
[89] See Adiel Kadari, "Talmud torah, mystyqah ve-eskatologiah: ʿal beit ha-midrash shel ha-qadosh barukh hu be-midrash ha-meʾuḥar [Torah Study, Mysticism and Eschatology: 'God's Study Hall' in the Later Midrash]," *Tarbiz* 73, no. 2 (2004): esp. 187, and 189–190.
[90] Adiel Kadari, "Talmud torah be-Seder Eliyahu: ha-mishnah ha-raʿeinit be-heqesherah ha-histori-chevrati [Talmud Torah in Seder Eliyahu: The Ideological Doctrine in its Socio-Historical Context]," *Daat* 50–52 (2003): 35–59.

The problem of the work's polemics has been approached from diverse perspectives. Whereas Aptowitzer argued that the minority against which *Seder Eliyahu* polemicises are the Christians living in Babylonia under Muslim rule,[91] Wilhelm Bacher and Moshe Zucker suggested that the work addresses the Karaites as its opponents.[92] Discussing an article by Jacob Elbaum in which the characteristics of late midrashim are summarised,[93] Myron Lerner argued that Elbaum failed to mention anti-Karaite polemics in particular as one of the two fundamental criteria for the identification of a document as a late midrash, the second being a tendency to pseudepigraphy:

> The Karaite schism begun by Anan b. David during the latter half of the eighth century evoked various forms of response from the leaders of Rabbinic Judaism and it was only natural that anti-Karaite polemics would find their way into contemporary midrashic literature. Surprisingly enough, however, this phenomenon is not too widespread and there is only sporadic evidence for such occurrences in midrashic works dating from the eighth to the tenth centuries. Bacher et al. have argued that certain halakhic passages in *Seder Eliyahu* as well as those stressing the importance of Mishna study, instead of concentrating exclusively

---

[91] See Aptowitzer, "Seder Elia," 14.
[92] Bacher, "Antikaräisches"; Zucker, *Rav Saadya Gaon's Translation*, 116–126 and 203–219. On this problem, see also chapter 5 below. The idea that *Seder Eliyahu* documents the controversy with the Karaites had already been formulated by others; see Chayyim Oppenheim, *Bet Talmud* 1 (1881): 265–270, 304–310, 337–346, and 369–377; Jacob Samuel Fuchs, *Ha-Maggid le-Yisrael* 11 (1897): 22–23, 34–35, 45–46, and 57–58. Fuchs went so far as to identify Anan, Karaism's founder with the third century amora R. Anan who is mentioned in the Talmud passage dealing with the redaction of *Eliyahu Rabbah* and *Eliyahu Zuta* .
[93] See Jacob Elbaum, "Bein arikhah le-shikhtuv: le-ofyah shel ha-sifrut ha-midrashit ha-meʾucheret [Between Redaction and Rewriting: On the Character of the Late Midrashic Literature]," in *Proceedings of the Ninth World Congress of Jewish Studies: Division B: The History of the Jewish People (From the Second Temple Period until the Middle Ages)*, vol. 1 (Jerusalem: Magnes Press, 1986), 57–62. Elbaum summarized the characteristics of late midrashim – works composed between 700 and 900 CE, such as *Midrash Tanchuma, Pirqe de Rabbi Eliezer*, or *Seder Eliyahu* – as distinct from those of earlier periods in the following terms: "1. Definite signs of usage of the classical Amoraic Midrashim (e.g. Genesis Rabba) and the reworking of their contents; 2. Possible usage of the Babylonian Talmud; 3. The disappearance of 'early' linguistic phenomena and the transition to a purely Hebrew mode of expression; 4. A synthesis between the exegetical and the homiletical methods of midrash or an organization of the material according to large formats (subject matter or organizational patterns); 5. Rhetorical expressions and extended speech; 6. Differing perspectives in the mention of the names of sage: on the one hand, a tendency to employ anonymity in the quotation of midrashic teachings (i.e., by eliminating the names), and on the other, the addition of various titles and epithets to the names of certain rabbis; 7. Style and content which are similar to the format of medieval Bible commentary." This quotation follows Lerner, "Works of Aggadic Midrash," 151–152. See also Lehmhaus, "Between Tradition and Innovation," 215n11.

on the Bible, reflect the author's staunch opposition to Karaism. However, this conclusion has been challenged by some scholars, or simply ignored by others. ... Needless to say, the presence of polemical material against Karaite beliefs and practices in a particular midrash most likely attests to a ninth century or even later origin. However, the somewhat surprising paucity of such material in supposed later midrashic works raises some serious doubts as to the date which scholars have attributed to these works.[94]

Incidentally, it is in an attempt to draw a general picture of the main contributions of Karaism to Jewish culture in the tenth century that Rina Drory observes that midrash composed at this time tried to efface any trace of the time of composition, a characteristic that would account for the difficulty of dating *Seder Eliyahu*, as seen in the brief review of scholarship dedicated to giving an answer to that problem.

> In the field of midrash too, classicist models, also originated in oral activity (as surviving written exemplars indicate), prevailed. Its norms and repertoire of items had been established centuries earlier. Its poetics dictated absolute acceptance of the literary paradigm created in previous generations; literary creativity was exclusively confined to the reproduction of that paradigm. Accordingly, every effort was made to conceal a work's contemporariness, presenting it as written in antiquity.[95]

Drory argues that a collateral result of this effacement of the time of composition is the previously mentioned tendency to pseudepigraphy, of which, in her view, *Seder Eliyahu* partakes: "Texts were therefore ascribed to ancient personae (usually Mishnaic or Talmudic: Pirke de R. Eliezer, Tanna de bei Eliyahu, Alfā Betā de Ben Sīrā)."[96] She also concedes that "[a]lternately, works were left anonymous, conveying as it were a collective, superpersonal and supertemporal message by obscuring or concealing any detail that might disclose the work's time or place of writing: realia, place names, indications of time, etc., were omitted or replaced by old, ready-made items."[97] I will discuss the problem of *Seder Eliyahu*'s alleged pseudepigraphy in chapter 2.

Some other contributions to the study of *Seder Eliyahu* have dealt with the nature of the text, approaching it in a more immanent manner, analysing its language and style, its structure, and its hermeneutics. According to Ephraim Urbach – who published a detailed analysis of the language used in the first chapter, in which he focuses primarily on what the author borrowed from earlier sources –

---

94 Lerner, "Works of Aggadic Midrash," 153.
95 Rina Drory, *Models and Contacts: Arabic Literature and its Impact on Medieval Jewish Culture* (Leiden: Brill, 2000), 150.
96 Drory, *Models and Contacts*, 150.
97 Drory, *Models and Contacts*, 150.

the language of *Seder Eliyahu* is classicist and devoid of the simplicity characteristic of the language of daily life.[98] Similarly, Günter Stemberger describes the language of the work as "reines, doch mit eigenartigen Ausdrücken und zahlreichen neuen Wendungen geschmücktes, blumenreiches 'klassizistisches' Hebräisch."[99] Gershom Scholem observed that *Seder Eliyahu* shares a "periodic style" and the use of strings of adjectives in the description of God with the hymnology of Hechalot literature.[100]

William Braude describes its language as "lucid and fluid," as well as fundamentally asyndetic, which is why he argues that a so-called "scientific method" in translation – a literal translation – is not an adequate option, for it would mean exposing "Rabbinic literature to ridicule."[101] Ulrich Berzbach refers to a personal communication with Jacob Elbaum during the EAJS summer colloquium "Jewish Bible Exegesis in the Middle Ages," which yielded the expression "piyyutic prose" to describe the style and language of *Seder Eliyahu*.[102]

Several innovative literary strategies in *Seder Eliyahu Zuta* are examined by Lennart Lehmhaus in an attempt to revise established notions of Rabbinic scholarship, according to which late midrash constitutes a "mere afterglow of the Golden Age of classic (i.e., amoraic) midrash," attesting to the stagnation of Rabbinic culture in post-talmudic times. [103] These include the special use of introductory formulas of classical Rabbinic terminology[104] and the link between the semantic and lexical examination of keywords and exposition on a certain topic or thematic cluster.[105] Lehmhaus concludes that "the absence of polyphonic discourse and attributions as well as the departure from midrashic exegesis and talmudic dialec-

---

[98] See Urbach, "Le-sheelat leshono u-meqorotaw shel Sefer Seder Elijahu [On the language and the sources of Seder Eliyahu]," 184.
[99] Stemberger, *Einleitung*, 379.
[100] See Gershom Scholem, *Jewish Gnosticism, Merkabah Mysticism, and Talmudic Tradition* (New York: Jewish Theological Seminary of America, 1960), 24 and 42; and Johann Maier, "Serienbildung und 'numinoser' Eindruckseffekt in den poetischen Stücken der Hekhalot-Literatur," *Semitics* 3 (1973): 36–66.
[101] Braude, "Conjecture and Interpolation," 78. This is the reason why Braude opts for the use of interpolations that provide the transitions a reader of English literature is bound to expect from a text. (See 79)
[102] Ulrich Berzbach, "The Varieties of Literal Devices in a Medieval Midrash: Seder Eliyahu Rabba, Chapter 18," in *Jewish Studies at the Turn of the Twentieth Century: Proceedings of the 6th EAJS Congress, Toledo, July 1998*, ed. Judit Targarona Borrás and Ángel Sáenz-Badillos (Leiden: Leiden, 1999), 389.
[103] Lehmhaus, "Between Tradition and Innovation," 215.
[104] See Lehmhaus, "Between Tradition and Innovation," 226–230.
[105] See Lehmhaus, "Between Tradition and Innovation," 231–236.

tics mark a major difference in the text's overall character" – that is, with respect to earlier Rabbinic literature.¹⁰⁶ In a later contribution, Lehmhaus is concerned with the use of liturgical elements which, in the non-liturgical context of *Seder Eliyahu Zuta*, are intertwined with the rest of the work's literary forms.¹⁰⁷

Some studies have focussed on the work's hermeneutics and literary forms. Zwi Werblowsky provides a close reading or "textual analysis" of two chapters of *Seder Eliyahu*, chapters 10 and 11, which he regards as "primarily a midrash on Deborah."¹⁰⁸ His initial appreciation of the text is not exactly enticing: "The midrash known as *Seder Eliyahu* (SE) or *Tanna debe Eliyahu* (TdbE) is, by common consent, one of the most baffling and intractable midrashim in our possession. ... This text is admittedly faulty and corrupt, often beyond restoration."¹⁰⁹ He concedes, nevertheless, that the character of the text is "well-rounded, closely knit," which makes it a "genuine *midrash* as distinct from a *yalkut*." He describes the text as follows: "Its pericopes are coherent, well-developed expositions of specific themes, although it may often be difficult to follow the thread of the argument in the maze of incidental matter and tangential excursions."¹¹⁰ In an analysis of two segments, he attempts to show that *Seder Eliyahu*'s versions of aggadic material appear "baroque" when compared with talmudic versions.¹¹¹ This comparative reading of small units furthermore enables Werblowsky to conclude that the form of the texts themselves reveals their diverse situatedness: A *maʿaseh* on the power of *tsedakah* told in *Bereshit Rabbah*, *Midrash Shemuʾel*, and *Seder Eliyahu* is read in terms of "edifying stories meant to exhort the audience or reading public to practise charity," whereas its parallel version in bRH 18a "is no sermon; it is meant as proof. It is advanced as empirical evidence in order to settle an argument."¹¹²

William Braude published a short article in which he provides examples from the first three chapters of *Seder Eliyahu Rabbah* of what he considers exegetical

---

106 Lehmhaus, "Between Tradition and Innovation," 238.
107 Lennart Lehmhaus, "'Blessed be He, who Remembered the Earlier Deeds and Overlooks the Later': Prayer, Benedictions, and Liturgy in the New Rhetoric Garb of Late Midrashic Traditions," in *"It's Better to Hear the Rebuke of the Wise Than the Song of Fools" (Qoh 7:5): Proceedings of the Midrash Section, Society of Biblical Literature*, ed. W. David Nelson and Rivka Ulmer (Piscataway, NJ: Gorgias Press, 2015), 95–140.
108 Werblowsky, "A Note," 202.
109 Werblowsky, "A Note," 201.
110 Werblowsky, "A Note," 201.
111 See Werblowsky, "A Note," 208.
112 Werblowsky, "A Note," 209.

innovations by its author.¹¹³ In an article on the literary devices employed in *Seder Eliyahu Rabbah* – focussing on the third part of the book, chapters 18–29 – Ulrich Berzbach argues that chapter 18, the longest in *Seder Eliyahu Rabbah* (and one which, in Friedmann's view, was not integral to the original text), can be read as containing evidence for four structuring principles that operate throughout the work, on the chapter level as well as on the macro-structural level of the entire book.¹¹⁴ These principles determine the characteristic architecture of a midrash, whose richness of literary devices – among which Berzbach highlights the use of keywords to link exegetical units, a hermeneutic operation he terms "masoretic association," and the use of lists – is interpreted as a evidence of the work's "medievality."¹¹⁵ After a brief analysis of the chapter's structure and literary forms he concludes with a remark that seems to apply to the whole work:

> None of these genres is unique to *SER*, but the high degree of combination and the interwoven texture created by the constant employment of all of them might be considered unusual for a "classical Rabbinical" midrash, together with the lack of a structure and organisation that is obvious at first glance. All this might point to a "medieval-minded" author, who consciously employed all material and all literary devices available to him, in order to create an educational as well as literary work with a structure and a flavor of its own.¹¹⁶

The illustrative function of *meshalim* in *Seder Eliyahu* is discussed by David Stern, who attributes to the late midrash *Seder Eliyahu* an inaugural role in the history of the parable:

> In literature from the Rabbinic period, one can find other parables of this illustrational kind. But it is not until post-Rabbinic early medieval Jewish times that the use of the *mashal* as an illustration becomes the prevalent form. It occurs initially in the ninth-century composition *Tanna de-Bei Eliyahu*, and becomes even more prevalent in subsequent philosophical works by such authors as Maimonides.¹¹⁷

In the following chapters, I will concentrate on different aspects of the Rabbah and the Zuta parts of *Seder Eliyahu*; in some cases, I will also draw on material from *Pseudo-Seder Eliyahu Zuta*. My main concern will be the use of narrative

---

113 See William G. Braude, "Novellae in Eliyyahu Rabbah's Exegesis," in *Studies in Aggadah, Targum and Jewish Liturgy in Memory of Joseph Heinemann*, ed. Jacob J. Petuchowski and Ezra Fleischer (Jerusalem: Magnes Press, 1981), 11–22.
114 These are a) the principle of continuous expansion, b) the principle of symmetry, c) the principle of linking units within parts of *Seder Eliyahu Rabbah*, and d) the principle of reversion of orders.
115 See Berzbach, "Varieties," 384.
116 Berzbach, "Varieties," 391.
117 Stern, *Parables*, 45.

within the non-Rabbinic discourse of a post-classical midrashic document. I will present narrative forms, describe them, analyse them, and see how they interact with non-narrative co-texts.[118] Throughout the book, for want of more appropriate terminology, the non-narrative discourse that contrasts with the narrative discourse is said to be ethical-homiletical, even if its chapters are most certainly not actual homilies.

1.2 Narratological Readings of *Seder Eliyahu*

> Rather than possessing a hermeneutics, a systematic base for interpretation, midrash may be said to have been impelled by a narrative of interpretation. Accordingly, the goal of a theoretical study of midrash would be less a matter of hermeneutics, of learning the system of interpretive procedures, than a project of constructing a narratology.[119]

With these words David Stern summarises his reflections in the book of essays *Midrash and Theory*, on what he describes as "the most clearly definable form of narrative in midrash, the parable or *mashal*."[120] In this essay, Stern is not concerned with the parabolical narrative per se, but primarily with recovering what these narratives say about themselves, about their being told for the sake of interpretation, in short, he is concerned with the poetology, which is an important aspect of the "literariness" of the Rabbinic parable in midrash.

Since the publication of Geoffrey Hartman and Sanford Budick's of the collected volume *Midrash and Literature* in 1986,[121] the study of the literary character of Rabbinic documents, and of Rabbinic narrative in particular, has developed into a legitimate approach to these texts, one with *Erkenntnisgewinn* – that is, findings in its own right. This is manifest in the wide range of publications on Rabbinic texts and subjects which rely on notions from different schools of literary theory,

---

118 The term "co-text" refers to the immediate linguistic environment of an expression, sentence, or passage, whereas with "context" I refer to the wider textual environment (an entire chapter or even the entire *Seder Eliyahu*) and to the non-linguistic situation of the text. See John Lyons, "Text and Discourse; Context and Co-text," chap. 9 in *Linguistic Semantics: An Introduction* (Cambridge University Press, 1995).
119 See David Stern, *Midrash and Theory: Ancient Jewish Exegesis and Contemporary Literary Studies* (Evanston, IL: Northwestern University Press, 1996), 53.
120 See Stern, *Midrash and Theory*, 39.
121 Geoffrey H. Hartman and Sanford Budick, eds., *Midrash and Literature* (New Haven, CT: Yale University Press, 1986).

including new criticism, new historicism, cultural studies, feminism, gender studies, and narratology, to name but a few.[122]

Parallel to these developments in the field of Jewish studies a boom in narratology can be ascertained in literary studies. Narratology emerged in the 1970s as a structuralist theory of narrative (a phase generally referred to as classical narratology) and developed from the 1980s onwards into several kinds of theoretical and applied post-classical narratologies.[123] Characteristic of the latter is a different, larger corpus, which includes non-literary sources; sources might be non-written or non-fictional texts – in short, sources from contexts other than fictional narratives of the nineteenth and twentieth centuries, including visual arts, culture, society, and gender. These new types of sources determine new sets of questions – for example, pertaining to a given text's narrativity.[124] The questions asked by these post-classical narratologies are also determined by a transfer of theory from disci-

---

[122] See, among others, Susan A. Handelman, *The Slayers of Moses: The Emergence of Rabbinic Interpretation in Modern Literary Theory* (New York: State University of New York Press, 1983); Ofra Meir, *Ha-sipur darshani be-bereshit rabbah [The Exegetical Narrative in Genesis Rabbah]* (Tel Aviv: Ha-kibutz Ha-meuchad, 1987); Daniel Boyarin, *Intertextuality and the Reading of Midrash* (Bloomington, IN: Indiana University Press, 1990); Yonah Fraenkel, *Darkhe ha-agadah veha-midrash [The Hermeneutics of Aggadah and Midrash]*, 2 vols. (Givatayim: Yad La-Talmud, 1991); Yonah Fraenkel, *Sipur ha-agadah, aḥdut shel tokhen ve-tsurah: Kovets mekharim [The Aggadic Narrative: Harmony of Form and Content]* (Tel Aviv: Ha-kibutz Ha-meuchad, 2001); Stern, *Parables*; Michael Fishbane, *The Midrashic Imagination: Jewish Exegesis, Thought, and History* (Albany, NY: SUNY, 1993); Jeffrey Rubenstein, *Talmudic Stories: Narrative Art, Composition, and Culture* (Baltimore: The Johns Hopkins University Press, 1999); Stern, *Midrash and Theory*; Judith Hauptmann, *Rereading the Rabbis: A Woman's Voice* (Boulder, CO: Westview Press, 1998); Judith Baskin, *Midrashic Women: Formations of the Feminine in Rabbinic Literature* (Hanover, NH: Brandeis University Press, 2002); Joshua Levinson, *Ha-sipur she-lo supar: omanut ha-sipur ha-miqraʾi ha-murchav be-midreshe chazal [The Twice-Told Tale: A Poetics of the Exegetical Narrative in Rabbinic Midrash]* (Jerusalem: Magnes Press, 2005); Carol Bakhos, *Ismael on the Border* (Albany, NY: State University of New York Press, 2006); Carol Bakhos, ed., *Current Trends in the Study of Midrash* (Leiden, Boston: Brill, 2006); Dina Stein, *Textual Mirrors: Reflexivity, Midrash, and the Rabbinic Self* (Philadelphia, PA: University of Pennsylvania Press, 2012); Inbar Raveh, *Feminist Rereadings of Rabbinic Literature* (Waltham, MA: Brandeis University Press, 2014).

[123] The expression "post-classical narratology" was introduced by David Herman, "Scripts, Sequences, and Stories: Elements of a Postclassical Narratology," *PMLA* 112, no. 5 (1997): 1046–1059.

[124] See Matei Chihaia, "Introductions to Narratology: Theory, Practice and the Afterlife of Structuralism," *Diegesis* 1, no. 1 (2012): 27. For recent examples of reflection on the narrativity of legal documents in the field of Jewish studies, see Barry Wimpfheimer, *Narrating the Law: A Poetics of Talmudic Legal Stories* (Philadelphia, PA: University of Pennsylvania Press, 2011) and Moshe Simon-Shoshan, *Stories of the Law: Narrative Discourse and the Construction of Authority in the Mishnah* (Oxford: Oxford University Press, 2012).

plines such as cultural studies, anthropology, media studies, and gender studies, among others. In this post-classical context of the widened scope of narratology's object of study ancient and medieval sources have come to be considered suitable for narratological readings.[125]

It is at the crossroads of both of these trends – the reading of the texts of Rabbinic Judaism as literary texts and the practice of narratological criticism on sources from discursive contexts other than narrative fiction – that the present study is situated. It seeks not to define what the work of late midrash known as *Seder Eliyahu* or *Tanna debe Eliyahu* is, or to read it in search of passages that can be valued as historical sources, but rather to describe some of its constitutive parts – the narrative ones – by presenting and discussing them with a view to elucidating how they interact with the non-narrative context in which they are found. Midrash is a discourse that makes frequent use of narrative.[126] That is why narrative in midrash never occurs on an independent level of communication, but could be described as framed by midrashic discourse.

A post-classical narratological approach to narrative that is part of (i.e., instrumentalised by) a non-narrative discourse, such as that of midrash, can contribute to addressing a series of important questions for the study of Rabbinic texts. As

---

[125] For the major trends in post-classical narratology, see e.g., Ansgar Nünning and Vera Nünning, "Von der strukturalistischen Narratologie zur 'postklassischen' Erzähltheorie: Ein Überblick über neue Ansätze und Entwicklungstendenzen," in *Neue Ansätze in der Erzähltheorie* (Trier: WVT, 2002), 1–33; Ansgar Nünning, "Narratology or Narratologies," in *What is Narratology? Questions and Answers regarding the Status of a Theory* (Berlin: De Gruyter, 2003), 239–275; Monika Fludernik, *Erzähltheorie: Eine Einführung* (Darmstadt: Wissenschaftliche Buchgesellschaft, 2006), 103–123; Sandra Heinen and Roy Sommer, "Narratology and Interdisciplinarity," in *Narratology in the Age of Cross-Disciplinary Narrative Research*, ed. Sandra Heinen and Roy Sommer (Berlin: De Gruyter, 2009), 1–10; Jan Alber and Monika Fludernik, eds., *Postclassical Narratology: Approaches and Analyses* (Columbus, OH: Ohio University Press, 2010), 1–31.

[126] A plethora of definitions have been proposed. For descriptions of what midrash is and how it operates, see e.g., Addison Wright, *The Literary Genre Midrash* (Staten Island, NY: Alba House, 1967); James Kugel, "Two Introductions to Midrash," in *Midrash and Literature*, ed. Geoffrey H. Hartman and Sanford Budick (New Haven, CT: Yale University Press, 1986), 77–103; Avigdor Shinan and Yair Zakovitch, "Midrash on Scripture and Midrash within Scripture," *Scripta Hierosolymitana* 31 (1986): 257–277; Gary Porton, "Defining Midrash," in *The Study of Ancient Judaism*, ed. Jacob Neusner, vol. 1: *Mishnah, Midrash, Siddur* (New York: Ktav, 1981), 55–92; Arnold Goldberg, "Die funktionale Form Midrasch," in *Rabbinische Texte als Gegenstand der Auslegung*, vol. 2 of *Gesammelte Studien*, ed. Margarete Schlüter and Peter Schäfer (Tübingen: Mohr Siebeck, 1999), 199–229 (originally published in *Frankfurter Judaistische Beiträge* 12 [1984]: 1–45); Gary Porton, "Definitions of Midrash," in *Encyclopedia of Midrash*, ed. Jacob Neusner, vol. 1 (Leiden, Boston: Brill, 2005), 520–534; Alexander Samely, *Forms of Rabbinic Literature and Thought* (Oxford: Oxford University Press, 2007), ch. 4, 5, and 10.

the survey in the first part of this chapter (1.1) has attempted to demonstrate, such an approach to a comprehensive study of *Seder Eliyahu* has not yet been done. For a long time, the work has been studied primarily with the aim of dating it or of determining whether it is of Babylonian, Palestinian, or even European origin, and seldom with a view to analysing it in its own right, as a work of Rabbinic *literature*.[127]

Chapter 2 deals with the apparently multiple voices of *Seder Eliyahu* and is concerned with the question of whether the categories of author, narrator, or author-image are viable when reading a work of late midrash such as this one. I will first consider the problem of the work's alleged pseudepigraphy and then turn to the voice that speaks in the first person, both in narrative and in non-narrative contexts. I shall also examine whether this voice can be seen as related to the figure of the prophet Elijah – that is to say, the Rabbinic reception of the prophet Elijah – and the question of what the reader learns from this voice, the text's governing voice[128] – about the image the author gives of himself – when it addresses its audience, when it speaks as a Rabbinic interpreter, and when it narrates stories.

Chapter 3 provides a preliminary typology of the narrative forms of *Seder Eliyahu*. Before turning to these, I discuss selected textual passages that are not considered of a narrative character. Among the narrative texts I distinguish small, simple forms, such as the *maʿaseh* and the *mashal*, and longer, composite, complex ones, such as the first-person narrative and the exegetical narrative. In the case of the latter, it might be argued that function is not as intrinsically related to form as might be the case with the simple forms (as appears to be more evident in earlier Rabbinic documents, in any case).

In the two subsequent chapters, I address the most conspicuous of these literary forms. For my discussion of the parables in chapter 4, I expand on the classification proposed in the typology of the previous chapter. Out of a corpus of 78 parables, I discuss selected examples for each of the following parable types: exegetical parables; not explicitly exegetical, narrative-recapitulative parables; those I designate as meta-exegetical parables; and parables that seem to provide an answer to a rhetorical question. I pay special attention to the way the parable interacts with its immediate linguistic co-text, but also with the wider thematic context of which it is a part; these are thematic agendas of *Seder Eliyahu*, among which

---

127 Max Kadushin's more detailed readings in *The Theology* and *Organic Thinking* attempt to abstract from the disparate text passages a series of theological and ethical concepts – an organon, the ideological structure of the work.
128 See n. 22.

the exaltation of the "disciples of the wise" – the Rabbinic class – is particularly remarkable.

Contributions by Wilhelm Bacher and Moshe Zucker provide the point of departure in chapter 5. According to Bacher and Zucker, a prominent feature of the late midrash *Seder Eliyahu* is the fact that its "author" depicts himself as impersonating an apologetical discourse on Rabbinic Judaism in the face of the challenge of Karaism.[129] The passages in question are dialogical passages set within a brief narrative frame and are, in the context of this study, designated as first-person narratives. I discuss them in order to reconsider the problem of *Seder Eliyahu*'s anti-Karaism, or the positivistic certainty with which scholarship has ascertained such an agenda in a work that so decidedly resists being dated and located.

In the last chapter, I attempt to apply notions of feminist narratology to readings of selected passages on the world of women in *Seder Eliyahu*. The passages discussed – for example, on women as legal personae, on nameless Rabbinic women in domestic contexts, on biblical women, on women as mothers, wives, or martyrs – are found in contexts dealing with legal questions (hence the designation "halakhic contexts") or with matters of scriptural interpretation (hence "exegetical contexts").

The texts discussed in chapters 3, 4, 5, and 6 are just segments of *Seder Eliyahu*, some of them probably more representative than others. In any case, as we have seen from the survey in 1.1 and pointed out above, a narratologically informed study of *Seder Eliyahu* represents a new approach to the work.

---

[129] See Bacher, "Antikaräisches"; and Zucker, *Rav Saadya Gaon's Translation*.

2 The Voices of *Seder Eliyahu*

Although most of the names of the rabbinic tradents quoted in midrashic literature are generally taken on face value and considered to be reliable, there are, nevertheless, certain midrashic works in which no authenticity whatsoever can be vouched for the names of the rabbis cited, and so these traditions must actually be considered pseudepigraphic.[1]

Myron Lerner points out that a distinctive characteristic of late midrashim is its tendency to pseudepigraphy. However, he does not refer to entire documents, such as the Book of Enoch and other Jewish hellenistic literary works which make use of pseudepigraphy as a literary convention[2] – that is, the false attribution of a text to a well-known person from the biblical past in order to lend the text authority. In the passage quoted above, Lerner instead refers to the way single traditions contained in late midrashic works are intentionally attributed to rabbis who were not the first to express them.[3] Since classical Rabbinic literature (Mishnah, Tosefta, Talmudim and Midrashim) is not "author literature," but rather the collective work of the community and, as Martin Jaffee argues, "'said,' 'received' or 'heard,' and 'transmitted'" but "not 'authored,'"[4] attribution remains a micro-

---

[1] Lerner, "Works of Aggadic Midrash," 152.
[2] See Ruben Zimmermann, "Pseudepigraphie / Pseudonymität," in *Religion in Geschichte und Gegenwart: Handwörterbuch für Theologie und Religionswissenschaft*, ed. Hans D. Betz et al. (Tübingen: UTB Mohr Siebeck, 2008), 1786–1788; and James H. Charlesworth, "Pseudepigraphen des Alten Testaments," in *Theologische Realenzyklopädie*, ed. Gerhard Müller, vol. 27 (Berlin: De Gruyter, 1997), 639–645.
[3] See Michael E. Stone, "Pseudepigraphy Reconsidered," *The Review of Rabbinic Judaism* 9 (2006): 1–15. For a general overview on the subject of pseudepigraphy in the literature of the Second Temple period, see Loren T. Stuckenbruck, "Pseudepigraphy and First Person Discourse in the Dead Sea Documents: From the Aramaic Texts to the Writings of the Yahad," in *The Dead Sea Scrolls and Contemporary Culture*, ed. Adolfo Daniel Roitman, Lawrence H. Schiffman, and Shani Tzoref (Leiden, Boston: Brill, 2011), 293–326. The works discussed by Stuckenbruck all name a biblical figure and present this as tradent of the whole or of the majority of the material comprised in the work. On the role of creative attribution in Rabbinic pseudepigraphy, see Marc Bregman, "Pseudepigraphy in Rabbinic Literature," in *Pseudepigraphic Perspectives: The Apocrypha and Pseudepigrapha in Light of the Dead Sea Scrolls*, ed. Esther Chazon (Leiden, Boston: Brill, 1999), 27–41.
[4] Martin S. Jaffee, "Rabbinic Authorship as a Collective Enterprise," in *The Cambridge Companion to the Talmud and Rabbinic Literature*, ed. Charlotte Elisheva Fonrobert and Martin S. Jaffee (Cambridge, New York: Cambridge University Press, 2007), 17. On the problem of authorship specifically in the context of the Babylonian Talmud, see Sacha Stern, "The Concept of Authorship in the Babylonian Talmud," *Journal of Jewish Studies* 46 (1995): 183–195; Sacha Stern, "Attribution and Authorship in the Babylonian Talmud," *Journal of Jewish Studies* 45 (1994): 28–51.

DOI 10.1515/9783110531879-002

phenomenon related to sayings but not to works or documents[5] – at least until post-talmudic times, when works such as the *Pirqe de Rabbi Eliezer* can be seen as an example of a whole work indirectly attributed to Eliezer b. Hyrkanos,[6] as part of a larger trend toward attribution in post-talmudic literature.

When we look at *Seder Eliyahu*, a series of questions related to the problem of (individual) authorship, as well as to the very categories of author and narrator, arises. Is it legitimate to consider a work which presents its material anonymously to be a pseudepigraphon just because different sources apparently refer to it with titles that include the name of Elijah?[7] Was the apparently pseudepigraphic title chosen by the author? To what extent can it be considered a work of pseudepigraphy if there is, as I will argue, no evident authorial intention to attribute the text to the prophet Elijah – or to any other person with the name Elijah – *within* the text which has come down to us? Related to these questions is the problem of single authorship itself – that is to say, is it possible for a work to be authored by a single person and still be regarded as belonging to the Rabbinic corpus? These are some of the issues I will consider in this chapter, focussing on different perspectives from which to describe the text's *Urheber*, its authorial and narratorial instances, as transmitted both in the text itself and in some of its paratexts.[8]

I shall first consider the problem of the title or titles as the main paratexts of the work in order to approach its apparent pseudoepigraphical character, as evidenced mainly in a passage of the Babylonian Talmud. Secondly, I will attempt to give an overview of the instances in which the main voice of the document (its "governing voice") makes use of the first person, both in narrative and non-narrative contexts. Thirdly, I will discuss the reception of Elijah within *Seder*

---

5 See Petr Pokorný and Günter Stemberger, "Pseudepigraphie," in *Theologische Realenzyklopädie*, ed. Gerhard Müller, vol. 27 (Berlin: De Gruyter, 1997), 657. For the tendency of the redactors of the Bavli to attribute anonymous compilations such as the Mishnah or certain *baraitot* to individual authors, see Stern, "The Concept of Authorship," 193.
6 See Lerner, "Works of Aggadic Midrash," 153.
7 *Seder Eliyahu* has sometimes been regarded as an example of pseudepigraphy, e.g., by Graetz, *Geschichte der Juden*, 294, who writes: "Dieses Werk ... läßt zwar den Propheten Eliah erzählen, ermahnen, predigen ... Der Prediger unter Eliah's Verkappung räumt zwar ein, daß ein Nichtjude gleich einem Israeliten des göttlichen Geistes theilhaftig werden könne je nach seinen Thaten." In a similar vein, Güdemann, *Geschichte des Erziehungswesens*, 52, claims: "Das Buch ist das Werk eines unter der nicht durchweg festgehaltenen Maske des Propheten Elias schreibenden Reisepredigers, der viele Länder und Menschen kennen gelernt, viel erlebt und erfahren hat und nun theils in zusammenhängenden Reden, theils in einzelnen Maximen im Wege selbstständiger Auslegung des Schriftwortes oder an ältere Auslegungen anknüpfend die Summe seiner Erfahrungen und seine Lehren darlegt."
8 On the concept of paratext, see Gérard Genette, *Paratexts: Thresholds of Interpretation*, trans. Jane E. Lewin (Cambridge: Cambridge University Press, 1997).

Eliyahu in order to argue that the narrator cannot be seen as conceived after the fashion of the biblical character of the prophet Elijah. Finally, I will turn to the category of the implied author and attempt to draw some conclusions regarding the image the author gives of himself in the text and how these textual strategies place *Seder Eliyahu* in the history of Jewish literature.

2.1 The Title

2.1.1 Paratext 1: bKet 105b–106a

> A man once brought to Rav Anan a basket of small fish. He said to him, What is your business here? He said to him, I have a lawsuit. He did not accept it [the fish] from him. He said to him, I am disqualified [to be the judge at] your lawsuit. He said to him, I do not want your judgement. Will the Master accept my present that I may not be prevented from offering my first fruits? For it was taught, *And there came a man from Baal-shalishah, bringing food from the first fruits to the man of God: twenty loaves of barley, and fresh ears of grain in his sack* (2 Kgs 4:42). But was Elisha entitled to eat first fruits? This is to tell you that one who brings a present to a scholar [is doing as good a deed] as if he had offered first fruits. He said to him, It was not my intention to accept [your present], but now that you have given me a reason I will accept it. He sent him to Rav Nachman and sent to him [the following message], Will the Master try [the action of] this man, for I, Anan, I am disqualified [to be the judge at] his lawsuit. From the fact that he has sent to me, [I may] infer that he must be a relative of his [Anan's]. An orphans' lawsuit was then in progress before him. He said: This is a positive precept and this is a positive precept. The positive precept of showing respect for the Torah takes precedence. He suspended the orphans' lawsuit and dealt with the man's suit. When the other party noticed the honour he [Nachman] showed him he remained speechless. [Until that happened] Elijah was a frequent visitor of Rav Anan whom he was teaching the Order of Elijah (סדר דאליהו). But as soon as he did this [Elijah] went away. He [Anan] spent his time in fasting, and in prayers for [God's] mercy, [until Elijah came to him again; but when he appeared he greatly frightened him. Thereupon he made a box [for himself] and in it he sat before him until he concluded his Order with him. And this is [the reason] why they speak of *Seder Eliyahu Rabbah* and *Seder Eliyahu Zuta* (סדר אליהו רבה, סדר אליהו זוטא).[9]

According to this passage of the Babylonian Talmud, someone brings Rav Anan some fish as a present and asks him to act as the judge in a lawsuit in which the unnamed person is himself the litigant. Even though Anan refuses to be involved at first, the man persuades him to keep the present, and he eventually fulfils the man's request and assigns him another judge, Rav Nachman. Assuming that Anan

---

9 With minor modifications, this text follows that of Isidore Epstein, ed., *Kethuboth*, vol. 2 of *The Babylonian Talmud: Seder Nashim*, trans. Samuel Daiches and Israel W. Slotki (London: Soncino, 1936).

is prevented from acting as the judge because he is related to the man, R. Nachman postpones another case he was presiding over and acts as the judge in the man's case, which is interpreted by the other party as a sign of partiality towards the unnamed man. So goes the first part of the story. Only in the second part does Elijah make his narrative appearance, to punish his friend and disciple Anan for his carelessness: The reader is told that until this day, Elijah has regularly visited Anan, whom he has taught the Order of Elijah (i.e., *Seder Eliyahu*). From that day onwards, Anan fasts and prays for mercy, but Elijah refrains from appearing to him. When he eventually does come to see Anan, it is such a frightening sight for the latter that he is said to shut himself up in a box to write down the Order of Elijah. Why Anan would resort to making a box in which to hide especially from Elijah the text does not explain, but the preceding context in bKet 105a–b hints at its possible meaning: Even if Anan ultimately did not act as the judge, accepting a present and suggesting another judge were actions that could be interpreted as showing an inclination for the unnamed man. The image of the box in which Anan hides is a vivid warning of the terror the rabbi must have experienced, as well as evidence of his urgent need to demonstrate repentance by putting down on paper what Elijah had taught him both before and after the incident with the present and the lawsuit. To close the passage, the anonymous voice of the talmudic narrator explains that it is to distinguish between Elijah's teachings to Anan before and after the incident of the lawsuit that we speak of *Seder Eliyahu Rabbah* and *Seder Eliyahu Zuta*.

Friedmann interpreted this passage as evidence that Elijah authored the work and, as Max Kadushin puts it, "that the entire text of Seder Eliahu was the result of abnormal mysticism."[10] This notion is expressed in his notes and preface in German.[11] In his lengthier Hebrew introduction, Friedmann adduces numerous talmudic passages which relate how the prophet Elijah revealed himself to rabbis and others.[12] Thus the transmission of *Seder Eliyahu* would not be an isolated occurrence in Elijah's Rabbinic tradition. Braude and Kapstein also appear to follow Friedmann's theory when they remark in the introduction to their translation of

---

10 Kadushin, *Organic Thinking*, 239.
11 Friedmann, *Seder Eliahu*, Vorwort, V, writes: "An stilistischer Schönheit, an ethischer Tiefe und Reichhaltigkeit, an Anregung zur Liebe der Thora wie des Volkes Israel kommt ihm [*Seder Eliyahu*] kein Buch in der aggadischen Literatur gleich. Ähnlichen Tones sind wohl einzelne Beraithoth zu finden, aber kein Buch, und dennoch war dieses Buch, wie oben gesagt wenig verbreitet. Es scheint, dass die tonangebenden Lehrer es mit Absicht vermieden, dem Buche beim Volke Eingang zu verschaffen, seines mystischen Ursprunges halber, um mystischem Aberglauben nicht Thür und Thor zu öffnen."
12 See Friedmann, *Seder Eliahu*, introduction, 2–44.

the work "that the legendary account of the work's origin is closer to the truth than the common sense of scholars is willing to accept."[13] Furthermore, they argue:

> If Rav Anan was a man open to such direct experience of the supernatural, he would have had no doubt that it was Elijah the prophet in person who, in the guise of a scholar, was visiting and instructing him in wisdom from above.[14]

It is beyond the scope of this chapter to examine whether this account was ever thought of as a factual narrative of how men who are open to the experience of the supernatural can access wisdom. As explained above, Elijah is said to have appeared to the printer Samuel Haida in Prague in the seventeenth century, aiding him in his publication of a purportedly correct version of *Seder Eliyahu*.[15]

2.1.2 Paratext 2: Codex Vat. ebr. 31.

The titles and colophons of the two parts of the work in the only manuscript which transmits both parts, which was copied in 1073,[16] all contain the name *Eliyahu*, without any epithet. The word *seder* is only used for the *Zuta* part, which is referred to as *Seder Eliyahu Zuta* in both the title and the colophon.[17] The *Rabbah* part is designated as *eliyahu rabbah* in the title and as *midrash eliyahu rabbah* in the colophon (see table 2.1.)

---

13 Braude and Kapstein, *Tanna děbe Eliyyahu*, Introduction, 10.
14 Braude and Kapstein, *Tanna děbe Eliyyahu*, Introduction, 10.
15 See above p. 6.
16 The manuscript was copied in the year 1073, as stated in the colophon of *Sifra*, the first work transmitted in the manuscript, according to two chronologies: "and it was concluded in the year 833 since the creation of the world and in the year 1005 since the destruction of the Temple. Let it be rebuilt soon. Amen." (ונגמר בשנת תתלג ליצירה ובשנת אלף וחמש לחרבן הבית שיבנה במהרה בימינו אמן). The first one, the traditional Jewish chronology, should be read as 4833 years since the creation of the world (3670 years are subtracted for the Gregorian chronology). The second date assumes that the destruction of the Temple took place in the year 68 CE.
17 MS Parma 2785 introduces *Seder Eliyahu Zuta* with the phrase סדר אליהו זוטה אתחיל. See Berzbach, "Textual Witnesses," 69, who points out that, apart from MS Vat. ebr. 31, this is the only one which assigns *Seder Eliyahu Zuta* a name.

Table 2.1: Titles and Colophons of Codex Vat. ebr. 31

Type of Paratext	Wording and Location
Title of *Seder Eliyahu Rabbah*:	יסייעיני להתחיל ולגמור אליהו רבה ("Let Him help me begin and conclude *Eliyahu Rabbah*") (fol. 112)
Colophon of *Seder Eliyahu Rabbah*:	סליק מדרש אליהו רבא בסיוע דגול מרבבה ("The *Midrash Eliyahu Rabbah* is concluded with the help of the chiefest among ten thousand") (fol. 159)
Title of *Seder Eliyahu Zuta*:	יסייעיני להתחיל ולגמור סדר אליהו זוטא ("Let him help me begin and conclude the *Order [Seder] Eliyahu Zuta*") (fol. 159)
Colophon of *Seder Eliyahu Zuta*:	הדרן עלך סדר אליהו זוטא ("We will come back to you, *Order [Seder] Eliyahu Zuta*"[18]) (fol. 167)

2.1.3 Paratext 3: Talmudic Passages

The work is also known as *Tanna debe Eliyahu* or the "Teaching of the School of Elijah," a title that goes back to a number of passages in the Babylonian Talmud introduced with the phrase תנא דבי אליהו.[19] However, only three of these are actually transmitted in *Seder Eliyahu* as it has been preserved: bSan 97a–b (par. bAZ 9a), bPes 94a, and bShab 13a–b.[20]

---

18 This wording reminds one of the scribal formula at the end of the Talmud tractates containing the Hadran prayer, which is said upon completion of the study of the tractate.
19 For their text, see appendix 1 (2.4.1) at the end of this chapter.
20 Regarding the origins of the Talmud passages and their intertextual relation to *Seder Eliyahu* Louis Ginzberg, *Notes to Volumes III and IV: From Moses in the Wilderness to Esther*, vol. 6 of *The Legends of the Jews* (Philadelphia, PA: Jewish Publication Society, 1928), 330–331n70, remarked: "The nine haggadic Baraitot cited by the Talmud from Tanna de be Eliyyahu ... are very likely taken from a haggadic compilation by a Tanna called Elijah. ... In the above-mentioned Midrashim attributed to Elijah these nine Baraitot are incorporated (see Friedmann, *loc. cit.*), and in three passages the Talmudic תנא דבי אליהו is changed to משום דבי אליהו הנביא by the author (authors?) of these Midrashim. This shows that at a comparatively early date דבי אליהו of the Talmud was misunderstood to refer to the prophet Elijah." Those passages introduced with משום דבי אליהו הנביא are not transmitted in the Talmud, but only in the first chapter of *Seder Eliyahu Zuta*. They are listed in appendix 2 (2.4.2) at the end of this chapter.

In their discussion of the previously quoted passage bKet 105b–106a, Braude and Kapstein suggest that Rav Anan can be viewed as the author of an attribution, one that consisted in naming both his own third-century school and "the discourses comprising Tanna debe Eliyyahu"[21] – the work that has come down to us – after the prophet Elijah out of respect for him. According to this view, Anan would be the undisclosed author of a work whose authority he attributes to Elijah. According to yet another hypothesis, *Tanna debe Eliyyahu* could have originated not at Anan's school, but at one led by a certain Abba Eliyahu, who would also have lived in the third century. The name of the head of the school would have led people to attribute the work to the celebrated prophet. Subsequently, the legendary account in bKet 105b–106a would have been forged in order to legitimate this attribution.[22]

The work is also designated as *Teni Eliyyahu* in *Bereshit Rabbah* 54:4,[23] as *Elijah* in *Bemidbar Rabbah* 4:20,[24] and as *Tanna debe Eliyyahu Rabbati* by Eleazar b. Judah of Worms (ca. 1165–1230) in his *Rokeach*, § 329, § 361. Natan b. Yechiʾel's *Arukh* in turn specifies that the parts of the work are called *Seder Eliyahu Rabbah* and *Seder Eliyahu Zuta*, coinciding with the Talmud passage bKet 106a–b.[25]

2.2 The "Metaleptic" Governing Voice

There are few studies on the category of the narrator in Rabbinic literature. One of them is an article by Ofra Meir, in which she presents the results of research based upon 679 stories found in *Bereshit Rabbah*, *Tanchuma* on Genesis, and the tractates *Berakhot* in both Talmudim.[26] Meir distinguishes between so-called "independent," "homiletical," and "Talmudic-type" stories[27] whose narrators reveal themselves in different ways by applying different "methods of intervening in the

---

21 See Braude and Kapstein, *Tanna děbe Eliyyahu*, introduction, 10.
22 See Braude and Kapstein, *Tanna děbe Eliyyahu*, introduction, 10.
23 The passage introduced with *teni eliyahu* has a parallel in ER 58.
24 This passage contains a parallel to ER 65–66 in *Seder Eliyahu*.
25 See Natan ben Yechiel, *Aruch completum*, 27.
26 See Ofra Meir, "The Narrator in the Stories of the Talmud and the Midrash," *Fabula* 22 (1981): 79–83.
27 The independent stories are those which, according to Meir, are not dependent on context and remain meaningful even without surrounding co-text. According to Meir, "The Narrator," 79, the context-dependent ones, such as the homiletical stories (stories that "come as part of the exposition upon a Biblical verse or passage") or the talmudic-type stories (stories that "are part of the instruction of Mishnaic 'Halacha'") "would lose their entire meaning if divorced from their contexts."

story." Meir argues that "intervention integral to the development of the story" – such as the description of characters' thoughts or feelings or the application of "judgemental" epithets – is infrequent, in spite of the fact that all the stories she analyses have omniscient narrators.[28] Instead of using description to mould his characters, the talmudic or midrashic narrator opts to let them present themselves using direct speech. If we consider Meir's results as expressed in numbers, it becomes clear that action other than speech, as part of the story transmitted by the narrator, does not play a central role in these texts:

> 19.6 % of the stories are composed *entirely* of direct speech – with only such parenthetical phrases as "he said" or "he asked" added; in 43.3 % there is only one narrated action, while all the rest of the story unfolds through direct speech; in 31.7 % there are several actions, in addition to direct speech; and in only 5.4 % there is a total absence of direct speech.[29]

Furthermore, Meir distinguishes what she terms narrator interventions through remarks that are not integral to the story. Among these interventions, authorial comments are quite frequent and take many different forms, such as addresses to the audience, rhetorical questions, and supplementary citations of Bible verses, among others.[30] This is especially the case in the "homiletical" stories of the midrashim *Bereshit Rabbah* and *Tanchuma*. Since narrator comments often take the form of addresses to the audience, Meir concludes that it is likely that the stories in which they are inserted "originate from oral sermons addressed to a listening audience."[31]

Most of the stories Meir analyses have an omniscient,[32] heterodiegetic narrator – a narrator who is not part of the world of the story he[33] narrates – but there is a group of eleven "independent," "Talmudic-type" stories which are told in the first person. Interestingly, no "homiletical" story is told in the first person, since, according to Meir, "[t]he characters in 'homiletical' stories are always Biblical, and there is no way the narrator can substitute himself for one of them."[34] The

---

[28] Meir, "The Narrator," 80.
[29] See Meir, "The Narrator," 80.
[30] Phrases such as "he avenged the insult to his mother" or "they did not know where they were going," which according to Meir are interpretive and explanatory commentaries that belong to this class of intervention, appear to me to be integral to the diegesis, and therefore not commentary in character.
[31] See Meir, "The Narrator," 82.
[32] Another term used for a narrator who is "'above' or superior to the story he narrates is 'extradiegetic.'" See Shlomith Rimmon-Kenan, *Narrative Fiction: Contemporary Poetics*, 2nd ed. (London, New York: Routledge, 2002), 95.
[33] Rabbinic narratives generally have male narrators.
[34] See Meir, "The Narrator," 83. This is valid for Rabbinic literature, but not for pseudepigrapha.

main function of the use of the first person is, as Meir points out, the credibility it bestows on the content of the narrative.[35]

It is clear from this brief summary of Meir's analysis that it focuses on the story itself, irrespective of its being "independent" or "context-dependent." Whereas independent stories "can be understood equally well in the absence" of the contexts in which they are inserted, context-dependent ones "would lose their entire meaning if divorced from their contexts."[36] Unfortunately, no example of this kind of loss of meaning is given. In her conclusions, Meir deals briefly with the way the broad context – Midrash compilation or Talmud tractate – might determine the type of narrator.

When we turn to *Seder Eliyahu*, we notice that the homodiegetic narrator – a narrator who is a character in the world he narrates – is not the exception, as in the corpus analysed by Meir, but rather a recurring feature.[37] The first person is used not only in first-person narratives, but also in non-narrative segments.

The stories told in the first person[38] in *Seder Eliyahu* could be described as independent, insofar as they are comprehensible if extracted from their respective homiletical or exegetical contexts, although they are clearly used to expand upon notions brought forward therein. They consist mainly of direct speech in the form of dialogues. In none does the narrator name himself[39] or describe himself explicitly, except by using direct speech. The degree of perceptibility of the narrator is thus, despite his participation in the stories he narrates, quite low.[40] What we come to know about him is rather little: If we take all the stories as being

---

35 See Meir, "The Narrator," 83.
36 Meir, "The Narrator," 79.
37 See Günter Stemberger, "Münchhausen und die Apokalyptik: Bavli Bava Batra 73a–75b als literarische Einheit," in *Judaica Minora II: Geschichte und Literatur des rabbinischen Judentums* (Tübingen: Mohr Siebeck, 2010), 299–316; and Dina Stein, "The Blind Eye of the Beholder: Tall Tales, Travelogues, and Midrash," chap. 3 in *Textual Mirrors: Reflexivity, Midrash, and the Rabbinic Self* (Philadelphia, PA: University of Pennsylvania Press, 2012), on the tall tales told in the first person in the first part of the unit bBB 73a–75b. Stein points out that the tales in this unit constitute an anomalous form of discourse in the Rabbinic corpus; she designates them as "discursive others." (61)
38 Zunz, *Die gottesdienstlichen Vorträge*, 120–121, identifies the narrator of these passages with Elijah: "Es ist dies Elia, wie aus dem Buch selber und aus Parallelstellen hervorgeht, obwohl der Autor diese Einkleidung auch vergisst und von Elia in der dritten Person redet."
39 It should be noted that the last chapter of *Seder Eliyahu Zuta* contains a first-person narrative featuring R. Jose as narrator. *Pseudo-Seder Eliyahu Zuta* contains two first-person narratives whose narrator can be identified as R. Jochanan.
40 Rimmon-Kenan, *Narrative Fiction*, 97, with respect to the narrator's degree of perceptibility, observes that it "ranges from the maximum of covertness (often mistaken for a complete absence of a narrator) to the maximum of overtness."

narrated by one and the same narrator, as constituting his fragmentary autobiography,⁴¹ then he depicts himself as spending most of his time going from place to place or as having arrived in this or that city – which, depending on the information he provides, can be identified as Jerusalem, Ctesiphon, or an unnamed city in Babylonia⁴² – and discussing diverse matters with people who address him or with people he addresses. This fragmentary autobiographical account is not concerned with the work's poetology. The narrative voice does not address either the reasons the historical persona of the author composed the work we know as *Seder Eliyahu* or the historical setting in which this happened.⁴³

---

41 This is for example the assumption of Güdemann, *Geschichte des Erziehungswesens*, 301, who claims: "Der Verfasser unseres Buches war, was von allen anerkannt wird, ein weitgereister Mann." See also Mann, "Changes in the Divine Service," and Ephraim Urbach, "Lesheelat leshono u-meqorotaw shel Sefer Seder Elijahu [On the Language and the Sources of Seder Eliyahu]," in *The World of the Sages* (Jerusalem: Magnes Press, 2002), 418–432. In her analysis of "biographical sketches" in *Bereshit Rabbah*, Maren R. Niehoff, "Biographical Sketches in Genesis Rabbah," in *Envisioning Judaism: Studies in Honor of Peter Schäfer on the Occasion of his Seventieth Birthday*, ed. Raʿanan S. Boustan et al., vol. 1 (Tübingen: Mohr Siebeck, 2013), 269, points out: "Given the popularity and cultural importance of biographical writing in the Hellenistic period, it is time to ask whether this genre altogether passes by the rabbis. Did they remain unaware of the intellectual and educational potential of the biography? A close reading of GR shows that while the rabbis did not write complete biographies, they were eager to insert biographical sketches of biblical heroes, thus making their stories livelier and more accessible to the reader. Indeed, this Midrash enthusiastically participates in the biographical discourse and engages in a creative reconstruction of the childhood as well as the inner lives of biblical figures." *Seder Eliyahu* does not contain the type of "biographical sketches" that participate in the Hellenistic biographical discourse as represented by Plutarch and Philo. Neither do we find in it anecdotes that illustrate specific character traits of known outstanding individuals, such as Abraham, Joseph, or Jacob.
42 Is this a remarkable fact that should be stressed? Or could it be taken as an indication of multiple narrative voices? Gérard Genette, "Discours du Récit: Essai de Méthode," in *Figures III* (Paris: Seuil, 1972), 227, observed that "s'il est remarquable que les aventures d'Ulysse soient racontées par deux narrateurs différents, il est en bonne méthode tout aussi notable que les amours de Swann et de Marcel soient racontées par le même narrateur."
43 The main voice of the document (on how to designate it, see below) does reveal a certain familiarity with the notion of authorship and transmission of authored written material: God, for example, is depicted as the material author of the Torah; he speaks of himself as having written or created it, or having had Moses write it down. E.g., כך אמר להן הקב״ה לישראל, בניי לא כך כתבתי
אמר לו, דוד בני לא כך כתבתי בתורתי אף על פי שאין (ER 4, l. 13); לכם בתורתי, לא ימוש ספר התורה הזה מפיך
אמר לו, עמוס עמוס לא (ER 16, l. 4); בכם דברי תורה אלא דרך ארץ ומקרא בלבד ורדפו מכם חמשה מאה וגו'
באותה שעה ביקש הקב״ה להחריב (ER 33, l. 9); כך כתבתי בתורה על ידי משה רבך, אשריך ישראל מי כמוך וגו'
את כל העולם כולו, אמר לא נתתי תורתי לאילו (לא) [אלא] שיקראו וישנו בה וילמדו הימנה דרך ארץ אלא לא כך
כתבתי בתורתי אף על פי שאין בהן דברי תורה אלא מדרך ארץ ורדפו מכם חמשה מאה (ER 56, l. 27).

Generally addressed by his interlocutors as "rabbi" and replying with "my son," the dialogue situations the narrator depicts consist, with one exception,[44] of one or more questions posed by the interlocutors and monologic answers given by the rabbi-narrator. Only in two cases are his interlocutors disciples; they also include a Zoroastrian priest, old men, men who know Scripture but no Mishnah,[45] an anonymous man, a widow, non-Jews, a woman, a fisherman, and more. The rabbi's answers leave no room for doubt. Even if he engages in a conversation with the sages, before whom he is "no more than dust under the soles of their feet,"[46] it is he who gives the answers.

Ginzberg – who, contrary to what has just been said, appears to be of the opinion that *Seder Eliyahu* does identify the first-person narrator with the prophet Elijah, – notes in any case that the narratives do differ from those about the legendary Elijah:[47]

> These Midrashim quite often introduce the prophet as narrating events and incidents of his life, but they lack the simplicity of legend, and one immediately sees that the author put into the mouth of Elijah his own views concerning God, Israel, and the Torah.[48]

Given the fact that they expand upon or illustrate statements made in the preceding co-text, the first-person narratives could be viewed as narrative digressions (or rather dialogical parables), which owe part of their explanatory force to the very presence of a first-person narrator. The arguments presented within these narratives appear to be especially valid because a Rabbinic persona first uttered them and recounts them as a witness, as it were, when he narrates the stories. Even if he chooses to remain veiled in anonymity, the instance of the first-person narrator lends authenticity to what he tells his Rabbinic audience.

In general terms, however, the non-narrative context of these and other narratives is not characterised by a voice in the first person, though occasionally a first person can be presupposed, as will be shown later on. The characteristic voice of *Seder Eliyahu* is rather that of an omniscient, anonymous speaker, a voice that can be designated as the "governing voice" – to use the expression introduced by Alexander Samely et al. in their *Inventory of Structurally Important Literary Fea-*

---

44 It could be argued that the story in chapter 18 of the master who died because of the conduct of his disciples (ER 100, l. 32–ER 101, l. 6) inverts the usual teaching situation and makes the angel into a teacher and the rabbi into a disciple.
45 On this subgroup of first-person narratives, see chapter 5.
46 See ER 9, l. 11, ER 49, l. 15, ER 51, l. 8, and ER 122, l. 1.
47 See the next section in this chapter for the passages in *Seder Eliyahu* which deal with the prophet Elijah.
48 See Ginzberg, *Notes to Volumes III and IV*, 330–331n70.

*tures in Ancient Jewish Literature*⁴⁹ – a voice which fulfils a number of functions, among others the interpretation of scriptural verses to provide an ethical message.

A close look at *Seder Eliyahu* shows that the governing voice and that of the first-person narrator can be identified as the same (literary) voice. It is as if, from time to time, the governing voice of non-narrative segments transgresses the limits of this type of discourse, which can be globally designated as "homiletical discourse," and changes modus, adopting a narrative discourse. This transgression and mutation could be viewed as signalling a sort of *metalepsis*.⁵⁰ I use this term as defined by Gérard Genette in his treatment of the narrative voice in "Discours

---

49 The inventory was originally published online, as the partial outcome of the research project Typology of Anonymous and Pseudepigraphic Jewish Literature of Antiquity (TAPJLA), Manchester-Durham 2007–2011, funded by the Arts and Humanities Research Council (UK), and is still accessible online. See Alexander Samely et al., *Inventory of Structurally Important Literary Features in Ancient Jewish Literature (Version Zero)* (Manchester, 2012), B. Perspective, http://www.manchester.ac.uk/ancientjewishliterature and final publication of the project: Samely, *Profiling Jewish Literature*. On the concept of "narrative voice," a modus the governing voice may adopt, see see Sophie Marnette and Helen Swift, "Introduction: Que veut dire « voix narrative » ?," *Cahiers de Recherches Médiévales et Humanistes* 22 (2011): esp. 1–7.

50 A special case of narrative metalepsis comparable to the case of apparently alternating voices in *Seder Eliyahu* is found in the Acts of the Apostles, where an extradiegetic-heterodiegetic narrator alternates with the first-person plural (in Acts 16:10–17; 21:1–18; 27:1–28:16). Anja Cornils, "La Métalepse dans les Actes des Apôtres: Un Signe de Narration Fictionnelle?," in *Métalepses: Entorses au Pacte de la Représentation*, ed. John Pier and Jean-Marie Schaeffer (Paris: Éditions de l'École des Hautes Études en Sciences Sociales, 2005), 103, describes it as follows: "Le narrateur passe de sa position artificielle de chroniqueur à la position historique réelle du témoin oculaire qui participe aux événements. Tandis que le narrateur de la première moitié des Actes ne figure pas comme personnage dans l'histoire qu'il raconte, dans la seconde partie du texte, il est identifié avec un groupe de personnages au niveau de la diégèse, devenant du coup un narrateur homodiégetique. Ce brusque changement du type de narration est ressenti par le lecteur comme la violation d'une norme implicite. ... Le constat d'une rupture dans la composition (des sources qui n'ont pas été suffisamment remaniées et rédigées avant leur adaptation) aussi bien que dans la conception (un récit à la troisième personne qui passe brutalement au récit à la première personne du pluriel) représente depuis toujours un problème grave pour l'exégèse du Nouveau Testament." Pokorný and Stemberger, "Pseudepigraphie," 646, interpret the first-person plural passages in Acts as an example of aesthetically and hermeneutically grounded pseudepigraphy: "In der antiken Historiographie und den verwandten literarischen Gattungen wird das Berichtete oft rekonstruiert und interpretiert. So ist es auch mit den Reden der Apostelgeschichte oder den Briefen und Texten von Verträgen, die wir inever manchen biblischen Büchern finden (z. B. Esr 1,2–4; 4,8-10.11–16 u. a.; I Makk 8,23–30; 10,52–56 u. a.), welche nachträglich zur Illustration verfaßt sind. ... Ähnlich sind vielleicht auch die Wir-Stücke der Apostelgeschichte entstanden (Act 16,10–17; 20,5–15; 21,1–18; 27,1–28,16), in denen das 'Wir' ein dramatisches Mittel sein kann wie in der Schilderung des Seesturms bei Petronius." On metalepsis in Rabbinic literature, see Lieve Teugels, "Blending the Borders between Literature and Commentary, Interpretation and

du récit," in the broad sense of a transgression of the representational level.[51] David Herman, whose understanding of metalepsis as a transgression of narrative frames could prove to be more suitable for the study of *Seder Eliyahu*,[52] observes:

> metalepsis occurs when normative expectations about the modal structure of narrative universes – expectations activated by textual cues included in the narrative discourse at issue – are then deliberately subverted and countermanded.[53]

He explains metalepsis in its formal and functional aspects as follows:

> Formally speaking, metalepsis can be described as one or more illicit movements up or down the hierarchy of diegetic levels structuring narrative discourse. In order to describe such metaleptic movements, we would need to identify textual markers proper to the embedding and the embedded diegetic level(s), respectively. Then we would need to show how a given narrative, by transporting particular classes of textual markers across such levels, fails to respect (or actively abolishes) the hierarchy presumed by our initial taxonomy. Such formal transpositions can be more or less obvious and pervasive, and hence narrative featuring metalepsis can be more or less amenable to classical models for narrative structure itself – models which differentiate between, and differently rank, embedding and embedded diegetic levels of narration. ... Functionally speaking, metalepsis signifies a transgression of the ontological boundaries pertaining to the diegetic and more broadly illocutionary levels structuring a given narrative text.[54]

These definitions are based on examples from genres of narrative fiction, texts quite different from that (or those) studied in this context – *Seder Eliyahu* does

---

Self-Reflection: Metalepsis in Rabbinic Midrash," in *Metalepse in Text- und Bildmedien des Altertums*, ed. Ute E. Eisen and Peter von Möllendorff (Berlin, Boston: De Gruyter, 2013), 405–430.

51 See Genette, "Discours du Récit," 244–245. Genette's concepts have been further developed over the course of the last decades, but his conceptualisation remains one of the most important points of reference. It should be noted that none of the five types of metalepsis described by Genette is found in *Seder Eliyahu*: the reason for this is that, whereas Genette's examples and those of most narratologists come almost exclusively from novels, we are not dealing with an essentially narrative text, but with many short narrative segments embedded in a non-narrative context. See Genette's more recent contribution to this topic, *Métalepse: De la Figure à la Fiction* (Paris: Seuil, 2004); and the essay collection edited by John Pier and Jean-Marie Schaeffer *Métalepses: Entorses au Pacte de la Représentation* (Paris: Éditions de l'École des Hautes Études en Sciences Sociales, 2005).

52 David Herman, "Toward a Formal Description of Narrative Metalepsis," *Journal of Literary Semantics* 26, no. 2 (1997): 136, bases his assumptions on Ervin Goffman's definition of "frame," which he paraphrases as follows: "The frame, then, is Goffman's generic label for the set of principles organizing interactional events of all sorts, including the events connected with the construction and elaboration of (narrative and other) discourse."

53 Herman, "Toward a Formal Description," 136.

54 Herman, "Toward a Formal Description," 133–134.

not consist exclusively of narrative discourse. The concepts of embedding and hierarchy are here related not just to narrative levels, but also to types of discourse, one of them being of narrative character.⁵⁵

In what follows, I will try to describe aspects of the text of *Seder Eliyahu* which could be viewed as instances of metalepsis, as a crossing of discursive borders and a transgression of narrative levels.

One such manifestation of metalepsis, understood as crossing the limits of homiletic and narrative discourse, pertains to the very use of the first person. The first person is a recurrent feature in several narratives,⁵⁶ but it is also present in the discourse within which these narratives are embedded – for example, in formulas. Thus, the voice of the narrator of first-person narratives and the voice that says "I" in other, non-narrative contexts may be (in most cases) identified as belonging to the same textual persona. A characteristic formula of the homiletic discourse which uses the first person is the expression "I call heaven and earth to witness" (מעיד אני עלי שמים וארץ or מעיד אני את השמים ואת הארץ). It is found ten times in *Seder Eliyahu Rabbah*, three times in *Seder Eliyahu Zuta*, and once in *Pseudo-Seder Eliyahu Zuta*.⁵⁷ In one case the formula is used *within* a first-person narrative, which can be seen both as a marker pointing to the stylistic unity of non-narrative and narrative, and as an indicator of the "metaleptic" character of the governing voice of *Seder Eliyahu*.⁵⁸ This also allows named Rabbinic characters to use its characteristic language, as attested by R. Dosa b. Orkinas's use of the formula.⁵⁹

Another strategy with which the governing voice of *Seder Eliyahu* draws attention to its own *persona* in the text, thus situating its voice, is the direct address of a counterpart (or a midrashic audience). This is done using formulaic language containing verbal and pronominal forms in the second-person singular, but also

---

55 It has been pointed out that the phenomenon is not known only in modern and post-modern fiction, but that it goes back to the Renaissance and even to antiquity, e.g., to Homer. See Monika Fludernik, "Changement de Scène et Mode Métaleptique," in *Métalepses: Entorses au Pacte de la Représentation*, ed. John Pier and Jean-Marie Schaeffer (Paris: Éditions de l'École des Hautes Études en Sciences Sociales, 2005), 87.
56 See chapter 5.
57 See ER 17, l. 19, ER 26, l. 24, ER 36, l. 6, ER 48, l. 20, ER 70, l. 20, ER 91, l. 32, ER 124, l. 10, ER 145, l. 17, ER 163, l. 11, ER 164, l. 7, EZ 169, l. 7 (in this case it is R. Dosa b. Orkinas who speaks the formula), EZ 175, l. 14, EZ 197, l. 10 and PsEZ 24, l. 1. The formula is known from other Rabbinic documents, such as bYev 16a, bAr 16b, SifDev 1, BerR 2:4, MidTeh 137:1, MidMish 16:10, MidTan 1:1, among others. However, it is significant that among thirty-eight occurrences in Rabbinic literature, fourteen stem from *Seder Eliyahu*. In Sifra Qedoshim, parashah 2, pereq 4:1, we find the expression מעידני עלי שמים וארץ. See Lehmhaus, "Between Tradition and Innovation," 222n26.
58 See ER 70, l. 20.
59 See EZ 169, l. 7.

in the inclusive first person plural.⁶⁰ Examples of verbal and pronominal forms in the first-person plural are למדנו,⁶¹ מה עלינו לעשות.⁶²

Other expressions which appear to directly address an audience in verbal or pronominal forms make use of a second-person singular. They include, among others, -תדע לך שכן צא ולמד מ⁶³ and וכי עלתה על דעתך⁶⁴ – both of which generally introduce retellings of biblical accounts – as well as אלא ללמדך,⁶⁵ בוא וראה,⁶⁶ and כיוצא בדבר אתה אומר.⁶⁷ The governing voice uses the second person even to address

---

60 See Steven Fraade, "Rewritten Bible and Rabbinic Midrash as Commentary," in *Current Trends in the Study of Midrash*, ed. Carol Bakhos (Leiden, Boston: Brill, 2006), 62. The following observation may be especially relevant in this context: "I wish to argue that in many ways Rabbinic midrash, both legal and narrative, may itself be viewed as containing aspects of 'rewritten Bible' beneath its formal structure of scriptural commentary. For example, even as Rabbinic midrash formally presents itself as simply disclosing the meaning(s) of particular scriptural words, following the scriptural sequence, it more subtly often speaks itself in the voice of Scripture, addressing its midrashic audience *in the second person* much as God and Moses do in the Torah, often assuming (pseudepigraphically) the voice of either or both. Likewise, through its very methods of localized commentary, it commonly displaces scriptural words from their sequential order so as to reread (or retell) them intertextually in other, often surprising, scriptural contexts, much as do works commonly included under the rubric of 'rewritten Bible.'" (384, emphasis added.)
61 The expression is used very frequently in Rabbinic literature. In *Seder Eliyahu*, "we learn" is followed by an adverbial, where biblical characters are mentioned as examples (not sources) – "from Abraham" (ER 59, l. 22; ER 128, l. 18), "from Gideon" (ER 60, l. 22), "from Manoah" (ER 60, l. 24), "from Isaac" (ER 128, l. 35), "from Jacob" (ER 129, l. 3), "from our fathers" (ER 129, l. 5) –, rulings pertaining to the carrying of the sacrificial ram to the altar (ER 36, l. 20) and the immersion of the *niddah* (ER 75, l. 15), and theological concepts such as faith in the reward (PsEZ 22, l. 16) and fear of sin (PsEZ 22, l. 21). The two last occurrences are the direct speech of R. Jochanan b. Zakkai in first-person narratives.
62 See ER 69, l. 8. The phrase is also used as spoken by members of two families of priests within the narrative context of a *maʿaseh* (ER 53, l. 8) and within a first-person narrative by the rabbi who narrates in the first person (ER 71, l. 28). It is also found elsewhere in Rabbinic literature, e.g., MekhY *Beshallach* 2, MekhSh 14:14, SifBem *Naso* 45, ShemR 23:9, WayR 30:3–4, MidTeh 105:13. With a total of 15 occurrences it is not very frequent, though.
63 Variant readings are צא למד מ תדע לך שכן and שכן לך שתדע. There are a total of 17 occurrences of the phrase in Rabbinic literature – two in WayR, the rest in *Seder Eliyahu*.
64 This phrase is found twice in *Seder Eliyahu*, ER 82, l. 27 (within first-person narrative) and ER 87, l. 13 where it introduces a dialogue between Elijah and Elishah. Elsewhere in Rabbinic literature it is not a frequent expression, see ySan 9:3 (27a), SifDev 342 (שמב), *Pitron Torah*, *Zot chuqqat ha-torah*.
65 Eight occurrences.
66 14 occurrences. Both phrases are very frequent in Rabbinic literature.
67 11 occurrences, and very frequent elsewhere in Rabbinic literature.

God. Whenever this is the case, the governing voice represents itself as taking part in dialogues with God.[68]

These formulas suggest a male implied reader[69] engaged in a learning situation. The verbs in the formulas denote cognitive processes; the formulas themselves anticipate maxims to be learned or hint at a hermeneutic decision made by the governing voice. More explicitly characterised than the governing voice's addressee are his narrative alter ego's interlocutors in the first-person narratives. Most of them are men in a didactic or polemic dialogical situation.

As Ofra Meir observed in the article discussed above, there are several ways in which a narrator can intervene in his or her narration. One of these is the use of rhetorical questions. In *Seder Eliyahu*, the governing voice makes use in non-narrative segments not only of introductory formulas, but also of rhetorical questions (which can be formulaic), thus intervening in his own discourse and drawing attention to the discursive task he is performing. Rhetorical questions are posed to introduce passages of explicit exegesis or homiletical-exegetical passages that do not use scriptural wording. At the opening of chapter (9) 10, Judg 4:4 is quoted, followed by the question: "What was the nature of Deborah that she judged Israel and prophesied over them?" (וכי מה טיבה של דברה שהיא שפטה את ישראל ומתנבאת עליהם). Thus the formulaic question sets the perspective from which the quoted verse is to be interpreted. Chapter 4 opens without quoting any verse, posing instead a more general question: "Why did Moses merit a radiance of countenance in this world, which the righteous are to be given in the world to come?" (מפני מה זכה משה למאור פנים בעולם הזה ממה שעתיד ליתן לצדיקים לעתיד לבא). This question is followed by an explanation in the form of an exegetical narrative. We are dealing with exegesis in both cases – the first type could be described as explicit, while the second is implicit exegesis; in both passages, the textual presence of the governing voice – the agency of someone posing an interpretive query – is made clear.

What has been described here as metalepsis is a phenomenon which, in accordance with Genette's understanding, produces and transgresses a limit. In the particular case of *Seder Eliyahu*, the limits are not only between narrative levels, but also and especially between discourse types – between the world of the homilet-

---

68 See, e.g., ER 90, l. 9.

69 This can also be designated as the addressee or narratee, depending on the communicative situation. Rimmon-Kenan, *Narrative Fiction*, 105, defines the narratee as "the agent addressed by the narrator." See also Genette, "Discours du Récit," 265–267; and Seymour Benjamin Chatman, *Story and Discourse: Narrative Structure in Fiction and Film* (Ithaca, NY: Cornell University Press, 1978), 253–261. Direct addresses can be regarded as markers of a metalepsis crossing the ontological limit between the textual and the extratextual. See Brian McHale, *Postmodernist Fiction* (New York: Methuen, 1987), 222–227.

ical discourse (that of the *petichah*, homily, or literary sermon) and the narrated worlds within it. *Seder Eliyahu* presents a multi-faceted or polyfunctional voice, which may have surprised its readers, if these characteristics were, as one is inclined to assume, not the norm in previous Rabbinic literature.[70] Another aspect of this presence of the same voice across discourse boundaries is that it produces – temporarily – an apparent incoherence, breaking what on the surface appears to be textual unity and coherence. However, it is *because* this voice permeates the entire text that a new type of coherence in the context of late Rabbinic literature emerges.

2.3 The Biblical Character of Elijah in *Seder Eliyahu*

Is this governing voice, which at times narrates episodes in the life of a wandering rabbi, at any point in *Seder Eliyahu* confused with the person of the biblical prophet Elijah or with one of his manifestations in a post-biblical afterlife? This is the question I am concerned with in this section.

The post-biblical reception of Elijah pictures the prophet in his afterlife in multiple roles.[71] As Louis Ginzberg puts it: "Sometimes he looks like an ordinary man, sometimes he takes the appearance of an Arab, sometimes of a horseman, now he is a Roman court-official, now he is a harlot."[72] The biblical prophet Elijah is the protagonist in a number of short exegetical narratives in *Seder Eliyahu*. In some others, he is rather a secondary character. The first narrative[73] is one of a series of exegetical narratives told in chapters 4–6 which are all introduced with similar formulaic wording.[74] This Elijah-narrative opens with the question: "Why did Elijah merit the ability of bringing a dead man back to life?" – a question that

---

70 On surprise as one of the effects of metalepsis, see Dorrit Cohn, "Métalepse et Mise en Abyme," in *Métalepses: Entorses au Pacte de la Représentation*, ed. John Pier and Jean-Marie Schaeffer (Paris: Éditions de l'École des Hautes Études en Sciences Sociales, 2005), 123. In any case, for modern readers of Rabbinic literature, this conspicuous voice installs an alternative norm with respect to the plurality of voices in classical Rabbinic documents.
71 For an overview, see Karin Hedner-Zetterholm, "Elijah's Different Roles: A Reflection of the Rabbinic Struggle for Authority," *Jewish Studies Quarterly* 16, no. 2 (2009): 163–182; and Kristen H. Lindbeck, *Elijah and the Rabbis: Story and Theology* (New York: Columbia University Press, 2010).
72 Louis Ginzberg, *Bible Times and Characters from Joshua to Esther*, vol. 4 of *The Legends of the Jews* (Philadelphia, PA: Jewish Publication Society, 1913), 203.
73 See ER 22, l. 24–29.
74 The series comprises narratives on Moses (ER 17), Elijah (ER 22), (Elisha (ER 22), Ezekiel (ER 23), Abraham (ER 27), Jacob (ER 29), and Jethro (ER 30).

presupposes the scriptural story of the resurrection of the widow of Zarephath's son (1 Kgs 17:17–24).[75] The answer, on the other hand, combines an allusion to the entire account of Elijah's activities in the books of Kings – "Elijah did the will of God," "was anxious for the honour of God and Israel" – with Rabbinic reworkings of the prophet's existence after his ascension: He is said to be present "in every generation." His treatment of the righteous whenever he encounters them is described with characteristic phraseology of *Seder Eliyahu*: "He would take the righteous in his arms, hold them close and kiss them and bless, praise, exalt, magnify, and hallow the name of Him at whose word the world came into being" (היה מגפפן מחבקן ומנשקן ומברך ומרומם ומשבח ומגדל ומקדש לשמו של מי שאמר והיה העולם הקב״ה). On the problem posed by the fact that the governing voice of *Seder Eliyahu* narrates this Elijah-narrative in the third person, and not in the first – that it does not identify itself with the person of the prophet Elijah – Friedmann observes that it is an analogous phenomenon to that of the Mosaic authorship of the Torah. It does not preclude the narration of stories about Moses in the third person.[76]

In the second narrative in which Elijah appears, it is rather as a secondary character, while Elisha is the protagonist.[77] The narrative is presented as surpassing the previous one by posing the opening question: "Why did Elisha merit being able to bring *two* dead back to life?" What the exegetical narrative that follows the question illustrates is the exemplarity of Elisha's following Elijah and renouncing ownership, but above all the importance of being under the general guidance of scholars. In contrast to the first story, this one makes explicit use of the biblical account it engages with by selectively quoting from 1 Kgs 19:15–21. The exegetical narrative closes with the maxim: "From here they taught: Attendance [on scholars] is greater than learning."[78]

Immediately following the Elisha narrative, the text presents a third Elijah text. This time, the passage opens with a Rabbinic statement: "From here they taught: No man should take leave of his colleague, but after [having brought up] a matter of halakhah." In the narrative that follows this statement, master and disciple are both main characters, engaged in matters of halakhah before taking leave of each other – the scriptural passage used as foil for this narrative is 2 Kgs 2:11, the account of Elijah's ascension to heaven while he was walking with his disciple. Without attempting to reveal the whereabouts of Elijah, the story implies that no harm could have come to him on that occasion, for he was clearly doing the right

---

[75] The same motif, of Elijah as agent of the revival of the dead, also appears in ER 14.
[76] See Friedmann, *Seder Eliahu*, 22n18.
[77] See ER 22, l. 30–ER 23, l. 18.
[78] ER 23, l. 5. On the meaning of שימושה in this context, see Braude and Kapstein, *Tanna děbe Eliyyahu*, 128nn71–72, on ER 37, l. 22.

thing, discussing matters of Torah with his disciple. The story closes with the following statement and proof-text: "Two men who are walking along and engage in matters of Torah, no harm can befall them, for it is said, *As they continued walking and talking[, a chariot of fire and horses of fire separated the two of them, and Elijah ascended in a whirlwind into heaven].*"[79]

In chapter 17, Elijah is again the main character in an exegetical story that retells his building of the altar and trench on Mount Carmel and thereby accounts for how the people of Israel became men in awe of Heaven.[80] The narrator of *Seder Eliyahu* focuses on the trench Elijah makes around the altar and on how it miraculously comes to be filled with water after Elijah asks his disciples to fill four jars of water and pour them on the burnt offering and the wood, as stated in the quotation of verse 34. After this verse, the narrator addresses the audience with the rhetorical question: "Should you wonder how twelve[81] jars of water could fill the entire place with water?" (introduced with the phrase וכי עלתה על דעתך) and explains the nature of the miracle: When Elisha approaches his master and pours the water from his jar over the latter's hands, ten springs begin to flow out of Elijah's hands and into the trench until it is filled with water. At the close of the story, we read that, at the time of the evening offering, Elijah prays and the fire of the Lord consumes the burnt sacrifice and the water in the trench. These signs[82] persuade Israel to acknowledge that there is only one God, which is why they learn to fear Heaven in the days of Elijah.

The governing voice of *Seder Eliyahu* opts for a reconfiguration of the dramatis personae of the scriptural account: In his version there is no mention of Ahab, nor of the prophets of Baal. The people Elijah addresses in Scripture are replaced by disciples, and among them the only one named is Elisha; Baal is replaced by the more generic Rabbinic expression for idolatry (עבודה זרה).

The post-biblical Elijah also appears in the context of a sages narrative,[83] where several unnamed authorities discuss the genealogy of the prophet. Some

---

79 ER 23, l. 16–18.
80 See ER 87, l. 9–20. The scriptural narrative on which this midrashic passage is based is concerned with Elijah's triumph over Baal's priests (1 Kgs 18:17–40). *Seder Eliyahu* focuses on the latter part, vv. 30–40, quoting partially vv. 32, 34, 36, 37, and 38. The opening of this narrative is a variation on the opening of the two narrative passages that precede it, which recount how "Israel took the rule of Heaven upon themselves." The first is set in the time of Joshua, the second in the days of the prophet Samuel.
81 This number presupposes the fact that Elijah asked the people three times to pour four jars of water on the burnt-offering. See vv. 33–34.
82 These contrast with "pending" signs from Baal in the immediately preceding co-text of the biblical account (1 Kgs 18:25–29).
83 See ER 97, l. 32–ER 98, l. 2.

state that he is a descendant of Rachel; others state that he is a descendant of Leah. Elijah himself appears to settle the matter by affirming that he is a descendant of Rachel, for which he (and the governing voice) adduces a proof-text (1 Chr 8:27). Not satisfied with this answer, the sages argue that, due to the episode with the widow of Zarephath, he is considered a priest, and that he is a descendant of Leah. Elijah himself interprets for the sages what he meant when he spoke to the widow, saying: "but first make me a little cake of it and bring it to me, and afterwards make something for yourself and your son" (1 Kgs 17:13). The son he spoke of was the Messiah son of Joseph, and Elijah himself hinted at his going down to Babylonia, after which the Messiah would come. The narrative contains a number of gaps, and only some of them can be filled with parallel passages in other works of Rabbinic literature.[84] In chapter 15, *Seder Eliyahu Zuta* contains what can be regarded as an "internal" parallel of this narrative.[85] The text is shorter and ends with Elijah stating that he is a descendant of Leah – which Friedmann corrects to "Rachel." It is worth noting that both of these short stories identify women as the starting point of genealogies, whereas the sages in the parallel version in BerR 71:9 discuss whether Elijah's genealogy has its origins with Benjamin, Gad, or Levi.

In the first chapter of *Seder Eliyahu Zuta*, Elijah is referred to as a companion of the Messiah; at the end of a sages narrative, he is referred to as his forerunner.[86] In chapter 3, an eschatological account of the so-called *Pirqe de Rabbi Eliezer* – that is, *Pseudo-Seder Eliyahu Zuta* – relates how Elijah will be brought together with the Messiah, his companion, as the bearer of the messianic oil, rather than as forerunner.[87]

Chapter 8 of *Seder Eliyahu Zuta* is an exegetical narrative, which has Elijah as its main character.[88] The story sets out to illustrate Israel's obstinacy in the error of idolatry; it ends up explaining how a major prophet, Elijah, cannot forgive their

---

84 A longer discussion among the sages as to which tribe Elijah – Benjamin or Gad – belonged is found in BerR 71:9, which makes use of more biblical quotations, interpreted in turn by named rabbis (Nehorai, Leazar, Philippi [אמר ליה ר׳ פליפי]). This passage is similarly brought to an end by the appearance of the prophet himself, who uses the same words as in *Seder Eliyahu*. On the other hand, Elijah is regarded as a Levite in bBM 114b and PesRab 4:2, since, according to legend, he and the High Priest Pinchas, Aaron's grandson, were identical.
85 See EZ 199, l. 6–9.
86 See EZ 169, l. 13–16.
87 See PsEZ 34, l. 12–13. Elijah is also referred to in non-narrative contexts, such as the interpretation of the four blacksmiths of Zech 2:3, as "Messiah son of David, Messiah son of Joseph, Elijah, and the Righteous Priest." See ER 96, l. 32–33.
88 EZ 185, l. 21–EZ 186, l. 16. The narrative engages with selected passages from the first part of the scriptural Elijah cycle; the verses quoted are 1 Kgs 16:29–17:1–2; 18:1; 19:3–18.

errors as God wishes. Due to his own obstinacy, Elijah is forced to name his own successor – Elisha.

In all of the passages briefly discussed above, Elijah is either the character in a narrative or functions as the mouthpiece of an interpretation. Whenever his direct speech is represented, it does not contain the characteristic phraseology with which the governing voice of *Seder Eliyahu* constructs its persona. It could be argued that this is at least a clear internal signal that the author of *Seder Eliyahu* did not intend his readers to identify him with the prophet, nor his work with the post-biblical words of Elijah. As far as *Seder Eliyahu Rabbah* and the passages of *Seder Eliyahu Zuta* that we have examined are concerned, the author keeps the biblical character Elijah and the Rabbinic traditions around him separate from the work's governing voice.

Things appear to be slightly different when we consider certain passages of *Seder Eliyahu Zuta*. This part opens with a formula that names Elijah the prophet as the head of a school in whose name ethical teachings were transmitted. This formula, used three times in chapter 1,[89] is a variation on the one that introduces the previously mentioned *baraitot* in the Babylonian Talmud.[90] There we read תנא דבי אליהו (one of the possible translations is: "a teaching of the School of Elijah"),[91] whereas here the wording is "they [the sages] said in the name of the School of Elijah the prophet" (משום דבי אליהו הנביא אמרו). Only at this point does the author of *Seder Eliyahu* specify that the school with which the transmitted teachings are believed to originate was headed by none other than the *prophet* Elijah. However, he is not presented as the speaker of these words, but rather as constituting their original authority. So the part of the book or the chapter (section) introduced with this formula can be seen as collectively authored (i.e., said) by his school, though the teachings are ultimately transmitted by the sages and by the governing voice that quotes them. This is the nearest the biblical character comes to being depicted as author of the text we read, so that we are dealing with an alleged collective authorship and an indirect transmission of the original teachings.[92]

---

89 EZ 167, l. 1, l. 14, and EZ 169, l. 17.
90 See appendix 2 (2.4.2) at the end of this chapter. According to Berzbach, "Textual Witnesses," 70, this is a distinctive trait of the Italian manuscript tradition of *Seder Eliyahu Zuta*.
91 On the ambiguity of this phrase, see below, 2.4.1.
92 There is still another important issue related to this formula. Neither this phrase nor its talmudic correlate seem to refer to the whole work we know as *Seder Eliyahu*. However, if we had in *Seder Eliyahu Zuta* the same phrase that introduces the baraitot in the Talmud, it could be a case of auto-referentiality, since scholars are persuaded that *tanna debe eliyahu* is an alternative title for the work. Thus, by capitalising the phrase the Soncino translation of the Babylonian Talmud treats the phrase as a title for the work.

The name Elijah is used at the beginning of chapter 15 in another *inquit*-formula: "Father Eliyahu, remembered for good and remembered for blessing, said" (אמר אבא אליהו זכור לטוב וזכור לברכה). In this case, it is this very teacher, Elijah, who uses a characteristic phrase that the governing voice uses in the first person: "I call heaven and earth to witness." This same chapter contains a short version of a sages narrative on the origins of Elijah, which was previously discussed.[93] In this version of the narrative, Elijah is referred to using the phrase "Elijah, remembered for good" (אליהו זכור לטוב), wording that can be understood to refer back to the "authorial" figure mentioned at the beginning of the chapter in the opening formula: "Father Eliyahu, remembered for good." This chapter, which some have argued does not belong to the original conception of *Seder Eliyahu*,[94] contains evidence of a conflation of the biblical character and an authorial figure, which is not present in the other passages dealing with the prophet Elijah in *Seder Eliyahu*, as previously discussed.

To sum up: *Seder Eliyahu* contains several exegetical narratives that engage with episodes from the scriptural Elijah cycle – such as the widow of Zarephath, Elijah's triumph over the priests of Baal, and Elijah's ascension to heaven – and some narratives containing legendary, post-biblical subject matter. With the exception of the passages introduced in *Seder Eliyahu Zuta* with the formulas משום דבי אליהו הנביא אמרו or אמר אבא אליהו זכור לטוב וזכור לברכה, none of the Elijah narratives or non-narrative passages discussed in this section depict Elijah as authoring statements or an entire corpus of wisdom, or as engaging in any activity related to the transmission, written or oral, of the work of which these narratives are a part. Nevertheless, the work's reception was very probably influenced by its being attributed to Elijah.[95]

---

93 See EZ 199, l. 6–9.
94 E.g. by Zunz, *Die gottesdienstlichen Vorträge*, 123: "Demnach ist alles von Cap. 15 an bis zum Ende des Elia sutta eine spätere Compilation, wozu Eliahu rabba, Eliahu sutta, Aboth derabbi Nathan, Boraitha Aboth, ältere Erzählungen, die Talmude und spätere Midraschim die Bestandtheile geliefert haben; das echte Eliahu sutta muss mithin mit dem 14. Capitel geschlossen werden, womit sogar Handschriften übereinzustimmen scheinen." See also Stemberger, *Einleitung*, 379.
95 Even in scholarly writings of the twentieth century, the governing voice is somehow identified with Elijah. Both Friedmann, *Seder Eliahu*, in his introduction and notes; and Aptowitzer, "Seder Elia," refer to "Abba Elia" as the work's author.

2.4 Abba Eliyahu, Elijah, anonymous I: The Governing Voice of Seder Eliyahu

Considering that the formulas *mishum eliyahu hanavi* and *tanna debe eliyahu*[96] have the same function as the standard Rabbinic *inquit*-formula *amar rabbi*,[97] – that is, they introduce sayings – they cannot be interpreted as hinting at attributing the authorship of the entire work to any of the individuals named in these passages. The pseudepigraphy of *Seder Eliyahu* is not an intrinsic characteristic of the work, but rather a paratextual phenomenon, attested by the titles which refer to it in the manuscript tradition and later on in print editions, as well as by the baraitot of the Babylonian Talmud introduced with *tanna debe eliyahu*. So the following distinction can be made: Whereas these titles point towards pseudepigraphy or pseudonymity,[98] the text itself consistently opts for anonymity.[99] One of

---

[96] The first is used to introduce statements in the first chapter of *Seder Eliyahu Zuta*; the second introduces statements in the Babylonian Talmud that have parallels in *Seder Eliyahu Rabbah*.
[97] The formula *amar rabbi* is present both in *Seder Eliyahu Rabbah* and in *Seder Eliyahu Zuta*. The following sages are thus named as tradents; in some cases, however, the rabbis' names are found within Mishnah quotations: R. Simeon b. Gamaliel (ER 34), R. [Aqiba] (ER 61), R. Simeon (ER 69), R. Eleazar (ER 101) (not in Friedmann's edition, but in the manuscript within a Mishnah quote), R. Eleazar b. Mathia (ER 109), Rabban Gamaliel (ER 122), R. Aqiba (ER 133), R. Natan (ER 147), R. Ishmael b. Eleazar (EZ 179), R. Jose (EZ 199). These few names in *Seder Eliyahu Rabbah* and *Seder Eliyahu Zuta* contrast with the numerous ones in the relatively short *Pseudo-Seder Eliyahu Zuta*. These include: R. Simeon (PsEZ 1), R. Shimon ben Jochai (PsEZ 2), R. Eliezer b. Jacob (PsEZ 3), R. Joshua (PsEZ 3), R. Aqiba (PsEZ 3), R. Nehemia (PsEZ 3), R. Judah (PsEZ 3), Rabbi (PsEZ 3), R. Eliezer b. Jacob (PsEZ 4), R. Simeon (PsEZ 4), R. Eliezer (PsEZ 7), R. Jose (PsEZ 7), R. Eliezer b. Jacob (PsEZ 8), R. Ishmael b. Elisha (PsEZ 8), R. Joshua (PsEZ 8), R. Jose (PsEZ 9), R. Eliezer (PsEZ 10) (2x), R. Eleazar b. Parta (PsEZ 11), R. Judah (PsEZ 11), R. Yannai (PsEZ 11), R. Jochanan (PsEZ 11), R. Nehorai (PsEZ 11), R. Nehemia (PsEZ 12), R. Jochanan (PsEZ 12), R. Eliezer b. Yakob (PsEZ 12), R. Jose b. Qisma (PsEZ 12), Jochanan b. Pinhas (PsEZ 13), R. Aqiba (PsEZ 13) (2x), R. Shimon b. Yochai (PsEZ 14), R. Eliezer (PsEZ 14), R. Joshua b. Levi (PsEZ 15), R. Eliezer (PsEZ 15), R. Joshua b. Levi (PsEZ 17), R. Simeon b. Judah (PsEZ 19), R. Shimon b. Mansi (PsEZ 19–20), Jochanan b. Bag Bag (PsEZ 20), R. Chanina b. Akshi (PsEZ 21), R. Eleazar b. Azariah (PsEZ 21), R. Simeon b. Laqish (PsEZ 22), R. Jochanan (PsEZ 22), R. Jochanan b. Zakkai (PsEZ 22), R. Jochanan (PsSE 24).
[98] See Lerner, "Works of Aggadic Midrash," 151. The pseudepigraphy of the titles could be described with Pokorný and Stemberger, "Pseudepigraphie," 648, as a type of "pseudepigraphy based on attribution to a tradition"; with regard to how this type of pseudepigraphy operates, they point out: "Im Prozeß der Überlieferung hat man mehrere anonym tradierte Texte einem anerkannten traditionellen Bereich zugeordnet, was man als eine Art der 'Kanonisierung' betrachten kann."
[99] Anonymisation of Rabbinic traditions in general is also a feature of the *Seder Eliyahu*, and of other late midrashim.

the most characteristic, if not programmatic manifestations of this affirmation of anonymity is the introduction of Mishnah quotations with formulas such as *amru chakhamim*, as well as the introduction of alleged Rabbinic sayings with the formula *mikan amru*.[100]

The text of *Seder Eliyahu* does not depict the character of the prophet Elijah on any single occasion as authoring the work we read, contrary to what Ginzberg and others have stated regarding the identification of the author of the work with the prophet Elijah. The only instance of an apparent conflation of the author of this work (or a previous version of it) and the post-biblical prophet Elijah is evidenced in the *Ketubbot* passage discussed previously,[101] which incidentally makes of Rav Anan, if not an author, at least a scribe of Elijah's *Seder*. In the extant *Seder Eliyahu*, Elijah is at most the "author" of those passages in direct speech which he himself utters. Apart from the paratexts in MS Vat. ebr. 31, the entire work is not presented as having been written in the name of the prophet Elijah, nor in anyone else's name. In the *Ketubbot* passage, Elijah is a "supernatural oral author" of a text that is said to have been memorised and written down by someone else – R. Anan.

The main text of *Seder Eliyahu* itself, however, presents a governing voice, which is heard in both non-narrative and narrative passages, but which is not depicted as having authored the text in either an oral or a written manner – that is, as responsible for the creation of an original and autonomous work. This voice tells us (and its original readers and listeners) nothing about how the anonymous author (or authors) went about composing his (or their) work.[102] The text does allow us to describe its *implied author*[103] – the reader's construction of the per-

---

100 On these two tendencies, see Lehmhaus, "Between Tradition and Innovation," 228–230. He suggests that the anonymity of the quotations in *Seder Eliyahu* "makes these traditions function quite independent from a specific socio-cultural and regional milieu (e.g., the *yeshivot* in Babylonia and Palestine) and distances the from a certain intellectual or literary ideal (like the dialectic discussions of the Talmudim)." (238)
101 See section 2.1.
102 See Samely, *Profiling Jewish Literature*, 107–108.
103 The category of the "implied author" has been controversial ever since its introduction by Wayne C. Booth in *The Rhetoric of Fiction* (Chicago, IL: University of Chicago Press, 1961). As Ansgar Nünning, "Implied Author," in *Routledge Encyclopedia of Narrative Theory*, ed. David Herman, Manfred Jahn, and Marie-Laure Ryan (London, New York: Routledge, 2005), 39, observes, there is "no widespread agreement about what the term actually designates." See also Tom Kindt and Hans-Harald Müller, "Der 'Implizite Autor': Zur Explikation und Verwendung eines umstrittenen Begriffs," in *Rückkehr des Autors: Zur Erneuerung eines umstrittenen Begriffs*, ed. Fotis Jannidis et al. (Tübingen: Niemeyer, 1999), 273–287; Sandra Heinen, "Überlegungen zum Begriff des "Impliziten Autors" und seines Potentials zur kulturwissenschaftlichen Beschreibung von inszenierter Autorschaft," *Sprachkunst* 33 (2002): 327–377; Susan Lanser, "(Im)Plying the Author," in *Narrative Theory II: Special Topics*, ed. Mieke Bal (London, New York: Routledge, 2004), 11–18.

sona (behind the governing voice) during the reading process, based both on the text and on the reader's prior extratextual background information. In the case of a work such as *Seder Eliyahu*, this construction is based on how a midrash goes about interpreting Scripture or, more generally, how Rabbinic documents deal with given topics. Rimmon-Kenan, on the other hand, pleads for a "depersonified" understanding of the implied author (to which she refers, however, in terms of the "agent of the communicative situation"):

> Thus, while the narrator can only be defined circularly as the "narrative voice" or "speaker" of a text, the implied author is – in opposition and by definition – voiceless and silent. In this sense the implied author must be seen as a construct inferred and assembled by the reader from all the components of the text. Indeed, speaking of the implied author as a construct based on the text seems to me far safer that imagining it as a personified consciousness or "second self."[104]

Sandra Heinen suggests yet another conceptualisation of what might be termed "the reader's idea of the author":[105] "Aus all diesen Informationen textuellen, paratextuellen und kontextuellen Ursprungs kann in der Vorstellung des Lesers ein Bild des Autors entstehen."[106] Even if the reader of an anonymous work has less prior knowledge about the author than the reader of a tale by Jorge Luis Borges, he must still build an image of the author on the basis of the text's characteristics: "Darüber hinaus vermittelt der Text durch seinen Stil, die Thematik und explizite oder implizite Wertungen einen Eindruck vom Autor."[107] Alexander Samely argues similarly when he states:

> Every text can be understood as creating some identity for its speaking voice. This identity is a function of the text's surface, not of the author "behind" it. The text may not have one person responsible for all its features, a single historical "author." In fact, this is routinely assumed for the anonymous and pseudepigraphic texts of Jewish antiquity. But even where a text has such a complex genesis, its actual structures will still forge an identity for its speaking voice. For such an identity is merely a function of *reading all its sentences together*

---

104 Rimmon-Kenan, *Narrative Fiction*, 88. See Nünning, "Implied Author," 240: "About the only thing that seems uncontroversial is that the implied author can be distinguished from the narrator and the characters, both of which are identifiable as textual speakers with clearly delimited speech segments. However, the notion of the implied author refers to a 'voiceless' and depersonified phenomenon, which is neither speaker, voice, subject, nor participant in the narrative communication situation."
105 See Nünning, "Implied Author," 240
106 Heinen, "Überlegungen," 337.
107 Heinen, "Überlegungen," 337.

(if that is impossible, other kinds of analysis are necessary). The contours of that voice's identity are thus determined by the boundaries of what the reader accepts to be one text.[108]

In what follows, I attempt to briefly sketch some traits of the persona of the governing voice of *Seder Eliyahu*. To begin with, we are dealing with a *male* identity.[109] He is keen on encouraging his audience to recognise his work as belonging to the Rabbinic tradition by using typically Rabbinic exegetical techniques and hermeneutic expressions as well as by explicitly quoting the Mishnah. He also adheres to this tradition in avoiding any mention of his own name.[110] The documents of formative Judaism were not created by single authors, but were rather the result of repetition and explanation of what had been revealed long before. In Martin Jaffee's words, the author of *Seder Eliyahu* adheres to a tradition within which texts "just happened."[111] His inclination towards anonymity is evidenced in his systematic effacing of authorities in the traditions that he quotes – a tendency which is less evident in *Seder Eliyahu Zuta*.[112]

On the other hand, it could be argued that he aims for his work to be perceived as a consistent unity of style and thought (as can be achieved by a single author). Max Kadushin has provided plenty of examples in his two monographs to prove that *Seder Eliyahu* is informed by an organic unity of thought.[113] In the chapter of his *Einleitung* dealing with methodological questions, Günter Stemberger points out that the work belongs to those few late Rabbinic works that can be studied *redaktionsgeschichtlich*, whereby the implied author or the persona of the governing voice is understood as the textual counterpart of a single historical, authorial personality.[114]

Among the traits that contribute to the text's consistency is a characteristic *phraseology*.[115] Certain phrases used by the governing voice in the homiletical dis-

---

108 Samely, *Profiling Jewish Literature*, 102.
109 Grammatical evidence of this is found in narrative (פעם אחת הייתי יושב, he is addressed as רבי) as well as in non-narrative segments (מעיד אני עלי את השמים ואת הארץ).
110 Not even in the first-person narratives does the governing voice of *Seder Eliyahu* allow the reader to speculate on a single, historical, identifiable person.
111 Jaffee, "Rabbinic Authorship," 32.
112 See n. 97.
113 See Kadushin, *The Theology*, and more systematically *Organic Thinking*. In several passages of the latter, Kadushin appears to consider the work as the product of collective authorship, referring to "one of our authors." See, e.g., *Organic Thinking*, 22, 45, 55, 67, 84, 95, 137, and 207.
114 See Stemberger, *Einleitung*, 69.
115 Friedmann, *Seder Eliahu*, introduction, 118–129, provides a list of those expressions which appear more than once in the text, which he refers to using an expression from the main text of *Seder Eliyahu*, כפולין.

course tend to recur not only in other contexts of the same type of discourse, but also within narratives that are themselves part of that discourse – in the voices of the Rabbinic or biblical characters who express themselves in direct speech. This is true of several expressions. To give but one example: Within an exegetical narrative on the covenant between David and God (2 Sam 7) in chapter 18 of *Seder Eliyahu Rabbah*, David addresses God in prayer with the words:

> My Father, who art in heaven, may Your great name be blessed for ever and ever and ever and may You find contentment in Israel Your servants in all the places of their dwellings, for You magnified us, You exalted us, You hallowed us, You extolled us, You bound [on] us a crown with the words of Torah from one end of the world to the other. (ER 89, l. 25–29)

David again utters a very similar prayer in the context of an exegetical narrative on Ahitophel's plot against him (2 Sam 17:23). The order of the words in the Kaddish-style tetracolon varies, and instead of "crown of the words of Torah" (כתר דברי תורה) it is with "a knot to the words of Torah" (קשר בדברי תורה) that Israel is bound:

> My Father, who art in heaven, may Your great name be blessed for ever and ever and ever and may You find contentment in Israel Your servants in all the places of their dwellings, *for You magnified us, You hallowed us, You extolled us, You exalted us, and from one end of the world to the other You have bound us with a great knot to the words of Torah.* (ER 157, l. 27–30)

The wording of David's second prayer is used, with a minor variation – "*a great knot to the words of Torah*" (קשר גדול בדברי תורה) – by the governing voice in a prayer with which it addresses God while interpreting Song 1:4:

> *We will exult and rejoice in you* (Song 1:4), in that *You magnified us, You hallowed us, You extolled us, You exalted us, and from one end of the world to the other You have bound us with a great knot to the words of Torah.* (ER 32, l. 25–29).[116]

Another recurring tetracolon is "with wisdom, understanding, knowledge, and insight" (בחכמה בבינה בדעה בהשכל): This is how God blesses Abraham (ER 29). The same qualities are predicated of all that is said in the Torah (ER 73),[117] of God as He created the world (ER 91), hypothetically of the nations of the world in the context of a midrash on Song 1:3 (ER 37) and Hezekiah in an exegetical narrative (ER 47).

---

116 This last prayer is in turn spoken by David in in the context of an exegetical narrative on Ahitophel's plot against him (2 Sam 17:23). See ER 157.
117 In this case, we are dealing with the tricolon "with wisdom, understanding and knowledge" (בחכמה בבינה ובהשכל). This is also found in several scriptural passages (e.g., Exod 31:3; 1 Kgs 7:14; and Prov 3: 19–20, 24:3–4) quoted in PRE 3 as evidence that the Tabernacle and the Temple were made according to these three attributes.

They are assured to him who teaches Torah to multitudes, does not favour the rich or the poor, and has both read Scripture and recited Mishnah (ER 63); the narrator affirms that they were given to him (ER 70) and to the rest of humanity to distinguish them from cattle (ER 70). The phrase is atomised in a *mashal* and reunited in its *nimshal* as the strength with which God provides the righteous (ER 84). These are but a few of the occurrences of this phrase, which, like several others, contributes to the book's conspicuous, periodic style.

The unity of the work's conception is perceived in the way the chapters are structured – as more or less closed homilies which generally address a topic or cluster of topics using either single scriptural verses as lemmas or several consecutive verses of a passage of Scripture, quoting them in sequence, and interpreting them in distinct hermeneutic operations, in what Alexander Samely designates as "lemmatic chain."[118]

The first-person agent who gives homiletical expositions, interprets scriptural verses, narrates his own experiences,[119] quotes sages' traditions, and addresses the audience is probably one of the most tangible indicators of the conceptional unity (and probably also of the historical, individual authorship) of *Seder Eliyahu*. Precisely this agent might be seen as the factor that holds together the *Rabbah* and *Zuta* parts of the text in the eyes of the reader, and at the same time distinguishes the so-called *Pseudo-Seder Eliyahu Zuta* as spurious. Here, it is no longer the anonymous rabbi, but Rabbinic authorities who utter sayings and tell stories or interpret scriptural verses.

The apparently contradictory tendencies which have been discussed, and which can be subsumed under "anonymisation" and "pervading traces of individual authorship," can help situate the work as the literary product of a time between the fundamental collective authorship of classical Rabbinic literature[120]

---

118 On this structuring device, see Alexander Samely, *Rabbinic Interpretation of Scripture in the Mishnah* (Oxford: Oxford University Press, 2002), 317. For an example of the way it operates in a concrete case in *Seder Eliyahu*, see Constanza Cordoni, "Biblical Interpretation in Seder Eliyahu," in *"Let the Wise Listen and Add to Their Learning" (Prov 1:5): Festschrift for Günter Stemberger on the Occasion of his 75th Birthday*, ed. Constanza Cordoni and Gerhard Langer (Berlin, Boston: De Gruyter, 2016), 413–430. Another feature which can be regarded as an indicator of compositional unity is the way chapters are grouped into so-called dovetailing units in *Seder Eliyahu Rabbah*, as pointed out by Berzbach, "Varieties."

119 Although his stories might not always give the impression of being consistent, closed units, the narrator is given the task of signalling that they are: As part of his answer to a question posed by his dialogue partner, the narrator reminds him of what has been said before – not just by repeating part of an answer, but by explicitly stating that what comes has already been uttered: "Is this not as in the first answer which I gave you at the beginning?" (ER 73)

120 See Stern, "The Concept of Authorship."

and the time when authors brought their self-conception as authors into the text
– for example, by writing a prologue and presenting their motivation for writing, translating or commenting on an existing work.

2.4.1 Appendix 1: Talmud Passages Introduced with the Formula *tanna debe eliyahu*

The text of the nine baraitot that are introduced in the Babylonian Talmud with the Aramaic formula *tanna debe eliyahu* and their English translation are given below. Friedmann discusses the *baraitot* and their wider talmudic co-texts in the fifth section of his introduction.[121]

1. תנא דבי אליהו: כל השונה הלכות מובטח לו שהוא בן עולם הבא, שנאמר אהליכות עולם לו, אל תקרי הליכות אלא הלכות

A teaching of the School of Elijah (*tanna debe eliyyahu*): Whoever repeats *halakhot* may rest assured that he is destined for the future world, for it says, *His ways [halikhot] are eternal* (Hab 3:6). Read not *halikhot* but *halakhot*. (bMeg 28b)[122]

1'. תנא דבי אליהו: כל השונה הלכות בכל יום מובטח לו שהוא בן העולם הבא, שנאמר ההליכות עולם לו, אל תקרי הליכות אלא הלכות

A teaching of the School of Elijah (*tanna debe eliyyahu*): Whoever repeats halakhot every day may rest assured that he will be a child of the world to come, for it says, *His ways [halikhot] are eternal* (Hab 3:6). Read not *halikhot* but *halakhot*. (bNid 73a)[123]

2. תנא דבי אליהו: צדיקים שעתיד הקדוש ברוך הוא להחיותן אינן חוזרין לעפרן, שנאמר כטוהיה הנשאר בציון והנותר בירושלים קדוש יאמר לו כל הכתוב לחיים בירושלים, מה קדוש לעולם קיים - אף הם לעולם קיימין

A teaching of the School of Elijah (*tanna debe eliyyahu*): The righteous, whom the Holy One, blessed be He, will resurrect, will not revert to dust, for it is said,

---

[121] See Friedmann, *Seder Eliahu*, introduction, 47. Three of them – namely 1, 3, and 5 – he considers to contain halakhic material, the rest aggadic.
[122] The quotation follows Isidore Epstein, ed., *Pesaḥim*, vol. 2 of *The Babylonian Talmud: Seder Moʿed*, trans. Harry Freedman (London: Soncino, 1938).
[123] The quotation follows Isidore Epstein, ed., *Niddah*, in *The Babylonian Talmud: Seder Ṭohoroth*, trans. Israel W. Slotki (London: Soncino, 1948).

Whoever is left in Zion and remains in Jerusalem will be called holy, everyone who has been recorded for life in Jerusalem (Isa 4:3): *just as the Holy One endures for ever, so shall they endure for ever.* (bSan 92a)[124]

3. תנא דבי אליהו: ששת אלפים שנה הוי עלמא, שני אלפים תוהו, שני אלפים תורה, שני אלפים ימות המשיח. ובעונותינו שרבו - יצאו מהם מה שיצאו

A teaching of the School of Elijah (*tanna debe eliyyahu*): The world is to exist six thousand years. In the first two thousand there was desolation; two thousand years the Torah flourished; and the next two thousand years is the Messianic era, but through our many iniquities all these years have been lost. (bSan 97a–b)[125]

3'. תנא דבי אליהו: ששת אלפים שנה הוי העולם, שני אלפים תוהו, שני אלפים תורה, שני אלפים ימות המשיח, בעונותינו שרבו יצאו מהן מה שיצאו מהן

A teaching of the School of Elijah (*tanna debe eliyyahu*): The world is to exist six thousand years; the first two thousand years are to be void; the next two thousand years are the period of the Torah, and the following two thousand years are the period of the Messiah. Through our many sins a number of these have already passed [and the Messiah is not yet]. (bAZ 9a)[126]

4. תנא דבי אליהו: לעולם ישים אדם עצמו על דברי תורה כשור לעול וכחמור למשאוי

A teaching of the School of Elijah (*tanna debe eliyyahu*): In order to study the words of the Torah one must cultivate in oneself the [habit of] the ox for bearing a yoke and of the ass for carrying burdens. (bAZ 5b)[127]

---

124 This and the next passage are quoted following Isidore Epstein, ed., *Sanhedrin*, vol. 3 of *The Babylonian Talmud: Seder Nezikin*, trans. Jacob Shachter and H. Freedman (London: Soncino, 1935).
125 The immediate subsequent co-text in the Talmud mentions the prophet Elijah: "Elijah said to Rav Judah, the brother of Rav Salla the Pious: The world shall exist not less than eighty five jubilees, and in the last jubilee the son of David will come. He asked him, At the beginning or at the end? – He replied, I do not know. Shall [this period] be completed or not? – I do not know, he answered. Rav Ashi said: He spoke thus to him, Before that, do not expect him; afterwards thou mayest await him." This passage has a parallel in ER 6, l. 30–ER 7, l. 2.
126 This and the next passage are quoted following Isidore Epstein, ed., ʿ*Abodah Zarah*, vol. 4 of *The Babylonian Talmud: Seder Nezikin*, trans. A. Mishcon and A. Slotki (London: Soncino, 1935).
127 This passage has parallels in ER 8, l. 6–7, EZ 198, l. 17f., and l. 22f.

5. תא שמע, דתנא דבי אליהו, רבי נתן אומר: כל הישוב כולו תחת כוכב אחד יושב. תדע, שהרי אדם נותן עינו בכוכב אחד, הולך למזרח - עומד כנגדו, לארבע רוחות העולם - עומד כנגדו. מכלל דכל הישוב כולו תחת כוכב אחד יושב! - תיובתא

Come and hear what was taught at the School of Elijah (*de-tanna debe eliyyahu*): R. Natan said: The whole of the inhabited world is situated under one star. The proof is that a man looks at a star, [and] when he goes eastward it is opposite him [and when he goes] to the four corners of the world it is opposite him. This proves that the whole of the inhabited world is situated under one star. This is indeed a refutation. (bPes 94a)[128]

6. תנא דבי אליהו: אף על פי שאמר רבי עקיבא עשה שבתך חול ואל תצטרך לבריות, אבל עושה הוא דבר מועט בתוך ביתו. מאי נינהו? - אמר רב פפא: כסא דהרסנא. כדתנן, רבי יהודה בן תימא אומר: הוי עז כנמר וקל כנשר רץ כצבי וגבור כארי לעשות רצון אביך שבשמים

A teaching of the School of Elijah (*tanna debe eliyyahu*): Though R. Aqiba said, "Treat your Sabbath like a weekday rather than be dependent on men," yet one must prepare something trifling at home. What is it? Said R. Papa: Fish hash. As we learned, R. Judah b. Tema said: Be strong as the leopard and swift as the eagle, fleet as the deer and valiant as a lion to do the will of thy Father in heaven. (bPes 112a)

7. תנא דבי אליהו: הואיל ונשים דעתן קלות /קלה/ עליהן

A teaching of the School of Elijah (*tanna debe eliyyahu*): Because women are temperamentally light-headed. (bQid 80b)[129]

8. תני דבי אליהו: מעשה בתלמיד אחד ששנה הרבה וקרא הרבה, ושימש תלמידי חכמים הרבה, ומת בחצי ימיו. והיתה אשתו נוטלת תפיליו ומחזרתם בבתי כנסיות ובבתי מדרשות, ואמרה להם: כתיב בתורה כי הוא חייך ואורך ימיך, בעלי ששנה הרבה וקרא הרבה, ושימש תלמידי חכמים הרבה - מפני מה מת בחצי ימיו? ולא היה אדם מחזירה דבר

A teaching of the School of Elijah (*tanna debe eliyyahu*): It once happened that a certain scholar who had studied much Bible and Mishnah and had served scholars much, yet died in middle age. His wife took his tefillin and carried them about in synagogues and complained to them, It is written in the Torah, *for that means life*

---

[128] This and the next passage are quoted following Epstein, *Pesaḥim*.
[129] The quotation follows Isidore Epstein, ed., *Ḳiddushin*, vol. 4 of *The Babylonian Talmud: Seder Nashim*, trans. H. Freedman (London: Soncino, 1936).

to you and length of days (Deut 30:20): my husband, who read [Bible], learned [Mishnah], and served scholars much, why did he die in middle age? And no man could answer her. (bShab 13a–b)[130]

9. תנא דבי אליהו: גיהנם למעלה מן הרקיע, וי"א - לאחורי הרי חשך

A teaching of the School of Elijah (*tanna debe eliyyahu*): Gehenna is above the firmament; some, however, say that is behind the Mountains of Darkness. (bTam 32b)[131]

It is not evident how one is supposed to translate the formula *tanna debe eliyahu*. In the case of bPes 94a (nr. 5), the expression *tanna*, because it is preceded by the particle *de-*, appears to be used as a verb. In the rest of the *baraitot*, *tanna* may be understood as meaning either the same verb (in which case *debe eliyyahu* would be a sort of subject or an adverbial, i.e. "The school of Elijah taught" resp. "It was taught at the School of Elijah") or a noun (an unnamed sage of the tannaitic period, somehow associated with a/the school of Elijah, or a tannaitic teaching of that school). If *tanna* is taken to be a noun, the introductory formula is seen as presupposing a *verbum dicendi*, which is not spelt out.

2.4.2 Appendix 2: Passages in *Seder Eliyahu Zuta* Introduced with the Formula *meshum debe eliyahu hanavi amru*

1. משום דבי אליהו הנביא אמרו, לעולם יהא אדם ערום ביראה, ומענה רך בפיו, ומשיב חמה, ומרבה שלום עם אביו ועם אמו ועם רבו ועם חבירו, בשוק אפילו עם גוי, כדי שיהא אהוב מלמעלה ואהוב מלמטה, כדי שיתקבל על הבריריות וכדי שיתמלאו ימיו בטובה.

In the name of the School of Elijah the prophet they said: A man should always be wise in his fear [of God]; *his answer soft* (Prov 15:1), turning away wrath, he should be on the best of terms (lit. "increase peace") with his father, with his mother, with his master, with his fellow Jew in the street, even with a heathen. Thus he will be

---

[130] This quotation follows Isidore Epstein, ed., *Shabbath*, vol. 1 of *The Babylonian Talmud: Seder Moʿed*, trans. H. Freedman (London: Soncino, 1938). The *maʿaseh*, of which the quoted passage is only the beginning, has a parallel in ER 76, l. 3–28.
[131] Quoted following Isidore Epstein, ed., *Tamid*, vol. 3 of *The Babylonian Talmud: Seder Ḳodashim*, trans. Maurice Simon (London: Soncino, 1948).

loved on high and be well regarded here below; his company will be welcomed by his fellows, and his days will be filled with good. (EZ 167, l. 1–4)

2. משום דבי אליהו הנביא אמרו, לעולם יהא אדם כשור לעול וכחמור למשאוי, כבהמה שהיא חורשת בבקעה, כך יהא אדם עוסק בדברי תורה, שנאמר אשריכם זורעי על כל מים [וגו'] , אשריהם ישראל, בזמן שעוסקין בתורה ובגמילות חסדים, יצרן מסור בידן ולא הם ביד יצרן אין זריעה אלא צדקה, שנאמר זרעו לכם לצדקה וגו', ואין מים אלא תורה, שנאמר הוי כל צמא לכו למים

In the name of the School of Elijah the prophet they said: A man should always be as an ox under the yoke, as an ass under its burden, as cattle plowing in the furrow. So should he occupy himself in words of Torah, for it is said, *Happy will you be who sow beside all waters* (Isa 32:20). Blessed are Israel when they occupy themselves with Torah and with loving-kindness: their Impulse [to Evil] is then made surrender to them, not they to the Impulse. By *sow* in the verse cited above is meant the giving of charity, for it is said, *Sow for yourselves charity* (Hos 10:12). And by *waters* is meant Torah, as in the verse, *Ho, everyone who thirsts, come to the waters* (Isa 55:1). (EZ 167, l. 14–19)

3. משום דבי אליהו הנביא אמרו, גדולה צדקה, שמיום שנברא העולם ועד עכשיו כל הנותנה הרי הוא משתבח, וקולט עצמו מדינה של גיהנם, שנאמר אשרי משכיל אל דל ביום רעה ימלטהו ה', אין יום רעה, אלא יום דינה של גיהנם, שנאמר הסר כעס מלבך והעבר רעה מבשרך, ואומר אשרי שומרי משפט עושה צדקה בכל עת

In the name of the School of Elijah the prophet it is taught: Great is charity, for from the day the world was created until the present, he who gives it is especially favored and spares himself punishment in Gehenna, as it is said, *Happy are those who consider the poor; the Lord delivers them in the day of trouble* (Ps 41:2). The day of evil can only mean the day of punishment in Gehenna, as implied in the verse, *Banish anxiety from your mind, and put away pain from your body; for youth and the dawn of life are vanity* (Eccl 11:10), for *Happy are those who observe justice, who do righteousness at all times* (Ps 106:3). (EZ 169, l. 17–22)

3 A Typology of Narrative Forms of *Seder Eliyahu*

The presence or absence of a story is what distinguishes narrative from non-narrative texts. However, non-story elements may be found in a narrative text just as story elements may be found in a non-narrative text. A novel may well include the description of a cathedral, and the description of a cathedral, say in a guide book, may include the story of its construction.[1]

Rabbinic literature is only of a narrative character in certain passages. It makes use of narrative, but it is primarily a scholarly discourse concerned with law and with the linguistic meaning of Scripture.[2] In recent times, scholarship started to focus on the interaction of legal and narrative discourses that is especially characteristic of an important part of the Rabbinic corpora. Moshe Simon-Shoshan's book *Stories of the Law* is a good example of this trend.[3] According to his examination of the first chapter of the Mishnah tractate *Shabbat*, its forms belong to one of three classes: irrealis texts, realis texts, and speech acts.[4] The table below summarises the more complex charts in which Simon-Shoshan presents his classification:

Table 3.1: Simon-Shoshan's Typology of Mishnaic Forms

Irrealis texts	Realis texts	Speech acts
Apodictic formulations	Repeated events	Attributed statements
Casuistic formulations	One-time events	Dialogues/*Beit midrash*-stories
	Ritual narratives	
	Stories: *maʿasim*	

---

1 Rimmon-Kenan, *Narrative Fiction*, 15.
2 For this definition of Rabbinic literature I follow Samely, *Forms*, 2.
3 Simon-Shoshan, *Stories*. Together with Wimpfheimer, *Narrating the Law: A Poetics of Talmudic Legal Stories*; Jane Kanarek, *Biblical Narrative and the Formation of Rabbinic Law* (New York: Cambridge University Press, 2014), to name just monographs.
4 In order to arrive at this classification Simon-Shoshan describes and analyses mishnaic forms with reference to their relative narrativity, dynamism, and specificity. Simon-Shoshan, *Stories*, 22, points out, "The categories and definitions of 'narrativity,' 'dynamism,' 'specificity,' 'narrative,' and 'story' create a precise yet flexible framework in which texts can be classified and compared in terms of their place within the broader category of narrative discourse. Most importantly for our purposes, they will provide us with the tools to analyze the place of narrative discourse in the Mishnah."

The irrealis texts comprise apodictic and casuistic formulations, only the latter of which are considered narratives. Among the realis texts and speech acts, only ritual narratives, *maʿasim*, and so-called *Beit midrash*-stories attain the level of narrativity to be regarded as either narratives or stories.[5] Due to the character of the Mishnah's textuality and structure, many of the examples Simon-Shoshan analyses would never be regarded as belonging to narrative discourse at all by conventional narratological standards.[6]

Simon-Shoshan closes his chapter with what he terms "a case study" in the form of a chart that represents the constitutive forms, both narrative and non-narrative, of the first chapter of the Mishnah tractate *Shabbat*. He sums up his results as follows:

> To sum up, the first chapter of Shabbat integrates a wide range of forms with varying levels of narrativity into a flowing exposition of activities forbidden on the eve of the Sabbath. The Mishnah easily moves back and forth between various forms of prescriptive statement, between abstract, stative clauses and detailed narratives, and between prescriptive statements, stories, and repeated events. This practice is representative of the way in which the level of narrativity in the Mishnah can fluctuate widely even within a single chapter.[7]

Like the Mishnah and Rabbinic literature in general, *Seder Eliyahu* is not a narrative text, but one in which a non-narrative discourse concerned with Rabbinic ethics makes use of Rabbinic hermeneutics and narrative discourse,[8] or rather one in which the former provides an encompassing frame for the latter.[9] Given that the chapters of *Seder Eliyahu* often take the form or style of a proemium (or

---

[5] In Simon-Shoshan's view, some texts of the Mishnah may still be regarded as narratives even though they are not stories. The latter are, in his terminology, narratives with a higher level of specificity. Simon-Shoshan, *Stories*, 20, sees stories as belonging to the wider category of narrative which he defines in the following terms: "(1) narratives are representations of events; (2) narratives present two or more events in sequence; (3) these events must be inherently interrelated in such a way as to portray some change in the world represented by the text. Given the centrality of dynamism to the traditional definitions of narrative, I will term any text which displays the above three features a 'narrative.'"
[6] E.g., in the case of apodictic formulations in the form of nonverbal clauses.
[7] Simon-Shoshan, *Stories*, 58.
[8] See Zunz, *Die gottesdienstlichen Vorträge*, ch. 7. There are, however, chapters, which give the impression of being primarily of a narrative character. See chapter (11) 12, which consists of a series of exegetical narratives and has very few of what we term ethical-homiletical passages.
[9] E.g., the structure of chapter (12) 13 itself illustrates the embeddedness of narrative discourse within one of a different nature: a) a homiletical opening states apodictically how a man is to behave in a given situation; b) a series of narrative forms exemplify the statement; c) a summary closes the chapter with a saying of the sages, the wording of which is a slightly modified version of the statement at the beginning of the chapter.

petichah, i.e. the introductory part of a homily), this encompassing discourse could be described as "ethical-homiletical."

Whereas this ethical-homiletical discourse of *Seder Eliyahu* is characterised by its intended universal validity – reflected, among other things, in the consistent use of the present tense[10] and apodictic statements,[11] – its narrative discourse is constituted by a wide range of textual forms, for which Simon-Shoshan's definition of story appears to be valid: Story is "any representation of a sequence of at least two interrelated events that occurred once and only once in the past."[12] In what follows I will be following the terminology suggested by the narratologist Shlomith Rimmon-Kenan, and instead of referring to the textual representations of events as "stories," I will refer to them as "narrative texts" or simply "narratives."[13] In Rimmon-Kenan's terminology, "story" denotes "the narrated events, abstracted from their disposition in the text and reconstructed in their chronological order, together with the participants in those events."[14] Rimmon-Kenan's "story" thus appears to correspond to the "events" whose representation constitutes a story according to Simon-Shoshan's definition. Rimmon-Kenan explains the difference between story and text as follows:

> Whereas "story" is a succession of events, "text" is a spoken or written discourse which undertakes their telling. Put more simply, the text is what we read. In it, the events do not necessarily appear in chronological order, the characteristics of the participants are dispersed

---

10 Generally expressed with participle and imperfect forms.
11 Including exhortations, *ashre*-passages, and benedictions.
12 Simon-Shoshan, *Stories*, 20. Within the field of Rabbinics, story has also been defined by Jacob Neusner, *The Precedent and the Parable in Diachronic View*, vol. 4 of *Rabbinic Narrative: A Documentary Perspective* (Leiden, Boston: Brill, 2003), 27, who distinguishes it from the rest of narratives in that they are "accounts of sequences of events, things said or done, things that happen and bear meaning, involving character-development, sequences of actions, a beginning, middle and end." According to the narratologist Gerald Prince, "Narrative," in *A Dictionary of Narratology* (Lincoln, NE: University of Nebraska Press, 2003), 58, the story a narrative represents can consist of less than two events: "The recounting ... of one or more real or fictitious EVENTS communicated by one, two, or several (more ore less overt) NARRATORS to one, two or several (more or less overt) NARRATEES." For definitions of "story" in narratological literature, see Rimmon-Kenan, *Narrative Fiction*, 3–4; Monika Fludernik, *An Introduction to Narratology* (London, New York: Routledge, 2009), 1–2; Matías Martínez and Michael Scheffel, *Einführung in die Erzähltheorie*, 9th ed. (Munich: Beck, 2012), 112, i.a.
13 This would be a translation of Genette's *récit*, though it should be noted that Genette distinguishes three meanings of the word: *récit* as narration or narrative act (i.e., as process); *récit* as *discours*, narrative text or utterance (i.e., as product); and *récit* as *histoire* or story told in a narrator's narrative (i.e., the abstracted events or fictional world). See Fludernik, *Introduction*, 2.
14 Rimmon-Kenan, *Narrative Fiction*, 3.

throughout, and all the items of the narrative content are filtered through some prism or perspective ("focalizer").[15]

Even if I refer in the following pages to a number of passages as "narratives," what will be presented, classified, and discussed in these pages are narrative texts in the sense of the above-quoted definition – texts that are found in Friedmann's edition of *Seder Eliyahu* (i.e., primarily in MS Vat. ebr. 31,) as well as in his edition of *Pseudo-Seder Eliyahu Zuta*, for which he follows the *editio princeps* Venice 1598 and MS Parma 3111 (de Rossi 1240).[16] The diagram below provides an overview of the five narrative forms I will discuss, though it should be anticipated that not all of the subtypes listed there will be illustrated (see figure 3.1).

3.1 Non-narrative Texts

Before I turn to the narrative texts themselves, a number of other textual forms with which narrative texts contrast and which contribute to the textual topography of *Seder Eliyahu* should be briefly discussed. This is the case with many passages which possess a certain level of narrativity (or story-structure) but are not the textual representation of at least two interrelated events which have already taken place in the past.[17] To this group belong texts that can be described as prophetic or eschatological, for they deal with the days of the Messiah and the

---

15 Rimmon-Kenan, *Narrative Fiction*, 3.
16 The work's (abstractable) macro-story, the "drama inherent in the *Tanna*," namely that which begins in chapter 1 with "God's departure from earth after the fall of man out of the Garden of Eden and ends with man's return to the earthly paradise in the time to come" in chapter (31) 29 of the *Seder Eliyahu Rabbah*, is not part of this classification. Braude and Kapstein, *Tanna děbe Eliyyahu*, introduction, 21–22, point out that the work has yet another dramatic macro-story, "*Tanna děbe Eliyyahu* is dramatic in a way that a piece of fiction or a play is dramatic: it presents us with a plot, the essence of which is a conflict that rises to a climax and comes to a conclusion. However, here the drama does not develop in a straight line as it usually does in a novel or play, for the work's intention, as we already have reason to understand, is didactic. We are given the drama not for its own sake, as a vicarious experience, entertaining and thrilling, but rather for what it teaches." On *Seder Eliyahu Rabbah*'s macro-story as a framing device, see Elbaum, "Between a Midrash and an Ethical Treatise"; and Lehmhaus, "Between Tradition and Innovation," 225.
17 Some of these non-narrative forms can be described with Suzanne Fleischman, *Tense and Narrativity: From Medieval Performance to Modern Fiction* (London: Routledge, 1990), 104, as "verbalizations of experience that is unrealized either because it is predicated on taking place in the future or because it is in some sense hypothetical."

64 — 3 A Typology of Narrative Forms of *Seder Eliyahu*

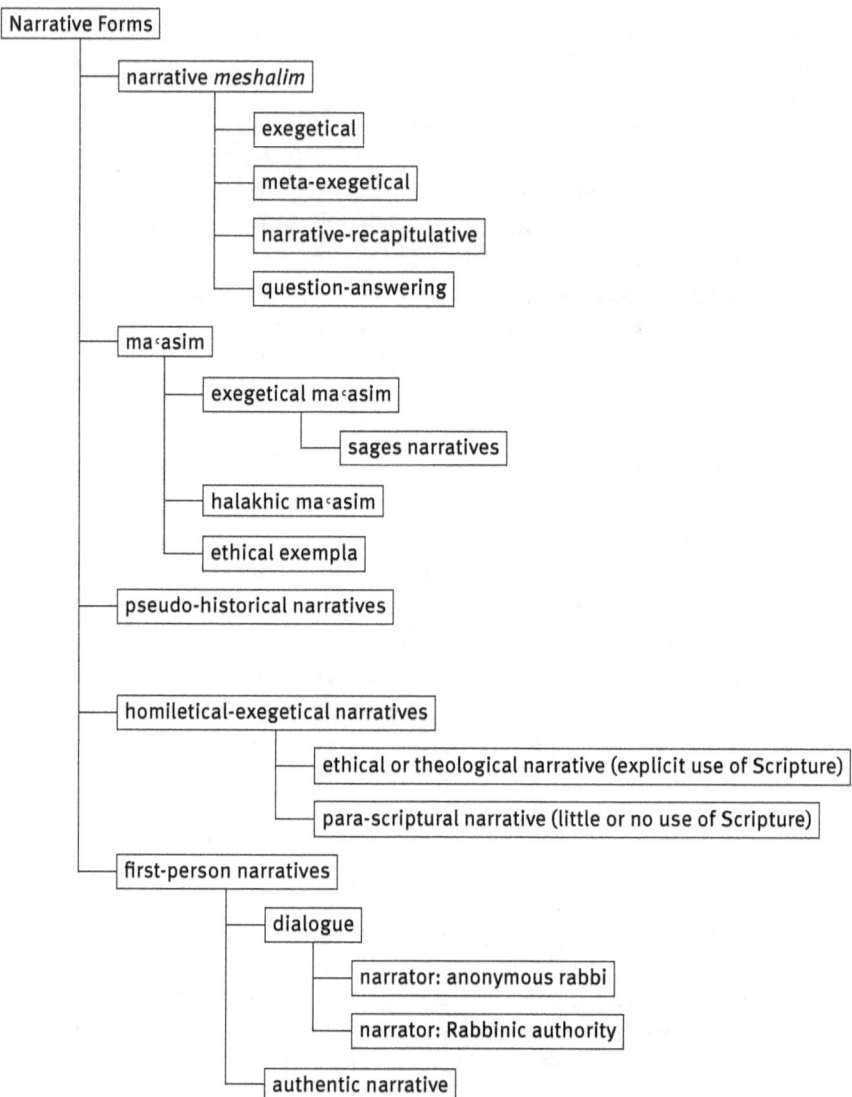

Figure 3.1: Typology of Narrative Forms in *Seder Eliyahu*

world to come.[18] *Seder Eliyahu Rabbah* actually ends with one such outlook on the messianic age:[19]

> And all those who rise to life again in the days of the Messiah will go to the land of Israel; they will never return to the dust they came from, for it is said, *Whoever is left in Zion and remains in Jerusalem will be called holy, everyone who has been recorded for life in Jerusalem* (Isa 4:3). Where will they go? In the hour when the Holy One, blessed be He, receives the righteous in the time to come, they will go before Him like children before the[ir] father and like servants before their master and like disciples before their teacher, for it is said, *And you shall flee by the valley of the Lord's mountain, for the valley between the mountains shall reach unto Azal [and the Lord my God shall come, and all the saints with him]* etc. (Zech 14:5). (ER 164, l. 24–ER 165, l. 3)

It could be argued, however, that in cases such as this, we are dealing with examples of "anterior narration," a less frequent temporal relation between narration and story than the standard one – that is, narration after the events. In anterior or predictive narration, the narrative communication precedes the events,[20] as for example in Scripture's prophetic books and in eschatological literature in general.[21]

---

18 So, for example, ER 24, l. 25ff. (on how God will feed Gog's and his allies' flesh to the birds of heaven); ER 81, l. 11ff. (Israel's pilgrimage in the time to come); ER 113, l. 23ff. (the nations in the days of the Messiah will enrich Israel); and ER 120, l. 25ff. (the nations in the days of the Messiah will melt to dust). Extensive eschatological passages are also found in chapters 20 and 21 of *Seder Eliyahu Zuta* (PsEZ 30–33). Further passages with a chronological setting in the time to come which are more of a descriptive, static nature, deal with God's Beit midrash. The representation of the world to come as a great academy is a recurring motif. Cf. ER 4, l. 3; ER 15, l. 4; ER 20, l. 25; ER 51, l. 26; and ER 68, l. 21, as well as PsEZ 33, l. 1. See Kadari, "Torah Study," 187, and 189–190. Another type of predictive narrative combines an account of man's reproachable conduct in this world and its future consequences: "Transgressors in (lit. "of") Israel. What will their fate be in that hour (of Judgement)? Because they commit transgressions and press on the feet of the Presence, in relation to whom it is said, *The whole earth is full of his glory* (Isa 6:3), because they transgress and desire the destruction of the world, therefore they will be banished from their homes to a land of sojourn and they will not be brought back, but they will be led to a wasteland, for it is said, *I will purge out the rebels among you, and those who transgress against me[; I will bring them out of the land where they reside as aliens, but they shall not enter the land of Israel]* etc. (Ezek 20:38)." (EZ 194, l. 20–24).
19 On a text ending with eschatological subject-matter, see Samely et al., *Inventory*, 1.4; and Alexander Samely, "War Scroll," in *Database for the Analysis of Anonymous and Pseudepigraphic Jewish Texts of Antiquity*, ed. Alexander Samely et al., http://literarydatabase.humanities.manchester.ac.uk.
20 These future events, even if we see them as "unique" rather than "generic," they are still events that pertain to a collective, not to individuals.
21 Rimmon-Kenan, *Narrative Fiction*, 91, describes this less usual type of temporal relation between narration and story in the following terms: "It is a kind of predictive narration, generally

66 — 3 A Typology of Narrative Forms of *Seder Eliyahu*

In some other passages, the governing voice makes use of forms, some of which would count as narratives according Simon-Shoshan's classification of mishnaic forms, but which I exclude from the analysis here. These comprise the representation of habitual actions (example 1 below), of what the governing voice presents as exemplary behaviour (example 2), and of hypothetical situations in the form of casuistic formulations (example 3).²² These passages can easily be identified as non-narrative by their choice of tense:²³ Whereas habitual actions are generally expressed with participial forms, and exemplary conduct with imperfect forms, the tense of the narrative sections is in the preterite or the periphrastic structure *haya + qotel*.²⁴

---

using the future tense, but sometimes the present. Whereas examples abound in Biblical prophecies, complete modern texts written in the predictive vein are rare."

22 Simon-Shoshan, *Stories*, 34, argues that, given that the protasis and apodosis of casuistic formulations present two interrelated events, taken together they "are almost always narratives."
23 This can be seen as a case of what is termed, after Paul Grice, "conversational implicature." Lyons, "Text and Discourse," 275, points out in this respect: "many fully lexical expressions are descriptively synonymous, but differ in respect of their social and expressive meaning. Most, if not all, of this difference would seem to fall within the scope of Grice's definition of conversational implicature. That is to say, morphological and syntactic distinctions, as well as differences between lexemes and particles may be associated with what many semanticists, following Grice, would classify as conversational implicatures."
24 There are, however, exceptions to this general rule. In eschatological passages, for example, imperfect and participle forms might be used. A few examples might illustrate that the author of *Seder Eliyahu* works with a certain flexibility with respect to the choice of tense forms. In the following passage, a series of hypothetical casuistic formulations is expressed using preterite forms in the protasis and participles in the apodosis: "When a man increases (הירבה) his language of falsehood and his lies with his father and with his mother, with his wife and his children, with his teacher who taught him Scripture and with his teacher who taught him Mishnah and wisdom, and with everyone in the world; when a man behaves (pret. נהג) impertinently toward his father and his mother, toward his wife and his children, toward his teacher who taught him Scripture and toward his teacher who taught him Mishnah and wisdom, and toward everyone in the world; when a man defies (pret. העז) his father and his mother and him who is better than he, leprosy will appear (part. מרעין) on his body. If he then repents (pret. חזר ועשה תשובה), they will heal him (part. מרפאין). If he does not, he [will remain] in its hold till the day of his death." (ER 76, l. 28– ER 77, l. 4). Apart from its occurrence in *Seder Eliyahu*, in few piyyutic texts and in the *Megillat Achimaʿats*, the form הירבה is extremely rare and not used at all in classical Rabbinic literature. See Maʾagarim. Similar cases of the use of preterite forms in the protasis and participle forms in the apodosis are found in ER 77, l. 7 and ER 122, l. 17. On the other hand, there are cases in which the use of the participle can be understood as referring to an action that took place in the biblical past: "And so David says (part. אומר), *I will not give sleep to my eyes, or slumber to my eyelids*. And it [Scripture]/he [David] says (part. אומר), *Until I find out a place for the Lord*, etc. (Ps 132:4–5). Because of this he merited (pret. זכה) great rewards." (ER 113, l. 9–10) This short exegetical narrative explains how David came to merit his reward. As regular citation formulas, these instances of

Example 1. But the King who is King of kings, blessed be He, may His great name be blessed for ever and ever and ever, is not like that [i.e., like the mortal king of a *mashal*]. He sits on His throne of glory, a third of the day He reads Scripture and recites Mishnah, a third of the day He passes judgement, and a third of the day He provides and nourishes the righteous and the disciples of the wise with wisdom, understanding, knowledge, and insight, for it is said, *He gives power to the faint[, and strengthens the powerless]* (Isa 40:29). (ER 84, l. 32–36)[25]

Example 2. Happy is the man who has plenty of food in his house, so that his servants and the members of his household come and enjoy with him at his table. Of him Scripture says, *You shall eat the fruit of the labour of your hands; you shall be happy* (Ps 28:2). (ER 136, l. 3–5)

Example 3. If a poor man who is himself son of one so poor that he never had a roof over his head, comes to repent of his misdeeds, he is [accounted] a righteous man afflicted with adversity. If he does not [repent], then he is [accounted] a wicked man afflicted with adversity. (EZ 181, l. 12–13)

3.1.1 Reports of Single Events

Passages which narrate single events – even if their narration occurs within a list of statements, each of which narrates a single event that is not causally related to the others – do not count as narrative texts; nor is the representation of single events that *imply* second events, which are merely alluded to, considered a narrative text. Given that the reporting of single events is a recurrent phenomenon in *Seder Eliyahu*, such passages are briefly discussed here as a type of non-narrative text. In the passage quoted below, a list of causally unrelated events is contained in the three comparisons presented by the governing voice:[26]

> He can become like the High Priest Aaron who had the intention and increased peace between Israel and their Father in heaven. He can become like David who had the intention and increased an abundance of loving-kindness between Israel and their Father in heaven.

אומר are generally translated in the present tense, even if they can be understood and translated as "David said," i. e., in his psalm.
25 The same events are told in a passage that constitutes a first-person narrative, but whose narrator is God himself; see ER 61, l. 21ff.
26 For a discussion of the form and function of a specific type of list – namely, that of allusions to scriptural passages – see Wayne Sibley Towner, *The Rabbinic "Enumeration of Scriptural Examples:" A Study of a Rabbinic Pattern of Discourse with Special Reference to Mekhilta D'R. Ishmael* (Leiden: Brill, 1973). As Samely, *Forms*, 13–15, points out, the list is one of the most characteristic small forms of Rabbinic literature. See also Samely, *Profiling Jewish Literature*, 293–294 (8.1.10/11) and 312–313 (9.3).

> He can become like Rabban Jochanan b. Zakkai who had the intention and had his disciples rejoice with him in halakhah.[27] (ER 136, l. 5–8)

In the next example, the answer given to a questioner in a first-person narrative exemplifies the manner in which the reporting of single and unrelated events synecdochally implies a series of biblical narratives. With the vertical line | I mark the beginning of each item in the list of reported single events; narrative texts – those consisting of at least two events – are set in bold type to distinguish them from the rest of the items in the list:

> He said to me, Rabbi, now according to this, he who carries out a command is given the reward he deserves, and he who commits a transgression is likewise given a reward as though he deserved it. I replied, My son, | can you consider the requital of the ancient serpent who proceeded to corrupt the whole world a reward? | Can you consider the requital of Adam and Eve who disobeyed the command a reward? Can you consider the requital of Cain who slew his brother Abel a reward? | Consider what, on the other hand, was the reward of Lamech who mourned the death of his father's father. Consider what was the reward of Shem who honoured his father as compared with the requital of Ham who did not honour his father. | **And consider also what was the reward of Noah who proceeded to upbraid multitudes of men for all of one hundred and twenty years, so that the punishment that had been decreed for them would not befall them. Wherefore Scripture said in praise of him, praise announced to all the generations after him,** *for I have seen that you alone are righteous before me in this generation* **(Gen 7:1).** | Consider, too, what was the reward of the great Shem who for four hundred years prophesied to all the peoples of the world who would not, however, heed him. | **Consider what was the reward of Abraham who rose up and demolished all the idols in his world. Nevertheless, because he said something improper to God, his children had to go down into [slavery] in Egypt. What he said was,** *O Lord God, how am I to know that I shall possess it?* **(Gen 15:8), and on account of the doubt implied in his question, his children had to go down into Egypt.** | Consider, also, what was the reward of Ishmael who went and buried his father. | Consider what was the reward of Isaac who said to his father, Bind me well and only lay me upon the altar lest I, who am only thirty-seven, young and full of strength, kick you or strike you and thus incur a double death penalty from Heaven. | **Consider what was the reward even of Esau who because he shed two tears before his father was given Mount Seir upon which rains of blessing never cease. And because the sons of Seir received the sons of Esau affably, they, too, were given their reward.** | Consider the reward of Jacob who, for all of his life, declared the truth [that the Lord is God] and in his heart also acknowledged that truth. | Consider what was the reward of the twelve Tribe-fathers who carried out the will of their father Jacob. Of them it is said, *Like grapes in the wilderness, I found Israel. Like the first fruit on the fig tree, in its first season, I saw your ancestors* (Hos 9:10). | Consider finally what was the reward of Abraham, Isaac, and Jacob, men of the one nation out of the nations that speak the seventy languages of the world, who instilled fear of God in them-

---

[27] In all three cases, the preterite form נתכוון is followed by participial forms, מרבה and משמח, although elsewhere it is usually followed by infinitive forms.

selves, in their children and in their children's children to the end of all generations. (EZ 174, l. 6–EZ 175, l. 8)

It could be argued that the items in the enumeration that are not set in bold face also consist of two events, the first being the explicit allusion to a biblical narrative, and the second the mention of a reward, which is not the same as the narration of how this happened. In his typology, Simon-Shoshan argues that from narrated single events, implied related events can be retrieved.[28] But then, even if implied events may be inferred from narrated ones, this does not mean that narrative itself can be retrieved from any one sentence. As was previously stated, and following Rimmon-Kenan, I opt in this study to exclude single-event narratives from my working concept of narrative texts in *Seder Eliyahu*.[29] In the example just quoted, the first event is told – the serpent corrupted the whole world, Adam and Eve disobeyed, etc., though what exactly happened to them afterwards the reader does not know from *this* text – from the text of *Seder Eliyahu*.

3.1.2 Speech Acts, Mishnah Quotations, and *mikan amru* Statements

When they are not part of a dialogue, reported speech acts constitute another form of narrated single event.[30] In *Seder Eliyahu*, they generally belong to the direct discourse type – they consist of a syntactical subject (pronoun or proper name),

---

28 In his discussion of a one-time event example in mPes 7:2 ("One may not roast the Passover offering on either a [metal] spit or grill. R. Zadok said, It once happened that R. Gamliel said to his servant Tevi, 'Go out and roast us the Passover offering on the grill'"), Simon-Shoshan, *Stories*, 45, argues that even if the *mishnah* does not qualify as a narrative or story, "the student can easily reconstruct the events leading up to and following this event. ... On the basis of this account, the student can easily fill in R. Gamliel's activities before and after he tells Tevi to roast the paschal sacrifice." If actions are predicated of a human being, common sense or familiarity with the law might help the reader in the work of reconstruction; if, however, actions are predicated of God, only a reader familiar with a specific corpus of literature might be able to reconstruct the events that precede and follow the event represented in statements such as "the Holy One, blessed be He, divided His world into two manners, that of the righteous and that of the wicked" (ER 87, l. 27–28), or "Therefore the Holy One, blessed be He, turned them into a sanctuary of His in the world." (ER 85, l. 19)
29 Rimmon-Kenan, *Narrative Fiction*, 3, argues: "Although single-event narratives are theoretically (and perhaps also empirically) possible ..., I speak of a succession of events in order to suggest that narratives usually consist of more than one."
30 Samely, *Forms*, 101, designates this form as a mini-narrative, pointing out that "the format 'speech report + statement' is not usually treated as narrative."

a *verbum dicendi*, an optional indirect object ("the Holy One, blessed be He, said to Moses"), and the reported utterance, with a broad variety of form and length:

> Thus said the Holy One, blessed be He, to Israel, My sons, what happiness does man have in this world? Nothing apart from the words of Torah. He who rejoices in silver, gold, precious stones, and pearls, what joy does he have after the hour of his death? After your joy there is death, so what profit does your whole joy have? You should rather come and rejoice with Me with a perfect joy the way I rejoice in you for ever and ever and ever, for it is said, *But be glad and rejoice* etc. (Isa 65:18). (ER 92, l. 30–34)

The reported utterance itself can be a descriptive or expository proposition,[31] but it can also consist of the report of a single event or of a narrative text. In the latter case, we are dealing with a level of discourse other than that on which the governing voice (in discursive or narrative modus) operates, for this narrative text is framed by the speech act, which is itself usually framed by the ethical-homiletical discourse of *Seder Eliyahu*.

Speech acts in *Seder Eliyahu* are represented both as taking place in the present and therefore as always being valid – such as in the case of scriptural quotations introduced with "it [Scripture] says" (הוא אומר) – and as having taken place in the past. The speaking agents of the latter vary, though many of them have God as the speaker: "the Holy One, blessed be He, said" (אמר הקב״ה). The words can be scriptural quotations or "new" midrashic words attributed to him:

> And the Holy One, blessed be He, spoke thus to Adam, My son, from the day I put you on earth do good things and learn Torah, but protect yourself from doing wrong, from sin and from vile acts. Therefore it is said, *On the day of prosperity be joyful, and on the day of adversity consider* (Eccl 7:14). Consider what you have done to deserve chastisements come upon you. (ER 67, l. 13–17)[32]

---

31 Speech acts can fulfil an explicit exegetical function, as for example in the following passage, where the speech act is the dictum of a midrashic unit: "*from your own kin do not hide yourself* (Isa 58:7). The Holy One, blessed be He, spoke thus to every man, My son, the days I have given you on earth perform good deeds and engage in study of Torah, keep distant from transgression and unseemly behaviour, hence it is said, *from your own kin do not hide yourself.*" (ER 139, l. 5–7) On the midrashic unit as Rabbinic small form, see Samely, *Forms*, 65–69. Sayings by named sages do not abound in the *Rabbah* and *Zuta* parts of *Seder Eliyahu*, but are frequently found in *Pseudo-Seder Eliyahu Zuta*.

32 In *Seder Eliyahu*, it is quite often difficult to tell in which precise moment the governing voice takes over from the characters it allows to speak. In this case, it could be argued that God's speech ends at this point and is followed by the words "For chastisement comes upon man (Adam) only for his good, in order to bring out of his hands everything he has done (wrong). And the sages taught in a *mishnah*." If God himself had spoken these words in direct speech to Adam, we would not expect him to refer to Adam in the third person.

Prayers, benedictions (*berakhot*), and vows[33] constitute a special type of speech act, whose agents can be the governing voice itself, biblical characters, or even God. The following example has the former as the speaker of words that include another speech act, which is attributed to God:

> My Father in heaven, may Your great name be blessed for ever and ever and ever and may You find contentment in Israel Your servants in all the places where they dwell, for You said, I shall receive their transgressors [if they come] in repentance, for even if a man heaps up a hundred transgressions, one above the other, behold, in mercy I receive him [if he comes] in repentance. For even if a man stands up and curses Heaven, but then retracts, the Holy One, blessed be He, forgives everything, for it is said, *then the lame shall leap like a deer* etc. (Isa 35:6). The lame man is none other than the one lacking in knowledge and lacking in good deeds, *For waters shall break forth in the wilderness, and streams in the desert* (Isa 35:6). (ER 121, l. 20–26)

Within another prayer, this time spoken by David, narrated speech act-like actions, such as "write" or "ordain" are used to explain the fact that the world still exists and has not been destroyed by God:

> And it [Scripture] says, *A prayer of one afflicted, when faint and pleading before the Lord* (Ps 102:1). In the manner of a lowly man when he is faint, David stood in prayer before the Holy One, saying: Master of the universe, had You not *written* on our behalf that in this world punishment for iniquity is to be put off for three generations, no man would remain alive on the face of the earth, and the entire world – all of it – would be destroyed. But in Your wisdom and Your understanding what did You do in our behalf? You *ordained* that until the very end of time, punishment for iniquity in this world be put off for three or four generations. Certainly, *The Lord is slow to anger, and abounding in steadfast love* (Num 14:18). (ER 98, l. 5–10)

One subgroup of speech acts are those composed of an introductory formula, such as "the sages recited" or "the sages said,"[34] followed by a quotation from the Mishnah. The verb form שנו is used in several formulas, which hint at the source being not Scripture, but Mishnah. The formula "the sages taught in a mishnah" (שנו חכמים במשנה) introduces 17 quotations;[35] less frequent are the formulas "the sages

---

33 The governing voice repeatedly uses the vow formula "I call heaven and earth to witness" (מעיד אני את השמים ואת הארץ), which is characteristic for Rabbinic literature of the amoraic period, to introduce its statements.
34 The names of the sages in *Seder Eliyahu Rabbah* are seldom mentioned; see, for example, R. Simeon, ER 69, l. 16.
35 I.e., mSan 4:5 (ER 10, ER 53, ER 127), mMen 5:8 (ER 37), mYom 8:9 (ER 38), mAv 4:10 (ER 56), mAv 1:7 (ER 67), mAv 4:4 (ER 68), mAv 3:12 (ER 141), mMak 3:15 (ER 73), mQid 4:1 (ER 100), mQid 4:13 (ER 101), mQid 4:14 (ER 101) (Friedmann omits one of the quotations in his edition), mAv 4:18 (ER 103), mAv 3:18 (ER 112), mAv 5:20 (ER 116), mAv 3:13 (ER 141), and mAv 5:16 (ER 141).

taught" (שנו חכמים),³⁶ "for so the sages taught" (שכך שנו חכמים),³⁷ "our masters taught in a mishnah/the Mishnah" (שנו רבותינו במשנה),³⁸ and "they taught us this mishnah" (שנו לנו את המשנה הזה).³⁹ The second most characteristic verb used to introduce mishnaic quotations is "said" (אמר). In this case, the syntactic subject might be spelled out – as in "the sages said" (אמרו חכמים),⁴⁰ "r[abbi]. said" (אמר ר'),⁴¹ "R. Simeon said" (אמר ר' שמעון)⁴² – or not, as in the characteristic introductory formula "on the basis of this, they said" (lit. "from here they said" מיכן אמרו).⁴³ The formula "for it is said" (שנאמר) – which introduces mBM 4:10 (ER 106) – represents a special case, since this expression is otherwise used to introduce scriptural quotations, not only in *Seder Eliyahu*, but in Rabbinic literature in general.

The speech act consisting of the formula "from that moment the sages instituted that halakhah" (מאותה שעה תקנו חכמים אותה הלכה) which introduces mKet 13:3 and mBB 9:1 in ER 122, l. 8, appears to be part of an etiological narrative that links the origins of the quoted *mishnayot* to the times of famine alluded to by the prophet Jeremiah in Lam 5:10–11, the interpretation of which precedes the mishnaic quotation.⁴⁴

3.2 Narrative in *Seder Eliyahu*: Preliminary Considerations

The typology and readings in the pages and chapters which follow can be considered one of several experiments in so-called "post-classical narratology," insofar as we are dealing with texts that lie beyond the corpus that "classical narratol-

---

36 Used to introduce mAv 4:18 (ER 83).
37 Used to introduce mHul 2:1 (ER 72).
38 Used to introduce mEd 2:10 (ER 15).
39 Used to introduce mAv 4:14 (ER 72).
40 E.g., mEd 5:7 (ER 104).
41 Emended by Friedmann to "R. Aqiba said" (אמר ר' עקיבא). See mAv 3:14 (ER 61, l. 13).
42 mMak 3:15 (ER 69, l. 16).
43 mSot 1:7 (ER 59). Most of the *mikan amru* formulas which abound in *Seder Eliyahu*, however, are not followed by mishnaic quotations. As with a very small subgroup of speech acts whose agents are individual sages, "R. Eleazar b. Matthia said" (ER 109, l. 17), the *mikan amru* formulas introduce sayings attributed to a collective Rabbinic voice, but not necessarily attested in other Rabbinic documents. On the use of this formula in tannaitic sources, see Günter Stemberger, "Leviticus in Sifra," in *Judaica Minora II: Geschichte und Literatur des rabbinischen Judentums* (Tübingen: Mohr Siebeck, 2010), 493–496; and Israel Azzan-Yadin, "'On the Basis of This, They Said': Mikan ᾽Amru and the Role of Scripture," chap. 4 in *Scripture and Tradition: Rabbi Akiva and the Triumph of Midrash* (Philadelphia, PA: Pennsylvania University Press, 2014), 73–100.
44 See ER 122, l. 5–12.

ogy" studies. The toolkit put to use is, however, one provided by Rimmon-Kenan, a rather conservative representative of classical narratology.[45] Unlike Simon-Shoshan, who pleads for "a fundamental reconception of the nature of narrative and narrativity,"[46] I will describe textual forms in *Seder Eliyahu* which do not need to be "justified" as narrative texts, but which could readily be recognised as such, at least by a reader acquainted with the peculiarities of Rabbinic literature.

Among the aspects which need to be addressed is the question of the fictionality of these narrative texts. Even if it is considered only (epigonally) related to Rabbinic literature, *Seder Eliyahu* distinctly suggests a self-conception according to which the work transmits Rabbinic ideology, somehow belongs to the Rabbinic corpus, and is therefore Oral Torah. Seen from this perspective, the question of the fictionality of some of its parts (e.g., its narrative texts) is a delicate one.[47] If, however, we understand fiction as an acceptable term for narrative texts which are not based on eyewitness accounts or on reliable sources, and if we agree with Jan P. Fokkelman when he states that in texts of the Old and New Testaments, a disciplined use of imagination predominates, then Rabbinic narrative and the narrative texts of the *Seder Eliyahu* can also be considered fictional.[48] The narratives of *Seder Eliyahu* contain certain textual markers which point to their fictionality, for example, the use of verbs for internal processes regarding third persons or even for

---

45 Rimmon-Kenan, *Narrative Fiction*.
46 Simon-Shoshan, *Stories*, 20.
47 As Gerhard Langer pointed out to me in a personal communication, "Gerade der in der Narratologie so heftig diskutierte Begriff des Fiktiven könnte vor allem in seiner Anwendung auf Texte im religiösen Kontext, selbst wenn diese nicht auf 'Offenbarung' beruhen, auf Probleme stoßen."
48 Jan P. Fokkelman, "Fiktion/Fiktionalität. I. Alttestamentlich," in *Lexikon der Bibelhermeneutik: Begriffe – Methoden – Theorien – Konzepte*, ed. Oda Wischmeyer (Berlin, Boston: De Gruyter, 2013), 178, observes: "F[iktion] ist ein akzeptabler Terminus für Erzählungen, die offensichtlich nicht auf Augenzeugenberichten oder verlässlichen Quellen basieren. Der größte Teil, wenn nicht der gesamte Erzählstoff von Gen und Exod ist ein Produkt der Intuition und entspricht den Bedürfnissen (wie der Etablierung einer spirituellen Identität) und religiösen Konzepten des alten Israel als eines sesshaften Volkes. Der Inhalt der Bücher Est und Dan ist F[iktion] im engeren Sinne. Der Großteil des atl. Erzählstoffes ... setzt sich dagegen aus Formen der nationalen Geschichtsschreibung zusammen. Diese Art Historiographie jedoch basiert auf Voraussetzungen, die sich grundlegend von den Ansprüchen und Prinzipien der modernen Geschichtsschreibung unterscheiden. In der Erzählung seiner Vergangenheit bedient sich Israel narrativer Formen und bejaht dichterische Freiheit, anstatt sie abzulehnen; Rhetorik und guter Stil werden favorisiert. Daher muss die Definition von F[iktion] dahingehend ausgeweitet werden, dass extensiver, aber disziplinierter Einsatz von Imagination ein anerkannter Teil der F[iktion] wird. Die hebräischen Erzähler und die Autoren ntl. Erzählungen fühlen sich dazu berechtigt, Lücken auszufüllen, die Innenwelt ihrer Charaktere wiederzugeben und zu interpretieren, und sie bleiben ihrer religiösen Vision treu, was ihnen hilft, den berichteten Geschehensabläufen Form zu verleihen."

God: "At that time the Holy One, blessed be He, said in His heart" (ER 85, l. 31).[49] Following Käte Hamburger, Monika Fludernik observes that one of the aspects which actually distinguishes narrative from non-narrative discourse is precisely this property of narrative: "Narrative is the one and only form of discourse that can portray consciousness, particularly another's consciousness, from the inside, and it is this capacity ... that provides narrative with a niche in the field of competing discourses, historical or otherwise."[50]

Another important part of the description of the forms has to do with the characters who act in the represented world. Who are the characters in the narratives – individuals (unnamed characters, types, biblical or post-biblical figures, Rabbinic authorities, God, other supernatural beings, animals) or collective bodies (Rome, thousands of human beings, myriads of angels)? With regard to their specificity, a problem posed by many narrative passages in *Seder Eliyahu* is that they deal not with named or unnamed individuals, but with collective agents, such as Israel and the peoples of the world, the transgressors, or the righteous among Israel. Although these passages do relate at least two events in the past, they lack the specificity narratology associates with narratives. In the case of the examples below, even if both texts purport to illustrate the same point – they both deal with the notion that the fear of God precedes the performance of good deeds – and their structure is quite similar, the lower narrativity of the second passage is due to depiction of the collective experience of Israel's forefathers during the exodus, whereas the first deals with Isaac's experience:

> We learnt from Isaac that from the beginning of his deeds he feared the Holy One, blessed be He. Isaac was seventy-five years old when Abraham entered his eternal abode. He said, Woe is me! Perhaps there are not good deeds in me as were in my father. What will happen to me before the Holy One, blessed be He? At once the compassion of the Holy One, blessed be He, was moved and He spoke to him then, for it is said, *And that very night the Lord appeared to him [and said, I am the God of your father Abraham; do not be afraid, for I am with you and will bless you and make your offspring numerous for my servant Abraham's sake]* etc. (Gen 26:24). (ER 128, l. 35–ER 129, l. 3)

> We learnt from our first forefathers that from the beginning of their deeds they feared the Holy One, blessed be He, for it is said, *Israel saw the great work [that the Lord did against the*

---

49 See Martínez and Scheffel, *Einführung in die Erzähltheorie*, 18: "Anders als der reale Sprecher einer faktualen Rede ist das fiktive Aussagesubjekt der fiktionalen Rede als eine nicht-empirische Person nicht an natürliche Beschränkungen menschlicher Rede gebunden. So gehören zu den textinternen Fiktionssignalen die Anwendung von Verben innerer Vorgänge auf dritte Personen ... sowie eine Erweiterung des Tempussystems der Sprache."
50 Monika Fludernik, *Towards a Natural Narratology* (London, New York: Routledge, 1996), 27.

Egyptians. So the people feared the Lord and believed in the Lord and in his servant Moses] etc. (Exod 14:31). (ER 129, l. 5–6)

How does characterisation operate in the narratives of *Seder Eliyahu*? Characters are predominantly indirectly presented, through actions predicated of them, including the representation of their direct speech. The representation of characters' thoughts or feelings is not a common feature.[51] Among their actions, conversing is probably the most common, which is true not only of sages as narrative characters, but also of biblical characters in their new Rabbinic clothes.

In her discussion of the problem of the subordination of character to action or of its independence – in other words, the problem of characters doing or being – Rimmon-Kenan claims it is possible to understand both types of subordination (character to action and action to character) as predominant in certain kinds of narrative: "There are narratives in which character predominates (so-called psychological narratives) and narratives in which action does (apsychological narratives) ... Between the two extremes, there are – of course – different degrees of predominance of one of the other element."[52] If the narratological question of whether character or action predominates is asked of *Seder Eliyahu*, it can be asserted that characters are there for the sake of their action, which generally consists in saying something (or quoting something or someone).

Time, "the relations of chronology between story and text,"[53] is an important aspect of a narrative text's constitution, but one on which I will not focus in my readings. Narratology distinguishes story-time (the time period covered by the story) from text-time (the time period during which the story is told). The relations between story-time and text-time, which are generally of discrepancy, were first systematically discussed by Gérard Genette with respect to the three aspects of order, duration, and frequency.[54] Under duration Genette subsumes the paces, which go from summary to scene, chosen by the narrative to represent a period of story-time. On this Rimmon-Kenan points out:

---

51 On the expression "lest a man think" (כדי שלא יאמר אדם לעצמו, lit. "say to himself"), it may be argued that, rather than being used to introduce a character's thought, it represents what the governing voice assumes to be the probable thoughts of the intended readers of the work.
52 Rimmon-Kenan, *Narrative Fiction*, 36.
53 Rimmon-Kenan, *Narrative Fiction*, 44.
54 See Genette, "Discours du Récit," 77–182: a) order (several forms of anachrony), b) duration (the possible paces, ranging from summary to scene [dialogue], with which the text can choose to represent a given story-period), and c) frequency (relation between the number of times an event appears in a story and the number of times it is narrated in the text; this can be singulative, repetitive, or iterative).

Theoretically, between these two poles [or paces, i.e. acceleration and deceleration] there is an infinity of possible paces, but in practice these are conventionally reduced to summary and scene. In summary, the pace is accelerated through a textual "condensation" or "compression" of a given story-period into a relatively short statement of its main features. The degree of condensation can, of course, vary from summary to summary, producing multiple degrees of acceleration.[55]

As was previously stated, conversing is one of the most typical actions characters perform in *Seder Eliyahu*. Therefore, much of the textual material from these narratives can be considered as examples of scenes, theoretically with no discrepancy between story- and text-time with respect to duration.[56] This means that it takes roughly as long to tell (or read) the dialogue as it took to conduct it.

Considering that most of the narratives in *Seder Eliyahu* are told by the same (governing) voice which speaks the entire document – the voice that quotes Gen 3:24 at the beginning of the book and sometime in the course of the first chapter says "I" for the first time – and considering that this anonymous I-speaker alternately assumes non-narrative and narrative modes of communication, we can claim that the narratives this voice tells are situated on the same communicative level as its non-narrative, ethical-homiletical discourse, even if the latter seems to encompass the former. The predominant narrative instance can be described (with Genette) as an extradiegetic narrator – one situated outside the narrated world. There are, however, narrative instances, in which the narrator is situated within the narrated world.[57] There are several further questions to pose with respect to the problem of the narrative levels: Are the narrators present or absent in the stories they narrate, in narratological terminology, are they "homodiegetic" or "heterodiegetic narrators"?[58] Who is the narratee – who is addressed with these narratives? Since most narratives in this midrash are hermeneutic tools with which the governing voice explains Rabbinic ideas, interprets scriptural verses, and transmits sayings of the sages, David Stern's suggested term "implied interpreter," a modification of Wolfgang Iser's "implied reader," could be considered as an alternative to the usual narratological term "narratee."[59] Certain

---

55 Rimmon-Kenan, *Narrative Fiction*, 53.
56 See Rimmon-Kenan, *Narrative Fiction*, 54: "In scene, as was said before, story-duration and text-duration are conventionally considered identical. The purest scenic form is dialogue."
57 In Genette's terminology, "Discours du Récit," 239, such narratives are designated "metadiegetic": "L'instance narrative d'un récit premier est donc par définition extradiégetique, comme l'instance narrative d'un récit second (métadiégétique) est par définition diégétique, etc."
58 See Rimmon-Kenan, *Narrative Fiction*, 96–97.
59 Stern, *Parables*, 86–87, defines the implied interpreter as "a figure in the text, inscribed as part of the fictional or exegetical structure of the *mashal*."

expressions point to the voice of the midrash addressing someone who is explicitly external to its narrative discourse (for example, "here you learned" [הא למדת], "go and learn" [צא ולמד]). Other expressions make use (and not only in narrative contexts) of the first-person plural – for example, in "we learnt" (למדנו), "our forefathers" (אבותינו), or "our father Abraham" (אברהם אבינו) – suggesting that the implied interpreter is thought of as belonging to the same community as the narrating governing voice.

Focalisation, or the perspective from which a story is presented,[60] can be a fruitful category of narratology when applied to the description of the narratives in *Seder Eliyahu* (and in other documents of Rabbinic literature as well). Focalisation is said to be external or narrator-bound when the narrator tells what they perceive. When the narrator narrates what a character in a story perceives, focalisation is said to be internal or character-bound. The subject of the focalisation or the focaliser is "the agent whose perception orients the presentation, whereas the object (the 'focalized') is what the focalizer perceives."[61] Among the facets of focalisation that Rimmon-Kenan distinguishes, the ideological facet is probably especially appropriate for the description of the so-called exegetical narratives, in which a Rabbinic voice renews the biblical discourse.[62]

A number of questions concerning the style rather than the narrative theory of these Rabbinic narratives need to be addressed in their description: Are scriptural verses quoted or not? If they are, are they used as lemmata or as proof-texts. Are they linked with verses from other books of Scripture, in the manner of the *petichah*? What kind of narrative openings can be distinguished? Is a story told with the same phraseology and/or structure as another or others in the same chapter, so that it seems to constitute a pair or a series of narratives? Does the narrator interrupt their narration with commentary or rhetorical questions? What kind of endings can be distinguished? Is there an ethical maxim appended to the narrative, or does the narrative follow an ethical maxim?

---

[60] There is no real consensus in narratology on whether focalisation is something essentially different from "point of view" or "perspective." I use the term as a synonym for perspective, without emphasising the visual aspect. The concept was introduced into the narratological discussion by Genette, "Discours du Récit," 203–224. It has been reformulated by Mieke Bal, *Narratology*, 3rd ed. (Toronto: Toronto University Press, 2009), 145–167, among others. For an overview, see Manfred Jahn, "Focalization," in *Routledge Encyclopedia of Narrative Theory*, ed. David Herman, Manfred Jahn, and Marie-Laure Ryan (London, New York: Routledge, 2005), 173–177; Manfred Jahn, "Focalization," in *The Cambridge Companion to Narrative*, ed. David Herman (Cambridge: Cambridge University Press, 2007), 94–108; and Rimmon-Kenan, *Narrative Fiction*, 72–86, where she applies the concept to the scriptural narrative of the Akedah.
[61] Rimmon-Kenan, *Narrative Fiction*, 75.
[62] See below, 3.4.1.

Related to this problem is the question of the narratives' relative autonomy and comprehensibility. As already stated, narratives in *Seder Eliyahu* are not told for their own sake, but primarily in order to elucidate an ethical or exegetical point made in the ethical-homiletical context of which they are a part. Narrative forms vary with regard to their comprehensibility when isolated from their homiletical frame. Whereas the meaning of parables (*meshalim*) depends to a large extent on their co-texts, more complex structures – such as those found in *maʿasim*, pseudo-historical, and homiletical-exegetical narratives – appear to be more stable in meaning, if isolated from their co-texts.

In my discussion of representative examples in the following pages, I will not be able to focus on every one of these aspects, but only on those most relevant to the passage in question. I propose to distinguish between "simple narratives" and "composite narratives." The former are self-contained, small forms; the latter integrate smaller structures.

3.3 Simple Forms

3.3.1 Narrative *Meshalim*

The expression *narrative mashal* in this study designates a short literary form with a narrative structure,[63] generally introduced in *Seder Eliyahu* with the opening

---

[63] Narrative *meshalim*, both those introduced with a fixed formula and those otherwise introduced, are distinguished from non-narrative, descriptive, static *meshalim* or similes, which consist of an image or a series of images but do not represent a sequence of causally related events. Alexander Deeg, *Predigt und Derascha: Homiletische Textlektüre im Dialog mit dem Judentum* (Göttingen: Vandenhoeck & Ruprecht, 2006), 372, refers to the narrative *meshalim* in terms of "narratives" ("Erzählungen") and to the non-narrative in terms of "static images" ("Standbilder"); Clemens Thoma and Simon Lauer, *Pesiqta de Rav Kahana (PesK) : Einleitung, Übersetzung, Parallelen, Kommentar, Texte*, vol. 1 of *Die Gleichnisse der Rabbinen* (Bern: Lang, 1986), 36, suggest the distinction between "event parables" ("Geschehnis-Gleichnisse") and "dramatic parables" ("Dramatik-Gleichnisse"). Samely, *Forms*, 189, distinguishes the *mashal* proper or *mashal* in the narrow sense, with its two-stage structure, from the "hermeneutic simile," which "has no 'before and after,' but is static." Examples of non-narrative *meshalim* or comparisons in *Seder Eliyahu* include: "What does he resemble? A threshold upon which all step; a plank over which all pass; a tree into whose shade all come; a lamp which provides light for the eyes of many" (ER 62, l. 31–ER 63, l. 2), and "What is he like? He is like a foot put in a well-fitting shoe and thereby saved from any sort of ache or pain" (ER 84, l. 1–2). There is yet another type, that of *meshalim* which consist of a single, explicitly narrated event, as for example in: "They told a parable. What does the matter resemble? It is like a king of flesh and blood who prepared a banquet for all the notables in his kingdom who came to his palace" (ER 117, l. 8–10).

formula "they told a parable: What does the matter resemble? It is like..." (משלו משל למה הדבר דומה ל-), which is rarely found in this full wording in early midrashim.⁶⁴ Less frequent are the short versions of this formula, namely "it is like..." (משל ל-) and the question formula, "What does the thing/he/the House of Israel resemble? It is like..." (למה הדבר / הוא / בית ישראל דומה ל-).⁶⁵

As has already been explained by – among others – David Stern in his seminal work on Rabbinic parables, *meshalim* or parables consist of two parts: a fictional (or rather a typifying, hypothetical) narrative, the *mashal* proper part, and its interpretation or application, the *nimshal*.⁶⁶ The latter is also generally introduced with a formula, such as "so" (or "likewise," "similarly," כך, וכך), or "therefore" (לפיכך).⁶⁷ In classical midrash, the latter usually comes to a close with the quotation of a Bible verse.⁶⁸ There is seldom a one-to-one correspondence between the elements of the *nimshal* and the elements of the *mashal*, so that the interpretation of this correspondence rests with the reader. With respect to the incongruence or uncertainty that arises between the two parts of the parabolical passages David Stern observes the following:

> By reproducing the message in duplicate, the structure of the *mashal* provides a framework for the interpretive act that its audience must perform. The duplication serves both as a hermeneutical safeguard – since the audience can "check" their interpretation of the narrative against their understanding of exegesis, and vice versa – and as an opening for additional subtleties of meaning, since by inserting discrepancies into the space between the *mashal* proper and the nimshal, by introducing differences into the larger pattern of resemblance, the mashal's author can deliberately complicate his audience's act of interpretation as well as the mashal's own message.⁶⁹

Braude and Kapstein sum up their appraisal of the characteristics and use of the *meshalim* in *Seder Eliyahu* as follows:

> Sometimes the point of the parable is given in advance so that the story serves as down-to earth illustration, an acting-out of the point. At other times the parable is given first, with

---

64 The order of these first two words is inverted once: משל משלו (ER 128, l. 20).
65 Stern, *Parables*, 214, observes that "[i]n striking contrast to Rabbinic texts, which often seem to have been written in a kind of scribal shorthand, nearly all the *meshalim* in TDE [*Tanna debe Eliyahu*] leisurely begin with the complete form of the standard formula *mashlu* mashal *lemah ha-davar domeh le*. In TDE, this formula effectively acquires the meaning of 'Once upon a time....'"
66 See Stern, *Parables*, 8. See also Samely, *Forms*, 189. Deeg, *Predigt und Derascha*, 371, describes *mashal* as a surface structure, of which the *nimshal* is a deep structure.
67 The *nimshal* is also introduced in *Seder Eliyahu* with several other expressions, such as "but" (אבל), "rather" (אלא), "so they resemble" (לכך נמדו), and "for it is said" (שנאמר).
68 See Stern, *Parables*, 8.
69 Stern, *Parables*, 9.

its point held off to the end. In any event, the teacher takes no chance that his audience will miss the point. Most often in *Tanna debe Eliyyahu* the parable serves to dramatize and explain God's actions by analogy with the actions of a mortal king. In this way God is brought down to earth, so to speak, and the awesome, remote Being is made understandable in terms of mortal speech and action. Indeed the opening sentence of many a parable seems to be a familiar folktale formula: "Once there was a king who lived in a city far across the sea" – a formula that suggests not only the sovereignty of Israel's King, but also the mystery of His power, remote and awesome.[70]

On the use of *meshalim* in *Seder Eliyahu*, David Stern observes: "Among the literary-rhetorical forms that TDE [*Tanna debe Eliyahu*]'s author borrowed from classical midrash and altered to suit his own purposes the *mashal* holds a prominent place."[71] Moreover, when comparing these forms with their counterparts in documents of classical midrash, he states: "Most of the Greek and Latin loanwords and the imperial terminology so common in Amoraic king-*meshalim* have disappeared from TDE; so have the rhetorical specifics, the everyday allusions, and the unstudied down-to-earth spontaneity of earlier midrashic parables."[72] In Stern's view, *Seder Eliyahu* exemplifies the increasingly rhetorical character of *meshalim* as illustrations of abstract ideas or beliefs.[73]

Most of *Seder Eliyahu*'s narrative *meshalim* are so-called king parables.[74] The *Rabbah* and *Zuta* parts include a total of 70 narrative *meshalim*, 62 of which are

---

70 Braude and Kapstein, *Tanna děbe Eliyyahu*, 23.
71 Stern, *Parables*, 211.
72 Stern, *Parables*, 214.
73 See Stern, *Parables*, 49.
74 On Rabbinic king parables as a type, see Stern, *Parables*, 19–21; and Alan Appelbaum, *The Rabbis' King-Parables: Midrash from the Third-Century Roman Empire* (Piscataway, NJ: Gorgias Press, 2010). Surprisingly, Appelbaum states that there are no king parables in *Seder Eliyahu*: "This possibility is reinforced by the fact that there are no parables about kings, but only about 'one' or 'rich men' or 'lords' in the quite late *Tanna debe Eliahu*. If indeed this is by a single author, it may simply mean that he did not share this preference. Or its composition in post-Muslim Iraq, if indeed that was hwere it was composed, resulted in less emphasis on kings or emperors" (60n184). A classical analysis is Ignaz Ziegler, *Die Königsgleichnisse des Midrash beleuchtet durch die römische Kaiserzeit* (Breslau: Schottlaender, 1903). Ziegler studied the king parables as a reflection of the historical background of the Roman Empire. The king parables were, according to Ziegler, not merely constructs imagined by the rabbis, but reflected their real experience – "nicht Phantasiegebilde, sondern reale Wirklichkeit" (xxiii). Stern, *Parables*, 20, argues against this assumption, though he concedes that "the many references in the *meshalim* to the larger world in which the Rabbis lived certainly show how profoundly familiar the sages were with that world and its culture, and how creatively they were able to turn that knowledge into material for their imaginative narrative compositions." Deeg, *Predigt und Derascha*, 373, points out that even if we are not to take king *meshalim* as historical sources, as Ignaz Ziegler's study suggested, they do operate within a political discourse: "Die Rabbinen nehmen sich die Freiheit, mit König und

king parables. The question underlying the different opening formulas quoted above – which can be paraphrased as, "To what is the matter comparable?" – is answered in the majority of cases with the words, "to a king of flesh and blood" (למלך בשר ודם) or just "to a king" (למלך). This is also characteristic of what Stern calls the regularised form of the Rabbinic *mashal*.[75] The rest of the narrative *meshalim* have other protagonists (or characters mentioned in the first place) as subjects – schoolchildren and a teacher[76] or a king's daughter.[77] Apart from the king, who can but need not be the protagonist of the narrative, the other characters include his wife, his servants, and/or his children.

Characterisation in *meshalim* takes place by indirect presentation: The mortal king of the parables is not said to be generous or tolerant; rather, his actions and speech present him as such or otherwise. The same is true of the rest of the characters, none of whom is ever given a proper name. *Meshalim* narrate action or represent dialogue in the form of direct speech in order to depict God's relation to Israel. *Meshalim*, it has been argued, are not full narratives in that they do not report a unique sequence of events, but rather hypothetical or typical ones. Therefore, the characters of *meshalim* are not individuals, but types.[78]

Meshalim are textual forms found in the non-narrative discourse of *Seder Eliyahu*; they are therefore narrated by the work's governing voice, which operates as an extradiegetic narrator. They can also be used in the context of those dialogues which are here collectively referred to as first-person narratives, in which the governing voice narrates its own experiences, which generally consist of dialogues with non-Rabbinic others.[79] Whereas in the first case the narrator addresses an extradiegetic audience with the *meshalim* – the reader or listener – in the second he addresses a diegetic narratee, one of his non-Rabbinic interlocutors. *Meshalim* can also be narrated by a character in an exegetical narrative. An interesting example of the latter is a case in which God himself is the narra-

---

Königshof auf der Figurenbühne der Meschalim zu "spielen" und dokumentieren so eine theologisch begründete Üerlegenheit entgegen aller realen politischen Machtverhältnisse. Das sicher nicht selten als übermächtig erfahrene Römische Reich lässt sich auf die Tora hin zuordnen und in der Schriftauslegung gebrauchen. – In dieser Hinsicht können Königsgleichnisse auch als politische Demonstration gelesen werden."
75 See Stern, *Parables*, 19.
76 See ER 114, l. 3.
77 See ER 149, l. 27.
78 See Samely, *Forms*, 189.
79 See section 3.4.2 in this chapter and also chapter 5.

tor of a king parable.[80] In only two cases does the governing voice let Rabbinic authorities, R. Ishmael[81] and R. Jose the Galilean,[82] take over to narrate *meshalim*.

The voice that narrates the *meshalim* seldom interrupts its narrative – the *mashal* proper – for example, with a rhetorical question[83] or a scriptural quotation;[84] it comes to the fore at the beginning of the *mashal* proper and at its end, when it speaks words that connect the two parts of the *mashal*, introducing the application of the narrative.

According to their immediately preceding co-texts (in brackets in the diagram below), narrative *meshalim* in *Seder Eliyahu* can be classified in the following four groups:

Table 3.2: Types of Narrative *meshalim* in *Seder Eliyahu*

Co-text	*Mashal* Type
Scriptural verse	Exegetical
Rabbinic statement	Meta-exegetical
Narrative of biblical subject-matter	Narrative-recapitulative
Rhetorical question	Question-answering

The majority belong to the exegetical *mashal* or "exegetical parable" group, to borrow Jacob Neusner's expression.[85] Their function is the elucidation of the meaning of a word or phrase in a verse. "The task of the exegetical parable or theological parable is to clarify not a law but a statement of Scripture."[86] In the German-speaking world, Arnold Goldberg's highly influential contribution "Das Schriftauslegende Gleichnis" provided a precise delimitation of the exegetical parable:

> Unter den Textsorten der rabbinischen Literatur, die mit "Maschal" bezeichnet werden, kann besonders im Unterschied zum "Vergleich" (aber auch zur Parabel) eine Textsorte als "Gleichnis" bestimmt werden. Gleichnisse sind kurze fiktionale narrative Texteinheiten, die zur Darstellung eines anderen Sachverhaltes, einer 'Sache' dienen. Unter den Gleichnissen kann eine Textsorte "Schriftauslegendes Gleichnis" (SG) bestimmt werden. Im Schriftauslegenden Gleichnis ist die "Sache," die der Erklärung bedarf, eine kleine Texteinheit der

---

80 See ER 20, l. 2.
81 See ER 143, l. 18.
82 See ER 150, l. 13.
83 See ER 69, l. 1.
84 See ER 5, l. 8.
85 Neusner, *Precedent*, 135. I discuss this type of *mashal* in more detail in section 4.2.
86 Neusner, *Precedent*, 135.

Offenbarungsschrift, ein Lemma ('L'), das in seinem Ko- oder Kontext fraglich ist. Die Gleichniserzählung dient dazu, das Lemma zu erklären, auszulegen.[87]

On the *mashal* proper, which he designates "Relat," Goldberg observes:

> Das Relat, die Gleichniserzählung, hat im S[chriftauslegende] G[leichnis] eine operationale Funktion und hat als Erzählung keinen eigenen propositionalen Gehalt. Es hat und behält immer seine eigene (fiktionale) Referenz.[88]

For an example of this type in *Seder Eliyahu*, we can briefly discuss the first *mashal* in the work: It consists of (1) an illustrand[89] (scriptural verse and interpretation), (2) an introductory formula, (3) the *mashal* proper, and (4) a short *nimshal* confirming the interpretation:

> 1. Another interpretation, *The days were fashioned and one of them belonged to Him* (Ps 139:16). That is Israel's Day of Atonement, a day of great joy before Him who spoke and the world came into being, given in great love to Israel. 2. They told a parable. What does the matter resemble? 3. It is like a king of flesh and blood whose servants and members of his household used to take the refuse and throw it out before the king's doorway. But when he [the king] came out [of the palace] and saw the refuse, he[90] rejoiced with great joy. 4. Therefore (לכך) it is like[91] the Day of Atonement, which the Holy One, blessed be He, gave in great love and joy. (ER 4, l. 24–29)

Even though it lacks the characteristic closing of classical *meshalim* with the same scriptural verse by which it was occasioned, this *mashal* is the one example Stern singles out among those of *Seder Eliyahu* as "almost perfectly classical in form and function."[92] On the other hand, Stern's next observation on the inadequacy of the

---

87 Arnold Goldberg, "Das schriftauslegende Gleichnis im Midrasch," in *Rabbinische Texte als Gegenstand der Auslegung*, vol. 2 of *Gesammelte Studien*, ed. Margarete Schlüter and Peter Schäfer (Tübingen: Mohr Siebeck, 1999), 195–196 ("Among the textual forms of Rabbinic literature which are designated as 'mashal' a form can be singled out as 'Gleichnis' especially in contrast with 'comparison' (though also with parable). 'Gleichnisse' are short fictional narrative units used for the representation of something else, a 'matter.' Among the 'Gleichnisse' an exegetical type can be distinguished (SG). In an exegetical Gleichnis the matter which needs to be explained is a small portion of Scripture, a lemma ('L') which in its co-text and context is unclear. The parabolic narrative helps to explain the lemma, to interpret it."
88 Goldberg, "Das schriftauslegende Gleichnis," 197 ("The Relat, the narrative of the parable, has an operational function in the exegetical parable, but as a narrative it does not have propositional content. It has and always maintains its own [fictional] reference.")
89 This is Stern's terminology.
90 Friedmann emends היה to הוא.
91 Friedmann emends נאמר to נדמה.
92 Stern, *Parables*, 216n63.

so-called illustrative model for *meshalim* seems to apply to this example as well: "the narratives of most meshalim, which according to this view are supposed to facilitate the understanding of their lessons, are actually far more enigmatic and difficult to understand than the nimshalim themselves."[93]

Exceptional manifestations of the exegetical *mashal* in *Seder Eliyahu* include an "antithetical *mashal*" – one which represents the actions of a king that do *not* resemble those of God[94] – and a series of parables, which can be termed hypothetical *meshalim*. The latter are told by the governing voice in the context of an interpretation of Hos 5:15. Addressing its audience in the second person with a variation of the usual *mashal* formula,[95] the governing voice introduces not one but three parables in which the addressed listener or reader is also part of the constellation of characters:

> By the [Temple] service! Each and every day, each and every moment I read this verse, *I will go and return to my place* (Hos 5:15), *my heart crushes within me* (Jer 23:9). Behold, it is as if someone were replying to <the deeds of> my brother Benjamin. I shall tell (אמשול) you a parable, and tell (ואומר) you what the substance of the matter [the meaning of its words] is. A parable: [Imagine.] Here you have a servant in your house and you raised him from the day he came into the world until the day he reached maturity, and you married him to a woman who bore him sons and daughters. And they were raised in grief, servitude, homelessness, trouble, oppression, and lack of food. After some time <you said> to him, Speak to your sons they are to do with you a work privately. He proceeded to kill them all at one and the same hour, at one and the same moment. This one, what is he to you? <Therefore it is better> for him if he had not come to the world.
>
> Or, [imagine] <you have> a son in <your house> and you raised him from the day he came into the world until the day he reached maturity, and you married him to a woman, and you built him a house, and you filled the house with wheat, barley, beans, lentils, and all kind of pulse. After some time when you were seated at a table he stood behind you, struck you and laid you low on the ground. This, who is he to you? If he is <your son> you would not let him remain in <your house> not even an hour.
>
> Or, [imagine] <you have> a son in your house with an ardent desire to commit transgressions, while saying, There is nothing to it; with an ardent desire to rob, while saying, There is nothing to it; with an ardent desire to shed blood, while saying, There is nothing to it, and

---

93 Stern, *Parables*, 49.
94 See ER 84, l. 30. On the antithetical *mashal*, see Stern, *Parables*, 22–23; and Talia Thorion-Vardi, *Das Kontrastgleichnis in der rabbinischen Literatur* (Frankfurt am Main: Lang, 1986).
95 Wilhelm Bacher, *Die bibelexegetische Terminologie der Tannaiten*: vol. 1 of *Die exegetische Terminologie der jüdischen Traditionsliteratur* (Leipzig: J. C. Hinrich'sche Buchhandlung, 1899), 121–122, argues that the word *mashal* as an introductory formula might be an elliptical form of the original *emshol lekha mashal*, which is used once in *Seder Eliyahu Rabbah* and twice in *Pseudo-Seder Eliyahu Zuta*. See also Wilhelm Bacher, *Die Bibel- und traditionsexegetische Terminologie der Amoräer*, vol. 2 of *Die exegetische Terminologie der jüdischen Traditionsliteratur* (Leipzig: J. C. Hinrich'sche Buchhandlung, 1905), 121.

being slothful at the house of study and considering himself exempt from doing there Torah, so that he would make his wife, his sons, and the members of his household punishable [as well]. This, who is he to you? He is one subject to the four death penalties which are imposed by the court <and to all the> death penalties mentioned in the Torah.
They know that their children die because of their transgressions, for it is said, *Also on your skirts is found the lifeblood of the innocent poor[, though you did not catch them breaking in]* etc. (Jer 2:34). (ER 110, l. 15–ER 111, l. 15)

Instead of a king parable narrating causally linked past events, what follows is the reporting of three evidently hypothetical situations depicting the relationship between the addressed reader or listener and his servant or his son. In all three, therefore, the addressee of the parable "replaces" the king, which is how readers or listeners are invited to think of themselves not as Israel, but as God. All three hypothetical *meshalim* close with a commentary and a proof-text.

Some parables in *Seder Eliyahu* do not interpret a scriptural verse, but illustrate a saying of the governing voice instead. For want of a better term, I will call these *meshalim* "meta-exegetical parables."[96] Consider the following parable of this type:

From here they said: If a man has just [knowledge of] right conduct and Scripture, he is given an angel to watch over him, for it is said, *I am going to send an angel [in front of you, to guard you on the way and to bring you to the place that I have prepared]* etc. (Exod 23:20). If a man reads Torah, the Prophets, and the Writings, they give him two angels to watch over him, for it is said, *For He will command His angels concerning you [to guard you in all your ways]* etc. (Ps 91:11). If a man reads Torah, the Prophets, and the Writings, recites Mishnah, Midrash, Halakhot, and Aggadot, and waits upon the sages, the Holy One, Himself, blessed be He, watches over him. They told a parable. What does the matter resemble? It is like a king of flesh and blood who walked with his son in the desert. When the sun was high and the heat intense, his father stood in the sun above him and made shade for his son, lest he should come in contact with the sun and the heat, for it is said, *The Lord is your keeper; the Lord is your shade at your [right] hand* etc. (Ps 121:5). (ER 100, l. 1–9)[97]

What the parable explains is not a difficulty posed by a scriptural verse, but the meaning of the third saying of the governing voice concerning the reward implied in pursuing the ideal Rabbinic curriculum. Whereas the first two sayings are solely confirmed with a proof-text, the third is first made clear by means of the parable of the king in the role of a protective father, after which a proof-text is quoted to provide the parable with its entire *nimshal*.[98]

---

[96] I discuss this type of *mashal* in more detail in section 4.4.
[97] A slightly different version of this parable is found in ER 155, l. 21.
[98] As will be shown in 4.4, other parables belonging to this group have a more detailed *nimshal*.

A small number of *meshalim* in *Seder Eliyahu* are of the type Neusner calls the "narrative-recapitulative parable."[99] Like the meta-exegetical parable, this type of parable is not intended to explain an aspect of a scriptural verse, either directly following a scriptural quotation or as confirmation of an interpretation. Instead, it rephrases or recapitulates a narrative (exegetical or otherwise) that precedes it.[100] In the example that follows, the *mashal* retells the last part of an exegetical narrative dealing with how Moses reconciled God to Israel after the episode of the golden calf:

> Why did Moses merit in this world the radiance of countenance that is to be given to the righteous in the time to come? ... I call heaven and earth to witness that the Holy One, blessed be He, did not say to Moses he was to stand *in the gate of the camp* and say *who is on the Lord's side* (Exod 32:26) and say *thus says the Lord, the God of Israel* (Exod 32:27), but that it was Moses who judged himself *a minori ad majus*, saying, If I say to Israel, *each of you kill your brother, your friend, and your neighbour* (Exod 32:27), Israel will reply, Have you not taught us, "A Sanhedrin that puts one man to death in a week of years is called 'destructive'" (mMak 1:10)? Why then do you kill three thousand in a [single] day? Therefore, he attached [these words] to the Glory that is above, for it is said, *Thus says the Lord* etc. (Exod 32:27). What is the subject matter [of the verse] after this one? *The sons of Levi did as [Moses] commanded* etc. (Exod 32:28). Then Moses stood in prayer before the Holy One, blessed be He, saying, Master of the world, You are just and kind, and Your deeds are all [done] in truth. Because of three thousand who worshipped [the calf] with a whole heart should six hundred thousand die, among them twenty-year-olds and those younger? Eighteen-year-olds, fifteen-year-olds, two-year-olds and one-year-olds? And many strangers and servants who have attached themselves [to Israel]? There is no end to the matter. At once the mercy of the Holy One, blessed be He, prevailed and He reconciled Himself with them in that moment. They told a parable. What does the matter resemble? It is like a king of flesh and blood whose first-born behaved offensively in his presence. He took him by the hand and turned him over to his servant the steward. He spoke to him, Go and kill this one and give him to the beasts and dogs. What did that servant do? He took him out away from his presence and left him <in his home and ran>[101] back and came to stand before him [the king]. After thirty days, as the king was kindhearted, his servants and members of his household assembled in his presence. When he lifted his eyes and did not see his first-born son he would store up grief and sighing in his heart and no creature except his servant the steward would understand. At once he set off running and brought him and put him in his place. The beautiful crown that was resting in front of him he took in his hand and placed on his servant the steward's head. <Therefore it is like Moses the righteous>.[102] (ER 17, l. 7–8.19–ER 18, l. 8)

---

99 See Neusner, *Precedent*, 217–218, where he illustrates this parable type with two examples from *Ekhah Rabbah*. I discuss the type in more detail in section 4.3.

100 In Neusner's terms, we are dealing with a narrative that is "perfectly clear in its own terms, followed by a metaphor built on the model of the transactions of the story" (218).

101 The MS here reads בבית ארץ, which Friedmann emends to ורץ לביתו.

102 Friedmann emends the MS reading למה נדמה במשה צדיק to לכך נדמה משה צדיק.

The bracketed expression <Therefore it is like Moses the righteous> following the *mashal*, which stems from the *Yalqut*, is the brief *nimshal* element that follows after the *mashal* narrative. The bulk of this parable's *nimshal* precedes the *mashal*-narrative, as an anticipated *nimshal*.

Characteristic of the last type of *meshalim* is that it does not explicitly resolve an exegetical problem[103] posed by a verse, nor does it provide an interpretation of a Rabbinic statement, or retell a narrative,[104] but rather answers a (formulaic) question that replaces the *ha-davar* in the usual *mashlu mashal* formula with a proper name (e.g., Israel, the generation of Manasseh) or with more specific subject matter ("When a man honours his father and mother in their old age, whom does he resemble?"). Whereas the *ha-davar* stands for a preceding co-text – a preceding co-text is required for the reader or listener to identify the terminus comparationis – the formula in this type of narrative *mashal*, which, for want of a better expression, I call "question-answering parables," provides the *mashal*'s co-text. Because it is self-contained, this type of *mashal* tends to be found at the opening of a chapter in *Seder Eliyahu* or at the start of new thematic sections of the ethical-homiletical discourse within a chapter. One such *mashal* is found in chapter (24) 22 of *Seder Eliyahu Rabbah*, a chapter which deals primarily with the biblical villain Esau:

> What do the wicked Esau, Eliphaz the Temanite, his son Amalek, Jeroboam son of Nebat, Nebuchadnezzar king of Babylon, and Haman the Agagite resemble? They are like one who found clothing on a road near a city. He took it in his hand, entered the city, and announced [his find] saying, To whom does this lost object belong? To whom does this lost object belong? All the citizens gathered to join him and said, See, how righteous so-and-so is, how kind<, how honest>. They proceeded to make him chief and magistrate of the city. A year, two years, three years [went by]; [in this time] he laid waste every province, [indeed] the whole country. This is what the wicked Esau, Eliphaz the Temanite, his son Amalek, Jeroboam son of Nebat, Nebuchadnezzar king of Babylon, and Haman the Agagite are like. Was it not because of the two tears that Esau shed in his father's presence that he was given Mount Seir upon which the rains of blessing never cease? Was it not because of the honour Eliphaz the Temanite accorded his father that his son Amalek was born? Was it not as a reward to Jeroboam because of the answer he gave the king that he was given the Ten Tribes? Was it not as a reward to Merodach because of the honour he accorded to our Father in heaven that from him Nebuchadnezzar came into the world? Was it not as a reward to Agag who wept and felt sorrow for himself at being kept in prison, who said, Woe is me, for my seed might perish for ever!, that from him the wicked Haman came into the world? *The thief breaks in, and the bandits raid outside* (Hos 7:1). (ER 125, l. 12–25)

---

103 In the sense of an irregularity in the text, a contradiction, a repetition, or redundancy.
104 I discuss this type of *mashal* in more detail in section 4.5.

In the *nimshal*, the wording of the opening question is taken up again as an affirmative answer, which in its turn is followed by a list of micro-narratives (in question form) dealing with every one of the mentioned villains, at whose head is the arch-villain Esau.

Considering the examples quoted and briefly discussed above, we can claim that whereas the *mashal* narrative is relatively stable, the *nimshal* is not, in that it can take several forms. The shortest are composed of an introductory formula – "for it is said" or "therefore it is said"– and a scriptural verse.[105] But the *nimshal* proper can also be a sort of parallel narrative (an exegetical narrative[106]) which connects the imagery of the *mashal* with the exegetical, theological, or ethical argument being made or, as in the last example, with a list of micro-narratives. Occasionally, the language of the *nimshal* pervades that of the *mashal* proper: For example, the mortal king asks his servants whether they had read Scripture and recited Mishnah.[107]

3.3.2 Maʿasim

A higher level of narrativity than that ascertained in *meshalim* can be found in those passages introduced with the formula "it happened to" (-מעשה ב).[108] In the fourth and final volume of his study *Rabbinic Narrative*, Jacob Neusner explores the development of the precedent or *maʿaseh* from the Mishnah through to the aggadic midrashim *Ekhah Rabbah* and *Shir ha-Shirim Rabbah*.[109] The *maʿasim* of *Seder Eliyahu* are more similar to the later documents Neusner analyses, in that they are neither formally uniform nor used as halakhic precedents. The expression with which they are introduced, designated by Neusner as a "marker," marks them as belonging precisely to that tradition of *maʿasim* that started with the Mish-

---

105 A similar case is that of ER 100, l. 13m in which the *nimshal* consists of the formula "the sages taught in a mishnah" and the quotation of mQid 4:1.
106 E.g., ER 128, l. 20.
107 See ER 93, l. 20. As Kadushin, *Organic Thinking*, 101n38 on ER 135, suggested, in more than a few cases the *nimshal* is just missing and has to be supplied by the reader: "Attention is to be called to the fact that in several places in the Seder Eliahu only the *mashal* (parable) is given while the application is to be supplied by the reader; cf., for instance, pp. 31–2, 40, 69 *bis*' – (L.G.)."
108 מעשה can be translated as "deed," "occurrence," or "event." On the wording of the translation "it happened to," see below n. 131.
109 See Neusner, *Precedent*.

nah.¹¹⁰ That is why this apparently minor formal aspect is taken as an indicator of genre.

In an appendix to his study of the Rabbinic parable, Stern discusses the *maʿaseh* as a form of non-parabolic narrative in Rabbinic literature without making special reference to its formal aspects, let alone to introductory formulas.¹¹¹ It could be argued, however, like *meshalim* and other narrative forms whose setting is a homiletical or exegetical discourse, that the *maʿaseh* also has a parabolical character, insofar as it is an embedded piece of text used to expand, illustrate, or emphasise an argument made in the text which contains it. Therefore, the *maʿaseh*, like the parable, points in a different direction than that of the framing discourse.¹¹²

According to Stern, the main characteristic of the *maʿaseh* is its claim to narrate an occurrence of the past.¹¹³ Stern contrasts the *mashal* as fictional narrative with the *maʿaseh*, which purports "to tell a story that actually took place."¹¹⁴ It is not that the *maʿaseh* and other narrative forms, such as the exegetical narrative,

---

110 See Arnold Goldberg, "Form und Funktion des Maʿase in der Mischna," in *Rabbinische Texte als Gegenstand der Auslegung*, vol. 2 of *Gesammelte Studien*, ed. Margarete Schlüter and Peter Schäfer (Tübingen: Mohr Siebeck, 1999), 22–49.
111 See Stern, *Parables*, 240–246. *Maʿaseh* is in Stern's view, a narrative genre which comprises a number of sub-genres, such as sages narratives, villain narratives, romances, and fulfilment narratives. Common to all of them is their claim to historicity.
112 In this sense, it could be argued that every narrative form in *Seder Eliyahu* is used parabolically or, borrowing an expression from Rüdiger Zymner, "uneigentlich" ("non-actually"); see Rüdiger Zymner, "Parabel," in *Historisches Wörterbuch der Rhetorik*, ed. Gert Ueding, vol. 6 (Tübingen: Max Niemeyer, 2003), 503. Narratives in *Seder Eliyahu* are used "parabolically" insofar as they are told in the service of another discourse, they constitute evidence of the actual discourse of Rabbinic ethics in *Seder Eliyahu*, and they are instrumentalised like parables in the narrow literary sense are. Characteristic of these, as Zymner explains, is their implicit and explicit signals of a transfer, which make the reader/listener realise that the meaning of what is narrated differs from the wording of the text and invite him to search for an alternative meaning; ("Eine P[arabel]. ist ein (1) episch-fiktionaler Text mit (2) mindestens einem impliziten oder expliziten Transfersignal [z.B. 'Das Himmelreich ist gleich einem Mann, …'], das darauf aufmerksam macht, daß die Bedeutung des Erzählten vom Wortlaut des Textes zu unterscheiden ist, und das eben dadurch zudem dazu auffordert, eine vom Wortlaut des Textes unterschiedene Bedeutung zu suchen, also eine 'Richtungsänderung des Bedeutens' vorzunehmen. Diese Richtungsänderung wird (3) entweder durch Ko- oder Kontextinformationen gelenkt, oder sie bleibt offen im Rahmen des Bedeutungspotentials des Textes. … das Kriterium (2) unterscheidet die P. weiter durch ihre gattungsspezifische Appellstruktur der Uneigentlichkeit von Literatur im allgemeinen mit ihrer allgemeinen hermeneutischen Disposition, deutendes oder vom Wortlaut eines Textes abweichendes, sinnkonstituierendes Verstehen zu ermöglichen." [Zymner, "Parabel," 502–503]).
113 See Stern, *Parables*, 240.
114 Stern, *Parables*, 13.

are not considered fictional, but rather that – unlike the *mashal*, which is "the only narrative form in Rabbinic literature to openly acknowledge its fictionality" – they make a point of not being fiction.[115]

As with *meshalim*, with *ma'asim* the identification of their specific contexts can also contribute to their classification. In the Mishnah, Jacob Neusner identifies three types of *ma'asim*: the normative-legal *ma'aseh* or precedent (which has a juridical setting), the domestic-exemplary *ma'aseh* or case (which has a household setting), and the story.[116] In the later documents of the corpus Neusner examines, a fourth form is identified – that of the exegetical *ma'aseh*.[117] Of a total of fourteen *ma'asim* identified in *Seder Eliyahu*, only two fulfil an exegetical task,[118] two deal with halakhic questions,[119] and the rest can be described as *ethical exempla*, told after the statement of an ethical maxim or apparently not illustrating the immediately preceding co-text, but rather illustrating an ethical topic dealt with in the wider co-text of the *ma'aseh* (e.g., the chapter in which the *ma'aseh* is found).

Only some of the *ma'asim* include sages as characters. In one of themm Rabban Jochanan b. Zakkai advises two families on how to prevent their children from dying;[120] another depicts a disciple of Rabbi Judah the Prince demonstrating God's will concerning the dispersion of Israel as implied in Judg 5:11, in front of a Roman commander.[121] Furthermore, there are a number of texts with named or unnamed sages as characters which are not introduced with the marker *ma'aseh be-*, but which could still be related to the genre of the *ma'aseh*: a) two short anecdotes on R. Zadoq and R. Natan entering the Temple area after its destruction;[122]

---

115 See Stern, *Parables*, 237. That Stern himself regards *ma'asim* as of fictional character to a certain extent is evident from his observation that "the claim to historicity [does not] entail a claim to naturalism: very frequently, ma'asim contain supernatural or miraculous elements" (242). In fact, among the types of "historical" or "history-like" narratives he regards as belonging to the genre of the *ma'aseh* are miracle-stories and fantastica. See Stern, *Parables*, 244.
116 See Neusner, *Precedent*, 8–31. He describes the corresponding context or setting only for the first two.
117 See Neusner, *Precedent*, 90–106.
118 See ER 54, l. 11 and PsEZ 39, l. 5. The first *ma'aseh* follows an "illustrand" consisting of the quotation of Judg 5:11 and a commentary upon this verse; the second *ma'aseh*'s "illustrand" consists of the quotation of Isa 58:1 and an interpretation of it.
119 I.e., ER 66, l. 18 and ER 76, l. 3.
120 See ER 53, l. 5ff.
121 See ER 54, l. 11. Dispersion is praised in similar terms in bPes 87b. PsEZ 7, l. 11 tells a *ma'aseh* of R. Joshua.
122 See ER 148, l. 8ff. These are introduced with the Hebrew words for "once" (פעם אחת), a formula which the governing voice uses primarily to narrate alleged episodes from its (or his) own life (see below 3.4.2).

b) the story of Rabban Simeon b. Gamaliel and R. Ishmael as they are about to be slain, a legend which depicts the two sages as martyrs;[123] c) the story of R. Dosa b. Orkinas's ruling pertaining to the exemption of a daughter's co-wife from levirate marriage;[124] d) a dispute among the sages pertaining to Elijah's origins, with the apparition of the prophet, who settles the matter;[125] e) R. Joshua b. Qarcha's demonstration before a Roman emperor of how God is just, even when He lets certain people be born blind or deaf;[126] and f) R. Jochanan's deathbed conversation with his disciples.[127]

These passages hardly differ from those introduced with the maʿaseh formula in *Seder Eliyahu*, and so could be considered forms related to the maʿaseh of later Rabbinic documents,[128] about which Jacob Neusner observed:

> [I]n the process of adaptation, the form [i.e., maʿaseh] lost all precise definition and no longer served to limit expectations to some few functions of narrative. The marker in the later documents thus took on the meaning of the Yiddish *meiseh*, a fable, tale, anecdote, or other generic story, of no exclusive, distinguishing formal characteristics.[129]

In contrast with the "generic" character of *meshalim*,[130] these stories are characterised by their specificity. Characters can be referred to simply as "a man," "a young child," or "an unmarried woman," but they encounter sages, a sage with a proper name, the Roman emperor, or Ezra the priest, so that a more precise spatial-temporal setting than that characteristic of the *meshalim* is given. These events are presented as having taken place once in the past. Specificity is also achieved through the events narrated, which are attributable to more or less concrete socio-cultural contexts. The passage quoted below may be seen as a case in point. It is the negative exemplum of a priest, in which a halakhic issue is used to illustrate an ethical message:

> It happened to[131] a priest that a fire befell him, consuming thirty <pillows>, sixty garments, twenty-four jugs of wine, ten jugs of oil, and the rest of his possessions. He went and sat

---

123 See ER 153, l. 16ff.
124 See EZ 168, l. 13ff. For a discussion of this passage, see section 6.1.
125 See EZ 199, l. 6ff. and also above 2.3.
126 See PsEZ 41, l. 10ff.
127 See PsEZ 43, l. 14ff.
128 See Stern, *Parables*, 241–244.
129 See Neusner, *Precedent*, 106–107.
130 See Neusner, *Precedent*, 107.
131 Instead of the opening words "A story is told of a priest," which can be interpreted as explicitly pointing to the fictionality of the passage, I prefer to use the more neutral expression "it happened."

before the sages, saying to them, My masters, a fire has befallen me, consuming thirty <pillows>,[132] sixty garments, twenty-four jugs of wine, ten jugs of oil, and the rest of my possessions. This brought the sages pain and grief equal to his own. They said: They had not moved from there when a man came along who was not totally unfamiliar with Halakhah. He asked him [the priest], To feed an animal with heave-offering, what is that [i.e., permitted or forbidden]? He said <to him, It is permitted>.[133] He said, Maybe it is forbidden. He replied, No, it is not. He said further, I am a priest and fed my animal with heave-offering. When the sages heard what he said they answered as one, Blessed be the Omnipresent, blessed be He, who favours no man over another. For heave-offering that is not eaten and consecrated food that is not eaten <should go nowhere but to fire>, but <you did not proceed according to the law>. He said to them, Do we not read: "Heave-offering of bitter vetch be given as fodder to domesticated animals and wild animals and to fowl" (mTer 11:9)? <They replied,> They said that only because they feed animals [with bitter vetch] and human beings only eat [it] in years of famine. Therefore David decreed that in years of famine it be permitted to feed an animal [with it].[134] From here they taught: Whoever feeds his animal heave-offering, whether heave-offering from the Land or heave-offering from outside the Land, of him Scripture says, *he who is heedless of his ways will die* (Prov 19:16). And it [Scripture] says, *you shall not profane the holy gifts of the Israelites, on pain of death* (Num 18:32). And it [Scripture] says, *Whoever digs a pit will fall into it[; and whoever breaks through a wall will be bitten by a snake]* <etc.> (Eccl 10:8). From here they said: A man should not teach Torah in public unless he has read Torah, the Prophets, and the Writings and recited Mishnah and Midrash, for it is said, *Who can utter the mighty doings of the Lord[, or declare all his praise]?* etc. (Ps 106:2). (ER 66, l. 18–ER 67, l. 12)

An extradiegetic narrator, the governing voice, tells a story that basically consists of two parts, which correspond to two narrated events. The first event is the destruction of a priest's possessions by fire, the second the discussion of the event between the priest and the sages, as well as an apparently unrelated dispute between the priest and a man mistakenly taken for one ignorant in matters of Halakhah. So the second event is actually a dialogue, in which two individuals and a collective character, the sages, take part. The first event has an explicit spatial setting, the priest's house; the setting of the second, which is probably the house of study, is hinted at by the characters involved in the action. The mere presence of the sages could be said to situate the action in Rabbinic times, a time when the authority of the sages in matters of Oral Torah can be represented as higher than that of a priest. Characterisation is both direct and indirect: The priest is indirectly depicted as a rich person in the listing of his burned possessions and, in the course

---

[132] Following the *Yalqut*, Friedmann emends the MS reading זכרים ("male children," "the male of the flock") to כרים ("pillows").
[133] The manuscript has a lacuna here which Friedmann fills with the wording between angle brackets.
[134] Friedmann emends the MS reading אדם to בהמה.

of the dialogue, as not sufficiently familiar with Oral Torah; the apparent ignoramus is directly depicted as such by the governing voice (which may but need not be focalising the perception of the sages and/or the priest), but also revealed as more cognizant of the Halakhah than was initially assumed – his direct speech presents him as better informed than the priest. The sages' inner lives are directly represented when the narrator describes their reaction to the priest's loss and indirectly represented when he lets them speak a blessing over the just punishment of the priest.

The question at stake (and this is the reason why the priest seeks the help of the sages in the first place) – whether the priest is to be pitied for the fire that has consumed his possessions – is a very specific one, which seems to have its origins in the *mishnah* quoted in the passage, mTer 11:9. The priest clearly does not properly understand this ruling as is revealed by the answer he gives to his questioner; it is the sages who explain the ruling by contextualising it with a para-biblical etiological narrative: David declared the use of vetch as fodder in times of famine permissible. It should be noted that precisely the fact that he is questioned by someone apparently unversed in Halakhah emphasises the priest's lack of halakhic competence.

The two *mikan amru* statements make the relevance of the story for the Rabbinic present of the enunciation explicit, and the governing voice leaves the narrative modus and switches to the homiletical-ethical one. The moral of the counter-exemplum appears to have an ethical rather than a halakhic focus.

3.3.3 Pseudo-historical Narratives

The penultimate chapter of *Seder Eliyahu Rabbah* contains three narratives that deal with Rome's oppression of the Jewish people in Alexandria, in Bethar, and in an unspecified place.[135]

Elsewhere in the chapter, there are narrative treatments of historical subject matter – the three narratives of oppression are followed by an account of the martyrdom of R. Simeon and R. Ishmael and by the story of the deaths of the inhab-

---

[135] See ER 151, l. 9–17, ER 151, l. 18–24, and ER 151, l. 24–ER 153, l. 15. For a parallel, see bGit 57b. The third text, which I discuss in more detail in section 6.6, goes back to Jewish-Hellenistic sources – 2 Macc 7 and 4 Macc 8–17 – and has several Rabbinic parallels, including EkhR 1, PesR 43, YalqShim *Ki Tabo*, and EkhZ 1. In the Christian tradition, the fabula was used by Gregory the Great in his *Homilia* III on St Felicity's *dies natalis*). On the Christian cult of the Maccabean martyrs, see Leonard V. Rutgers, "The Importance of Scripture in the Conflict between Jews and Christians: The Example of Antioch's Maccabean Martyrs," chap. 1 in *Making Myths: Jews in Early Christian Identity Formation* (Leuven: Peeters, 2009), 19–48.

itants of the towns of the tribes of Judah and Benjamin, whom Nebuchadnezzar sent into exile by the waters of the Euphrates.

In contrast to the latter two narratives, the narratives of Rome's oppression are not told by the governing voice. The first two are told by R. Eliezer, the third by the sages, and all three are hermeneutic tools with which the superscription and the first part of the first verse of Psalm 79 are interpreted. Their function is thus an exegetical one.[136] I propose to consider briefly the first two narratives (again the vertical line | is used to mark the division between the two units):

> R. Eliezer the Elder says: *A Psalm of Asaph. O God, the heathen are come* etc. (Ps 79:1). Hadrian Caesar came and seized Alexandria of Egypt, where there were one hundred twenty myriads of human beings. He deceived them with words, saying to them, Go forth and settle in the valley of Yadaim, so that this people will not prevail over you. They went forth and settled in the valley of Yadaim. But he stationed fifty thousand holding swords at their rear and killed them until not one of them remained, for it is said, *They have poured out their blood like water* etc. (Ps 79:3). The sages said: Three rivers of blood would flow, beginning in the valley of Yadaim and running into the Great Sea. The sages evaluated the waters of the Great Sea and found that they were three parts blood to one part water. Some say: For seven years the nations of the world fertilised their vineyards with the blood of Israel. | R. Eliezer says: *A Psalm of Asaph.* (Ps 79:1). The kingdom of Rome came and slew Bethar. At that time four myriads of human beings were killed there, until blood would run out of doorways and water pipes and it looked as if Bethar were then in the rainy season. They said: They found three hundred baskets of tefillin in Bethar, each containing three measures, if you counted them you would have found nine hundred measures of tefillin. (ER 151, l. 9–24)

The characters in both narratives are mainly collective agents, Hadrian being a synecdoche of the Roman army he supposedly led in a campaign against Alexandria.[137] From among the oppressed Jewish people, no one is named, but they are referred to as "human beings." The choice of Hadrian's name appears to be based on the fact that he was understood at some point as substantially involved in the historical events alluded to in the second narrative, namely the Bar Kochba revolt, which had its stronghold in Bethar. Apart from Rome or the Roman period being explicitly named as the historical setting for these stories – both the first and the

---

136 That is also the case in bGit 57b, where the first two narratives are reduced to the mention of the single hyperbolical events of Hadrian's killing sixty myriads in Alexandria and Vespasian's killing of four hundred thousand myriads in Bethar in an interpretation of the redundant phrase "The voice is the voice of Jacob" (הקול קול יעקב) from Gen 27:22, and the lengthier third narrative, told by Rav Judah, interprets Ps 44:23.
137 Braude and Kapstein, *Tanna dĕbe Eliyyahu*, 370n21, point out that the attribution of the killings to Hadrian in the first narrative is an error, for the incident referred to "may have been the Roman devastation of the Jewish quarter in Alexandria in the days of Alexander Tiberius (first century C.E.)."

third narratives have Hadrian as one of their protagonists, while the second has the personified kingdom of Rome as a collective character – what the three narratives have in common is the hyperbolic numbers of victims reported. The designation "pseudo-historical narrative" hints at the lack of historical accuracy in these texts, which is partly manifest in their inclination to legend.[138] In the third story, it is not the number that is exorbitant – there are no *myriads* being killed here – but the fact that seven sons of one mother are killed in her presence before she takes her own life.

3.4 Composite Forms

3.4.1 Homiletical-exegetical Narratives

In his appendix on non-parabolical narratives in Rabbinic literature, David Stern describes what he terms the "homiletical-exegetical narrative" as "stories that elaborate upon the biblical text, either in the form of commentary or as independent, autonomous narratives."[139] Characteristic of the discourse of these narratives▯ is their juxtaposition of narrative and exegesis – that is, the recurrent interruption of the narration with "homiletical and interpretive asides."[140] As an example, Stern discusses a passage from *Ekhah Rabbah* which begins ("opens") as a homily on charity and interprets an expression from Ps 71:19 by means of a mythical narrative told by multiple narrators. The scriptural components of this exegetical narrative are both of non-narrative (e.g., the verse in lemmatic position) and narrative character.[141]

---

[138] The *maʿaseh* of PsEZ 21, l. 17 can also be considered a pseudo-historical narrative with a Roman setting.

[139] Stern, *Parables*, 237, observes that the genre is often referred to as "extra-biblical legend." The most important contributions to the study of the genre include Dan Ben-Amos, "Generic Distinctions in the Aggadah," in *Studies in Jewish Folklore*, ed. Frank Talmage (Cambridge, MA: The Association for Jewish Studies, 1980), 45–72; Fraenkel, *Darkhe ha-agadah*, 1:287–322; Joseph Heinemann, "The Nature of Aggadah," in *Midrash and Literature*, ed. Geoffrey H. Hartman and Sanford Budick (New Haven, CT, London: Yale University Press, 1986), 41–55; Meir, *Ha-sipur darshani*; Shalom Spiegel, "Introduction," in *Legends of the Bible*, by Louis Ginzberg (New York: Jewish Publication Society of America, 1956); Joshua Levinson, "Dialogical Reading in the Rabbinic Exegetical Narrative," *Poetics Today* 25, no. 3 (2004): 498–528; and Levinson, *Ha-sipur*.

[140] Stern, *Parables*, 238.

[141] The verses quoted are Ps 71:19, Ezek 10:7–9, and Lam 1:13. See Stern, *Parables*, 238–239.

More recently, Joshua Levinson has described the genre of the exegetical narrative as follows:[142]

> The exegetical narrative is composed of a story which simultaneously represents and interprets its biblical counterpart. As a hermeneutical reading of the biblical story presented in narrative form, its defining characteristic lies precisely in this synergy of narrative and exegesis. As exegesis, it creates new meanings from the biblical verses, and as narrative it represents those meanings by means of the biblical world. As exegesis, it is subservient to the biblical narrative, but as a story in its own right, it creates a narrated world which is different from its biblical shadow. It is obvious that the combination of these two elements creates a certain dissonance. Narrative and exegesis are two very different methods of persuasion, based upon divergent, if not opposing, presuppositions of "author-ity." It is specifically this tension between sameness and difference, subservience and creativity, which establishes the genre's identity.[143]

To illustrate what he terms the specific dynamics of reading in the exegetical narrative, Levinson discusses texts transmitted in the amoraic midrash *Bereshit Rabbah* and in the Babylonian Talmud, exegetical narratives which retell scriptural texts whose original contexts are exclusively of narrative character.[144]

In this study and for the typology proposed I use the expression "homiletical-exegetical narrative" to refer not to a homogeneous form, but rather to a group of Rabbinic narratives of a discernibly biblical theme, even if they do not retell a narrative passage of Scripture or quote a scriptural verse in lemmatic position (as is the case in the examples adduced by Levinson and Stern).

Unlike *meshalim*, *maʿasim*, or first-person narratives,[145] the homiletical-exegetical narratives of *Seder Eliyahu* are not introduced by any standard formula.

---

[142] To a certain extent, Levinson, "Dialogical Reading," 500–501, uses the expression "exegetical narrative" as a synonym for "rewritten Bible," though he acknowledges that the latter is a Jewish-Hellenistic literary genre in its own right, which flourished between the early second century BCE and the first century CE. The crucial aspects that distinguish the Rabbinic exegetical narrative from rewritten Bible, and by which "Rabbinic culture appropriated for its own uses this preexistent literary form," are a) the fact that the text of rewritten Bible does not distinguish between the old text of Scripture and the new one of the rewriting; b) that their exegesis is not explicit; and c) that their authority is anchored in revelation or in a first-person narrator.
[143] Levinson, "Dialogical Reading," 498.
[144] The verses are Gen 22:12; 29:12; and 33:8. It should be pointed out that neither Stern nor Levinson uses the expression "exegetical narrative" in the functional sense Jacob Neusner ascribes to it – namely, as any narrative, even of a non-biblical theme, used to explain a single biblical verse. Thus for example, in his discussion of a *maʿaseh* told to interpret the verse Song 6:12 in *Shir ha-Shirim Rabbah*, Neusner, *Precedent*, 101, observes: "The item qualifies as an exegetical narrative."
[145] See below section 3.4.2.

The beginning of one such narrative may be the quotation of a scriptural verse, but narratives may also begin with phrases with which the governing voice directly addresses its audience, such as "go and learn from" (-צא ולמד מ) or "we learnt from" (-למדנו מ).

One conspicuous feature of homiletical-exegetical narratives (but also of other documents of Rabbinic literature) is their composite character and double-voicedness. They bring together, whether explicitly or not, two voices – a scriptural and a Rabbinic one; two discourses – a narrative/non-narrative scriptural and a homiletical-exegetical one – whereby the latter's emphasis can be of theological or of ethical character; and two textual systems, that of the extant, already known, quoted, or alluded to biblical text, and that of the midrash, thus modelling the biblical material according to their own discursive needs. Because the reader of these narratives ideally had a relatively solid foreknowledge of the scriptural narrative accounts, the challenge faced by the narrative voice is of a special nature: it has to maintain its reader's interest by providing an alternative narrative to the scriptural account, but in the end, it is expected to retell an ending that is already known. As Levinson puts it:

> Since the exegetical narrative is both a new story and an exegetical rewriting of an old one, it is positioned on the fault line between sameness and difference, between received and innovative meanings.[146]

In what follows, I briefly discuss a number of examples that are representative of *Seder Eliyahu*'s repertoire of homiletical-exegetical narratives. Its corpus consists of a wide variety of forms, which range from extensive and elaborate texts to minimalistic ones that tell "just enough to respond to the exegetical difficulty at hand or to the immediate homiletical occasion," as Stern puts it.[147]

3.4.1.1 Standard Homiletical-Exegetical Narrative

Seder Eliyahu contains numerous passages that roughly qualify as exegetical narratives according to Levinson's use of the expression – that is, they retell a scriptural passage which is itself inherently narrative in character, as the following passage from chapter (11) 12 illustrates, in which a lengthy passage of Scripture, 1 Sam 2–6, is narrated anew:

> And because of the immoral deeds of Eli's sons Israel went to war and four thousand of them were killed. At that time Israel said, *Why has the Lord put us to rout today before the*

---

146 Levinson, "Dialogical Reading," 506.
147 See Stern, *Parables*, 240.

Philistines? etc. (1 Sam 4:3). And the Holy One, blessed be He, responded at that time, When the son's of Eli used to provoke me in the court of Israel and the women's court [in the Temple], you would not say, Where is it [the ark of the covenant]? Now when Israel went forth to war, they said, *Let us bring the ark of the covenant of the Lord here from Shiloh[, so that He may come among us and save us from the power of our enemies]* etc. (1 Sam 4:3). So they sent and fetched the ark of the covenant of the Lord, for it is said, *So the people sent to Shiloh, and brought [from there the ark of the covenant of the Lord of hosts]* etc. (1 Sam 4:4). Israel shouted a great shout, but it was not true. Of that time it [Scripture] says, *she has lifted up her voice against me, therefore I hate her* (Jer 12:8). The Philistines said, *Woe to us! Who can deliver us from the power of these mighty gods?* etc. *Take courage, and be men* etc. (1 Sam 4:8–9). At once Israel went forth to war and thirty thousand of them were killed and the ark of the covenant was captured and sent to Ashdod to the temple of Dagon, their god, for it is said, *When the people of Ashdod rose early the next day[, there was Dagon, fallen on his face to the ground before the ark of the Lord. So they took Dagon and put him back in his place]* <etc.> (1 Sam 5:3). They saw that this was the requital, for it is said, *So they sent and gathered together all the lords* etc. *and they replied, Let [the ark of the God of Israel] be brought across to Gath,* etc. (1 Sam 5:8). And also there it struck with a great stroke, for it is said, *But after they had brought it there, the hand of the Lord [was against the city, causing a very great panic; He struck the inhabitants of the city, both young and old, so that tumours broke out on them]* etc. (1 Sam 5:9). When they saw that this was the requital, they carried it to Ekron, for it is said, *So they sent the ark of the God of Israel to Ekron* (1 Sam 5:10). But also there it struck with a great stroke, for it is said, *the people of Ekron cried out[, Why have they brought across to us the ark of the God of Israel to kill us and our people?]* etc. (1 Sam 5:10). When they saw that this was the requital, they carried it to an open field (בשדה), for it is said, *The ark of the Lord was in the country [of the Philistines]* (בשדה) etc. (1 Sam 6:1). And also there it struck with a great a stroke, for it is said, *Then the Philistines called for the priests and the diviners* (1 Sam 6:2). The priests, though idolaters, did have a notion of proper conduct. And which was this their proper conduct? They told them, *If you send away the ark of the God of Israel, do not send it empty* (1 Sam 6:3).

And what was the plague the Holy One, blessed be He, brought upon them? He brought upon them mice, who would slay men,[148] and women, and children among them. From their houses they would go out to the open field and eat from them their wheat, barley, beans, lentils, and every kind of pulse, for it is said, *So you must make images of your tumours*[149] *[and images of your mice that ravage the land]* etc. *Why should you harden [your hearts as the Egyptians and Pharaoh hardened their hearts? After he had made fools of them, did they not let the people go, and they departed?]* etc. (1 Sam 6:5–6) At once they filled it [the ark] with silver and put it on the wagon. When they were walking on the way, <the> cows took up a song in their voices, speaking thus, Sing, o sing, acacia tree, soar in all of your glory, lovely in embroidery of gold, you are praised in the innermost of the palace, who are enfolded between the two cherubim, for it is said, *The cows sang* (וישרנה) *in the direction of Beth-shemesh* etc. (1 Sam 6:12) When they were at a distance of two thousand cubits by measure from Beth-shemesh, they said, We shall take the vestments and put them in a secluded

---

148 The MS reading has the proof-text 1 Sam 6:5 here. Friedmann moves it to the end of the sentence following this one.
149 The MS follows the Qere-reading, טחריכם.

place and we shall see what these do for their god whom we have so honoured and who <has treated us>¹⁵⁰ this way. At once they took the vestments and put them in a secluded place. The people of Beth-shemesh should have taken <their clothes> upon seeing the ark and <covered> with them <their faces>,¹⁵¹ then they should have gone and prostrated themselves before the ark for an hour, or two, or three until the ark was covered, so that the name of the Holy One, blessed be He, be magnified and sanctified from one end of the world to the other. They did not act like this. Instead, when they saw the ark they laughed and stood up, remained standing and then danced, and spoke too many words, for it is said, *Now the people of Beth-shemesh were reaping [their wheat harvest in the valley. When they looked up and saw the ark, they went with rejoicing to meet it.]* etc. (1 Sam 6:13) And they did not know who had left the ark [there]. They [the Philistines] took <the vestments>¹⁵² and went back, for it is said, *When the five lords of the Philistines saw it[, they returned that day to Ekron.]* etc. (1 Sam 6:16) Therefore fifty thousand from Israel fell and the Great Sanhedrin with them, for it is said, *And he killed some of the people of Beth-shemesh[, because they looked into the ark of the Lord; and he killed seventy men of them.]* <etc.> (1 Sam 6:19) And who killed all of them? They said: No one but the people of Beth-shemesh killed them, for they did not behave properly (lit. "did not have the proper conduct"). [This is] to teach you that not a penny is taken from Israel but as a form of judgement. (ER 57, l. 15–ER 58, l. 30)

In a sort of preamble to the narrative, reference is made to the immoral deeds of Eli's sons. There is neither a narrative account nor a quotation of scriptural material here; rather, this introductory passage presupposes 1 Sam 2:12–17.3:13 and alludes to 1 Sam 4:2,¹⁵³ thus suggesting a causality that is not evident in the scriptural account: Four thousand men were slain by the Philistines in the first battle as a direct consequence of Hophni's and Phinehas's misdeeds.

The narrative itself begins with a short dialogue between Israel and God, consisting of the question quoted from 1 Sam 4:3 and God's reproachful answer – the first evident expansion by the Rabbinic narrator. The new narrative is characterised by certain stylistic features. In God's reproach of Israel, the Rabbinic expressions for "men's compartment" (lit. "Israel's compartment") and "women's compartment" are used metaphorically to allude to two types of transgressions the sons of Eli committed, as narrated in 1 Sam 2:12–17.3:13 and 1 Sam 2:22. God, therefore, speaks Rabbinic Hebrew and helps the governing voice reproach Israel for their behaviour in times of trouble. The narrative continues with the account of Israel's next devastating defeat – the fall of thirty thousand (as reported in 1 Sam 4:10) and the abduction of the ark. The latter is mentioned no less than five

---

150 Friedmann emends MS reading עשה to עשינו.
151 Friedmann emends MS readings נוטל, בגדיו, and פניו to ליטול, בגדיהם, and פניהם, respectively.
152 The MS here reads הארן, which Friedmann emends to הבגדים.
153 No allusion is made to Eli admonishing his sons in 1 Sam 2:23–25, nor to the passages in Eli's narrative dealing with Samuel (1 Sam 2:18–21) and with the man of God (1 Sam 2:27–36).

times in 1 Sam 4 with forms of the verb נלקח ("to be taken away"); in the Rabbinic rewriting, a different expression is used – namely, נשבה ("to be captured").

The several stations of the ark among the Philistines constitute the next section in the narrative, characterised by the repetition of more or less the same account for each of these stations – the repetition-relation between the story events and their narration is therefore singulative, in the sense that we are told *n* times what happened *n* times.[154] The ark comes to one of the cities of the Philistines, causes havoc, and the Philistines realise that this is a punishment intended for them and have the ark sent to another city, until they eventually return it to Beth-shemesh. The nature of the havoc caused by the ark in these cities is not mentioned by the Rabbinic narrator at this point. It suffices for him to narrate that they had to move it from Ashdod to Gath, from Gath to Ekron, and from Ekron to an "open field," the last station before the ark is returned to Israel – the latter being an interpretation of "in the country [of the Philistines]" (1 Sam 6:1) in terms of an imprecise "open field." It is at this stage that their own priests suggest that the Philistines should not return the ark empty, which shows their *derekh erets* ("proper conduct" and maybe also "common sense") in spite of them being idol worshippers.[155]

But before the ark is returned to Beth-shemesh, the narrator inserts a short digression on the nature of the plague with which God struck the Philistines during the ark's sojourn with them, focusing on the mice mentioned in 1 Sam 6:5 and leaving the tumours of the scriptural account unmentioned.

Following the advice of their priests, the Philistines prepare a guilt offering to accompany the ark on its return. According to the priests in the scriptural account, the cows' return of their own accord in the direction of Beth-shemesh is evidence that the God of Israel had been punishing them all this time (1 Sam 6:9). The very expression which refers to this "miraculous" return of the cows, וישרנה – an imperfect form of the verb ישר ("to take the straight way"), read as a form of

---

154 According to Rimmon-Kenan, *Narrative Fiction*, 57, the standard singulative relation consists in telling once what happened once. With regard to the example of *Seder Eliyahu*, it must be noted that the little variation in the representation of the single events emphasises the repetitive nature more than the singularity of the events. This type of representation of frequency is most characteristic of *Seder Eliyahu*, not just of homiletical-exegetical narratives.
155 Kadushin, *Organic Thinking*, 120, points out that the Philistine priests' *derekh erets* is crucial to understand the whole passage: "Derekh Ereẓ here describes the reverence the priests of the Philistines felt for the Ark, and that reverence entitled them to be called priests. In contrast to the action of the priests was the behavior of the men of Beth-Shemesh who, instead of prostrating themselves before the Ark in reverence, laughed and remained upright and even spoke unseemly words, so that as punishment fifty thousand men, including the Great Sanhedrin fell in Israel."

the verb שיר ("sing") – is used as the appropriate occasion for a miracle narrative, that of the cows singing in praise of the ark.[156]

Somewhere about two thousand cubits from Beth-shemesh, the Philistines uncover the ark and hide its vestments. This addition to the scriptural narrative is followed by a commentary by the Rabbinic narrator on how the people of Beth-shemesh should have behaved in the presence of the ark, and then by the narration of how they actually behaved. All of this serves one purpose: to account for yet another massive loss in Israel, namely of fifty thousand people and the seventy members of the Great Sanhedrin, thus alluding to the number of casualties mentioned in 1 Sam 6:19.[157] It is not the Philistines this time, but the very people of Beth-shemesh who are made responsible for the punishment God inflicts on them. In contrast to the Philistine priests, they did not behave properly – they did not demonstrate proper conduct.

The Rabbinic exegetical narrative quoted above operates by selecting part of the narrative material presented in 1 Sam 2–6 – that is, it focuses on this selection and leaves the rest of the scriptural narrative aside. The focus is determined by the homiletical discourse that frames (or provides a wider co-text for) the narrative. This is how a retold biblical narrative can serve the purpose of eliciting a theological or ethical message in the midrash. In the case of the narrative quoted above, it is the last in a series of narratives[158] that expand upon the statement: "not a penny[159] is taken from Israel but as a form of judgement." The governing voice selects not only which verses, but also which parts of these verses it quotes and which ones it leaves unquoted. It is very often the case that precisely those parts of verses that are left unquoted provide the actual link to the Rabbinic interpretive retelling.[160] In the text quoted above, this is evident in several instances – for example, in the passages which quote the first part of 1 Sam 5:3.9 and 6:1.5.19.

---

[156] This has a parallel in BerR 54:4 and bAZ 24b. In the former, the parallel is introduced with the words תני אליהו.
[157] According the Commentary to the English Standard Version, in most Hebrew manuscripts the verse reads "struck of the people seventy men, fifty thousand men."
[158] The other narratives are based on passages of the Book of Judges.
[159] Friedmann does not emend the MS reading פרומה (which can be either a wrong reading of פרוטה ["cent"] oder a corrupt form of Aramaic פרומא ["a small liquid measure"]), even though a parallel of this statement in *Seder Eliyahu* (ER 55, l. 17) has the reading פרוטה.
[160] One could conjecture that the abbreviated expression "etc." (וגו׳) at the end of a scriptural quotation signals this fact, reminding the reader to search for the link not in the words spelt out, but rather in those alluded to – that is, text that in Scripture is adjacent or in proximity to the text actually quoted in midrash. However, as Alexander Samely pointed out to me, this may actually be more of an issue of scribal than of compositional practice.

The selection and transformation of scriptural material is also related to the type and number of characters. With the exception of God and the personified ark, which is said to cause havoc, the Rabbinic narrative, unlike its scriptural hypotext (the earlier text on which the Rabbinic text expands)[161] – which has Eli, the man of God, and even Hophni and Phinehas among its characters – includes only collective characters as its characters: Israel, the Philistines, their priests and their five lords, the Great Sanhedrin, the cows, and the people of Beth-shemesh.

3.4.1.2 Homiletical-exegetical Narratives in Series

As pointed out above, the narrative on the sons of Eli, the Philistines, and the people of Beth-shemesh is followed by a statement that appears to sum up its teaching. The segment which, in its turn, follows upon this statement and with which the chapter closes consists of a series of eight micro-exegetical narratives. These can be seen as summaries of and parallels to lengthier accounts in exegetical narratives found in the same and previous chapters.[162] Thus the last three of these minimal accounts are parallel accounts to the lengthy exegetical narrative found previously in chapter 12 (ER 57–58):

> But God in heaven knows that it was as | the reward of Deborah and her prophecy and of Baraq and his prophecy that great deliverance came through them. | The reward of Ahab and Jezebel was that they perished from this world and from the world to come and that their children perished with them. | The reward of the Tribes of Zebulun and Naphtali who did the will of [their Father in heaven and the will of their father] Jacob was that great deliverance came through them. | The reward of Jael, wife of Heber the Kenite, who did the will of her husband, was that great deliverance came through her. | The reward of Phinehas was that the children of Ephraim went to war and forty thousand of them were killed. | The reward of the Great Sanhedrin, whom Moses left, [while] Joshua and of Phinehas the son of Eleazar were with them, was that Israel gathered and went to war against the children of Benjamin and seventy thousand of them were killed. | The reward of the sons of Eli was that Israel went to war and four thousand of them were killed. | The reward of the elders was that Israel went to war and thirty thousand of them were killed and that the ark of the covenant was captured. |

---

161 For the concept of hypotext, see Gérard Genette, *Palimpsests: Literature on the Second Degree*, trans. Channa Newman and Claude Doubinsky (Lincoln, NE, London: University of Nebraska Press, 1997), 5.

162 In the first part of this segment, micro-narratives about individuals predominate. These refer back to ER 49 (on why Ahab and Jezebel were punished for their transgressions) or to ER 51 (on why Baraq and Deborah, the tribes of Zebulun and Naphtali, and Jael were rewarded for the deliverance they brought to Israel). In the second part, collective characters, seen as responsible for the killing of multitudes in Israel (the Great Sanhedrin, Eli's sons, the elders, the men of Beth-shemesh) predominate. These micro-narratives summarise the lengthier narrative of ER 57–58.

The reward of the men of Beth-shemesh, who did not conduct themselves properly, was that fifty thousand of them, of Israel, fell and the Great Sanhedrin with them. From here they said: "With what measure a man metes it shall be measured to him again." (mSotah 1:7) Indeed, Master of all the worlds, *Your righteousness is like the mighty mountains[, your judgements are like the great deep; you save humans and animals alike, O Lord.]* (Ps 36:7) (ER 58, l. 30–ER 59, l. 13)

The series segment quoted above, which is located at the end of a chapter (or a group of chapters), not only summarises but draws attention to the similarities between the lengthier narratives, endowing a corpus of stories about paradigmatic righteous and wicked characters with an unambiguous meaning.[163]

Elsewhere in *Seder Eliyahu*, this type of arrangement of homiletical-exegetical narratives in a series can be ascertained. The narratives can be identified as belonging to one and the same series, even if they are not placed adjacent to each other, because of their style (e.g., opening words), structure, and topic. In the example of chapter 17 of *Seder Eliyahu Rabbah* quoted below, the series consists of three adjacent narratives and a fourth, told after a digression on the third, in the governing voice's homiletical-discursive mode. The structure of each narrative in the series is relatively simple and stable; there is recurring phraseology, and even if the theological argument they illustrate is the same in all four of them, there is a clear variation in the use of scriptural quotation as well as in the alternation between narration (A, B, and C) and commentary (A', B', and C') (see Table 3.3).

None of these narratives can be regarded as successful in maintaining the anticipatory tension expected by a modern reader – not when read within their co-text, the series, or in isolation. There are good reasons to doubt that it was otherwise with the work's original audience, for *Seder Eliyahu* itself, like many other documents of Rabbinic literature, witnesses to a fully-fledged narrative culture, a context in which the texts quoted above appear as poor drafts of good Rabbinic narratives.

---

[163] On the righteous and the wicked being thus "listed" in midrash, Gerhard Langer, *Midrasch* (Tübingen: Mohr Siebeck, 2016), 229, observes: "Oft werden paradigmatische *Schurken* wie Kain, die Enoschgeneration, das Geschlecht der Flut, das Geschlecht des Turmbaus zu Babel, die Sodomiter oder die ägyptischen Sklavenhalter verglichen und in eine Reihe gestellt. Ihnen stehen wiederum paradigmatische *Gerechte* gegenüber, so in BerR 19 die drei Erzväter, Levi, Kehat, Amram, Mose." A list of narratives need not refer back to narratives already told. In answer to a question posed by a disciple in a first-person narrative, the rabbi replies with a series of micro-narratives, in which the first ten generations are said to illustrate how God let them live longer so that they could do deeds of kindness for their forefathers; see ER 80, l. 23ff.

Table 3.3: Homiletical-exegetical Narratives: A Series

	In Joshua's days	In Samuel's days	In Elijah's days	In Hezekiah's days
A.	In the days of Joshua Israel took upon themselves the Kingdom of Heaven[164] with love, for it is said, *Now if you are unwilling to serve the Lord[, choose this day whom you will serve, whether the gods your ancestors served in the region beyond the River or the gods of the Amorites in whose land you are living; but as for me and my household, we will serve the Lord.]* etc. Then the people answered, *Far be it from us that we should forsake the Lord [to serve other gods]* etc. (Josh 24:15–16).	In the days of Samuel Israel took upon themselves the Kingdom of Heaven in awe, for it is said, *The people of Israel said to Samuel, Do not cease [to cry out] to the Lord [our God for us, and pray that He may save us from the hand of the Philistines]* etc. (1 Sam 7:8). And he also replied to them on this subject, for it is said, *Moreover as for me, far be it from me that I [should sin against the Lord by ceasing to pray for you; and I will instruct you in the good and the right way]* etc. (1 Sam 12:23).	In the days of Elijah Israel were truthfully in awe of Heaven.	In the days of Hezekiah, king of Judah, Israel occupied themselves with Scripture, Mishnah, Midrash, Halakhot, and Aggadot.
A'.		From here they said: Whoever has the power to beseech mercy for his fellow man and for the community and does not do it, is called a sinner, for it is said, *sin against the Lord* (1 Sam 12:23).		

---

164 Kadushin, *Organic Thinking*, 7, argues that *Malkhut shamayim* should be translated not as "the kingdom of God," but as "the sovereignty of God."

Table 3.3: – continued

	In Joshua's days	In Samuel's days	In Elijah's days	In Hezekiah's days
B.	Israel's reward for having taken upon themselves the Kingdom of Heaven with love was that the Holy One, blessed be He, was forbearing with them for three hundred years in the days of the judges' rule, treating them like small children at their master's house or like children at their father's table.	Israel's reward for having taken upon themselves the Kingdom of Heaven in awe was that also He descended from the uppermost heaven, from the place of His glory and greatness and sovereignty, of His splendour and holiness, and dwelt with them during the war, for it is said, *So Samuel took a sucking lamb and offered it as a whole burnt-offering to the Lord; Samuel cried out to the Lord for Israel, and the Lord answered him* etc. (1 Sam 7:9).	Israel's reward for being truthfully in awe of Heaven was that also he [Elijah] stood and built an altar and made a place like a container for two measures of seed, for it is said, *with the stones he built [an altar in the name of the Lord. Then he made a trench around the altar, large enough to contain two measures of seed]* etc. (1 Kgs 18:32). He said to his disciples, *Fill four jars with water and pour it on the burnt-offering and on the wood. Then he said, Do it a second time and they did it a second time* (1 Kgs 18:33–34).	Israel's reward for occupying themselves with Scripture, Mishnah, Midrash, Halakhot, and Aggadot is that something that was meant to happen in the end, *This shall be the plague [with which the Lord will strike all the peoples that wage war against Jerusalem: their flesh shall rot while they are still on their feet; their eyes shall rot in their sockets, and their tongues shall rot in their mouths. this shall be the plague]* etc. (Zech 14:12), was carried out for Hezekiah and his generation.

Table 3.3: – continued

	In Joshua's days	In Samuel's days	In Elijah's days	In Hezekiah's days
B'.	Whence [do we infer this]? You should know that it is so. Go and learn from Gideon son of Joash, Abdon son of Hillel, and Ibzan of Beth-lehem. What is written of Gideon? *Now Gideon had seventy sons* etc. (Judg 8:30). What is written of Abdon? <*He had forty sons and thirty grandsons* etc. (Judg 12:14). What is written of Ibzan of Bethlehem?> *He had thirty sons. He gave his thirty daughters in marriage outside [his clan]* (Judg 12:9).	But if it is said *burnt-offering* why is it also said *whole*? To teach that he did not have room to skin the animal, for it is said, *As Samuel was offering up [the burnt-offering, the Philistines drew near to attack Israel; but the Lord thundered with a mighty voice that day against the Philistines and threw them into confusion; and they were routed before Israel]* etc. (1 Sam 7:10).	And you might wonder how twelve jars of water could have filled the whole trench with water, but he said to his disciples, He who has water left in his jar, let him come and pour it over my hands. Elishah said to him, I have water left in my jar. He said to him, Come and pour <it over my hands. And he went and poured it> over his hands.[165] Ten springs gushed from them until the whole place was filled with water, for it is said, *At the time of the offering of the oblation[, the prophet Elijah came near and said, O Lord, God of Abraham, Isaac, and Israel, let it be known this day that you are God in Israel, that I am your servant, and that I have done all these things at your bidding]* etc	How so? *[That very night] the angel of the Lord set out [and struck down one hundred and eighty-five thousand in the camp of the Assyrians; when morning dawned, they were all dead bodies]* etc. (2 Kgs 19:35).

---

[165] Singular in MS.

Table 3.3: – continued

In Joshua's days	In Samuel's days	In Elijah's days	In Hezekiah's days
		Answer me, O Lord, answer me[, so that this people may know that you, O Lord, are God, and that you have turned their hearts back] etc. *Then the fire of the Lord fell [and consumed the burnt-offering, the wood, the stones, and the dust, and even licked up the water that was in the trench]* etc. (1 Kgs 18:36–38). At that time they abandoned the idolatry they had in their hands and became truthful fearers of Heaven, for it is said, *When all the people saw it[, they fell on their faces and said, The Lord indeed is God; the Lord indeed is God]* etc. (1 Kgs 18:39).	

Table 3.3: – continued

	In Joshua's days	In Samuel's days	In Elijah's days	In Hezekiah's days
[B.]	Israel's reward for having taken upon themselves the Kingdom of Heaven with love was that the Holy One, blessed be He, was forbearing with them during the three hundred years of the judges' rule, treating them like small children at their master's house or like children at their father's table.			
C.	And He made permanent for them a blessing that is a good dispensation forever, for it is said, *So Joshua blessed them and sent them away[, and they went to their tents]* etc. (Josh 22:6).	And He made permanent for them a blessing that is a good dispensation forever, for it is said, *For the Lord will not cast away his people[, for his great name's sake, because it has pleased the Lord to make you a people for himself]* etc. (1 Sam 12:22).		And He made permanent for them a consolation that is a good dispensation forever, for it is said, *Comfort, O comfort my people* etc. *Speak tenderly* etc. (Isa 40:1–2).

Table 3.3: – continued

In Joshua's days	In Samuel's days	In Elijah's days	In Hezekiah's days
C'.			They told a parable. What does the matter resemble? It is like a mortal king who became angry at his wife. But he had a son by her who was some eighteen months old. Every day, as they brought him before him, he used to take him into arms, embrace him, and kiss him. He would take hold of him with both hands and seat him between his knees and speak to him thus, Were it not for my great mercy for you, I would have already thrown your mother from my house. So, *What shall I do with you, O Ephraim? [What shall I do with you, O Judah? Your love is like a morning cloud, like the dew that goes away early]* etc. (Hos 6:4). *I will not execute my fierce anger* (Hos 11:9).

Their structure is basically tripartite, though each of the main parts – A, B, and C – can be expanded upon with commentary: Of a certain biblical time, identified by the name of a biblical character, it is stated in a first part (A) that Israel acted exemplarily, either by accepting the kingdom of Heaven or, as in the last narrative, by engaging in the study of the Rabbinic corpus. The second narrative is the only one to provide a commentary passage on this first part (A'). The second narrative part (B) reports the reward for Israel's exemplary conduct in each of the chronological settings mentioned in A. The governing voice can opt in either the first or the second part to do without the explicit use of biblical material. All four narratives provide in B' a different kind of commentary on B: an explanation of how the narrator arrived at (derived) his statement in B in the Joshua-narrative; an exegetical digression on 1 Sam 7:9, quoted in the Samuel-narrative; a continuation of the Elijah-narrative, distinguished from the preceding text by the use of the formula of direct address, "and you might wonder" (וכי עלתה על דעתך); and a rhetorical question followed by a proof-text in the Hezekiah-narrative. The last part (C) follows, with slight variation, the same pattern in three of the texts, giving an account of God's permanent blessing of Israel.

The Elijah-narrative, the only one which clearly retells a scriptural passage (1 Kgs 18:30–40), comes to an end as in its biblical counterpart – with the end of idolatry. The Elijah-narrative is, moreover, the only one with more than one individual as its characters. The rest have Israel as a collective, primary character, the names of Joshua, Samuel, and Hezekiah being included almost exclusively to provide a temporal setting and hint at a scriptural hypotext. In this last narrative section, only the fourth narrative – that set in Hezekiah's time – expands by means of a *mashal*, in C'.[166]

---

[166] Another series of exegetical narratives is introduced with the same formula, "in the days of Uzziah/Manasseh/Hoshea/Zedekiah" in chapter 9 of *Seder Eliyahu Zuta* (EZ 186, l. 16ff.). The bulk of *Seder Eliyahu Zuta*'s tenth chapter consists of a series of exegetical narratives that open with the formula "it was God's intention to" (בדעתו של הקב"ה). Homiletical-exegetical narratives, especially short ones, also tend to be arranged in pairs of opposites, with an example (A) and a counter-example (B), so to speak, as in the following passage: "Another interpretation: *You shall not go around as a slanderer among your people[, and you shall not profit by the blood of your neighbour: I am the Lord]* (Lev 19:16). There are four measures in this verse. Two are measures of the righteous. Two are measures of the wicked. A. Two measures of the righteous, how so? Go and learn from Moses and Aaron who intended to and did make peace between Israel and their Father in heaven, between Israel and the sages, between a sage and his fellow, between a man and his fellow, between a man and his wife. Because of their ways a good name was established for them, for their children, and their children's children until the end of all generations. *It was Aaron and Moses* etc. (Exod 6:26). B. Two measures of the wicked, how so? Go and learn from Dathan and Abiram who meant to and caused strife between Israel and their Father in heaven, between Israel <and the Sages>, between a sage and his fellow, between a man and his fellow, between a man and his wife. Because of their ways a bad name was established for them, for them and for their children, and their children's children until the end of all generations. For it is said, *That is Dathan and Abiram* (Num 26:9)." (ER 106, l. 19–28)

3.4.1.3 Homiletical-Exegetical Narrative as Part of Ethical Discourse

Whether or not they occur in a series, homiletical-exegetical narratives can make use of a biblical theme in order to expand upon the ethical maxims of the work – that is, what the governing voice considers ideal Rabbinic conduct, as the following two brief narratives on Amram and Boaz illustrate. They purport to answer the rhetorical question that precedes them and are followed by a proof-text:

> Whence [do we infer that] when a man marries a woman for the sake of Heaven he will have children who deliver Israel in their time of distress? | Go and learn from <Amram who married a woman for the sake of Heaven. From him there issued Moses, Aaron, and Miriam, who caused Torah and commandments to increase in Israel. | Go and learn from> Boaz son of Salmon, son of Nahshon, son of Amminadab, who married for the sake of Heaven. Eventually there issued from him David and Solomon his son who caused Torah and commandments to increase in Israel. Of them, of the likes of them, of those who resemble them, and of those who act after their deeds, Scripture says, *For as the new heavens and the new earth, which I will make, shall remain before me, says the Lord, so shall your descendants and your name remain* (Isa 66:22). (EZ 177, l. 35–EZ 178, l. 5)

The narratives quoted above constitute a hermeneutic tool for the explanation of the meaning of the expression "to marry for the sake of Heaven."[167]

3.4.1.4 Multi-directionality of Homiletical-Exegetical Narratives with Explicit Use of Scriptural Material

With the next short example, I wish to point to an aspect of those homiletical-exegetical narratives which are explicit with regard to their composite character – not only in that they quote scriptural material, but also with respect to the characteristic practice in midrash that consists in linking unrelated scriptural verses. This aspect of homiletical-exegetical narratives can be described as their "multi-directionality." By retelling a biblical story, the midrash simultaneously interprets a verse (or part of a verse) that is part of the scriptural account of that story and a verse that is unrelated to that scriptural narrative (which can appear in a lemmatic position, as in the example below, but can also function as a proof-text). The verses are not merely connected, but also simultaneously interpreted and linked with Rabbinic notions:

---

167 This passage is the last in a series of similar structures concerned with four ways of life (lit. four measures in the way of the world [ארבע מדות בדרך ארץ]), related to the reward of marrying for the sake of satisfying one's lust, of money, of social status, or of Heaven. For a parallel without narrative segments, see PsEZ 9, l. 7ff.

> When you see the naked, cover them [and not ignore your own kin] (Isa 58:7). When the Holy One, blessed be He, may His great name be blessed for ever and ever and ever, saw Adam naked, He did not let an hour pass before He had dressed him, for it is said, *And the Lord God made garments of skins for the man and for his wife[, and clothed them]* (Gen 3:21). Indeed a man should not see his father and mother standing in shabby clothes and turn his face away, but he should dress them with comely clothes. If a man wears [clothes worth] five minas, then he should dress his father and mother with [clothes worth] ten minas. If a man wears [clothes worth] ten minas, then he should dress his father and mother with [clothes worth] fifteen minas. He should distinguish them in a manner that he is praised. (ER 136, l. 13–19)

This passage links the notion of the lemmatic verse Isa 58:7, that the naked are covered to the account of God's having mercy with the nakedness of Adam and his wife after the fall, of which Gen 3:21 is a part. The short exegetical narrative is a preamble to an ethical segment concerning the proper attitude towards one's parents, which is in turn part of the governing voice's exposition on the commandment "Honour your father and mother" (Deut 5:16). The midrash does not quote words of the verse in Isaiah which link the covering of the naked with being close to one's family.[168]

We find another example of exegesis that has more than one target in the following "aetiological" narrative dealing with the observance of festivals in the diaspora in the Rabbinic present of *Seder Eliyahu*:

> A. Another interpretation: *my children have gone from me, and they are no more* (Jer 10:20). *They are no more*, festivals are not [observed] according to their institution. B. The congregation of Israel spoke before the Holy One, blessed be He, Master of the universe, As long as I was on my soil, I used to observe [the festival] on one day and that was as it was established. But now, behold, I <observe [the festival]> on one day and two days[169] and not on one as was established. Master of the universe, who caused me to come to such a state? For it is said,[170] *My mother's sons caused me this grief*[171] (Song 1:6). Do not read, *My mother's sons* (בני אמי) *brought me to grief*, but "my own people (בני אומא שלי) caused me this grief" etc. But who are the sons of my people? Such as Hananiah the son of Azzur, Ahab the son of Kolaiah, and Zedekiah the son of Maaseiah, who spoke false prophecies to me, therefore it is said, *my mother's sons caused me this grief*. (ER 149, l. 1–7)

---

168 In the original context of the book of Isaiah, both are actions that qualify as an authentic fast from God's point of view.
169 MS reading: ושלושה.
170 Friedmann sets MS reading שנאמר between brackets, suggesting it is not the correct one.
171 Braude and Kapstein, *Tanna děbe Eliyyahu*, 353n1, suggest reading נחרו as "sought to bring me to grief." Cf. the rendering of the Jewish Version – *The Holy Scriptures according to the Masoretic Text* (Philadelphia, PA: Jewish Publication Society, 1917) – as "incensed against me."

The quotation of Jer 10:20 is followed by a midrashic unit that focuses on part of the verse and also by an exegetical narrative (B), which is actually a short dialogue set in the context of the exile, which is only alluded to. Israel (or the governing voice speaking on their behalf) and God are the only two acting – that is, speaking – characters. Israel express their displeasure at not observing (or being able to observe) the festivals as they were once instituted, and ask God how this could come about. The answer is given by God himself in the manner of the governing voice, – again quoting an unrelated scriptural verse as a proof-text (Song 1:6) and suggesting an adequate reading with the Rabbinic hermeneutic formula *al tiqrey*. When Israel in turn ask who God means when referring to "my own people" as responsible for their present situation, God names three biblical characters whose names function as metonyms for the account of their transgressions in two narrative passages of the book of Jeremiah.[172]

3.4.1.5 Para-Scriptural Narratives

Certain narrative passages are related to Scripture in the form of legends associated with biblical characters or events with little textual basis in Scripture, and therefore make correspondingly scarce use of scriptural quotations. The verses quoted in these passages are not in a lemmatic position, nor do they stem from narrative sections of biblical books, as the examples below illustrate. This sub-group of homiletical-exegetical narratives can be termed para-scriptural narratives. Two examples follow, one from the beginning of *Seder Eliyahu Rabbah* and one from the end of *Seder Eliyahu Zuta*:

> And in His wisdom and with His understanding God created His world and set it on its foundation. He then created Adam and threw him[173] before His presence. As He examined him till the end of all the generations, He foresaw that his descendants would provoke His wrath. Therefore He said, If I keep in it the sins of the first ones, the world will not endure; I must therefore have the first [sins] pass out of mind. And He had them do so. (ER 3, l. 8–11)

> It had been the intention of the Holy One, blessed be He, not to give the power of speech to animals, but when He gave the power of speech to the serpent, it corrupted the world, all of it. (EZ 190, l. 6–7)

Israel's history of salvation, especially the giving of the Torah at Mount Sinai, is the subject of recurring para-scriptural narratives, which can be paraphrased using Simon-Shoshan's wording as the "master narrative of exile and redemption of

---

172 I.e., Hananiah for Jer 28; Ahab and Zedekiah for Jer 29:22–23.
173 MS here reads השליכו which Friedmann emends to השליט.

Egypt."[174] Two examples of this type of narrative, whose beginnings I mark with a vertical line |, are found within the *berakhah* quoted below:

> My Father in heaven, may Your great name be blessed for ever and ever and ever, and may You have contentment <in Israel>,[175] your servants, in all the places of their dwellings. | For [in spite of] all the repulsive things and unworthy things which Israel committed before You, you did not have ill feeling or vengefulness against them, nor were You overbearing towards them, nor did You keep words of Torah from them. Rather You remembered on their behalf the good things and not the bad things – the good things they did in Your presence and not the bad things they did in Your presence. You said to them what your lips spoke, *[For I am about to create new heavens and a new earth;] the former things shall not be remembered or come to mind* etc. (Isa 65:17). | And when our fathers stood on Mount Sinai to take upon themselves the Kingdom of Heaven of their free will (בנדבה), He also came down from the upper heaven of heavens, from the place of His glory, of His greatness, of His splendour, and His holiness, and willingly (בנדבה) had His great name dwell with them. Hence Isaiah said, *But those who are noble* (נדיב) *plan noble things* (נדיבות) *[, and by noble things they stand]* etc. (Isa 32:8). (ER 83, l. 23–32)

As in many other passages, in this example God is one of the protagonists. He may also assume the role of a homodiegetic narrator explicitly addressing his narratees, the Rabbinic-minded Israel contemporary with the enunciation of *Seder Eliyahu*, as in the following example, in which we could claim that it is God himself who tells Israel a Rabbinic parable:[176]

---

174 Simon-Shoshan, *Stories*, 78. The narrative of Israel's transgressions is told on several occasions in *Seder Eliyahu Rabbah*. See, for example, ER 20, l. 5ff. (with God as the narrator) and ER 56, l. 26ff. A similar phraseology is applied to other characters in different narrative contexts, e.g., to Egypt in ER 40, l. 10ff., and to a group of young men who died in a city in Babylonia in ER 100, l. 29ff. The narrative of Israel's taking upon themselves the Kingdom of Heaven has several parallels within *Seder Eliyahu Rabbah*: ER 6, l. 14ff., ER 85, l. 21ff., ER 101, l. 17ff., ER 119, l. 21ff., and ER 122, l. 27ff. Another version of the Exodus narrative begins with the phrasing "when Israel were in Egypt" (כשהיו ישראל במצריים). Characteristic of these narratives is the phrase "all the repulsive and unworthy things" (כל דברים מכוערין ודברים שאינן ראויין).
175 Friedmann emends the MS reading ישראל to מישראל.
176 There is no clear mark of delimitation between the governing voice's discourse and God's speech, neither in the preceding co-text of the narrative, nor in the one following it (ER 20, l. 7ff.), with the governing voice taking over with a rhetorical question. We find the same type of transition in another passage where God is the narrator: "When your fathers did My will in the wilderness, I found contentment in them. What is said of them? *And they came, everyone whose heart was stirred[, and everyone whose spirit was willing, and brought the Lord's offering to be used for the tent of meeting, and for all its service, and for the sacred vestments]* etc. *So they came, both men and women* (Exod 35:21–22). Of this hour Scripture says, *I slept, but my heart was awake* (Song 5:2). And when I shaped the Torah of the priests and gave commands to your fathers, in which I disposed of men and women with a genital discharge, women with menstruation and women who

I made a covenant with you when you went out of Egypt, and I made a covenant with you in the Book of Admonitions. A song I spoke for you when you went out of Egypt, and a song I sang for you in the Book of Admonitions. This has taught you that the words of Torah are everywhere said twice. Not so according to you, though. You that *smear whitewash* (Ezek 13:11). You mock my words[177] as if they had no substance, making out of them a command, even though they are no command, [understanding as] hope what is no hope.[178] I gave you commands (ציויתי) when you went forth out of Egypt, I gave you commands in the Book of Admonitions. For four hundred and eighty years before the Temple was built I had hope (קויתי) in you. Then I had hope in you for four hundred and ten years after the Temple was built,[179] for it is said, *Precept upon precept, precept upon precept, line* (קו) *upon line, line upon line*, etc. (Isa 28:13). Neither here did I find in you contentment, nor there did I find in you contentment. What is your wage from me? They told a parable: What does the matter resemble? It is like a king of flesh and blood who became angry at his servant and ordered with regard to him that he be bound with a heavy chain, that the chain be pulled from behind so that they would have him fall on his face and they would kick him in his face and bowels, for it is said, *Therefore the word of the Lord will be to them[, Precept upon precept, precept upon precept, line upon line, line upon line, here a little, there a little; in order that they may go, and fall backwards, and be broken, and snared, and taken]* (Isa 28:13). And so on a hundred occasions you did repulsive things and unworthy things before Me, but My compassion for you goes first every day, always, for it is said, *You deliver the weak from those too strong for them, the weak and needy from those who despoil them* (Ps 35:10). (ER 19, l. 30–ER 20, l. 7)

Even if God is represented with anthropomorphic features – reported speech and thought, characterisation as a father – many of his actions are such as cannot possibly be predicated of a human being, so that the narrative becomes purely metaphorical, or rather non-mimetic.[180] Related to this is the problem of God as a main character in some of the narratives and the representation of a correspond-

---

have recently given birth, they did not criticise Me, they did not utter a word, but were of a perfect conduct in this regard. And of this hour Scripture says, *Just as you have been a cursing among the nations, O house of Israel and house of Judah, so I will save you [and you shall be a blessing. Do not be afraid, but let your hands be strong]* etc. (Zech 8:13)." (ER 86, l. 1–8) A series of short exegetical narratives that expound on Ezek 16:8 in chapter (25) 17 of *Seder Eliyahu Rabbah* show a different, clearer transition from the governing voice to that of the narrator, God. Here the former interprets Ezek 16:6 by uttering a hypothetical statement about God, and from then on lets God himself speak in the first person, addressing Israel directly: "When I said to Abraham your father, *Go from your country and your kindred* <etc.> (Gen 12:1), he hearkened to My words immediately. Therefore it is said, *see, you were at the age for love* (Ezek 16:8). (ER 138, l. 21–22)

177 Friedmann emends the MS reading דבר to דברײ.
178 MS reading: קואה. Friedmann, *Seder Eliahu*, 19n23, points out: "We have commandment ציווי and hope קיווי. The word קואה follows the pattern of צואה, where the waw has a qamats. The passage is defective in the Venice print. My version is in accordance with the subject matter."
179 Friedmann emends the MS reading משבנה to משגבנה.
180 E.g., "the Holy One, blessed be He, made them His sanctuary in the world" (ER 85, l. 19), or "and He gave the Day of Atonement for forgiveness." (ER 86, l. 19)

ing "supernatural" time and space – that is, when the narrated events are God's actions both before creation and in the world to come. Such spatial-temporal settings, which can be seen as indicators of the narratives' non-mimetic fictionality, are found in the following two passages:

> The sages taught: Nine hundred and seventy-four generations before the world was to be created, the Holy One, blessed be He, sat and inquired into, analysed, refined, and tested all the words of Torah two hundred and forty-eight times with the same painstaking care He gave to selecting and putting together the two hundred and forty-eight parts of the human body. Then the Holy One, blessed be He, <took them up and set them> in His Torah. (EZ 189, l. 31–EZ 190, l. 1)[181]

> She [Gehenna] was trembling. The Holy One, blessed be He, asked her, Why are you trembling? She replied, Master of the Universe, I tremble, I am agitated, I shake but because of the wicked among the nations of the world who stand and speak ugly things about Israel, for it is said, *Sheol beneath is stirred up to meet you when you come*, etc. (Isa 14:9). But then she began to tremble again. The Holy One, blessed be He, asked her, Why are you trembling? She replied, Master of the Universe, give me those who know her [the Torah], yet transgress her. So the Holy One, blessed be He, would argue with her, saying, Maybe you do not have room. But she swore that <she> did have room,[182] for it is said, *Therefore Sheol has enlarged itself [and opened its mouth beyond measure]* etc. (Isa 5:14). (ER 108, l. 9–16)

The first text contains an account of God's numerous steps in his meticulous work on the Torah, described as consisting of as many parts of the human body, before giving it its final form. In the second, a personification of the supernatural spatial setting, Gehenna or hell (the scriptural verses used as proof-texts use the term *sheol*), converses with God about her own emotions.[183]

The texts discussed previously show that *Seder Eliyahu* makes use of several types of texts that can be subsumed under the broad category of the homiletical-exegetical narrative. Common to them all is their composite character – one of the components being scriptural (whether explicitly quoted or not) and the other Rabbinic – which is directly related to what has been called double-voicedness.

---

181 For a parallel, see ER 9, l. 2ff. Further parallels of the chronological motif of God acting nine hundred and seventy-four generations before the creation of the world are found in ER 33, l. 14ff., ER 61, l. 21ff., ER 68, l. 27f., and ER 130, l. 7f. See Kadushin, *Organic Thinking*, 273n95.
182 Friedmann emends the MS reading מקום בי שיש לו ונשבעת to מקום בה שיש לו ונשבעת.
183 The narrative about Gehenna's tremor is preceded by a sort of parallel in the form of a comparison in the present tense: "The utter wicked, behold, they are like brine (כציר ומוריים) in the cauldron. What cauldron? One at the moment brine is given therein, it is suddenly still. Likewise Gehenna, when the transgressors in Israel are put inside her, is still." (ER 108, l. 7–9) In two passages of *Pseudo-Seder Eliyahu Zuta*, God converses with personifications: In chapter 3 (21) with the light that God created on the first day, and in chapter 5 (23) with the measure of judgement.

3.4.2 First-Person Narratives

First-person narratives – whose use is a very rare phenomenon in Rabbinic literature – are probably the most prominent feature of *Seder Eliyahu* and the most characteristic of all its narrative forms.[184] The corpus comprises twenty-three narratives with the following distribution: sixteen are found in *Seder Eliyahu Rabbah*, four in *Seder Eliyahu Zuta*, and three in *Pseudo-Seder Eliyahu Zuta*. In these narratives the governing voice takes on a mode of communication different from the purely discursive, homiletical one. It switches to a narrative mode to give an account in the first person of an event in the life of an anonymous rabbi. In four of the narratives, however, it is not this anonymous rabbi who functions as the first-person narrator, but R. Jose,[185] R. Jochanan,[186] and Rabban Jochanan b. Zakkai.[187] Nevertheless, they make use of the characteristic phraseology of the anonymous first-person narratives.

The nature of the narrated events is quite uniform: In most cases, they are conversations represented as direct speech.[188] On these first-person narratives Braude and Kapstein, point out: "The debates are not merely summarized for us: they are reported directly in the words of the speakers and have the dramatic force of living voices."[189] This observation is particularly relevant in connection with an aspect of time representation – namely, with duration as a relation between story-time and text-time. Being conversations, most of the first-person narratives in *Seder*

---

[184] The series of travel accounts by Rabbah bar bar Chana in bBB73a–74a are an important exception. On this see Stemberger, "Münchhausen und die Apokalyptik"; and Stein, "The Blind Eye." In tShab 15:8 there is a first-person account by R. Nathan on how he applied the ruling based on a case in a similar situation. Lennart Lehmhaus, "Were not Understanding and Knowledge Given to You from Heaven? Minimal Judaism and the Unlearned Other in Seder Eliyahu Zuta," *Jewish Studies Quarterly* 19 (2012): 236n18, points out that eighteen of forty occurrences of first-person narrative in post-tannaitic texts stem from *Seder Eliyahu*.
[185] See EZ 199, l. 6ff.
[186] See PsEZ 22, l. 11 and PsEZ 22, l. 16. Friedmann, *Pseudo-Seder Eliahu Zuta*, 22n51, suggests that this passage, which is attributed to R. Jochanan, is to be regarded as a *baraita* of R. Jochanan ben Zakkai.
[187] See PsEZ 22, l. 22.
[188] EZ 199, l. 6 is an exception to this rule, for it primarily represents action other than dialogue. This narrative by R. Jose tells how he once saw the emperor humbling himself in front of a young Jewish girl afflicted with leprosy who had been thrown on a dung heap. His role is that of a witness rather than of a first-person narrator involved in the events he narrates. See below, p. 122.
[189] Braude and Kapstein, *Tanna děbe Eliyyahu*, 21.

Eliyahu are therefore comparable in duration to scenes, for which story-duration and text-duration are by convention regarded as identical.[190]

3.4.2.1 Topics, Settings, Beginnings, and Endings

Thematic variation in the first-person narratives is determined by the different subjects discussed by the rabbi and his interlocutors – mainly individuals, though collective interlocutors are also possible – and, to a much lesser extent, also by the changing spatial settings of the conversations. Many conversations, however, are introduced as taking place while the anonymous rabbi (or a named rabbi) is walking – nine of them are introduced with "I was walking from one place to another" (הייתי מהלך ממקום למקום),[191] three with "walking on the road" (הייתי מהלך בדרך),[192] one with "walking in the greatest city of the world" (הייתי מהלך בכרך גדול שבעולם),[193] and finally one with "walking in the great city of Rome" (הייתי מהלך בכרך גדול של רומי).[194] Four conversations, three with the sages and one with a disciple, are set at the academy in Jerusalem (הייתי יושב בבית המדרש [ה]גדול שבירושלים),[195] and three at the synagogue (פעם אחת הייתי עומד אני והוא בבית הכנסת).[196] The only semi-private space in which we find the rabbi in conversation with someone is the courtyard of the building in which a widow lives.[197]

Some of the first-person narratives are long dialogues in which several questions are addressed. Most, however, are short passages that focus on a single topic. It is generally the rabbi's interlocutor who opens the conversation posing a question or uttering a statement to which the rabbi responds. Whereas the beginnings

---

190 Rimmon-Kenan, *Narrative Fiction*, 52, however, argues that this convention is not without problems: "Even a segment of pure dialogue, which has been considered by some a case of pure coincidence between story-duration and text-duration, cannot manifest complete correspondence. A dialogue can give the impression of reporting everything that was said in fact or fiction, adding nothing to it, but even then it is incapable of rendering the rate at which the sentences were uttered or the length of the silences. It is, therefore, only by convention that one speaks of temporal equivalence of story and text in dialogue."
191 Seven in *Seder Eliyahu Rabbah* and two in *Seder Eliyahu Zuta*.
192 One in *Seder Eliyahu Rabbah* (ER 35, l. 7ff.), one in *Seder Eliyahu Zuta* (EZ 171, l. 16ff.), and one in *Pseudo-Seder Eliyahu Zuta* (PsEZ 22, l. 22ff.)
193 ER 5, l. 24, probably in allusion to Ctesiphon.
194 See EZ 199, l. 10. R. Jochanan b. Zakkai is the first-person narrator here.
195 All of them in *Seder Eliyahu Rabbah*. In three cases, the academy is called "the great academy."
196 See ER 66, l. 9, and two in PsEZ 22, l. 11 and PsEZ 22, l. 16.
197 See ER 76, l. 6.

are formulaic[198] (they all begin with the phrase "once I was" [פעם אחת הייתי])[199]), their endings are frequently not so easily recognisable and are therefore not perceived as real closures or dénouements. After having addressed a given matter (or a series of topics) in direct response to the question or questions he has been confronted with, the rabbi's speech fades into the homiletical discourse of the governing voice, so that the reader does not have the impression that he (or she) is reading a narrative any longer – or rather a dialogue, in which the rabbi primarily addresses an intradiegetic interlocutor – and that he (or she) is part of an extra*diegetic* audience. Instead, the reader is once again being addressed as the recipient of a homiletical discourse by the governing voice, which has taken up its standard, homiletical-ethical communicative mode, thereby preventing the rabbi's interlocutor from reacting to the last answer he receives. Thus the rabbi's questioners do not get to explicitly acknowledge what they are told, a silence which may lead the reader to assume that they are persuaded by the rabbi's explanations.[200]

3.4.2.2 Discourse Interference and Characterisation of Interlocutors

An example may illustrate how these stories lack a dénouement. In chapter (15) 16 of *Seder Eliyahu Rabbah*, answering the last of several questions, the rabbi tells his interlocutor the *maʿaseh* of a man who died young, despite his diligence in Torah study. This narrative turns out to be another first-person narrative, which is itself embedded within the first one: The rabbi narrates how he met the man's widow and discussed her husband's behaviour with her until he (or both of them) realise why the man had to die prematurely. The dialogue with the woman has a blurred ending: The rabbi addresses the woman directly one last time before quoting Av 4:2, and then proceeds to interpret this *mishnah* without ever again mentioning or addressing the widow or the interlocutor of the upper narrative level.[201]

This phenomenon – the fading of the narrative into the homiletical discourse or the "interference" of both discourse types – can also be ascertained within more

---

198 With the exception of a narrative in chapter 2, which represents the rabbi in dialogue with the sages, and which is incidentally the only one that deals with astronomical matters.
199 On the phrase פעם אחת הייתי as a marker for a narrative unit in tannaitic literature, see Rivka Shemesh, "On the Narrative Discourse in Tannaitic Language: An Exploration of the *maʿaseh* and *paʿam ʾachat* Discourse Unit," *Hebrew Studies* 49 (2008): 99–125.
200 The narrative in EZ 167, l. 23ff. is an exception, in that the magistrate speaks a *berakhah* in response to the rabbi's answer. The parallel in ER 95, l. 11ff. has the rabbi himself speaking the *berakhah*.
201 On this passage, see pp. 206ff. I also deal with this *maʿaseh* in section 6.2.

extensive first-person narratives, in which case the shift in discursive mode can be perceived as an interruption of the narrative in the form of a homiletical digression. To name but one example of "interference" between homiletical and narrative discourses,[202] also in the first-person narrative of chapter (15) 16, the rabbi's answer to the question of whether cheating a non-Jew is permitted is followed by a digression on the eight reasons why the world has been destroyed, which is introduced with the characteristic formula *mikan amru* as a tradition of the sages, before the next question is posed.[203]

First-person narratives – like homiletical-exegetical narratives, though in a different sense – are also texts of a double-voiced nature. This manifests itself in the already mentioned interference of homiletical and narrative modes of communication or discourses as well as in the "homiletical endings" to all the passages that begin as first-person narratives. Another manner in which the narratives' double-voicedness is made evident is the fact that they combine not an old (scriptural) and a new (Rabbinic) discourse or textual system, but rather contemporary, competing discourses or ideologies – a Rabbinic and a non-Rabbinic.[204] Many of the first-person narratives put in the mouths of the rabbi's interlocutors a discursive problem which the rabbi successfully solves from a Rabbinic point of view. These challengers of Rabbinic ideology never get a chance at posing an authentic problem,[205] precisely because they act within someone else's first-person narrative. It is worth noting that, from a narratological point of view, the account of what happened (and of what was said) by a first-person narrator has to be regarded as less objective than if it were an account by a narrator situated outside the narrated events. As Monika Fludernik argues, unlike heterodiegetic narrators, first-person (or autodiegetic) narrators "have an agenda when telling their stories, which could come into conflict with a true representation of what happened."[206]

Some of the interlocutors are explicitly depicted as non-Rabbinic "others": They are directly presented as men familiar with Scripture, but not with Mish-

---

[202] For the concept of interference in narrative texts, see Wolf Schmid, *Narratology: An Introduction*, trans. Alexander Starritt (Berlin, New York: De Gruyter, 2010), 137–174, whose concept of text interference draws on notions taken from Mikhail Bakhtin and Valentin Voloshinov.
[203] On this passage, see pp. 202ff.
[204] To a certain extent, it could be argued that this special type of double-voicedness is probably true of the whole of *Seder Eliyahu*, not just of the first-person narratives.
[205] Which holds true not just for issues raised within first-person narratives.
[206] Fludernik, *Introduction*, 153.

nah;[207] as a Zoroastrian priest;[208] or as a Roman magistrate.[209] In these cases, the clash of discourses is more evident than in the narratives where the "otherness" of the interlocutors is not so explicitly emphasised.

Certain narratives deal not with "others" as interlocutors, but with members of the Rabbinic system. The *Rabbah* part contains three conversations with the sages, a sort of choir or collective interlocutor,[210] which take the form of an exposition the rabbi delivers after having sought the occasion to do so: He himself presents the problem he wants to discuss, as well as a solution to it. *Ex silentio*, the sages are depicted as good listeners. Two passages depict the rabbi's conversations with one of his disciples.[211] They also follow the usual pattern of question and answer. In the first one, the disciple is depicted both indirectly by his speech acts and directly in the narrative frame, wherein his relation to the rabbi is compared to that of a son approaching his father. The disciple in the second narrative is said to be "unversed in Halakhah" (שאינו בקי בהלכה). In four passages of *Seder Eliyahu Rabbah*, the anonymous rabbi converses with "an old man," who is himself indirectly characterised by the questions he poses.[212] Unlike the group of narratives with the men who know Scripture but no Mishnah, in which the questions tend to pertain to halakhic topics, the questions posed by the old men and by the disciples address a wide range of subjects, which is why it is not possible to infer from them which historical counterparts could thereby have been alluded to.[213]

Finally, the so-called *Pseudo-Seder Eliyahu Zuta* has a smaller corpus of first-person narratives, all of them told by Rabbinic authorities. In the first one

---

207 For example, ER 66, l. 9ff., ER 70, l. 7ff., ER 72, l. 9ff., and EZ 171, l. 16ff. Precisely this kind of characterisation has been interpreted as a key to the question of whom these first-person narratives address, or who their intended recipients could have been – namely, potential followers of the Karaites or of some of their scripturalist predecessors. On this, see chapter 5.
208 See ER 5, l. 24ff.
209 See ER 95, l. 11ff. and EZ 167, l. 23ff.
210 See ER 49, l. 15ff., ER 51, l. 8ff., and ER 122, l. 1ff.
211 See ER 80, l. 19ff. and ER 120, l. 24ff. The second is the only case in which the rabbi converses in the first part with one person, an old man, and in the second with another, a disciple.
212 See ER 99, l. 12ff., ER 113, l. 34ff., ER 120, l. 24ff., ER 123, l. 36ff.
213 One first-person narrative has an angel as the rabbi's interlocutor. Here an inversion of the usual hierarchy of teaching takes place: It is the rabbi who listens to the angel's explanation for the death of a group of young men and their teacher; see below, p. 123. In one of the four first-person narratives of *Seder Eliyahu Zuta* (a number which, given this part's length, shows that this type of narrative is especially well represented), the rabbi encounters a man he describes at the beginning as a scorner and a mocker; being asked about his profession by the rabbi, he replies that he is a fisherman. On this passage, see Kadushin, *Organic Thinking*, 45–46, who interprets this narrative as illustrating that every man with normal capacities is granted the chance of studying Torah.

R. Jochanan relates what he learned from conversing with an old woman and with an unmarried woman.[214] Both of these women are indirectly characterised, both by their speech and by Jochanan's interpretation of their words. The narrative told by R. Jochanan b. Zakkai has "a man gathering fagots" as his interlocutor, thus symbolically presenting him as a man who has been punished. The man's own report on his (previous) life further characterises him.[215]

Characterisation by indirect presentation is, therefore, a conspicuous feature in the first-person narratives of *Seder Eliyahu*; characters are constituted as such by the narrator's referring to them with a name (or a phrase), but mostly by their own actions, which are primarily of a linguistic nature – they are speech acts. A rare example of indirect presentation where both action other than speech come into play is found in EZ 199, l. 6ff., the last narrative in *Seder Eliyahu Zuta*, where the Roman "other" is presented as exemplarily acknowledging the Rabbinic worldview. Here, R. Jose tells how he witnessed the Roman emperor alighting from his horse to prostrate himself before a Jewish girl afflicted with leprosy. To the ensuing criticism by the Roman notables who, like R. Jose, witness the emperor's peculiar behaviour, the latter replies:

> Let it not grieve you. All the kings of the nations will prostrate themselves before them, for it is said, *Thus says the Lord, the Redeemer of Israel and his Holy One, to one deeply despised, abhorred by the nations, the slave of rulers, kings shall see and stand up, princes, and they shall prostrate themselves, because of the Lord, who is faithful, the Holy One of Israel, who has chosen you* (Isa 49:7). *The Holy One of Israel*, for He chose them. And it [Scripture] says, *Their descendants shall be known among the nations, and their offspring among the peoples; all who see them shall acknowledge that they are a people whom the Lord has blessed.* (Isa 61:9) (EZ 199, l. 14–19)

3.4.2.3 Narrative Levels

One narratologically interesting aspect of first-person narratives is their use of different narrative levels. A case in point is the first-person narrative in chapter (15) 16 which contains the *maʿaseh* of the man who died young mentioned previously.[216] During the dialogue, the first-person narrator tells his interlocutor a story. In this embedded narrative, the rabbi is one of the dramatis personae, he is the rabbi who lends an ear to the desperate widow and realises that her husband has been justly punished.[217] The first-person narrator, who depicts himself in his narratives as a

---

[214] See PsEZ 22, l. 11ff. and l. 16ff.
[215] See PsEZ 22, l. 22ff.
[216] See ER 76, l. 3–24.
[217] A similar combination of the formal features of the *maʿaseh* and a reporting first-person narrator is found in the *maʿaseh* of ER 66, l. 9–17.

rabbi, is also the (intradiegetic) narrator of other types of (metadiegetic) narratives, including *meshalim*[218] and homiletical-exegetical narratives. In such cases, his direct addressee is not the extradiegetic audience, but first and foremost his (fictional, diegetic) interlocutor. An example of a homiletical-exegetical narrative told within a first-person narrative is found in chapter 18: An old man asks the rabbi why some householders in Israel are prevented from having children. The rabbi explains to him that God purifies some householders in Israel by withholding from them the joy of having children for many years, not forever. He illustrates this idea with a series of summarised biblical passages (or para-scriptural narratives) that function as exempla on the nature of infertility and the reward for prayer:

> He said to him, My son, it is because the Holy One, blessed be He, loves them with a perfect love and rejoices in them, that He purifies them, so that they increase their prayers before Him. He said to me, No. Rather it is because they have lust in their hearts and take women not to be fertile and multiply. I said to him, My son, we have many householders in Israel who are ass-drivers and who have but one wife and are prevented from having children. You should know that it is so. | Go and learn from our father Abraham [and Sarah] who were barren for seventy-five years. They increased their prayers before Him until Isaac came and they rejoiced in him. | Go and learn from Rebekah who was barren for twenty years, but she increased her prayers before Him until Jacob was born and they rejoiced in him. | Go and learn from Rachel who was barren for fourteen years before her <two> children [were conceived], but she increased her prayers before Him until both came and they rejoiced in them. | Go and learn from Hannah who was barren for nineteen years and six months, but she increased her prayers before Him, and her son Samuel came and she rejoiced in him. So you should accept the first explanation I gave you at the beginning, that the Holy One, blessed be He, loves them with a perfect love and rejoices in them and purifies them, so that they increase their prayers before Him. (ER 99, l. 14–25)

It should be noted that it is not only the rabbi who functions as an intradiegetic narrator; his interlocutor can also assume this role, as for example when a man with no Mishnah tells the rabbi a *maʿaseh* about how he cheated a Gentile, which is then used against him by the rabbi.[219]

An example of a first-person narrative might better illustrate what these texts look like and how they operate:[220]

---

[218] In ER 70, l. 7, for example, the rabbi answers the four questions posed by his interlocutor with four *meshalim*.
[219] See ER 74, l. 25ff. and pp. 202ff. for a discussion of this passage.
[220] It must be pointed out that this narrative has a number of anomalies when compared to the rest of the corpus, but this does not lessen its relevance for our present purposes. On how first-person narratives operate, see chapter 5.

> A. One time while journeying among those in exile in Babylonia, I came into a great city which was entirely Jewish – there were no Gentiles at all in it. I found there a teacher of young men who had before him two hundred students, most of whom were between eighteen and twenty years old.[221] B. Because these young people disgraced themselves with immorality, their teacher died, his son died, and his grandson died, as did every one of the students, most of whom were between the ages of eighteen and twenty. C. As I was weeping and sighing for them, an angel came to me and asked, Why do you weep and sigh? I replied, Shall I not weep and sigh for those who came to possess knowledge of Scripture and Mishnah and are now gone as if they had never been? The angel said, It is fair that you weep and sigh. Still, why should these young men have followed filthy ways and committed unworthy deeds and disgraced themselves with immorality discharging their seed for no reason? Did they not know that death would lead them astray? (ER 100, l. 32–ER 101, l. 6)

The narrative does not – at least not obviously – illustrate the statement that immediately precedes it,[222] but rather anticipates arguments that come after its narration.[223]

Here the rabbi is not teaching someone else, but is first depicted as an observer, anguished at the "sight" of how a certain group of people ruined their lives and that of their teacher. Although there is no indication of the passage of time, two story-times can be distinguished, almost two scenes (A and B): In the first one, the young students and the teacher are said to be there, though there is no dialogue or action of any sort; in the second passage, the narrator laments the death of the teacher and his family, as of every single young student seen in the first scene. We assume that the narrator in C is still there weeping for the loss when he is approached, not by an old man or by a denier of the Oral Tradition, but by a supernatural being – an angel. Only now is there a short dialogue defining the nature of the immorality referred to in B: The students of this teacher have not been capable of restraining their sexual appetites and have been punished for "discharging their seed in vain." The angel only alludes to how these people were responsible for their own and their teacher's deaths.

As previously noted, the reader is given no clear indication of whether the dialogue comes to an end with the end of C, whether the angel scene in the Jewish city in Babylonia is then closed and whether the words quoted below as D–E

---

[221] According to the MS, this line is followed by: "Their teacher was not among them, there was only a son of his and a grandson."
[222] The governing voice expounds on the subject of intermarriage among the ten different classes that came up to the land of Israel from Babylonia after the exile.
[223] Common to both the passages preceding and following the narrative, however, is the fact that *mishnayot* from the fourth chapter of the tractate *Qiddushin* are quoted.

are already spoken by the governing voice resuming its homiletical discourse,[224] which appears to draw halakhic conclusions from the rather mysterious narrative about the premature death of a teacher, his family, and his students:

> D. If this be so, this is the measure of why this *mishnah* was given to the sages: "A man may not stay alone with two women." If you, however, say "a woman may be alone with two men" (mQid 4:12), [bear in mind that] the halakhah is not thus, for if one [of the men] should commit a sexual transgression with her, there would not be enough testimony. On the other hand, a woman may be alone with three men, for, should one of them commit a sexual transgression with her, then there would be enough testimony. And why is there a difference between two and three [men with whom a woman may stay alone]? Those who taught that [a woman may be alone with] three meant disciples of the wise and great sages. But if they are licentious, she may not be alone even with a hundred of them. The sages taught in a *mishnah*: "An unmarried man may not tend cattle, nor may two unmarried men sleep together under the same cover" (mQid 4:14). And also this halakhah is widespread in Israel: One whose business is with women must not be alone with women, for example net makers, carders, [handmill] cleaners, wool dressers, tailors, spice peddlars, barbers, and launderers. E. If you wish to learn and take delight in the words of Torah, go and learn from what happened at the very beginning of it all. When our fathers stood at Mount Sinai to receive upon themselves the Torah from Sinai, the Holy One, blessed be He, said to Moses, *Go to the people and consecrate them [today and tomorrow. Have them wash their clothes]* etc. (Exod 19:10). Moses went and said to them, *Prepare for the third day[; do not go near a woman]* etc. (Exod 19:15). But is it really so that he warned them only against women? What he said was, Abstain from transgression, from theft, and from improper acts, so that you are pure when you stand at Mount Sinai. (ER 101, l. 6–22)

Two of the three quotations of the Mishnah tractate *Qiddushin* in D as well as the minimal exegetical narrative in E focus on women as the core of a discussion on how to avoid the immoral behaviour of sexual transgressions.[225] Seen in the light of D–E that follows upon it, the narrative of A–C – where women are not even mentioned – is understood as a warning exemplum against more general situations which can lead to or be interpreted as sexual transgressions involving women.

---

224 There is no clear delimitation at the end of the narrative passage, so it could be argued, that it is the angel who provides a sort of application of the narrative that points to a wider context than that of the schoolhouse as the setting for immoral behaviour.

225 Only by the end of E does the governing voice relativise the role of women in this context, depicting Moses warning Israel with respect to all sorts of immorality, not just with respect to restraint in sexual conduct. The two text passages D and E are characteristic of the homiletical discourse of *Seder Eliyahu*. The governing voice addresses its reader (with a masculine personal pronoun *atah* or verbal forms with masculine endings) as if he were a potential questioner, posing questions they could have had and answering them itself. The narrative of the students is never explicitly taken up or commented upon again – only indirectly, implicitly, in this passage where a shift of focus towards the two *mishnayot* can be ascertained.

3.5 Conclusions: Homiletical Narration

> *For the mighty are ruined!*[226] (Zech 11:2). These are the mighty in Israel whose ruin He hates, for it is said, *By the rivers of Babylon [– there we sat down and there we wept when we remembered Zion]* etc. (Ps 137:1). It is surely not said, "<There we sat down> and wept,"[227] but *There we sat down and there we wept [when we remembered Zion]*, which teaches that they wept, they were silent, and then wept again. What does Scripture teach when it says, *when we remembered Zion*? Just that when they[228] remembered Zion, they wept, burst forth in one loud cry of agony, and then they wept again. Therefore it is said, *when we remembered Zion*. (ER 149, l. 20–24)

Is there a narrative in the quoted verse from the psalm, or rather a single event consisting of two simultaneous "actions"? Does the meticulous reading of the midrash constitute a narrative? We are told "that they wept, then they were still, and then they wept again." We are told, in yet another interpretation, "that when they remembered Zion, they wept in a loud cry of agony, and (then) they wept." Is this a micro-exegetical narrative about the mighty of Israel? What are the narrated events? Is the relation between them of a causal nature? The passage quoted above shows that the midrash can be concerned with explicitly naming events implied in a scriptural verse, but that the resulting matrix of scriptural text and Rabbinic statement need not always constitute a narrative. As has been shown in this chapter, *Seder Eliyahu* contains several narratives that need not be "explained" or "justified" as such, but are probably easily recognisable as narratives by a reader with little familiarity with Rabbinic literature.

Even if the narrative texts in *Seder Eliyahu* to describe them they were generally isolated from their context in order to describe them, they are never independent, but are parts of a non-narrative, homiletical-ethical whole. Narratives not only interact with the non-narrative discourse that encompasses them, but often with other narratives. Short, simple forms such as the narrative *mashal* or the *maʿaseh* can be arranged in pairs or series, and they can also be embedded in other narratives, functioning as metadiegetic narratives. So to illustrate the ways in which narrative and homiletical modes or discourses interact in *Seder Eliyahu*, I propose closing the typology presented in this chapter with a case study:[229] A cursory reading of a chapter in *Seder Eliyahu*, chapter (11) 10. The description of the

---

[226] MT reads גַּם-בָּכִינוּ, MS גם ובכינו.
[227] MT reads אֲשֶׁר and the MS אשר. Friedmann puts the MS expression גם in brackets, although it appears to be the very word the midrash attempts to interpret in the verse from the psalm.
[228] Braude and Kapstein, *Tanna děbe Eliyyahu*, 367, translate "the Levites."
[229] For this idea, although not for the form of the exposition, I again follow Simon-Shoshan, *Stories*, 54–58.

narrative passages is set in block citation to distinguish it typographically from the discussion of the non-narrative discourse that encompasses these passages.

The chapter opens with the quotation of Judg 5:1 and its interpretation.[230] "Then Deborah and Baraq sang" (ותשר דבורה וברק), a formula that introduces the speech in the song of Deborah and Baraq in Scripture, is quoted and interpreted by means of a brief exegetical narrative. In it, the biblical speech act (a poem) is replaced, reformulated with Rabbinic discourse. To introduce this, the governing voice poses the question "What did Deborah prophesy to Israel?" and answers, "She just spoke to them as follows." Deborah's speech itself is yet another pairing of question and answer, one that seeks to explain the problematic redundancy in the infinitive absolute construction of Judg 5:2, בפרוע פרעות: "On account of whom does the Holy One, blessed be He, deliver (נפרע) Israel from among the peoples of the world?" Both question and answer have a low narrativity, since they are formulated in the *qotel* form,[231] and can be regarded as a non-narrative hermeneutic digression within a narrative passage (or as a hermeneutic passage within a narrative frame). The answer consists of three parts. The first part states that those men who go to the synagogue and to the house of study in the morning and in the evening and answer with Amen are the reason why God saves Israel from among the peoples of the world. As a (connecting) proof-text, Ps 55:19 is quoted. The second part explains Ps 55:19 as referring to the man who is one of ten in the synagogue in the morning and in the evening. According to the third, the verse also refers to the man who sustains not only the disciple of the wise, who reads Scripture and studies Mishnah, but also his wife and children and all those who read Scripture and study Mishnah with him. This last statement on charity is expanded upon with two further statements, followed by proof-texts: The first is an anonymous saying, supported by Deut 9:19; the second is a saying of the sages in the Mishnah (mSan 4:5), followed by Prov 21:14.[232] The emphasis on charity in the third and final part of the answer to the question posed by Deborah is also evident in that this statement is followed by a *ma'aseh* which illustrates the importance of charity.

> The formula "It happened to two priestly families" (מעשה בשתי משפחות של כהנים) introduces a narrative – an exemplum on the power of charity is related.[233] The passage's narrativity is clearly higher than that of the previous one; it is an account of events that happened

---

230 See ER 52, l. 17–ER 53, l. 4.
231 The unvocalised form נפרע could also be a form of the perfect. However, since all the answers are given in the active participle or *qotel* form, we assume that the question uses the same "tense."
232 Both of these verses are used in a passage of bBB 9b that discusses charity.
233 See ER 53, l. 5–11. A parallel is found in BerR 59:1.

once in the past, concerning two priestly families that consult R. Jochanan b. Zakkai on the premature death of their sons. He infers that they must be descendants of Eli's family, who were punished by the death of male descendants in their youth (1 Sam 2:33). The families do not comment on this, an embedded minimal para-scriptural narrative, but ask R. Jochanan for a remedy. He suggests that they estimate the value of their sons once they have reached puberty in goods and give the goods to charity. This is the only way they can reverse the curse on the descendants of Eli. The idea that charity preserves lives, as expressed in Prov 10:2 and quoted by R. Jochanan, connects this ma῾aseh with the previous narrative segment.

The narrative is followed by a segment of ethical-homiletical discourse dealing with charity and introduced with the connecting formula "and not only this" (ולא זו בלבד אלא).[234] The segment consists of five statements: a) a casuistic formulation in the form of a relative construction: "Whoever does X, of him Scripture says Y"; b) the report of a speech act which, represents God as posing a question and answering it himself – even though this passage uses qatal[235] and qotel forms, it does not deal with events in the past, but with ever-recurring ones; c) two parallel constructions of the form "Whenever Israel does X, what verse applies to them?" and the application of two verses to different ways in which Israel can behave with regard to charity; d) a berakhah followed by God's question in b) and an answer in the form of a rhetorical question, suggesting that it is not the charitable man, but God himself who redeems not only Israel but all of his creatures; e) Words of admonition addressed to the house of David, followed by Jer 21:12, a verse which contains two words that are almost leitmotifs of the narrative and homiletical unit (consisting of ma῾aseh and homiletical application): משפט and הצילו.

In the next segment,[236] the inquit formula "Deborah said" (דבורה אמרה) introduces a speech act attributed to Deborah. Its first part, which according to Friedmann is a sort of petichah,[237] consists of an apodictic statement and a proof-text (Prov 3:18). The second part is an atomising exegesis of Judg 5:10–11. Each verse is divided into three parts and analysed.[238] Why is the reader/listener to assume that these words were uttered in the past – that we are dealing with an event that took place in the past? The only indication of this is the verb in the introductory formula, amrah, which provides a frame for both the apodictic statement and the

---

234 See ER 53, l. 12–24.
235 The phrase "in that hour" (באותה שעה) was already used in the Mekhilta as a temporal marker for the past.
236 See ER 53, l. 25–ER 54, l. 10.
237 See Friedmann, Seder Eliahu, 53n10.
238 Apart from segmenting each verse into three parts, the interpretation of both verses seems to follow the same pattern, providing two explanations (davar acher) for the second verse part – בין משאבים resp. יובי על מדין.

exegetical passage. This way of reading the text makes of Deborah the "author" of her song and, at the same time, her own interpreter. It could be argued that Deborah only spoke the apodictic statement, but the exegesis that follows it is spoken by the governing voice itself.[239] The last part of Judg 5:11 is quoted, whereby an expression left unquoted, פרזונו, is interpreted in terms of Israel's dispersion (פיזר) as the merciful plan of God. This notion is illustrated in the exegetical *ma'aseh* that follows.

> The narrative, which opens with the formula "It happened that a Roman leader" (מעשה בהגמון אחד), is the account of an encounter between a Roman leader (*hegemon*) and the Patriarch Judah the Prince.[240] After being defied by the Roman, Rabbi lets one of his disciples, whose name is not mentioned, reply to the Roman and defeat him. His reply takes the form of a hypothetical parable: "Where would the master of the house put his vessels so that these come into the house when the master of the house returns?"[241]

> In order to provide an alternative interpretation, *davar acher*, of the verse part of Judg 5:11, שם יתנו צדקות ה׳ צדקות פרזונו בישראל, the governing voice lets an aetiological narrative explain how it came to pass that so many synagogues and houses of study are found in Israel. The narrative closes with the final part of Judg 5:11.[242]

A blessing in the form of an *ashre*-passage reopens the homiletical discourse. He who renews the words of Torah in one of the numerous houses of study in Israel is compared to one who is heard in heaven and who is directly spoken to by God. God's direct speech is represented and confirmed with the quotation of the first part of Judg 5:8.

---

239 See the exegesis of the first verse in bEruv 54b.
240 See ER 54, l. 11–27. In the Venice print, Rabbi's interlocutor is a כומר – a non-Jewish or idolatrous priest. A parallel in bPes 87b depicts the following characters instead: a sectarian, R. Chanina, and R. Oshaia.
241 The use of such a hypothetical parable is one of the many differences between this version of the story and its parallel in bPes 87b: "R. Oshaia said: What is meant by the verse, *Even the righteous acts of His Ruler in Israel?* (Judg 5:11). The Holy One, blessed be He, showed righteousness [mercy] unto Israel by scattering them among the nations. And this is what a certain sectarian said to R. Chanina, We are better than you. Of you it is written, *For Joab and all Israel remained there six months, until he had cut off every male in Edom* (1 Kgs 11:16); whereas you have been with us many years yet we have not done anything to you! Said he to him, If you agree, a disciple will debate it with you. [Thereupon] R. Oshaia debated it with him, [and] he said to him, [The reason is] because you do not know how to act. If you would destroy all, they are not among you. [Should you destroy] those who are among you, then you will be called a murderous kingdom! Said he to him, By the Capitol of Rome! with this [care] we lie down and with this [care] we get up." Quoted following Epstein, *Pesaḥim*.
242 ER 54, l. 28–32.

The chapter closes with an anonymous statement by the sages, introduced with *mikan amru*, "derived" from the preceding one (or just associated with it by the author of *Seder Eliyahu*). The statement is itself a hyperbolic narrative, according to which forty thousand men of Israel went to war but were not in need of shields – here, the last part of Judg 5:8 is interpreted – because two disciples of the wise were with them.

4 Parabolical Passages on the Disciples of the Wise

4.1 Preliminary Considerations

The following passage in *Shir ha-Shirim Rabbah* is often quoted as an example of what could be termed a Rabbinic poetology of the Rabbinic *mashal*, or according to David Stern, "a *mashal* about the mashal."[1] Five *meshalim* are told in this passage in order to illustrate how *meshalim* themselves illustrate:

> Another interpretation: *Song of songs*. This is what the verse says, *Besides (ויותר) being wise, the preacher* (Qoh 12:9). Had another man composed them [the books Proverbs, Qohelet, and Song of Songs] you would need to incline your ears (אוזניך) and listen to these words, all the more [so] (ויותר) since Solomon composed them; had he composed them from his knowledge, you would need to incline your ears and listen to them, all the more [so] (ויותר) since he composed them in the spirit of holiness. *Besides being wise, the preacher also taught the people knowledge, weighing (ואזן) and studying (וחקר) and arranging (תקן) many proverbs* (Qoh 12:9). Weighing the words of Torah and studying the words of Torah, he provided Torah with handles (אזנים). You find out that until Solomon came there was no illustration (דוגמא). Rav Nachman [gave] two [illustrations]. Rav Nachman said: Like a large palace which had many doors and anyone who entered would not find his way to the door. A clever man came and took a coil [of string] and hung it up along the way to the door, so that everyone went in and out [following] the way of the coil. So, until Solomon came no one could discern the words of Torah, and when Solomon came everyone began to understand Torah. Rav Nachman [used] another expression (לישנא חורי): Like a thicket of reeds which no one could enter, until a clever man came and cleared [part of it so that] everyone began to go in and out through the cleared area. So [it was with] Solomon. R. Jose said: It is like a big basket full of fruit with no handle (אזן) that could not be carried until a clever one came and made handles for it and so it began to be carried by the handles. So, until Solomon arose no one could discern the words of Torah, but when Solomon came, everyone began to understand Torah. R. Shila said: It is like a big ladle full of hot water without a handle to carry until one came and made a handle for it so that they began to carry it by its handle. R. Chanina said: Like a deep well full of water, its water being cold, sweet, and good, but no creature could drink from it, until a man came who joined rope with rope, and cord with cord to draw water out of it to drink. So everyone began to draw water and drink. So from word to word and from parable to parable, Solomon stood on the foundation of Torah, for it is written, *The proverbs (משלי) of Solomon son of David, king of Israel* (Prov 1:1), by means of Solomon's parables (

---

1 David Stern, "Forms of Midrash I: Parables of Interpretation," chap. 2 in *Midrash and Theory: Ancient Jewish Exegesis and Contemporary Literary Studies* (Evanston, IL: Northwestern University Press, 1996), 41. See also Daniel Boyarin, "Interpreting in Ordinary Language: The Mashal as Intertext," chap. 5 in *Intertextuality and the Reading of Midrash* (Bloomington, IN: Indiana University Press, 1990).

משלותיו) he understood the words of Torah. Our rabbis said: Let not the (lit. "this")[2] parable be light[ly esteemed] in your eyes, for by means of the parable a man can understand the words of Torah. It is like a king who lost the gold of his house or a precious pearl, does he not find it by means of a wick of very little worth? So the parable should not be light[ly esteemed] in your eyes, for by means of the parable a man can understand the words of Torah. You should know that it is so, for by means of the parable Solomon understood the subtlety of Torah. R. Judan said: It is to teach you that whoever speaks words of Torah in public merits that the spirit of holiness rest upon him. And from whom do you learn [this]? From Solomon, who, because he spoke words of Torah in public, merited that the spirit of holiness rested upon him and he composed three books: Proverbs (משלי), Qohelet, and Song of Songs. (ShirR 1:1:8)[3]

The task of the *mashal*, both according to this rare Rabbinic statement and as explained by Arnold Goldberg, is to illustrate the meaning of the words of Torah.[4] The *mashal* gains its worth not from its inherent value, but rather from the task it performs.

Other talmudic passages reflect upon the rabbis' understanding of the parable as belonging to the Rabbinic curriculum: in bBB 134a and bSuk 28a, for example, it is reported that Jochanan b. Zakkai studied not only Miqra, Mishnah, Gemara, Halakhah, and Haggadah, but also parables, which are referred to as "washers' proverbs" and "fox fables" (משלות כובסים ומשלות שועלים).[5] According to bSan 38b, one-third of R. Meir's lectures are said to have consisted of parables. By

---

2 Also in the following instances, the Hebrew original reads המשל הזה.

3 For this translation, I follow the text of ShirR of the Vilna edition, contained in the Bar Ilan University Online Responsa Project.

4 See Arnold Goldberg, "Das schriftauslegende Gleichnis im Midrasch," in *Rabbinische Texte als Gegenstand der Auslegung*, vol. 2 of *Gesammelte Studien*, ed. Margarete Schlüter and Peter Schäfer (Tübingen: Mohr Siebeck, 1999), 143.

5 The complete passage on Jochanan's curriculum in bBB 134a reads: "It was said of R. Jochanan b. Zakkai that his studies included the Scriptures, the Mishnah, the Gemara, the Halachoth, the Aggadoth; the subtle points of the Torah and the minutiae of the scribes; the inferences from minor to major and the [verbal] analogies; astronomy and geometry; washer's proverbs (ומשלות כובסים) and fox fables (ומשלות שועלים); the language of the demons, the whisper of the palms, the language of the ministering angels and the great matter and the small matter. The 'great matter' is the manifestation of the [divine] chariot and the small matter is the arguments of Abaye and Raba. Thereby is fulfilled the Scriptural text, That I may cause those that love me to inherit substance and that I may fill their treasuries. Now, if the least among them [was] so, how great must have been the greatest among them! It was related of Jonathan b. Uzziel [that] when he sat and studied the Torah, every bird that flew over him was burned." This quotation follows Isidore Epstein, ed., *Baba Bathra*, vol. 2 of *The Babylonian Talmud: Seder Nezikin*, trans. Maurice Simon and Israel W. Slotki (London: Soncino, 1935).

the times of R. Jochanan, who is assumed to have lived one hundred years after R. Meir, only three of the numerous fox parables he used to tell were still known.[6]

Rabbinic parables or *meshalim* – the words are used as synonyms in this study – have been at the centre of scholarly attention for a long time. Arnold Goldberg's survey in his seminal article "Das schriftauslegende Gleichnis" provides a concise overview of which aspects of these short texts scholarship has been addressing since the nineteenth century.[7] It should be noted that, among the vast material of Rabbinic parables, it is particularly the subgroup of so-called king parables that has received special attention,[8] and that most of the studies of Rabbinic *meshalim* focus on *tannaitic* and *amoraic* documents.[9] In contrast, the parables in post-talmudic documents have not received much attention. One exception is a chapter David Stern dedicates to the history of the *mashal* in Hebrew litera-

---

[6] "Whence do you know that? asked he [R. Ishmael]. – I heard it in a public discourse of R. Meir, [he answered]. Even as R. Jochanan said: When R. Meir used to deliver his public discourses, a third was Halacha, a third Haggadah, and a third consisted of parables (מתלי). R Jochanan also said: R. Meir had three hundred parables of foxes (משלות שועלים), and we have only three left, [as illustrations to the verses]. [a] The fathers have eaten sour grapes and the children's teeth are set on edge; [b] Just balances, just weights, [c] The righteous is delivered out of trouble and the wicked comes in his stead." This quotation follows Epstein, *Sanhedrin*.

[7] See Goldberg, "Das schriftauslegende Gleichnis," 135–136.

[8] Louis Isaac Rabinowitz, "Parable," in *Encyclopaedia Judaica*, ed. Michael Berenbaum and Fred Skolnik, vol. 15 (Detroit: MacMillan Reference, 2007), 621–623, provides a classification of Rabbinic king parables according to their motifs.

[9] To name but few of the most influential ones, apart from the article by Goldberg already mentioned (see n. 4): The first comprehensive study of a Rabbinic parable corpus was Ziegler, *Die Königsgleichnisse des Midrash beleuchtet durch die römische Kaiserzeit*; Clemens Thoma and Simon Lauer undertook the large-scale project of collecting, translating into German, and commenting the parables of *Pesikta de Rav Kahana*, *Bereshit Rabbah*, and *Shemot Rabbah* in the four volumes of *Die Gleichnisse der Rabbinen*, 4 vols. (Bern: Lang, 1986–2000); David Stern's 1991 book *Parables* is dedicated to the poetics and rhetoric of the *mashal*, with a special focus on the midrash *Ekhah Rabbah*; Alan Appelbaum's study *The Rabbis' King-Parables* (2010) is based on a tannaitic corpus of 232 king parables. The NWO research project "Parables and the Partings of the Ways" (2014–present), under the direction of Eric Ottenheijm, examines parables on family relations, on slavery and on common meals in Rabbinic corpora and the Synoptic Gospels in several interrelated studies in an attempt to describe the manner in which the late antique social and religious realities of Rabbinic Judaism and nascent Christianity were processed in the short fictions of the parables; see https://parabelproject.nl/; the special issue of NTT on parables, with several contributions on Rabbinic *meshalim*, such as Eric Ottenheijm, "De parabels van Jezus en van de Rabbijnen als 'media' van Tora," *Nederlands Theologisch Tijdschrift* 71, no. 2 (2017): 114–130 and Ronit Nikolsky, "De functie van parabels (*mesjalim*) in de *Tanchuma*," *Nederlands Theologisch Tijdschrift* 71, no. 2 (2017): 151–168; as well as Eric Ottenheijm, Annette Merz, and Marcel Poorthuis, eds., *Parables in Changing Contexts: Interreligious and Cultural Approaches to the Study of Parables* (Leiden: Brill, 2018).

ture, from ancient Near Eastern literature to Agnon. In this context, he discusses two texts from *Seder Eliyahu*,[10] and comes to the general conclusion that its author made use of a literary-rhetorical form of classical midrash but adapted it to his own (generic) purposes. Stern identifies four distinctive traits of the *mashal* in this post-talmudic text: First of all, he points out that, although the context of the parable appears to be exegetical, few features in the parable links it to the verse quoted at the opening. This leads Stern to posit that, unlike classical midrash, *Seder Eliyahu* uses the literary form as an illustrative rather than a rhetorical tool.[11] Related to this illustrative function is a tendency "to extending the narrative through its own logic rather than concentrating it upon a single rhetorical message," which Stern also describes as a "tendency to 'novelization.'"[12] When compared to its precedents in classical midrash, Stern argues, the *mashal* narrative in *Seder Eliyahu* is "less concentrated and increasingly romance-like – more of a story, or a miniature novella."[13] The third aspect Stern describes as especially characteristic of *Seder Eliyahu* – namely, an inconsistency between the *nimshal* and the co-text preceding the *mashal* proper – is probably present in more *meshalim* than the above-mentioned tendency towards novelisation. Finally, and related to the previous aspect, is the puzzling and implausible character of the narrative itself, which elicits the question from the reader: "What was this *mashal* actually about?" The ultimate consequence of such a transformation in the use of the *mashal* is the fact that "narrative and exegesis fail to intersect as they do in classical mashal."[14] It is worth noting at this point that the parables Stern discusses are representative of only part of the parable corpus of *Seder Eliyahu* – namely, of the (formally) exegetical parables.

In this chapter, I will discuss examples from *Seder Eliyahu*'s corpus of 78 parables,[15] focusing both on those characteristic traits described by David Stern and on further aspects that appear to constitute their specificity in contrast to the parables in earlier Rabbinic documents. For this purpose, I will present examples of every type of parable, as introduced in chapter 3: 1) exegetical parables; 2) narrative-recapitulative parables – parables with a biblical narrative (or a scriptural verse) as (part of) their preceding co-text, but which are *not explicitly exeget-*

---

10 See Stern, *Parables*, 211–216.
11 See Stern, *Parables*, 213. It is not evident, however, why an "illustrative" use should exclude a "rhetorical" one.
12 Stern, *Parables*, 213.
13 Stern, *Parables*, 213.
14 Stern, *Parables*, 213.
15 Stern, *Parables*, 216, states that "more than a hundred examples" can be found in *Seder Eliyahu*, which I cannot confirm using Friedmann's edition.

ical, at least not from a formal point of view; 3) meta-exegetical parables – parables told to explain not a scriptural verse, but rather a Rabbinic dictum; and 4) question-answering parables, parables that are told to (purportedly) provide an answer to a rhetorical question.

Delimiting a parable's co-text is no easy task. For heuristic purposes, I propose considering Friedmann's divisions of the text[16] as units of textual meaning that constitute the co-text of a parable (in some cases, of a series parables). With the expression "preamble," I refer to the co-text that precedes a parable. As noted above, the expression "context" denotes a wider textual environment as well as the text's cultural and historical situation.[17]

4.2 The Exegetical *Mashal*'s New Clothes

Seder Eliyahu contains a total of 42 exegetical parables: 36 in *Seder Eliyahu Rabbah*, two in *Seder Eliyahu Zuta*, and four in *Pseudo-Seder Eliyahu Zuta*. Most of them are king parables, but there are cases of narrative parables which do not feature a king and in which the protagonists are a householder (in two cases), an anonymous man (אדם ,אחד), "two/ten men" as a "collective" character, "a servant," "a princess," or "a poor girl."

Characteristic of the exegetical parable is the quotation of part of a scriptural verse or lemma. The lemma may sometimes – if the *mashal* is not the first attempt at explaining its meaning – be preceded by the hermeneutic expression דבר אחר ("another interpretation," lit. "another word/thing"). It is followed by a short comment on it and a narrative that illustrates this comment, though in some cases the comment is not present. After the narrative comes the *nimshal* – an application of the narrative or an explanation of the narrative's exegetical point, of how it illustrates. The table below lists the terminology proposed by three scholars who studied the Rabbinic parable: Arnold Goldberg, David Stern, and Alan Appelbaum:[18]

---

16 For which he, in his turn follows the manuscript's divisions. These include line breaks, but also a dot followed by several blank spaces between two words within a line of text. Friedmann represents this punctuation mark with a *sof pasuq*.
17 On this, see p. 22n118.
18 See Goldberg, "Das schriftauslegende Gleichnis," 146; Stern, *Parables*, 24; and Appelbaum, *The Rabbis' King-Parables*, 66–67.

Table 4.1: The Structure of the Rabbinic Exegetical Parable

Goldberg	Stern	Appelbaum
Lemma	Illustrand	Introductory word/phrase
Formular/ "Konnector des Vergleichs"	Introductory formula *mashal le-*	Marker of comparison
Relat	*Mashal* proper	Secular narrative
Entsprechungsformel		Marker of applicability
Korrelat/Sachhälfte	*Nimshal*	*Nimshal*
	Proof-text	

Alan Appelbaum terms the exegetical parable told immediately after the quotation of a scriptural verse as "direct parable" – that is, a parable that is told directly after the verse or part of the verse has been quoted.[19] Of this type, 21 parables can be identified. The rest of the exegetical parables in *Seder Eliyahu* have a lemma that consists of a quotation and an explicit interpretation preceding the *mashal* narrative.[20] After the *mashal* narrative (referred to as Relat, *mashal* proper or secular narrative), the application of this narrative (referred to as "Korrelat" or *nimshal*[21]) follows, generally introduced by a formula or "marker of applicability." There are, however, variations of this standard form of the exegetical parable, which lack some of the constituting parts – either there is no *nimshal* or the *nimshal* lacks the connecting "marker of applicability" or the characteristic proof-text.

The *nimshal* of exegetical parables in *Seder Eliyahu* takes very different forms. In some cases only the lemma verse, introduced with the formula "for it is said" (שנאמר), is quoted as a confirmation of the interpretation given. The lemma verse can also be quoted and commented upon with an exegetical narrative or with a statement on the end times. In many cases, however, the *nimshal* takes the form of a statement followed by a verse other than the lemma verse – a proof-text. The table below shows the range of *nimshal* types, categorised according to their constituent elements, in the exegetical parables in *Seder Eliyahu*:[22]

---

[19] See Appelbaum, *The Rabbis' King-Parables*, 65.
[20] It should be noted that in some cases, e.g., ER 11, l. 25, the lemma is not preserved in the MS, but has been introduced by Friedmann in his edition of the text.
[21] Unlike the expression *mashal*, the word *nimshal* is not found in the texts of the *meshalim*, but is rather a scholarly coinage.
[22] Here and in the following tables, the page and line numbers indicate the position of the formula *mashlu mashal*. With the expression "biblical narrative" I refer to a narrative based on biblical events or in which reference to the history of Israel is made, but in which no scriptural verses are quoted. With "biblical narrative + proof-text(s)," I refer both a biblical narrative (as just de-

Table 4.2: The *Nimshal* of Exegetical Parables

Elements	Examples
Lemma	ER 6. l. 26ff., ER 11, l. 25ff., ER 34, l. 3ff., EZ 181, l. 8ff.
Illustrand (Lemma + Statement)	ER 4, l. 26ff.
Lemma + Biblical Narrative	ER 34, l. 12ff.
Lemma + Statement	ER 31, l. 27ff., ER 93, l. 20ff.
Lemma and Following Verses + Interpretation	ER 107, l. 16ff.
Eschatological Narrative	ER 5, l. 8ff.
Biblical Narrative + Proof-text(s)	ER 11, l. 5ff., ER 49, l. 7ff., ER 82, l. 27ff., ER 119, l. 5, ER 150, l. 13ff., ER 150, l. 31ff., PsEZ 26, l. 5ff.
Biblical Narrative + Lemma	ER 29, l. 10ff.
Statement + Proof-text(s)	ER 84, l. 30ff., ER 110, l. 17ff., ER 120ff., l. 12ff., ER 155, l. 1ff., ER 160, l. 3ff., EZ 193, l. 8ff., PsEZ 28, l. 3ff., PsEZ 29, l. 16ff.
Statement + Proof-text + Lemma	ER 11, l. 13ff.
Statement + Lemma	ER 12, l. 15ff., ER 70, l. 23ff., ER 91, l. 7ff., ER 91, l. 20ff., ER 113, l. 29ff.
Proof-text	ER 12, l. 30ff., ER 20, l. 2ff., ER 100, l. 6ff., ER 125, l. 5ff.[23]
Mishnah + Statement	ER 100, l. 13ff.
Direct speech + Lemma	ER 143, l. 18ff.
None	ER 117, l. 8ff., ER 137, l. 1ff.

In order to deal with the question of how the exegetical parable operates in *Seder Eliyahu*, it might be useful to have a look at some examples. We can anticipate, however, that for most of these *meshalim*, Stern's claim that *Seder Eliyahu*'s parables are of a non-exegetical character in spite of their apparent exegetical intention is valid. The explanation of an unclear aspect of the verse quoted at the beginning is not itself the primary function of the *mashal*.

In the passage quoted below, two exegetical parables are told as part of the same textual unit in chapter 18:[24]

---

scribed) followed by an unrelated scriptural verse as well as an exegetical narrative – i.e., a biblical narrative which stands in relation to the verse(s) it quotes.

23 As transmitted, the *nimshal* of this parable consists of a single proof-text. Given that the passage has a lacuna, it could be assumed that it was otherwise originally.
24 As Berzbach, "Varieties," points out, this is the longest and structurally one of the most complex chapters in the work.

Happy are the righteous whose faith is such that they trust in their Father who is in heaven, who created the world with wisdom, understanding, knowledge, and insight. Therefore it is said, *They shall be like a tree planted by water, [sending out its roots] by the stream (יובל). [It shall not fear when heat comes, and its leaves shall stay green; in the year of drought it is not anxious, and it does not cease to bear fruit]* etc. (Jer 17:8). And it [Scripture] says, *At that time a gift will be brought (יובל) to the Lord of hosts [from a people tall and smooth, from a people feared near and far, a nation mighty and conquering, whose land the rivers divide, to Mount Zion, the place of the name of the Lord of hosts]* etc. (Isa 18:7). They told a parable: (ER 91, l. 7) What does the matter resemble? It is like a king of flesh and blood, <whose servant> brought him an ephah of wheat as a present (דורון). Had he ground it (טחנה), but not sifted it (ביררה), it would have been an ugly thing. Had he sifted it, but not ground it, it would have been an ugly thing (דבר מגונה). Had he sifted and ground it, but not made out of it fine flour, it would have been a mediocre manner [of giving a present]. But if he had sifted it, ground it, and made fine flour out of it, this would have been a perfect manner. So (כך) it is with the disciples of the wise in this world with respect to the words of Torah. If a man reads Scripture, but does not study Mishnah, this is a reprehensible thing (דבר של גנאי). If he studies Mishnah, but does not read Scripture, this is a reprehensible thing. If he reads Scripture and studies Mishnah, but does not wait upon the disciples of the wise, this is a mediocre manner. But if a man reads Torah, the Prophets, and the Writings, if he studies Mishnah, midrash, halakhot, and aggadot, and waits upon the disciples of the wise, this is the perfect manner. Therefore it is said, *At that time a gift will be brought (יובל) to the Lord of hosts* etc., [that is to say,] to do the will of their Father who is in heaven is like [giving] a gift to a king. | <And it [Scripture] says,> *On the banks, on both sides of the river, there will grow [all kinds of trees for food]* (Ezek 47:12). What is there in this river? There is Torah in it, Scripture, Mishnah, midrash, halakhot, and aggadot, but also good deeds and study of Torah, all of which are drawn from and go out from the Divine Majesty, and flow through Israel and through the disciples of the wise from here and from there, and everything is set in order and put down before them. They told a parable: (ER 91, l. 20) What does the matter resemble? It is like a king of flesh and blood who had his servants and members of his household assembled before him at table. When he saw that they ate and that the food delighted them, that they drunk and that the drink delighted them, he himself proceeded to bring together piles and piles without end before them. So (כך) it is with the disciples of the wise in this world with respect to the words of Torah. When they read Scripture and study Mishnah and it delights them, the Holy One, blessed be He, shows them mercy, rewarding them with wisdom, understanding, knowledge, and insight, as well as good deeds and study of Torah. Therefore it is said, *On [the banks, on both sides of] the river, there will grow <all kinds of trees for food. Their leaves will not wither nor their fruit fail>* etc. What is this olive tree (זית) like? It does not drop [its leaves], neither in the days of sun nor in the days of rain, for it is said, *A Song of Ascents. Happy is everyone who fears the Lord[, who walks in his ways]* (Ps 128:1). You could say that even the strangers and servants who are fearers of heaven are *happy*. If it were <not> so, Scripture should state, Happy the wise, happy their disciples, happy those who teach them, but from the subsequent verse one learns, *You shall eat the fruit of the labour of your hands; you shall be happy* (Ps 128:2). I call heaven and earth to witness that every disciple of the wise who eats of what is his own, enjoys the fruits of his own labour, and does not enjoy the fruits of the congregation's labour at all, he is implied by [the expression] *happy*. And any table which a disciple of the wise does not enjoy is not blessed, for it is said, *There is no remnant (שריד) left after they had eaten[; therefore their prosperity will not endure]* etc. (Job 20:21). And *remnant* means nothing but the disciples of the wise, for it is said, *and among the survivors (שרידים) shall be those whom the Lord calls* (Joel 3:5). (ER 91, l. 4–36)

The co-text preceding the first parable connects an *ashre* statement (a sort of Hebrew beatitude) on the righteous with Jer 17:8, and this verse in its turn with Isa 18:7. The link between these verses appears to be the quoted homograph יובל, though its different meanings are of no explicit interest to the governing voice in the first place. Instead, it takes the second verse as the lemma, as the occasion for a narrative *mashal* that provides a sort of extended parallel to the verse – that is, it retells the verse, phrasing it as a *mashal*. Whereas the verse contains a description of a future landscape, the *mashal* narrative consists of a single event in the past tense and, instead of a second event, a series of conditional statements based on the report of first event: A servant brings the king a measure of wheat. The narrator then proceeds to comment on the different manners in which this very present can be given and the implied effect it can have on him who is receiving it. Even though the narrative does not reveal which of the four manners the servant chooses at the time of giving his present to the king, the *nimshal* suggests that it was the last – namely, the one described as perfect. The *nimshal*, which opens with the "marker of applicability" כך, identifies the way of the disciples of the wise as the perfect manner of approaching Torah. As in the *mashal* proper, in the *nimshal* also four possibilities ranging from the least worthy to the perfect are also described – in this case, approaches to the study of Torah, the fourth corresponding to the perfect manner of giving a measure of wheat as a present. The perfect way to be in the world is described as occupying oneself with reading the three parts of Scripture, studying the four parts of the Rabbinic curriculum, and waiting upon the disciples of the wise. The *mashal* closes with the quotation of the lemma, which is this time explained, again with a comparison: The complete Torah of the disciples of the wise is doing God's will, which is comparable to giving a king a perfect gift.

With respect to the *mashal*'s style, it should be noted that identical or similar expressions connect not only the two verses cited, but also the *mashal* proper and the *nimshal*. In the former we read, "Had he sifted it, but not ground it, it would have been an ugly thing (דבר מגונה)"; the *nimshal* makes use of another form of the same root when it states, "If a man reads Scripture, but does not study Mishnah, this is a reprehensible thing (דבר של גנויי)." The "perfect manner" has the same Hebrew wording, מדה שלימה, in both parts; God is referred to as "Father in heaven" both in the preamble of the parable and in the *nimshal*. On the other hand, there is variation as well. To denote a "present," the biblical expression שי is used in the quoted verse, while the *mashal* and *nimshal* choose two terms that are more characteristic in Rabbinic Hebrew: the expression מנחה and the Greek loanword דורון.

The exegetical intention is more evident in the second parable's preceding co-text or illustrand: Unlike the case of the first lemma, this parable's lemma, Ezek 47:12,[25] is commented upon in an allegorical fashion. The question "What is there in this river?" can be rephrased as "What do this *river* and *all kinds of trees for food* stand for?" The answer is Torah, which is used as an all encompassing term covering "Scripture, Mishnah, midrash, halakhot, and aggadot, but also good deeds and study," a variation on the "perfect manner" of the foregoing *mashal*. The illustrand anticipates that the parable will be about the disciples of the wise, who are those among Israel who occupy themselves with all the components of Torah.

In the *mashal* proper, a king's servants and the members of his household rejoice in food and drink and are rewarded with even more refreshment. With the same formula used for the first parable – "So it is with the disciples of the wise in this world with respect to the words of Torah" – the *nimshal* again focuses on the centrality of Scripture and study of Mishnah in a man's life. The reward for the man who delights in the study of both Scripture and Mishnah is "wisdom, understanding, knowledge, and insight" (a recurrent tetracolon of near-synonyms in *Seder Eliyahu*), but also good deeds and study itself – that is, also Torah, as the wording of the illustrand suggests. Delight in study of Torah is therefore compared with physical delight in food. For this purpose, the text following the *nimshal* also makes rich use of expressions belonging to the semantic fields of food and positive emotions ("fruit" is mentioned four times, "happy" six times – אשריהם is incidentally the word with which the whole passage opens), which are linked to the disciples of the wise (who are themselves mentioned four times).

In both parables, the *mashal* proper is an extremely short narrative. The first parable is actually an incomplete narrative, in that it consists of a single narrated event. Both the speculations of the narrator regarding how the present came into being and the *nimshal* help the reader imagine what it could actually have looked like. But we are not told what the king thinks or says about the gift he eventually gets from his servant, or what he does with it. The second *mashal* is more of a regular narrative, consisting of two narrated events: First, the king's servants and the members of his household rejoice in eating and drinking, and as a consequence, the king generously provides them with more food and drink. In neither narrative is there evidence of the "novelisation" to which Stern refers. Instead, they present an austere, minimal narrative. In both cases, the *nimshal* takes a very standard form: It opens with the marker of applicability כך, followed by a statement in the present tense and the quotation of the lemma verse. In both cases, the relation be-

---

[25] This "river" motif refers back to the "stream" motif of Jer 17:8.

tween *mashal* and *nimshal* is one of analogy.[26] There is, however, neither equivalence between the lemma and the *nimshal* nor similarity between the lemma and the *mashal*, and this is due to the fact that these parables are not inherently exegetical. Rather than explaining verses, these parables associate ideas with the quoted verse or with a word it contains, so that the *mashal* and the *nimshal* together illustrate these ideas, which are themselves independent of the quoted verse. In both parables, the Rabbinic class and its way of life are idealised.

A peculiarity of certain parables in *Seder Eliyahu* is the fact that their *mashal* proper, or secular narrative, contains non-secular material – phraseology that either stems from Scripture or is generally found in other textual Rabbinic contexts. The *nimshal* thus appears to invade the *mashal*, producing a sort of hybridisation of the *mashal* narrative that is very seldom found in the classical Rabbinic *mashal*.[27] A case in point is the following parable from chapter 18, told in the exegetical context of Ezek 47:12:

> *Because the water for them flows from the sanctuary* (Ezek 47:12). Because a light commandment is like a weighty one, and a weighty commandment is like a light one, and both these and those are a remedy (רפואה) for Israel in this world, in the days of the Messiah, and in the world to come. And it [Scripture] says, *Their fruit will be for food, and their leaves for healing (לתרופה)* (Ezek 47:12). To loosen (להתיר) their mouth. When Israel does charity and justice, the Holy One, blessed be He, rejoices in them. This shows that the joy with which He rejoices in them is thousand thousand times for good, is twice as great as theirs, for it is said, *I went down to the nut orchard[, to look at the blossoms of the valley, to see whether the vines had budded, whether the pomegranates were in bloom]* etc. (Song 6:11). What is [there in] this garden? There are four houses in it. So every single sage in Israel who truly has [knowledge of] the words of Torah has wisdom, understanding, knowledge, and insight. They told a parable: (ER 93, l. 20) What does the matter resemble? It is like a king of flesh and blood who came to his house after a long time (לימים ושנים). When he examined his servants he did not examine them with respect to silver, gold, precious stones, and pearls, but asked, So-and-

---

26 See Goldberg, "Das schriftauslegende Gleichnis," 166.
27 Stern, *Parables*, 89, points out that there are certain parables, e.g., ShirR 7:18 and MidTeh 4:11, which explicitly represent what he calls the interpretive act by identifying it with the *qal wachomer*. The two examples he discusses have characters in the narrative utter the phrase ʿ*al ʾachat kamah ve-khamah*. Among the further examples he adduces, a *mashal* in SifDev 26, for example, mentions the sabbatical year in its secular narrative. In yet another context, that of the discussion of Jesus's parable of the Wicked Husbandmen (Mark 12:1–12 and parr.), he states: "In the light of Rabbinic practice, the possibility that Jesus would have used Scripture in reciting a *mashal* cannot be ruled out. The Wicked Husbandmen, however, is the sole parable in the gospels to use and interpret a scriptural proof-text in this way; the only other parable even to allude to Scripture is the parable of the Sower (Mark 4:3–20; Matt. 13:3–23; Luke 8:5–15), and there the verses involved, Isa. 6:9–10, are actually part of the so-called theory of parabolic speech that Jesus proceeds to expound to the disciples." (197)

so, my servant, has he read Scripture and studied Mishnah? They answered, He has read Scripture and studied Mishnah, and has done so more than his fellow. [He asked,] So-and-so, has he repented? They answered, He has repented and done so more than his fellow. At once the king praised [this servant] and left everyone [else].[28] Hence it is said, *I went down to the nut orchard* etc.: these are good deeds and study of Torah, which the wise in Torah look forward to. Whence does everything come? From the mouth of the Holy One, blessed be He, whose hands are stretched to the repentant. Everything is His and everything is the work of His hands. And the Holy One, blessed be He, does not leave anything in the world unrevealed to Israel, for it is said, *The friendship of the Lord is for those who fear him[, and he makes his covenant known to them]* etc. (Ps 25:14). *Surely the Lord God does nothing[, without revealing his secret to his servants the prophets]* etc. (Amos 3:7). (ER 93, l. 12–28)

The king examines his subjects according to their behaviour with respect to the study of Torah, explicitly *not* according to the "secular" attributes or behaviour which a king in a *mashal* would normally take as his criterion in testing his servants, his sons, or the members of his household. The servants in this *mashal* are exemplary not only in that they study Scripture and Mishnah, but also in their repenting. In a chapter in which he analyses the figure of God, Alan Appelbaum objects to the notion that the king in king parables is a stand-in for God, arguing that he is rather compared to God. Stern and others, on the other hand, understand the king and God as the same character, as "superimposed on one another."[29] Such a superimposition is made more evident in texts such as the example quoted above, where the king, like God (from a Rabbinic point of view), is concerned with placing the study of Torah at the centre of everyday life.

Such phraseology, which can be identified as belonging to the text that usually surrounds the *mashal* narrative, not only indicates that the mortal kings of Rabbinic parables are metaphors for God, but that the *mashal* genre has evolved into a new way of speaking about God and his creatures. The same phenomenon can also be ascertained in the following example:

The God of glory thunders[, the Lord, over mighty waters] (Ps 29:3). For I poured words of Torah for your sake like milk and oil passed silently from one vessel to another. Therefore it is said, *the God of glory thunders[, the Lord, over mighty waters. The voice of the Lord is powerful; the voice of the Lord is full of majesty* (Ps 29:4). They told a parable: (ER 12, l. 15) What does the matter resemble? It is like a king of flesh and blood who had distinguished sons. Some of them were masters of Torah; some of them masters of Mishnah, [and] some of

---

28 The expression מודה ועוזב, seldom attested in Rabbinic literature, but more often in piyyutim, stems from Prov 28:13 – "one who confesses and forsakes them [his transgressions] will obtain mercy." Following Leon Nemoy's interpretation, Braude and Kapstein, *Tanna děbe Eliyyahu*, 248, render the text as follows: "Forthwith the king is satisfied [that all his servants are men of high moral worth], and cuts short his inspection."
29 Appelbaum, *The Rabbis' King-Parables*, 101. See also Stern, *Parables*, 19.

them masters in the give-and-take [of trade]. He married another woman who was poor and had sons by her. He sent them [to learn] Scripture, Mishnah, and proper conduct (lit. "the way of the earth"). He would sit and hope, saying to them, When are you to become like my distinguished sons? After some time he went to them. No Scripture was in their hands, no Mishnah was in their hands, no proper conduct was in their hands. So he would sit down before them, clapping his hands [in grief] and saying, The houses I built for these, what [are they] for? The fields I bought for these, what [are they] for? The vineyards I planted for these, what [are they] for? So it is with Israel who resemble them in this world before our Father who is in heaven, whenever there are no words of Torah in them. Hence it is said, *The voice of the Lord is powerful … The voice of the Lord breaks the cedars* (Ps 29:4–5). (ER 12, l. 13–28)

In the passage above, God's voice and the governing voice appear to take turns in a joint interpretation of verses from Ps 29. God takes the liquid image of "mighty waters" in Ps 29:3 as a point of departure for a comparison of the giving of Torah with the gentle movement of passing milk and oil from one vessel to another – an image that obliterates the thunderous aspect of God's voice in the same verse. The subsequent *mashal* seems to follow the same line of thought, providing an explanation of Ps 29:4, where the voice of the Lord is described as both "powerful" (בכוח) and "full of majesty" (בהדר). Braude and Kapstein suggest that the author of *Seder Eliyahu* appears to have intentionally read חצר instead of הדר, hence their suggested translation "gentle."[30] This might be correct, and in fact, the king in the *mashal* does behave "gently." However, when the governing voice of *Seder Eliyahu* suggests an alternative spelling (and reading) of the Masoretic Text for the sake of his interpretation, this is generally indicated.[31]

But to return to the problem of discourse interference,[32] in the *mashal* proper, the mortal king's sons by his first wife are described as masters of Torah (in this context, Scripture or Written Torah), of Mishnah (Oral Torah), and as experienced businessmen. His sons by his second wife, herself described as poor, are sent in vain to learn Scripture, Mishnah, and proper conduct (instead of trade, though the triad is a parallel to the first one). These are not the usual activities of *mashal* princes, but rather projections of Rabbinic ideals onto the narrative discourse of the *mashal* proper. In his disappointment, the king asks them and himself what all his efforts for their sake have been for, but obtains no answer, for the *mashal* comes to an end with the three questions he poses. The *nimshal* explains that Is-

---

30 See Braude and Kapstein, *Tanna děbe Eliyyahu*, 64n59.
31 Anteposing such a reading, the formula "Do not read X, but Y" (אל תקרא ... אלא). In this case, it could be argued that the governing voice only implicitly reads הדר as חצר, so that God's voice is interpreted as meaning both "dignified, lordly, sublime," and "gentle."
32 On this concept, see p. 120n202.

rael resemble the sons who let the king down, which is why God's once-gentle voice does not remain unaffected, but shows its indignation by breaking cedars.[33]

Goldberg points out that Rabbinic parables can be classified according to their respective co-texts and functions, and observes:

> Es gibt Gleichnisse, die sind dem Kotext nach in einer bestimmten Situation von einer bestimmten Person vorgetragen, um eine Meinung zu erhellen, einem Argument Gewicht zu geben, um einen Gesprächspartner oder Kontrahenten mit diesen rhetorischen Mitteln zu überführen.[34]

Even though, as he concedes, all parables are in essence rhetorical, it is these particular parables that are aptly called *rhetorical parables*. Furthermore, he argues that this type of parable should be distinguished from the exegetical:

> Im Unterschied hierzu sei das Schriftauslegende Gleichnis bestimmt als eines, das allein zum Zweck der Schriftauslegung gebildet und vorgetragen wurde. Der Kotext is in der Regel nicht dialogisch, es gibt ja keinen zu überführenden Gesprächskontrahenten, der namentlich genannt wäre (die Ausnahme kann die Regel bestätigen), zu überzeugende Leser oder ursprüngliche Hörer werden nicht direkt angesprochen, der Ausgangspunkt im Kotext ist keine Gesprächssituation, sondern, sofern überhaupt auszumachen, eine Vortragssituation, der Vortrag der Schriftauslegung. Am Anfang steht ein Schriftvers, den es in irgendeiner Weise zu erklären gilt, und eines der Mittel der Erklärung ist das Gleichnis. Der Kotext, hier der Schriftvers, bestimmt die Form. Die übergeordnete Form des Gleichnisses ist hier "Mi-

---

33 Further examples of this hybridisation include ER 5, l. 8ff. (a scriptural verse is quoted in the *mashal* narrative); ER 6, l. 26 (the expression "angel of death" is used in the *mashal* narrative); ER 9, l. 21ff. (the king is said to act with "wisdom and understanding," a pair of near-synonyms the governing voice habitually makes use of); ER 12, l. 15ff. (just as in the *mashal* discussed above, a king sends his sons to learn Scripture, Mishnah, and proper conduct); ER 25, l. 4ff. (the two protagonists of the *mashal* are disciples of the wise); ER 69, l. 1ff. (the temporal expression for the duration of a feast in "the eight days of the feast" could be an allusion to the Feast of Tabernacles), ER 69, l. 25ff. (a king's sons and servants are described as being smart [or lame!], but also mute, deaf, or blind, which may be an allusion to Isa 42:18, while some others possess knowledge of Scripture, of Mishnah, or experience in the give-and-take of trade); ER 71, l. 2ff. (a king's servant teaches the king's sons "good deeds"); ER 84, l. 30ff. (the king learns from the elders of his kingdom "a word of wisdom, and a word of understanding, a word of knowledge, and a word of discernment," characteristic tetracolon used by the governing voice in non-narrative discourse); EZ 193, l. 8ff. (the king in the parable poses a rhetorical question, which he answers by quoting Exod 24:17).
34 Goldberg, "Das schriftauslegende Gleichnis," 141 ("There are parables which, in view of their co-text, are delivered by a certain person to illustrate an opinion, to reinforce an argument, to convince an opponent with these rhetorical means").

drasch", die Auslegung des Schriftverses, so wie die übergeordnete Form des rhetorischen Gleichnisses (z. B.) der Dialog oder die Anekdote ist.³⁵

A number of parables in *Seder Eliyahu* do appear within dialogues.³⁶ They are told by the anonymous rabbi to diverse dialogue partners in the so-called first-person narratives³⁷ and could therefore be considered rhetorical, following Goldberg, in the narrow sense of the term. In four cases, the co-text of these parables is not only conversational, but at the same time exegetical. The second of the consecutive parables quoted below illustrates how, in the context of a polemical dialogue, a scriptural verse is interpreted with the aid of a *mashal*, thus combining two functions which, in Goldberg's view, usually crystallise in different forms:

> I was once walking through the greatest city of the world, when there was a roundup. They seized me and brought me to the king's palace. On seeing spread couches, silver vessels, and gold vessels set out, I said, *O Lord, you God of vengeance, you God of vengeance, shine forth!* (Ps 94:1). A Parsee priest came to me and asked, Are you scholar (lit. "scribe," סופר)? I answered, Yes (lit. "what one is"). He said, If you reply to one thing I say <to you>, you will leave in peace. I answered, Speak. He said, You say fire is not a divinity. Why is then written in your Torah, *fire eternal* (Lev 6:6=Engl. 6:13)? I replied to him, My son, When our fathers stood at Mount Sinai to receive upon them the Torah, they did not see the image of a human being nor the image of any creature nor the image of a soul created by the Holy One, blessed be He, on the face of the earth, for it is said, *Take care and watch yourselves closely, for you saw no form on the day [that the Lord spoke to you at Horeb out of the fire]* (Deut 4:15), but the one God, *He is God of gods and Lord of lords* (Deut 10:17), whose kingdom endures in heaven and on earth, and in the uppermost heaven of heavens. And [yet] you say fire is a divinity! [Fire] is only like a rod, given to be used on human beings on earth. They told a parable: (ER 6, l. 20) What does the matter resemble? It is like a king of flesh and blood who took a lash and hung it up inside his house. He spoke to his children, to his servants, and members of his household, With this I [may] strike you, I [may] smite you, and I [may] kill you, so that they would then repent. Hence it is said, *fire eternal*. And it [Scripture] says, *For by fire will the Lord execute judgement* (Isa 66:16). You may [think you can] refute me quoting (lit. " and say

---

35 Goldberg, "Das schriftauslegende Gleichnis," 141 ("Unlike this the exegetical parable should be defined as one which is composed and delivered only for the sake of scriptural interpretation. The co-text is usually not dialogical, there is no named dialogue opponent (the exception confirms the rule), readers to be convinced, or original listeners that are directly addressed, the departure point in the co-text is no dialogue situation, but, if discernible at all, one of exposition, the exposition of scriptural interpretation. At the beginning there is a scriptural verse, which in one way or another is to be explained, and the parable is one of the means used for the explanation. The co-text, here the scriptural verse, determines the form. The superordinate form of the parable is in this case 'midrash,' the interpretation of the scriptural verse, just as the superordinate form of the rhetorical parable is the dialogue or the anecdote").
36 See ER 6, l. 20ff.; ER 6, l. 26ff.; ER 70, l. 23ff.; ER 71, l. 2ff.; and ER 82, l. 27ff.
37 For a discussion of first-person narratives, see chapter 5.

to me"), *For the Lord your God is a devouring fire* (Deut 4:24). However, they told a parable: (ER 6, l. 26) What does the matter resemble? It is like a king of flesh and blood whose <sons>, servants, and members of his household would not behave properly. He spoke to his sons, to his servants, and to the members of his household, A bear in ambush am I to you, a lion am I to you, the angel of death am I to you because of your ways. Hence it is said, *For the Lord your God is a devouring fire* (Deut 4:24). (ER 5, l. 24–28, ER 6, l. 13–29)

The parables are told to a Zoroastrian priest in the context of a polemical dialogue. He promises to let the Jew who narrates the encounter go[38] if he gives a satisfactory answer to certain questions he is about to confront him with. The Jew replies to the second and last of these questions with the help of rhetorical parables. The priest's question is an implied polemical statement: How can Jews affirm that fire is not a god (or even that their own God is not fire) when their own Scriptures assert the contrary? The verse the priest quotes, Lev 6:6, refers in its scriptural context to instructions for sacrifices, specifically to those concerning burnt offerings. Conversely, it is the verses the Jew himself brings into the dialogue that associate God rather than a sacrifice with fire, the most problematic of which is clearly Deut 4:24. As in the first parable, fire is explained as a metaphor for the fear-inspiring nature of God. Both *mashal* narratives basically consist of the report of a menacing speech by the king addressed to his children, his servants, and the members of his household. In both cases, the *nimshal* consists of the repetition of the lemma – the verse the parable purports to explain.

4.3 Narrative-Recapitulative Parables

A small subgroup of nine parables of *Seder Eliyahu* can be identified, using Jacob Neusner's terminology, as narrative-recapitulative parables.[39] The narrative that is recapitulated can be an extremely concise one – in fact, it can be as compact as "My son, it is their [the nations'] merit that Israel was set apart [by God] from among them" (EZ 174, l. 3). But they can also be more detailed, as in the first example below, in which the *mashal* rephrases an exegetical narrative.[40]

As already explained in chapter 3, the narrative-recapitulative *mashal* is not explicitly exegetical – it does not explain an expression within a scriptural verse by quoting the verse and explaining its meaning with a brief commentary and a *mashal* narrative. Rather, it rephrases or recapitulates an entire narrative, which

---

38 Elsewhere he is addressed as "rabbi."
39 See Neusner, *Precedent*, 217–218.
40 Other examples include ER 17, l. 31ff.; ER 149, l. 27ff.; and EZ 180, l. 27ff.

can be completely devoid of scriptural quotation, as is the case in five parables of this type.⁴¹ However, wherever the rephrased narrative is an exegetical one, the exegetical agenda can be even more evident than in exegetical parables proper.

Unlike the exegetical parables, the narrative-recapitulative parables make sparse use of the conspicuous topics and phraseology usually found in *Seder Eliyahu*'s discourse surrounding parables as well as in certain exegetical parables, which produces the sort of interference described previously. The co-text immediately preceding the *mashal* proper of narrative-recapitulative parables⁴² may include a Mishnah quotation or a *mikan amru* statement, and Moses may reason there with a *qal wa-chomer* inference, but the characteristic Rabbinic curriculum is not mentioned, nor are the disciples of the wise exalted in these parables, nor does their *mashal* proper contain any of the external elements of Rabbinic discourse.⁴³

These parables deal primarily with stories about biblical themes – with Moses, but also with Egypt, with the peoples of the world, or with Israel as collective narrative agents,⁴⁴ or with David, as in the following passage:

> *[Pour out your heart like water] before the presence of the Lord!* (Lam 2:19). What does Scripture teach? The mercies of the Holy One, blessed be He, are many for Israel, both for the wicked among them and for the righteous among them. And whence [do we infer this]? You should know that it is so. Go and learn from David, king of Israel. Because of the love with which He loved him and the joy with which He rejoiced in him, He let words be spoken fluently to him by Nathan the prophet. For it is said, *But that same night [the word of the Lord came to Nathan]* etc. *Go and tell my servant David[: Thus says the Lord: Are you the one to build me a house to live in?]* etc. *I have not lived [in a house since the day I brought up the people of Israel from Egypt to this day, but I have been moving about in a tent and a tabernacle]* etc. (2 Sam 7:4–6). From here they said: Whoever supports his friend even with a piece of bread with salt, or even with salad to dip,⁴⁵ or even with dates, or even with shrivelled olives, even if he who supports [his friend] had a hundred banquets every day like the banquet of Solomon's times, he [who is supported] should be grateful in his presence. Therefore it is said, *I have not lived in a house* etc. So when David heard [God], he prostrated the whole length of his body on the ground, then went and sat before the Presence, saying, My Father, who art in heaven, may Your great name be blessed for ever and ever and ever

---

41 See ER 40, l. 15ff.; ER 114, l. 3ff.; EZ 174, l. 3ff.; EZ 178, l. 11ff.; and PsEZ 36, l. 13ff.
42 A co-text which, in exegetical parables, is more clearly an illustrand.
43 As illustrated below, the *mashal* proper of these parables may contain scriptural material.
44 This expression is used by Uri Margolin, "Telling in the Plural: From Grammar to Ideology," *Poetics Today* 21 (2000): 592, who defines "a collective narrative agent" as "a group of two or more individuals represented as a singular higher oder entity or agent, a collective individual so to speak, with global properties or actions"; collective narratives are correspondingly narratives "whose main protagonist is a collectivity of some kind."
45 According to Maʾagarim, the phrase טובל ירק occurs only in *Seder Eliyahu*.

and may You find contentment in Israel Your servants in all the places of their dwellings, for You magnified us, You raised us, You hallowed us, You extolled us, You bound [on] us a crown with the words of Torah from one end of the world to the other. The Torah I carried out (lit. "did"), I only carried out with what is Yours; the deeds of love I did, I only did with what is Yours; and as a reward for the little Torah I did in Your presence I was given this world, the days of the Messiah, and the world to come, for it is said, *Then King David went in and sat before the Lord[, and said, Who am I, O Lord God, and what is my house, that you have brought me thus far?]* etc. (2 Sam 7:18). They told a parable: (ER 89, l. 32) What does the matter resemble? It is like a king of flesh and blood who had a servant, whom he loved with a perfect love. Everyday they would bring him into his presence and he would show him his esteem in front of all the [other] servants. The servant returned [once] to the king's presence and said, My lord king, what work have I done and which contentment have you found in me that you show me all this esteem in front of all your servants? Therefore it is said, *Then King David went in [and said, Who am I, O Lord God, and what is my house, that you have brought me thus far (עד-הלום)?]* etc. And further on it [Scripture] says, *Come here (הלום), all you leaders of the people* etc. (1 Sam 14:38). And it [Scripture] says, *Come no closer (הלום)* (Exod 3:5). Indeed it [Scripture] says, *thus far (עד-הלום)*, [but] what does *thus far* mean (lit. "is")? <It means "kingdom.">[46] And you should know that it is so. Because of all the good deeds which the Holy One, blessed be He, found <in David>, He will sit him to the right of the Presence, for it is said, *The Lord says to my lord[, Sit at my right hand until I make your enemies your footstool]* etc. (Ps 110:1). How so? Whenever a man does a little Torah for Your sake, You set aside his reward for him [thus multiplying it] a thousand thousand times for good, but no creature knows [what that reward is]. Whenever a man does a little charity and deeds of love for Your sake, You double his reward a thousand thousand times for good, for it is said, *And yet this was a small thing [in your eyes, O Lord God]* etc. (2 Sam 7:19) This is the world to come, where there is no death ever, not ever, and ever; *and this is the instruction of man (תורת האדם)* (2 Sam 7:19), for he does a little Torah for Your sake, my Lord God. And yet something else he said before Him, <*And what more can David say to you?*>[47] etc. (2 Sam 7:20). Happy is he who knows in his heart who he is with respect to his Father who is in heaven and all his deeds are [done] with faith in his Father who is in heaven. Happy is he who fears heaven privately (lit. "secretly") and relies on Him who holds a shield[48] in His hand, for it is said, *my God, my rock, in whom I take refuge[, my shield and the horn of my salvation, my stronghold and my refuge]* (2 Sam 22:3). For indeed we find in David that, although chastisements came over him, he relied for his deeds on Him who holds a shield in His hand, for it is said, *my God, my rock, in whom I take refuge* etc. *I call upon the Lord, who is worthy to be praised* etc. *for the waves [of death] encompassed me* etc. *in my distress I called upon the Lord* etc. (2 Sam 22:3–5.7). (ER 89, l. 18–ER 90, l. 20)

---

46 This interpretation, added by Friedmann, is transmitted in BerR 65:6, where the expression הלום in Exod 3:5 is interpreted as ואין הלום אלא מלכות, and 2 Sam 7:18 is quoted as a proof-text.
47 Friedmann emends the MS reading מהו ויוסף עוד דוד to the reading of the MT וּמַה־יּוֹסִיף דָּוִד עוֹד לְדַבֵּר.
48 This is the only record in Maʾagarim of the hendiadys מגן ותריס.

4.3 Narrative-Recapitulative Parables — 149

This passage contains a short *mashal* narrative framed by an exegetical narrative whose broad scriptural hypotext is 2 Sam 7, the account of Nathan's prophecy about God's choice of David as the beginning of a royal dynasty and David's prayer following the prophecy. What the exegetical narrative attempts to explain is condensed in a *mikan amru* statement according to which, following the example set by God, one is to be grateful even for a small token of generosity from someone else. God's gratitude for David's minimal good deeds is expressed in his choice of David and his descendants as his house and, in a concrete sense, as those who would build God's house in the land of Israel. David's gratitude towards God is expressed in the prayer with which he both acknowledges God's choice and shows that he is bewildered about the reasons for this choice.

Turning to the *mashal* narrative itself, it relates how a servant is openly singled out by the king as his favourite and how he comes to ask the king about the reasons for this choice. The narrative is immediately preceded by a passage of the exegetical narrative in which David addresses God in prayer, hinting at the question he poses in 2 Sam 7:18 by quoting only the first part of the verse that contains the question – "Who am I, O Lord God, and what is my house, that you have brought me thus far?" – but not quoting the question itself. Instead, the *mashal* has the king's servant formulate a parallel question to which not the king, but the continuation of the exegetical narrative – which functions as a *nimshal* – gives an answer. The *nimshal* opens with the same verse that precedes the *mashal* proper and is associated with two other verses that contain the expression הלום, which is understood – as Friedmann, following the reading of BerR 65:6 suggests – as meaning "kingdom." Even though what David did can be regarded as "little Torah" or as "a small thing," a reminder of the piece of bread in the *mikan amru* statement, God's reward for David – allowing him to become king of Israel and his descendant Solomon to build the Temple – is ineffably generous. The expression "a thousand thousand times" is a human attempt at describing this magnanimity, but as the governing voice explains, "no creature knows" what this reward is like – not even he who would become king of Israel knows, and this is why he is as perplexed in the exegetical narrative as the servant in the *mashal*.

The passage reflects on the inability of human beings to fathom mercy as one of God's attributes. For this purpose, *Seder Eliyahu* resorts to an exegetical narrative about David, at the hermeneutic nucleus of which is the adverb הלום. The manuscript of *Seder Eliyahu* does not transmit an explicit interpretation of the word in terms of "kingdom," as is the case with *Bereshit Rabbah*. Even though it is likely – as Friedmann suggests with the reading "It means 'kingdom'" – that this was the interpretation the author of *Seder Eliyahu* sought to transmit, it is also possible that he chose to leave out the explanation of the amoraic midrash and let his late midrashic audience understand הלום as a more general reward for the ordinary righteous people of his time.

Both the text preceding the *mashal* and that following it, as is the case with exegetical narratives generally in *Seder Eliyahu*, are not smooth texts. Due to their nature as composite texts, the language is inhomogeneous, alternating Rabbinic Hebrew with biblical Hebrew and narrative with commentary. In this textuality, the *mashal* narrative can be seen as the sole passage containing entirely uniform language; even if it does not explain much, it clearly relates that a servant was chosen from among others and that his reaction to this was bewildered gratitude. Still, even in this type of parable, the traditionally plain style of the *mashal* is nuanced in *Seder Eliyahu* through the interaction of "external" phraseology with the traditional, secular material of the *mashal* proper. In the next example, a scriptural quotation gives the *mashal* proper its special nuance:

> I was once travelling from one place to another when I came upon an old man. He said to me, Rabbi, why did the Holy One, blessed be He, divide His world between two nations, between two kingdoms? I answered him, My son, had the entire world been in the hand of one [nation], Sennacherib, king of Assyria, and Nebuchadnezzar, king of Babylon, would have proceeded to do their will. The Holy One, blessed be He, divided His world between two nations, between two peoples, but in order to protect Israel. They told a parable: (ER 114, l. 3) What does the matter resemble? It is like a schoolteacher's pupils, whose teacher used to take care that they would not go out and drown in the river, – so that they were like those who came up from Egypt (כעולי מצרים), for it is said, *Thus says the Lord: See, waters are rising (עולים) out of the north* etc. (Jer 47:2), that they would not go out and beat each other, that the sun would not smite them.[49] And why all this? In order to sanctify His great name. For it is said, *For the Lord is our judge, the Lord is our ruler[, the Lord is our king; he will save us]* etc. (Isa 33:22). And it [Scripture] says, *You shall eat in plenty and be satisfied[, and praise the name of the Lord your God, who has dealt wondrously with you. And my people shall never again be put to shame]* (Joel 2:26). There is no satisfaction apart from the words of Torah, for it is said, *The righteous have enough to satisfy their appetite[, but the belly of the wicked is empty]* etc. (Prov 13:25). Therefore it is said, *You shall eat in plenty and be satisfied, and praise the name of the Lord your God, who has dealt wondrously (להפליא) with you* (Joel 2:26). To distinguish (להפליא) between the deeds of the righteous and the deeds of the wicked, between the reward (<מתן> שכרן) of the righteous in the Garden of Eden and the reward (מתן פורענות) of the wicked in Gehenna, for each and every man who comes to the world is someone else's reward (לפי שכל אחד ואחד לפי שכרו בא בעולם). The Holy One, blessed be He, did not bring about that Abraham came into the world but as a reward for Shem, for he prophesied for four hundred years about the lands of the world but they would not heed him (lit. "accept from him"). The Holy One, blessed be He, did not bring about that the kingdom of Greece came into the world but as a reward for Japheth, for he covered his father's nakedness. The Holy One, blessed be He, did not bring about that the kingdom of Rome came into the world

---

49 Friedmann puts the phrase ויהיו כעולי מצרים. שנאמר כה אמר ה' הנה מים עולים מצפון וג' in brackets and moves it to the close of the *mashal*, after כדי שלא תכה אותן חמה.

but as a reward for Esau, for He wept and sighed because Isaac had blessed Jacob. The Holy One, blessed be He, did not bring about that the kingdom of Media came into the world but as a reward for Cyrus, for He wept and sighed when the nations destroyed the Temple. The Holy One, blessed be He, did not bring about that Sennacherib came into the world but as a reward for Asshur, for Asshur was a righteous man and was the counsellor (בן עצתו) of Abraham our father. And the Holy One, blessed be He, did not bring about that <Nebuchadnezzar came> into the world but as a reward for Merodach,[50] for he used to honour our Father in heaven. The Holy One, blessed be He, did not bring about that Haman came into the world but as a reward for Agag, for He wept and sighed when he was kept in prison. He said, Woe is me, for my seed might perish for ever! Therefore it is said, *And my people shall never be put to shame (יבושו)* (Joel 2:26). (ER 113, l. 34–ER 115, l. 5)

In this case, the *mashal* recapitulates not an exegetical narrative, but rather a narrative on a biblical theme, which is alluded to in the question an old man poses to the anonymous, wandering rabbi and the answer the rabbi gives. This is not a narrative about individuals set in a particular moment the history of Israel, but rather a macro-narrative resulting from the abstraction of several scriptural narratives that make up an important part of Israel's history. The content of this narrative can be paraphrased as follows: God divided His world between two kingdoms to protect Israel by preventing Sennacherib and Nebuchadnezzar from taking hold of the entire world – of the whole of the people of Israel in the land of Israel in biblical times.[51] The use of the periphrastic verb form היה משמרן in the *mashal* narrative might correspond to the recurrent events of the macro-narrative it reformulates.

With respect to the succinct *mashal* narrative, it should be noted that, although Friedmann moves the phrase ויהיו כעולי מצרים and the biblical quotation of Jer 47:2 to the close of the *mashal* proper, the biblical interference may have been intended as it is found in the MS reading and in the translation above. In this sense, instead of interpreting ויהיו כעולי מצרים as "those who had come under the *yoke* of Egypt," as Braude and Kapstein suggest,[52] a more literal reading makes sense as well – just as "those who *came up* from Egypt" did not drown in the Red Sea, so the schoolchildren do not drown in the nameless river.

If the question "And why all this?" and its answer belong to the *mashal* proper, then the *nimshal* consists of the quotation of two scriptural verses whose *unquoted parts* echo the *mashal* proper: Whereas Isa 33:22 appears to rephrase the propositional content of the first part of the *mashal* proper, namely "the teacher protects

---

50 The MS reads שלאויל מרודך, but Friedmann puts the first part of the name between brackets.
51 Even though the names of the kings are given here, this is one of several recurring narratives in *Seder Eliyahu* which depicts collective characters instead of individual ones.
52 See Braude and Kapstein, *Tanna děbe Eliyyahu*, 288n17.

his pupils" with "He will save us," Joel 2:26 confirms the wording of the answer "To sanctify His great name" with *You shall ... praise the name of the Lord your God*.

The text continues by quoting Joel 2:26 in its entirety and focusing on the expression להפליא – which, in the sense of "wondrously", might be said to refer back to "those who came up from Egypt," given that the crossing of the Red Sea is generally depicted as a wonder. This expression is explained as meaning "to distinguish," thus opening a digression on the distinction made between the righteous and the wicked. Seven micro-narratives with exactly the same structure but dissimilar characters illustrate the statement "each and every man comes into the world as a reward for someone else." Two of these, on Sennacherib and Nebuchadnezzar, refer back to the preamble of the *mashal*.

The passages preceding and following the *mashal* narrative are both challenging, highly elliptical pieces of literature that rely heavily on other Rabbinic and scriptural sources; only the reader who knows these will understand which kingdoms are meant by the "two kingdoms" in the preamble, or why Asshur is depicted in a positive light. By contrast, and in spite of making use of external elements, the *mashal* proper, with its unambitious character, is the one soothing moment in an otherwise difficult reading experience.

Less challenging is the text that precedes the following example from *Seder Eliyahu Zuta*. Conversely, its *mashal* narrative is a more sophisticated, or, in Stern's words, a more "romance-like" one:

> [Concerning] the first forty days that Moses was up on Mount Sinai to bring the Torah to his people [it can be argued:] were it not for [His] kindness, the Torah would not have been given to Israel. They told a parable: (EZ 178, l. 12) What does the matter resemble? It is like a king of flesh and blood who married a woman, whom he loved with a perfect love (אהבה גמורה). He sent for and was brought a man who would be a messenger between him and her. He showed him [the messenger] all his bridal chambers, all his rooms, and all his private rooms. He said to him, Go and say to that woman [that I say], I do not need you at all, but make me a small bridal chamber, so that I come and dwell with you. So will my servants, and the members of my household know that I love you with a perfect love. While the king was occupied with the measures of the bridal chambers and ordering his messenger to send plenty of gifts to his wife, they came and told him, Your wife has been unfaithful with another. At once the king left all he had in his hands, and the messenger was thrust out and went out terrified from the king's presence, for it is said, *While the king was on his couch[, my nard gave forth its fragrance]* (Song 1:12). (EZ 178, l. 11–20)

This parable is a good example of Stern's claim that the parables of *Seder Eliyahu* show a "tendency to extending the narrative through [their] own logic rather than concentrating it upon a single rhetorical message."[53] The short narrative on the

---

53 Stern, *Parables*, 213.

Mosaic covenant is retold with much more detail in the *mashal* narrative, which in a sense replaces its biblical counterpart. The brief *nimshal*, a scriptural verse quoted in part, alludes to the moment before the crisis in the *mashal* proper (or euphemistically to the wife's and Israel's transgression)[54]; it does not explain the point of the entire narrative or its parts.

Ever since Zunz pointed it out, it has been acknowledged that the structure and language of *Pseudo-Seder Eliyahu Zuta* are clearly different from those of *Seder Eliyahu Rabbah* and *Seder Eliyahu Zuta*. This is also true with respect to its parables. The passage quoted below – a parable and its immediate co-texts – is part of a *petichah* by R. Eliezer on the light created by God on the first day, which was hidden on the third day and put aside for Israel's exclusive use:

> The Holy One, blessed be He, and the righteous will be in the Garden of Eden, [the latter] will bow <there> and they will be seated there. And the Holy One, blessed be He, will be seated at the head of the righteous, and will bring the light that He had hidden for the righteous, increasing its radiance three hundred and forty-five times. They will say before Him, Master of the universe, we have longed for this light, for it is said, *My soul thirsts for God, for the living God. When shall I come and behold the face of God?* (Ps 42:3). He will reply, You now see My face. They will say before Him, Master of the universe, You shine for us with Your light, what is this darkness for? He replied to them, It is for the children of Esau and of Ishmael, for it is said, *For darkness shall cover the earth, and thick darkness the peoples; but the Lord will arise upon you, and his glory will appear over you* (Isa 60:2). And the Holy One, blessed be He, will speak to Israel,[55] My children, accept from Me now the cup of consolation. They will answer, Master of the universe, You were angry at us, and You drew us out of Your house, You banished us to be among the nations of the world<, so that we were like a condemned vessel for the nations of the world.> Now You come to us to be reconciled? He replied to them, I shall tell you a parable: (PsEZ 36, l. 13) What does the matter resemble? It is like a man who married his niece (lit. "sister's daughter"). He became angry at her and drew her out of his house. After some days he came to be reconciled with her. She said <to him>, You were angry at me and drew me out of your house. Now you come <to me> to be reconciled with me? He replied <to her>, <You are> my niece, you might have thought (lit. "said in your heart") <that after the day you left my house another woman entered it. By your life>,[56] neither have I entered it [ever since]. Thus spoke the Holy One, blessed be He, to Israel, My children, from the day that I destroyed My house below, I have not gone up and dwelt in My house above, but have sat<, in dew and in rain>. And if you do not believe Me, put your hands on My head <and you will feel the dew on it. Were it not written in Scripture, it would be impossible to utter it,> for it is said, *for my head is wet with dew, my locks with the drops of the night* (Song 5:2). And the Holy One, blessed be He, will clothe Zion in her strength (עוזה) on account of the words, *The Lord is my strength* (עזי) *and my might* (Exod 15:2), which Israel said at the [Red] Sea. <Whence [do we infer that] that the Holy One, blessed be He, will clothe

---

54 See Friedmann, *Seder Eliahu*, 178n2.
55 Friedmann emends the *editio princeps* reading להן to לך.
56 Here Friedmann follows the reading of MS Parma 1240.

Zion in her strength?> From the verse, *Awake, awake, put on your strength, O Zion!* (Isa 62:1). (PsEZ 36, l. 3–24)

The text preceding the *mashal* proper is a sort of eschatological narrative that depicts God conversing with Israel in the garden of Eden and offering them a reconciliation. Israel's reproachful reply to this offer is rephrased by God himself in a *mashal* he introduces with the rare formula "I shall tell you a parable" (אמשול לך משל), a formula *Seder Eliyahu Rabbah* uses on only one occasion.[57] The first part of the *mashal* narrative rephrases this reproach in the niece's speech. The husband's speech anticipates God's argument in His *nimshal*: Just as the former refrains from entering the house from which he has drawn out his wife, so God refrains from dwelling in His house during Israel's exile. The woman's and Israel's banishment are for her husband and God, respectively, a time of grief. The relation between the *mashal* and the *nimshal* is one of analogy. Before the governing voice lets the voice of R. Eliezer take over again to close the *petichah*, God as the narrator of the *mashal* emphasises his own anthropomorphic depiction one last time by offering to let Israel feel his wet head as evidence of his having dwelt out of doors. As is the case in many other passages in *Seder Eliyahu*, it is not possible here to determine who actually utters the proof-text "for my head is wet with dew, my locks with the drops of the night" – whether it is God or R. Eliezer as the speaker of the *petichah*.

What does the *nimshal* of narrative-recapitulative parables look like? As with the types of *mashal* discussed previously, the table below (4.3) represents the different types of *nimshal* according to their components. Five parables have a narrative *nimshal*; in only two cases is there an evident analogical relation to the *mashal* narrative.[58] In the rest of the parables, the *nimshal* consists primarily of proof-texts, which are either commented upon or follow a statement.

In his discussion of the origins of the *nimshal*, David Stern argues that, in the process of regularisation of the Rabbinic *mashal*, the *nimshal* compensated for a missing narrative with a "real-life setting" that had originally explained the *mashal* narrative – a narrative on how and why the parable came to be told:[59] "For a *mashal* preserved within a narrative context, that narrative supplies the information that makes it possible to understand the mashal's allusive meaning."[60]

---

[57] See ER 110, l. 17ff., where three consecutive parables are told. As was noted already in chapter 3, n. 95, these parables are rather anomalous, in that they are introduced with typical formulas for parables, but they depict hypothetical situations instead of narrating past events.
[58] See ER 149, l. 27ff. and PsEZ 36, l. 13ff.
[59] See Stern, *Parables*, 6–7, who provides an example from *Bereshit Rabbah*.
[60] Stern, *Parables*, 16.

So Stern claims that, "instead of a narrative frame, there is now an exegetical context, which is provided through the invention of the nimshal."[61] The parables discussed in this section have both a narrative frame, albeit not one that reproduces "a real-life setting," and a *nimshal*. Understanding their allusive meaning is thus made possible both by the preceding narratives and by the *nimshal*. The narratives preceding the *mashal* proper can be viewed as anticipated *nimshal*.

Table 4.3: The *Nimshal* of Narrative-Recapitulative Parables

Elements	Examples
Biblical Narrative	EZ 174, l. 3ff.
Biblical Narrative + Proof-text(s)	ER 17, l. 31ff., ER 149, l. 27ff., EZ 180, l. 27ff., PsEZ 36, l. 13ff.
Proof-text	ER 89, l. 32ff., EZ 178, l. 12ff.
Proof-texts + Comment	ER 40, l. 15ff.
Rhetorical question + Statement + Proof-texts	ER 114, l. 3ff.

4.4 Meta-Exegetical Parables

Parables told to illustrate a statement from Rabbinic discourse, instead of a scriptural verse, are here referred to as "meta-exegetical parables."[62] Seventeen such parables can be identified in *Seder Eliyahu*, four of which are in *Seder Eliyahu Zuta*.

The statement such parables illustrate can take different forms. It can be found without any preceding formula,[63] or introduced with a formula *Seder Eliyahu* characteristically employs to quote a tradition understood to go back to the collective authority of the sages, such as "from here they said" (*mikan amru*).[64] The following passage provides an example:

> Another interpretation: *at the beginning of the watches* (לראש אשמורות) (Lam 2:19). Even a small town in Israel where there is Torah is better in the eyes of the Holy One, blessed be He, than Samaria (שמרון), where there is no Torah, for it is said, *I am one of those who perfect*

---

61 Stern, *Parables*, 16.
62 Lehmhaus, "Between Tradition and Innovation," 220, sees in this type of parable evidence of a shift in the use of *meshalim* in *Seder Eliyahu* from an exegetical to a rhetorical function, arguing that the *mashal* is used not to merely to illustrate, but "to impart its core ideas."
63 See, for example, ER 69, l. 1ff. and l. 4ff.; ER 69, l. 25ff.; EZ 191, l. 15ff.
64 The formula is spelt מכאן אמרו, מיכן אמרו, and מכן אמרו; see p. 72n43.

(שלומי) *[the faithful in Israel; you seek to destroy a city that is a mother in Israel]* (2 Sam 20:19), even a small town where [there is Torah]. From here they said: Even if a man has only proper conduct and [knowledge of] Scripture, he is given an angel[65] to watch over him, for it is said, *I am going to send an angel [in front of you, to guard you on the way and to bring you to the place that I have prepared]* etc. (Exod 23:20). If a man reads Torah, the Prophets, and the Writings, he is given two angels to watch over him, for it is said, *For he will command his angels concerning you [to guard you in all your ways.]* (Ps 91:11) But if a man reads Torah, the Prophets, and the Writings, if he studies Mishnah, midrash, halakhot, and aggadot, and waits upon the disciples of the wise, the Holy One, blessed be He, Himself watches over him. They told a parable: (ER 100, l. 6) What does the matter resemble? It is like a king of flesh and blood who was walking with his son in the desert. When the sun and the heat of noon came, the (lit. "his") father would stand upon him against the sun (עמד עליו אביו בחמה) to make a shade for his son, so that the sun and the heat of noon would not touch him, for it is said, *The Lord is your keeper; the Lord is your shade at your [right] hand* (Ps 121:5). (ER 99, l. 26–ER 100, l. 9)

There is undoubtedly exegesis at work in the co-text preceding the *mashal* – in the interpretation of "watches" (אשמורות, Lam 2:19) as implying Samaria, as well as in the application of 2 Sam 20:19 to this interpretation. The tripartite statement beginning with "From here they said," however, attempts both to explain the wording of the Rabbinic dictum "Even a small town" – the notion that God loves a small town with Torah more than an important one where there is no Torah – and to describe the perfect Rabbinic way of life, which consists of the study of Scripture and Mishnah, and ministering to the disciples of the wise. Even if it can be argued that both the entire *mikan amru* statement and the parable explain the occurrence of שלומי ("perfect") in 2 Sam 20:19, the *mashal* proper is an image of how God rewards the one who dedicates himself perfectly to Torah in the third and last part of the statement.[66]

In five cases, the Rabbinic statement immediately preceding the *mashal* narrative is part of an answer the rabbi gives to a question posed by his interlocutor in a first-person narrative. To give but one example:[67]

He said to me, Rabbi, Israel was exiled twice. Once at the [time of the] First Temple and once at the [time of the] Second Temple. Why was the <duration (lit. "time")>[68] <for [the exile after

---

65 Friedmann emends the MS reading שני מלאכים to מלאך אחד.
66 The content of the statement reminds us of another *mashal* we have already discussed, ER 91, l. 7, in which the third manner is described as "perfect" (שלימה); see p. 137ff.
67 Further examples of this type of Rabbinic statement within a dialogue in first-person narratives are found in ER 71, l. 2ff.; ER 71, l. 13ff.; and EZ 173, l. 5ff.
68 The MS reads זיין, which Friedmann emends to זמן.

the destruction of] the first [Temple]> given [them], [but for[69] the exile after the destruction of] the second [Temple] no duration was given them? I said to him, My son, those living at the time of the First Temple, even if they were idolaters, had proper conduct. And what did this their proper conduct consist of? Charity and deeds of love, for it is said <...>.[70] They told a parable: What does the matter resemble? (ER 71, l. 22) It is like a king of flesh and blood, who had many sons and servants. Many of them were clever,[71] many of them were mute, many deaf, many blind (סומין). [Because] they acted offensively with their deeds, he swore that he would leave them, and separated from them. Then they would cry and follow him, so he told them, Turn away from me (חזרו מאחרי)! Look, I shall return to you in thirty days. Thus it is with Israel and the Holy One, blessed be He. Some of them possessed [knowledge of] Scripture, some of them possessed [knowledge of] Mishnah, some possessed [experience in the] give-and-take [of trade]. [Because] they acted offensively with their deeds, He swore that he would leave them and separated from them. Then they would cry and follow him, so he told them, Turn away from me (חזרו מאחרי)! Look, I shall return to you <...>.[72] How are we, therefore, to behave? We should pour out pleas of mercy and speak supplications and prayer to Him, we should find another door (פתח אחר) to the words of Torah among all the doors which were opened for us by His servants the prophets, for so it is written, *Yet even now, says the Lord, return to me [with all your heart, with fasting, with weeping, and with mourning]* (Joel 2:12). Perhaps His many mercies will be moved for our sake and upon us will be fulfilled what His lips said to us, for it is said, *The one who breaks out will go up before them[; they will break through and pass the gate, going out by it. Their king will pass on before them, the Lord at their head]* etc. (Micah 2:13). (ER 71, l. 18–32)

In this case, the statement the *mashal* is expected to illustrate is not as explicit as in the first example. The question and answer in the preamble to the *mashal* are part of a dialogue the anonymous rabbi maintains with a non-Rabbinic adversary. The question pertains to the different durations of the Babylonian exile, referred to indirectly as that of the "first [Temple]," and a second exile of indefinite duration, that associated with the aftermath of the destruction of the "second [Temple]."[73] While focusing on the people of Israel of the first exile, the rabbi seizes the occasion to criticise Israel of his own time by praising those exiled in Babylonia, which he does by projecting Rabbinic ideals back on them. Whereas the reason for the comparatively short duration of their exile, according to the preamble, was

---

69 The MS reads ובא אחרון ("but [the exile after the destruction of] the second [Temple] *came*"), which Friedmann emends to an alternative punctuation ובא. אחרון, so that the first exile is the one which "came [and ended].
70 Lacuna in MS.
71 The MS reads פקחים ("clever"), not פסחים ("lame").
72 Lacuna in MS.
73 On the problem of a second exile in Rabbinic literature, see Chaim Milikowsky, "Notions of Exile, Subjugation and Return in Rabbinic Literature," in *Exile: Old Testament, Jewish, and Christian Conceptions*, ed. James M. Scott, Supplements to the Journal for the Study of Judaism (Leiden: Brill, 1997), 256–296.

their proper behaviour, the *nimshal* states that Israel had knowledge of Scripture and Mishnah at that time, as well as of the give-and-take of trade.[74] A special feature of the *mashal* narrative itself is the use of the adjectives "smart" (or "lame"?), "mute," "deaf," and "blind" to describe the king's sons and servants.[75] The reader might have associated these adjectives with a number of scriptural verses (some of which are quoted elsewhere in *Seder Eliyahu* itself) in which reference is made to "the lame," "the blind," and "the deaf,"[76] as well as with earlier versions of the parable.[77]

A rather anomalous meta-exegetical parable is told in chapter 5 of *Seder Eliyahu Rabbah* as a comment upon the quotation of a statement first made in chapter 3 – namely, "The blood and flesh, and the destruction of Gog in the time to come upon the mountains of Israel [has already been] partially [foreshadowed by] the blood and flesh and the destruction of those who oppress us in this world, whom our eyes behold every day without fail."[78] The attentive reader of both chapters in the right order is expected to recognise the text quoted in chapter 5 as such – as an internal quotation of *Seder Eliyahu*, a self-quotation:[79]

---

[74] This is also one of the characteristic phrases with which the author of *Seder Eliyahu* designates the Rabbinic curriculum. See also, for example, ER 69, l. 25ff. (*mashal*) and ER 92, l. 1–16 (exegetical passage on Ps 128:3).

[75] The same characterisation is used in ER 69, l. 25ff.

[76] For example, Jer 31:8 (quoted in ER 69, l. 4); Isa 42:18 (quoted in ER 69, l. 25); and Isa 43:8 (quoted in ER 82, l. 7). The wording is not the same in all cases in biblical and Rabbinic Hebrew. The scriptural expression for "blind" (עיוורים) used in verses *Seder Eliyahu* quotes, differs from the Rabbinic Hebrew סומין, used to represent Rabbinic wording.

[77] On the Rabbinic parables of the lame and the blind, see Marc Bregman, "Excursus: The Rabbinic Versions of the Blind and the Lame," in *The Apocryphal Ezekiel*, ed. Michael E. Stone, Benjamin G. Wright, and David Satran (Atlanta, GA: Society of Biblical Literature, 2000), 61–68; and Lieve M. Teugels, "The Contradictory Philosophical Lessons of the Parable of the Lame and the Blind Guards in Various Rabbinic Midrashim," in *From Creation to Redemption: Progressive Approaches to Midrash*, ed. W. David Nelson and Rivka Ulmer, Proceedings of the Midrash Section 7 (Piscataway, NJ: Gorgias Press, 2017), 153–171.

[78] ER 15, l. 1–2.

[79] Both original and modern readers are helped by the fact that the textual segment preceding that in which the *mashal* is told also opens with a self-quotation of the same statement, first made in chapter 3. On the phenomenon of the self-quotation, or of *Seder Eliyahu* having its own *baraita* (the passage from a previous passage which is quoted) and a commentary that expands on it, see p. 14n75 and 77. Other examples of *Seder Eliyahu*'s *baraitot* and commentaries upon them include ER 63, l. 11ff. (*baraita*) and ER 63, l. 20ff. (commentary); ER 123, l. 3 (*baraita*) and ER 123, l. 5 (commentary); ER 128, l. 13 (*baraita*) and ER 139, l. 28ff.; ER 143, l. 25ff.; ER 156, l. 15ff. (commentary).

And "partially [foreshadowed by] the blood and flesh and the destruction of <those who oppress us>"⁸⁰ in this world, whom our eyes behold every day without fail. How so? (ER 25, l. 4) Two young children who studied Scripture at their teacher's house, who grew up and became disciples of the wise. When they used to pass the door of their teacher's house they would see the strap with which he used to flog them, and they would laugh (משחקין) together and say, With that strap he used to flog us. So (כך) the peoples of the world afflict Israel and oppress them and grind (שוחקין) their bones and flesh until their souls depart from them and they do not feel any pain. But later on, see, they will be on the mountains and hills, for it is said, *You have forgotten the Lord, your Maker, who stretched out the heavens [... who is bent on destroying (כונן להשחית)]* etc. (Isa 51:13). If Scripture had said, "[*me* the Lord,] who *am* bent on destroying," I would have interpreted, "who am bent on destroying you (כוננתי בעיניך להשחית)." It follows that it is only of Babylon that Scripture said [the verse], *who is bent on destroying. But where is the fury of the oppressor?* (Isa 51:13). See, they are on the mountains and the hills, and the birds eat their flesh from them. (ER 25, l. 3–12)

Even though there is no marker of comparison that introduces the narrative, and even though it is not a narrative about a king and his children and/or servants, or about a householder, but one about certain disciples of the wise, who are reminded of their former teacher's pedagogical methods – another case of discourse interference⁸¹ – the narrative *is* clearly a *mashal*. It is identified as a *mashal* because it is followed by one of the usual markers of applicability and what is read as a plausible *nimshal* or application – an eschatological account of events which refers back to the ersatz lemma, the Rabbinic statement with which the passage opens. The author of *Seder Eliyahu* is inclined to make use not only of repetition, but also of a kind of hermeneutic paronomasia⁸² in order to provide cohesion in his text: This we can also appreciate in this passage where, the *mashal* proper depicts the disciples laughing (משוחקין) while the nations of the world grind (שוחקין) Israel's bones, and God is bent on destruction (להשחית) in the *nimshal* and the following lines.

In some cases, and as we have seen in a previous example, the preamble to a meta-exegetical parable does contain a scriptural verse. As Goldberg himself conceded, one might have the impression that these are exegetical parables: Es gibt allerdings Gleichnisse, die im Zusammenhang eines Midrasch zunächst den Eindruck erwecken, als seien sie textauslegend, die sich aber dann als Teil thematischer Ausführungen erweisen.⁸³ In order to distinguish them from the exegetical parables, we could argue as follows: If the preamble to a parable contains verses

---
80 Friedmann emends the MS reading שלו חצים to של לוחצים.
81 On this concept, see p. 120n202.
82 One based on the partial overlap of consonants.
83 Goldberg, "Das schriftauslegende Gleichnis," 142 ("Yet there are parables that in the context of a midrash first appear to be exegetical, but then turn out to be part of thematic expositions").

that, instead of *occasioning* an "interpretation" by means of a parable, rather *follow* a statement and are used as proof-texts, then these parables can be identified as meta-exegetical, for it is not primarily scriptural exegesis, but the illustration (or explanation) of a Rabbinic statement (including the verbatim repetition of a statement made previously in the work, i.e., a self-quotation) which stands at the centre of this type of *mashal*'s attention. We find an example of such a preamble containing a scriptural verse functioning as a proof-text in the following parable:[84]

> Blessed be the Omnipresent, blessed be He, for He chose the sages, their disciples, and their disciples' disciples, for upon them is [the mishnah] fulfilled: "With what measure a man metes it shall be measured to him again" (mSotah 1:7). And when they sit in the synagogues and in the houses of study, and on every free day read Scripture for the sake of heaven and study Mishnah for the sake of heaven and fear [God] in their hearts and engrave the words of Torah on their mouths, it [the verse] is fulfilled upon them, *for the word is very near to you; it is in your mouth [and in your heart for you to observe]* (Deut 30:14). <And they took upon themselves the yoke of heaven for it is said, *You have put gladness in my heart* (Ps 4:8).> They told a parable: (ER 97, l. 5) What does the matter resemble? It is like a king of flesh and blood who had an orchard by his house. And he fertilised it, cleared it of weeds, and irrigated it <from a water-trough>,[85] and brought it manure at the requested time. [Of] each and every tree in it [i.e., in the orchard, it holds true that] the days of its old age were more beautiful to itself than the days of its youth. So [of] each and every sage of Israel who truly has words of Torah with him [it holds true that] the days of his old age are more beautiful to himself than the days of his youth, for it is said, *they shall not build <and another inhabit; they shall not plant> and another eat[; for like the days of a tree shall the days of my people be, and my chosen shall long enjoy the work of their hands]* <etc.> (Isa 65:22). And it [Scripture] says, *they shall not labour in vain* etc. (Isa 65:23). And it [Scripture] says, *but those who wait for the Lord shall renew their strength* etc. (Isa 40:31). This word [shows] how it will be at the end and how it is partly today. (ER 96, l. 34–ER 97, l. 12)

The co-text preceding the parable is a *berakhah* or blessing that praises God's choice of the sages, or rather the sages themselves, whose exemplary occupation consists in going to the synagogue and to the house of study and occupying themselves with the study of both the Written and Oral Torah. Deut 30:14 is quoted as confirming the notion that the sages have the words of Torah in their mouths as if "engraved." The *nimshal* furthers the exaltation of the sages' lifestyle by comparing the beauty of their old age with that of mature trees. To emphasise the analogical relation between the trees of the *mashal* proper and the sages of the *nimshal*, two statements are made, which have a parallel structure and also iden-

---

[84] Further examples can be found in ER 128, l. 20ff.; ER 136, l. 19ff.; and EZ 173, l. 5ff.
[85] Friedmann emends the uncertain מהשקה to מהשוקת.

tical wording in the second parts, and according to which both the trees and the sages are beautified with time and proper nurture.

As a final example of meta-exegetical parable, I propose the following passage of *Seder Eliyahu Zuta*:

> From the nature of His ways (ממידת דרכיו) one (lit. "he") learns that His compassion for the world is abundant. Why does He say, Give charity to the [average] poor (עניים), to the poor who longs for everything (אביונים), to those diminished in their property (דלים), and to the utterly poor (רשים)?[86] Does He not feed, provide for, and sustain (זן ומכלכל ומפרנס) all the inhabitants of the world, as well as all the work of His hands which He created in His world? Still, He says, Give charity to the [average] poor (עניים), to the poor who longs for everything (אביונים), to those diminished in their property (דלים), and to the utterly poor (רשים). He only means (lit. "says") the man who did something unworthy, decreeing harm over himself (קנסה עליו רעה) for as long as four generations. That is him of whom we say, "He is righteous but has trouble (צדיק ורע לו)." Not only this, but even more: Our teacher Moses himself used to judge with an *a minori ad majus* argument [as follows]: Maybe because Israel do not desire to stand on the ways of the Omnipresent, God forbid, they are sentenced (מתחתם) with the decree of punishment (גזר דין), and see, they are smitten each and every hour. They told a parable: (EZ 182, l. 18) What does the matter resemble? It is like a king of flesh and blood who married a woman and used to bring her with him from province to province. Whenever she acted offensively towards him, he would punish <her> with lashes. The king's father-in-law sent a messenger to the king. He said to him, Tell me, what does the king want? I shall tell my daughter [how] to succeed in doing what you want (שתעמוד בצורכך). The king sent him five sorts of fruit, and corresponding to them he wrote five letters, in which the king wrote and sent [a message of] what he desired. When the letters and the fruits reached the king's father-in-law, he read one of the letters, in which was written, These are so-and-so fruits. [In] the second was written, These are so-and-so fruits. [In] the third was written, These are so-and-so fruits. [In] the fourth was written, These are so-and-so fruits. When he realised (lit. "came to") what the king wished, he called for his daughter and said to her, The king loves truth, he loves peace, he loves justice, and charity. This [father-in-law] is what Moses resembles at that time, for it is said, *[Moses] said* etc. *Now if I have found favour in your sight, show me your ways[, so that I may know you and find favour in your sight. Consider too that this nation is your people]* (Exod 33:12–13). The Holy One, blessed be He, foresaw Moses's mind until its end, showing him each and every generation with its sages, each and every generation with its prophets, each and every generation with its interpreters [of Scripture], each and every generation with its community leaders, each and every community with its men on whose behalf miracles occur. He showed him the dimension of this world (מידת העולם) and the dimension of the world-to-come. Thereupon he said in His presence, Master of the universe, You <have shown me>[87] the dimension of this world (מידה של עולם); show me the manner (מידה) in which the world is to be conducted, for I see the righteous who does well, [but also] the righteous who has trouble, the wicked who does well, [and] the wicked who

---

86 The author lists four synonymous terms that express different senses of "poor" and which can be paraphrased in English as different categories of poverty.

87 Friedmann emends the MS reading הראיני to הראיתני.

has trouble; the rich who does well, [but also] the rich who has trouble, the poor who does well, [and] the poor who has trouble. He said, *Show me your glory, I pray* (Exod 33:18). The Holy One, blessed be He, said, Moses, you cannot understand my ways (מידותיי). However, I will let you know some of my ways. When I look at human beings, I see that there is no hope in their deeds nor in the deeds of their forefathers. Still, because they proceed to bless me, and supplicate, and multiply their prayers, I respond (נזקק) to them and double their provisions, for it is said, *He will regard the prayer of the destitute[, and will not despise their prayer]* etc. (Ps 102:18). And it [Scripture] says, *And he said, I will make all my goodness pass before you* (Exod 33:19). These are the thirteen attributes (מידות): *The Lord, the Lord, a God merciful and gracious, slow to anger, and abounding in steadfast love and faithfulness, keeping steadfast love for the thousandth generation, forgiving iniquity and transgression and sin* (Exod 34:6–7). If it were said "my goodness" instead of *all my goodness*, I would say that the days of the Messiah are not [included] here. But since it [Scripture] says *all my goodness*, the days of the Messiah are [included] here; *and I will proclaim before you the name, "The Lord"* etc. (Exod 33:19), and it [Scripture] says, *The Lord descended in the cloud [and stood with him there, and proclaimed the name, The Lord.]* etc. *The Lord passed before him, and proclaimed[, The Lord, the Lord, a God merciful and gracious]* etc. (Exod 34:5–6). When Moses saw that one [of His] ways (מידה) is loving-kindness and one [of His] ways is compassion, he wrapped himself [with a prayer shawl] and stood in prayer before the Holy One, blessed be He, for it is said, *He said, If now I have found favour in your sight[, O Lord, I pray, let the Lord go with us. Although this is a stiff-necked people, pardon our iniquity and our sin, and take us for your inheritance]* (Exod 34:9). (EZ 182, l. 11–ER 183, l. 20)

The passage opens with a statement concerning God's ways as evidence of His compassion, which is shown in His urging human beings to be compassionate towards the poor, towards any kind of poor person. To emphasise this, the author of *Seder Eliyahu* uses four adjectives – four near-synonyms with the meaning "poor." The last one, רשים, provides the immediate co-text for the parable that follows. רשים is explained metaphorically as those who bring harm to themselves by their own misdeeds. In a second step, רשים is paraphrased using what appears to be a popular saying, one probably known to the audience, as can be inferred from the use of the first-person plural. The third attempt at interpreting the term is a conjecture put into Moses's mouth,[88] according to which the reason why Israel are רשים, why they are constantly smitten (לוקין), is their own reluctance to get to know God's attributes. The *mashal* proper depicts a king beating (מלקה) his wife whenever she acts offensively towards him. At the request of his father-in-law, the king explains his wishes by sending him five sorts of fruit together with five letters describing them but not explicitly naming them. The father-in-law reveals his wisdom in being able to decipher four of the king's five metaphors for the king's

---

88 Despite being introduced as an *a minori ad majus* inference, Moses's argument does not have the characteristic Rabbinic structure and wording of this hermeneutic resource.

wishes. What the *mashal* does not tell us, is whether the king's wife followed the king's principles after her father explained them to her.

When we turn to the *nimshal*, it is clear that, corresponding to the *mashal* narrative, it turns the reader's attention towards the behaviour of Moses rather than Israel. It is not the wife's reproachable behaviour, but rather the ability of the king's father-in-law to understand the king's will and to transmit it to his daughter that the *mashal* proper is about. Whereas only four of the five types of fruit were allegorically interpreted in the *mashal* narrative,[89] the *nimshal* provides five classes of men as equivalents for the types of fruit.

This *mashal* can also be seen as representing the tendency towards novelisation which David Stern considered a main feature of *Seder Eliyahu*'s *meshalim*. The *mashal* proper does much more than merely illustrate how those unable to read metaphors bring harm to themselves by misbehaving. Likewise, the *nimshal* provides an extended account of how Moses came to be familiar with some of God's attributes.[90] This is the subject of an exegetical narrative, which takes "show me your ways" (Exod 33:13) as its lemma and closes with Moses's prayer in Exod 34:9. It explains that he utters this prayer after having realised that one of God's ways is His compassion – thus providing consistency and closure not just to the *nimshal* narrative, but to the whole passage that had set out to expound on compassion as a major divine attribute.

The examples discussed so far provide an overview of the various types of statements in *Seder Eliyahu* that are illustrated or explained with a *mashal*. As noted by Stern and observed previously with respect to exegetical parables, in the case of this type of parables, it is also true that the *nimshal* is more clearly connected to the *mashal* narrative, but only loosely to the preamble of the parable. The form of the *nimshal* in this subgroup of parables also varies, as can be seen in the following table:

---

89 Four is incidentally the number of types of "poor" God is said to urge his children to be charitable with at the beginning of the passage.

90 The repetitiveness of the passage is manifest in the frequency of the use of the expressions מידה and דרכיו, which are used twelve times in the passage quoted above. The expressions are used in the following phrases: מידת העולם ומידת העולם הבא, דרכיך, בדרכיו של מקום, מידת דרכיו, and מידה של חסד, שלש עשרת מידות, מקצת מידותי, מידותיי, מידת שהעולם מתנהג בה, של עולם רחמים.

Table 4.4: The *Nimshal* of Meta-Exegetical Parables

Elements	Examples
Statement	ER 9, l. 21ff., ER 71, l. 2ff.
Statement + Proof-text	ER 69, l. 25ff., ER 71, l. 13ff. (lacunae), ER 97, l. 5ff., ER 136, l. 19ff.
Statement + Proof-text + Biblical Narrative	EZ 182, l. 18ff.
Statement + Biblical Narrative	ER 71, l. 22ff.
Biblical Narrative	EZ 173, l. 5ff.
Biblical Narrative + Proof-text(s)	ER 128, l. 20ff.
Biblical Narrative + Eschatological Narrative + Proof-text	ER 25, l. 4ff.
Rhetorical Question + Proof-text	ER 69, l. 4ff.
Proof-text	ER 100, l. 6ff., ER 155, l. 21ff., EZ 191, l. 15ff.
None	ER 69, l. 1ff.

4.5 Rhetorical Questions and the Parables That (Do Not Always) Answer Them

Eleven parables are preceded by a variation of the usual formula *le-mah ha-davar domeh* that replaces the phrase *ha-davar* with a proper name – for example, Israel,[91] Esau, Amalek, Jeroboam,[92] Manasseh's generation[93] – the noun "man,"[94] or with questions following the structure "What is the difference between X and Y?"[95] In one case, the wording of the question is "What does the Holy One, blessed be He, compare the face of the righteous with?"[96] It is worth noting that precisely because the openings of this type of *mashal* do not contain a "matter" that refers back to a preceding co-text, these parables may be found at the beginning of either a chapter or a paragraph, functioning as a sort of preamble for the subsequent dis-

---

91 Alternatively, "the House of Israel"; e.g., ER 55, l. 7ff.; ER 82, l. 7ff.; ER 156, l. 7ff.; and ER 156, l. 10ff. The last parable can be seen as a hybrid case, since it is actually preceded by the regular formula, but at the same time, it provides an answer to the same question to which the immediately preceding parable (ER 156, l. 7ff.) responds.
92 E.g., ER 125, l. 12ff.
93 E.g., ER 162, l. 20ff.
94 E.g., ER 135, l. 11ff.
95 E.g., between love and awe in ER 140, l. 27ff.; between Scripture and Mishnah in EZ 171, l. 19ff. and EZ 194, l. 25ff.
96 ER 164, l. 1ff.

course.⁹⁷ In what follows, I shall discuss three examples of the use of this type of parable, designated in chapter 3 as a "question-answering parable,"⁹⁸ beginning with the opening text segment of chapter (11) 12 of *Seder Eliyahu Rabbah*:

> What did Israel resemble during the days of the judges' rule? (ER 55, l. 7) It is like a king of flesh and blood who had sons⁹⁹ and servants. Some of them were six years old. Some five years old. Some four years old. Some three years old. Some two years old. [Some] one year old. All of them he brought up at his table, where they would eat from what he ate and drink from what he drank. So he brought them up and built for them houses, planted vines, trees, and saplings (נטעים). He spoke to them, Do not disregard these saplings (נטיעות), do not disregard these trees, do not disregard these vines. Once they had eaten and drunk, they proceeded to uproot the vines, to fell the trees, and to destroy the houses and the saplings. Still, when he came and found them he took comfort¹⁰⁰ from them. He said, Look, they are like schoolchildren (lit. "children of a master's house"). What am I to do about (lit. "to") these? ...¹⁰¹ Bring them [to me]! And he hit them once, twice, and a third time. This is what Israel resembled (לכך נדמו ישראל) in the days of the judges' rule before our Father who is in heaven. They acted offensively with their deeds, so that he delivered them to a kingdom, but as soon as they repented he redeemed them at once, which teaches you that even the penny taken from Israel is a form of judgement and that everything [that happens to them] is nothing but part of [this] judgement. Maybe you ask why the forty-two thousand who were slain in the days of Jephthah the Gileadite were killed. Jephthah the Gileadite made an improper vow at the time when Phinehas son of Eleazar was designated [as High Priest for giving counsel]. Phinehas should have gone to Jephthah to release him from his vow. Jephthah should have gone to Phinehas and have himself released from his vow. But he did not go. This one said, I am High Priest, son of a High Priest, grandson of Aaron the priest, and should go to one who is an ignorant (עם הארץ)? The other said, I am the leader of all Israel, and should go to this one? This one and the other were guided by their pride in themselves. Woe unto the pride (גדולה) that buries those it possesses! Woe unto the pride that does no good in the world! [When] Jephthah the Gileadite made a vow that was improper – to offer his daughter on an altar –, the children of Ephraim gathered against him and were in serious argument with him over this. Phinehas should [then] have said to them, You did not come to him to release him from his vow. You came to him to engage in an argument. Phinehas neither forewarned the children of Ephraim, nor released Jephthah from his vow. He who sits on the throne, the righteous judge, may His great name be blessed for ever and ever and ever, said, After this one took his life in his hand and came and delivered Israel from the hand of Moab and from the hands of the children of Ammon, they came to engage in a serious argument with him. Therefore they gathered to wage war and he killed forty-two thousand of them, for it is said, *they said to him, Then say Shibboleth, and he said, Sibboleth* (Judg 12:6), this is an

---

97 In five cases, this type of textual location can be ascertained for these parables.
98 See p. 87.
99 Friedmann emends the MS reading בנים to בתים.
100 Friedmann emends the MS reading הרחיבה to הרחיקה.
101 Lacuna in MS.

expression for idolatry, as when a man says to his fellow (לחבירו) s*abul* (שאבול);[102] *for he could not pronounce it right. Then they seized him and killed him at the fords of the Jordan. [Forty-two thousand of the Ephraimites fell at that time]* (Judg 12:6). *And who killed all these? You should say, No one killed them but Phinehas son of Eleazar, who was in a dilemma as to whether to forewarn [them], but did not forewarn [them], as to whether to invalidate Jephthah's vow, but did not release him. And not only Phinehas, but every one who is in doubt whether to forewarn [someone else], but does not forewarn [them], who has the possibility of bringing back* (להחזיר) *Israel to goodness, but does not do it, the blood spilt by Israel is but spilt on his hands, for it is said, So you, mortal, I have made [a sentinel for the house of Israel; whenever you hear a word from my mouth, you shall give them warning* (הזהרת) *from me.] etc. If I say to the wicked[, O wicked ones, you shall surely die, and you do not speak to warn the wicked to turn from their ways, the wicked shall die in their iniquity, but their blood I will require at your hand.]* <etc.> *But if you warn the wicked [to turn* (לשוב) *from their ways, and they do not turn from their ways, the wicked shall die in their iniquity, but you will have saved your life]* <etc.> (Ezek 33:7–9). *Given that all [of] Israel are responsible for one another, what can they be compared with? With a ship one of whose compartments has been torn apart. They do not say, A compartment has been torn apart, but the entire ship has been torn apart, for it is said, Did not Achan son of Zerah break faith [in the matter of the devoted things, and wrath fell upon all the congregation of Israel? And he did not perish alone for his iniquity!] etc.* (Josh 22:20). (ER 55, l. 7–ER 56, l. 15)

The rhetorical question at the beginning of the quoted passage determines the subject matter of the chapter of *Seder Eliyahu* it opens: The whole of chapter (11) 12 deals with biblical narratives from the book of Judges, or rather with Rabbinic narratives associated with the time of the judges, as this is depicted in the scriptural accounts.[103] At this time, according to the *mashal* proper, Israel resemble a king's sons and servants, who act inexplicably rudely toward him, doing harm to the vines, trees, saplings, and houses they were expected to take care of. The king, although his affection for them remains unaltered, reprimands his sons and servants, whose behaviour resembles that of schoolchildren.

The short *nimshal* does not account for certain details of the *mashal* narrative: Why are the different ages of the children and the servants mentioned? What do the vines, trees, and saplings stand for? Is the description of the behaviour of the children and the servants more effective if they are said to destroy vines, trees,

---

102 Amos Geula, in a paper delivered at the Tenth Congress of the European Association of Jewish Studies (Paris 2014), suggested that the expression שאבול might be understood as referring to the Sibylla or to the sibylline books, thus hinting at a Greco-Roman context.

103 The narratives include a Rabbinic account of the reason for the quasi-extinction of the children of Benjamin; a passage on the place of the episode of Gibeah's crime against the Levite's concubine, according to Judg 19–21; and a lengthy narrative on the abduction of the Ark by the Philistines. These narratives attempt to explain why so many thousands among Israel fell in wars against their enemies.

and saplings, than if they destroy tens or hundreds of vines? There are no clear answers to these questions. The apparently superfluous detail of the *mashal* narrative might be evidence of the inclination of *Seder Eliyahu* towards novelisation and, in general, towards an instrumentalisation of the *mashal* that differs from that of its predecessors in classical midrash.

The *nimshal* consists of a summarised, vague biblical narrative – Israel offends God in the days of the judges, so he turns them over to an unspecified kingdom, but then forgives them once they have repented – and a closing maxim, according to which every chastisement that comes from God upon Israel is evidence of God's justice. This maxim is immediately followed by a question that addresses the reader directly – ושמא תאמר – and connects the message of the *nimshal* with an exegetical narrative.[104] This links the killing of forty-two thousand Ephraimites "in Jephthah's days" with a Rabbinic retelling of the biblical narrative of Jephthah's vow,[105] according to which Phinehas is said to have still been alive and held the office of High Priest at the time when Jephthah made an ominous vow which led him to sacrifice his daughter.[106] *Seder Eliyahu* explains that neither did Phinehas release Jephthah from his vow, nor did Jephthah ask him to do so. Moreover, Phinehas is made responsible for not intervening and forewarning the Ephraimites, who are said to have been in conflict with Jephthah because of his vow. The reason why the Ephraimites fell, as the midrash concludes, is that Phinehas failed to forewarn them. Therefore, Phinehas is understood to have killed them. From the individual case of Phinehas, the governing voice extrapolates the general rule that whenever anyone in Israel fails to be responsible for the rest, the whole of Israel is comparable to a ship, one part of which has been torn apart.

At least part of the message of the parable – the notion that during the times of the judges, God repeatedly allowed Israel first to be oppressed by the nations of the world and then to be redeemed – is illustrated by the exegetical narrative, or rather the exegetical narrative is expected to be read at least partly in the light of the *mashal* that precedes it: By allowing Phinehas to refrain from forewarning them, God punishes the forty-two thousand Ephraimites for being in conflict with Jephthah. Phinehas himself is also punished, insofar as the midrash makes him responsible for the mass killing and for Jephthah's vow being fulfilled.

---

104 The formula ושמא תאמר is also used to introduce the exegetical narrative on the killing of seventy thousand Benjaminites in Gibeah that follows this narrative.
105 See bTaan 4a; BerR 9:3; and TPsJ to Judg 11:39.
106 According to the biblical account in Judg 11:31, Jephthah vowed to sacrifice whatever came out of his house if he could defeat the Ammonites.

Instead of an illustration of something already expounded, the parable functions as a sort of preamble for a number of exegetical narratives; it anticipates in condensed form what is still to be narrated and expounded on, as if the exegetical narratives themselves were the illustrations of the parable.

Most parables of this type open with questions like the one in the previous example. In the next passage, the question, placed at the beginning of a paragraph (thus opening a thematic section), has a different form and is followed by the usual opening formula *mashlu mashal*:

> What is the difference between love and awe? They told a parable: (ER 140, l. 27) What does the matter resemble? It is like a king of flesh and blood who had to go away to a distant province.[107] He had two servants. The one loved the king and was in awe of him; the other was in awe of him, but did not love him. The one who loved him and was in awe of him planted gardens, and an orchard with all sorts of fine fruit. The one who was in awe of him did nothing at all until a letter was brought to him by a messenger. After some days the king came [back]. When he entered his house [i.e., that of the servant who loved him] and saw the figs and grapes and all sorts of fine fruit, he arranged [it all] corresponding to the understanding of the servant who loved him. When the servant who loved him came into the king's presence and saw all sorts of fine fruit [thus arranged], his mind was set at rest corresponding to the king's pleasure. The one who just feared him, on the other hand, did nothing at all. When the king came into his house and saw all sorts of ruined stuff (כל מיני חרבות בלום), he arranged before him all sorts of ruined stuff. His mind was shaken corresponding to the king's grief, for it is said, *He provides food for those who fear him* (Ps 111:5), this is the measure of judgement; *he is ever mindful of his covenant* (Ps 111:5), this is the world to come and the Torah that is with it; *He has gained renown by his wonderful deeds; the Lord is gracious and merciful* (Ps 111:4), this is this world and the Torah that is with it; *He is mindful of his covenant for ever* (Ps 105:8) and *he is ever mindful of his covenant* (Ps 111:5), this is the reward of the fearful. Whence [do we infer] the reward of the one who loves [Him]? Scripture says, *you shall have no other gods [before me. You shall not make for yourself an idol, whether in the form of anything that is in heaven above, or that is on the earth beneath, or that is in the water under the earth. You shall not bow down to them or worship them; for I the Lord your God am a jealous God, punishing children for the iniquity of parents, to the third and the fourth generation of those who reject me, but showing steadfast love to the thousandth generation of those who love me and keep my commandments]* etc. (Exod 20:3–6). From here you learn that the reward of the one who loves [and fears Him consists of] two portions, whereas the reward of the one who [just] fears [Him consists of] one portion. Therefore the peoples of the world have the privilege only of enjoying this world. Israel on the other hand has the privilege of enjoying two worlds, this world and the world to come. (ER 140, l. 27–ER 141, l. 12)

---

107 Immediately after this sentence, the MS reads: "He wanted to hand his son over to a wicked guardian. His courtiers and ministers said in his presence, Our lord, king, do not hand your son over to a wicked guardian. The king ignored (lit. 'transgressed') the words of his courtiers and ministers and handed his son over to a bad guardian." The sentence belongs to another passage and is erroneously placed here, which Friedmann indicates by putting it in brackets and a smaller typeface.

Taken together, both parts of the opening could be paraphrased as, "What does the difference between love and awe resemble?" The *mashal* proper responds with a representation of the difference between the two feelings of love and fear, characterising two servants in a different light. Whereas the loving and fearful servant is diligent and pleases the king by cultivating fruit, so that the king himself arranges it in a manner that pleases them both, the fearful one is idle and prepares "all sorts of ruined stuff" for the king to see. Why a fearful servant should behave so awkwardly, even though he has received a letter from the king which probably announces a meeting, remains unclear. The *mashal* narrative just shows that the king was displeased with him. The *nimshal* consists of two parts: The first one deals primarily with the fearful and their reward, quoting for this purpose verses from Ps 111 and Ps 105. Both in the scriptural verses and in their interpretation, word-forms for "love" and "fear" are used, linking the *nimshal* to the *mashal* proper. The second part focuses on the main notion the parable appears to have set out to illustrate: the idea that a double reward consisting in a double portion of this world and the world to come is foreshadowed by those (among Israel) who have a "double" feeling towards God – fear and love.

One last example illustrates the apparent textual inconsistency between the parts of the parable that David Stern refers to when he observes that the lesson of a *nimshal* "is not quite identical to the introductory thesis preceding the *mashal*, which it is supposed to illustrate":[108]

> What is the difference between Scripture and Mishnah? They told a parable: (EZ 194, l. 25) What does the matter resemble? It is like a king of flesh and blood who had sons and servants whom he loved with a complete love. He sent them to [study] Scripture and Mishnah, and to learn proper conduct. Then he would sit and look forward to [seeing] them, saying, When will they come so that I may see them? When he saw that they were not coming, he proceeded to go himself to them, and found them reading Scripture and studying Mishnah, and showing proper conduct. He seated them on his lap, embraced them, hugged them, and kissed them, some of them [he held] on his shoulders, some of them on his arms, some [he placed] in front of him, some of them behind him, for it is said, *He will feed his flock like a shepherd[; he will gather the lambs in his arms, and carry them in his bosom, and gently lead the mother sheep]* etc. (Isa 30:11). Maybe you say, Because He humbles Himself like a shepherd, He is an ordinary man. But then is it not written of Him, *Who has measured the waters in the hollow of his hand and marked off the heavens with a span[,enclosed the dust of the earth in a measure, and weighed the mountains in scales and the hills in a balance?]* etc. (Isa 30:12)? This refers to someone whose compassion is abundant. And whence [do we infer that] He finds them reading Scripture, studying Mishnah, and showing a proper behaviour? Because it is said, *They shall go after the Lord, who roars like a lion; when he roars, his children shall come trembling from the sea* (Hos 11:10). And *the sea* is but the words of Torah, for

---

108 Stern, *Parables*, 215.

> it is said, *All streams run to the sea[, but the sea is not full; to the place where the streams flow, there they continue to flow]* (Eccl 1:7). And it [Scripture] says, *They shall come trembling like birds from Egypt, and like doves from the land of Assyria[; and I will return them to their homes, says the Lord.]* etc. (Hos 11:11) (EZ 194, l. 25–ER 195, l. 8)

Unlike Stern's example, the parable quoted above has no "thesis" or lesson preceding the *mashal* narrative, that could be said to be "not quite identical" to what is argued after the *mashal* narrative. The *mashal* narrative is preceded by the notion that there *is* a difference between Scripture and Mishnah in the form of a straightforward question, but neither the *mashal* proper nor the *nimshal* deals in any obvious manner with this difference. Whereas the former praises the king's subjects, all of whom engage in the study of both the Written and the Oral Torah and are distinguished by their proper behaviour,[109] the latter focuses on the problem of an overly anthropomorphic understanding of Isa 30:11 – that is, how God rejoices when men outside the *mashal* world study Scripture and Mishnah and generally behave properly. Furthermore, the *nimshal* claims that God, as the king of the *mashal* narrative, finds his children engaged in the three activities mentioned in the *mashal*, providing scriptural evidence with the quotation and interpretation of "the sea" in Hos 11:10 as meaning the "words of Torah" and "all streams" in Eccl 1:7 as meaning "[*all* the] words of Torah."[110] So in this case, it cannot be argued that the *mashal* functions as a bridge between ideas that are not identical but similar,[111] but rather that it is a transition between two different, unrelated ideas.

The same type of question that opened the previous passage precedes another parable in *Seder Eliyahu Zuta*:

> He said to me, Scripture was given to us from Mount Sinai. Mishnah was not given us from Mount Sinai. And I answered him, My son, were not both Scripture and Mishnah uttered by the mouth of the Lord? What is the difference between Scripture and Mishnah? They told a parable: (EZ 171, l. 19) What does the matter resemble? It is like a king of flesh and blood who had two servants, whom he used to love with a complete love. He gave one a measure of wheat and the other a measure of wheat. He gave one a bundle of flax and the other a bundle of flax. The clever one of the two, what did he do? He took the flax and wove it into a linen cloth. He took the wheat and made a dish of fine flour out of it. He sifted and ground it [the grain], kneaded it [the dough], baked it, set it on the table, and spread the linen cloth

---

[109] Whereby once again the use of phraseology (דרך ארץ) usually found in the text surrounding the *mashal* proper can be ascertained as having been incorporated into it.
[110] Further examples of this apparent textual inconsistency are the parables in ER 162, l. 20ff. and ER 164, l. 1ff., which also fail to answer the question that precedes them. The focus of these parables clearly lies elsewhere – in the elucidation of a scriptural verse quoted in the *nimshal*.
[111] See Stern, *Parables*, 215.

over it, but left it [there] until the coming of the king. The foolish one did nothing at all. After some time the king came into his house and spoke to them like this, My sons, bring me what I gave you. One brought out [a loaf of] the dish of fine flour upon the table and the tablecloth spread over it. The other brought out the wheat in a basket and on top of it the bundle of flax. Oh, for such a shame! Oh, for such a disgrace! Alas, tell me, which of the two was dear to him? The one who brought out the table with [a loaf of] the dish of fine flour upon it. (EZ 171, l. 19–28)

In this case, there is an answer to the question: The difference between Scripture and Mishnah – or rather, the difference between understanding Torah as consisting only of Scripture and understanding it as encompassing both Scripture and Mishnah – is represented by two servants, one of whom is diligent in processing the raw materials given to him by the king, while the other is idle and leaves the materials he received untouched. The lengthy *nimshal*, interwoven with the continuation of the dialogue, argues that the Oral Torah is the result of the raw material of Scripture being elaborated upon with the aid of Rabbinic hermeneutics.[112]

As in all the preceding types of parables, the *nimshal* in this type can also have different components. Most of the *nimshal* examples consist either of biblical narratives followed by proof-texts or of proof-texts, as the table below shows:

Table 4.5: The *Nimshal* of Question-Answering Parables

Elements	Examples
Biblical Narrative(s) + Proof-text(s)	ER 82, l. 7ff., ER 125, l. 12ff., ER 156, l. 10ff.
Biblical Narrative + Statement	ER 55, l. 12ff.
Dialogue + Biblical Narrative + Proof-text	EZ 171, l. 19ff.
Proof-text	ER 135, l. 11ff., ER 162, l. 20ff., ER 164, l. 1ff., EZ 194, l. 25ff.
Proof-texts + Comments	ER 140, l. 27ff.
None	ER 156, l. 7ff.

4.6 Concluding Remarks

According to the passage of *Shir ha-Shirim Rabbah* quoted at the beginning of this chapter, the *mashal*'s task is to illustrate the meaning of the words of Torah. If Torah is understood not in the narrow sense as a part of Scripture, but in terms of

---

[112] For a discussion of this parable which considers its broader cultural context, see section 5.1.

both Written and Oral Torah – the latter in turn being an umbrella term that even includes the words of *Seder Eliyahu* – then the message of the *Shir ha-Shirim Rabbah* passage itself does not differ substantially from the function of the parable in *Seder Eliyahu*.

However, the parables included in ShirR 1:1,8 and those of *Seder Eliyahu* are different: The former use images of inanimate objects – a thicket of reeds, a basket, a ladle, a well – which a clever man adapts so that better use can be made of them, to illustrate how Solomon's use of *meshalim* ("proverbs" or "comparisons" rather than "narrative parables") have come to contribute to the understanding of Torah.[113] The parables in *Seder Eliyahu* do not deal with inanimate objects and clever men, but generally with a king, and they are not parables about the parable – they do not contain an explicit poetology of the *mashal*. On the whole, they can be described as belonging to the type of regularised king *mashal* described by David Stern in *Parables in Midrash*,[114] especially in that their *mashal* narratives make use of highly conventionalised language and of narrative patterns. There are, as will be summarised below, a number of aspects which set the instrumentalisation of these parables apart from their predecessors in classical midrash.

Even if Stern concedes in his article "Rhetoric and Midrash" that the Rabbinic *mashal* is seldom found in non-exegetical contexts, it is not on this rare type that he focuses, but on the regularised form, which is the exegetical *mashal*. The same can be said for *mashal* scholarship in general. Based on the discussion in this chapter, it appears that *Seder Eliyahu* contains an important corpus of parables, many of which differ from their predecessors in classical midrash from the amoraic period, as described by Stern and others, in the way they are put to use. Roughly half of the parables are not found in explicitly exegetical contexts; they do not purport to explain a scriptural verse, but either illustrate a statement from Rabbinic discourse, rephrase a narrative of biblical subject matter or an exegetical narrative, or constitute a reply to a rhetorical question, which is itself not explicitly related to a scriptural verse.

The *mashal* narratives are clearly fictional narratives about ahistorical events,[115] but in more than a few cases, the fictions include diction not found in what Stern describes as the "thesaurus of thematic, motific, and lexical stereotypes" of the

---

[113] For an analysis of this passage in terms of poetology of the parable see Stern, *Parables*, 65–67.
[114] See Stern, *Parables*, 16–24.
[115] Heinrich Lausberg, *Handbuch der literarischen Rhetorik: Eine Grundlegung der Literaturwissenschaft*, 2nd ed. (Munich: Max Hueber Verlag, 1973), Registerbd., s.v. παραβολή, who defines the term as "*similitudo*, die aus dem Bereich der Natur und des allgemeinen (nicht historisch fixierten) Menschenlebens genommen ist."

regularised form of the Rabbinic *mashal*.[116] In the case of the *mashal* proper with the disciples of the wise as characters, we could ask whether this is an approximation of the *mashal* to the rhetorical claim of the *maʿaseh* – a literary form that "purports to tell a story that actually took place," as David Stern describes it.[117]

In some cases, as was pointed out in my discussion of certain parables,[118] Stern's claim that there is evidence in *Seder Eliyahu* of a tendency towards novelisation appears to be valid. It cannot, however, be stated that this is a characteristic feature of the entire corpus, or even of the majority of its parables. On the contrary, for a considerable number of parables, Goldberg's description of the classical parable in terms of a "minimal narrative sequence" is more adequate.[119]

Another salient feature of the parables in this late midrash is that, except for two in *Seder Eliyahu Rabbah* and those told in *Pseudo-Seder Eliyahu Zuta*, the parables are never attributed to a Rabbinic authority. The teller of the remaining sixty-odd parables is the governing voice, which tells them either as itself, as part of its non-narrative discourse, or in its role as the narrator in a first-person narrative, thus having different direct addressees. Notwithstanding this choice to efface the names, much of what is accomplished with the parables in *Seder Eliyahu* is nothing but self-representation of the Rabbinic class. Even though they remain nameless for the most part, it appears that the sages, their mores and values, are at the centre of *Seder Eliyahu*'s discourse, and the parables are no exception in this respect. The "disciples of the wise" in many parables are the characters in the *nimshal*, so that the praise they receive appears to be the very reason why the parable is told. They can even be present *in* the *mashal* narrative, as has been shown. A further rhetorical strategy used by the author of *Seder Eliyahu* to explicitly put the disciples of the wise in focus is the use of the first-person plural in the contexts of parables praising the sages;[120] thus he not only identifies with the sages he praises, but also invites his audience to identify with them. The sages are said to be one of two or several classes within Israel; they are contrasted with "the ignoramuses with proper conduct,"[121] but also with heartless men who have

---

116 See Stern, *Parables*, 21.
117 Stern, *Parables*, 13.
118 E.g., EZ 178, l. 11, among others.
119 See Goldberg, "Das schriftauslegende Gleichnis," 146–147: "Da das narrative Relat eine minimale narrative Sequenz enthält, nämlich eine Ausgangssituation, ein darin enthaltenes oder ein geäußertes Problem und eine Folge, und diese beiden Teile des Relats in der Regel durch eine Relation des Grundes oder der Ursache ('weil': 'deshalb') oder der Bedingung ('wann': 'dann') stehen, seien die beiden Teile des SG 'Protasis' und 'Apodosis' genannt."
120 E.g., ER 25, l. 4ff.; ER 69, l. 4ff.; and ER 71, l. 22ff.
121 See ER 69, l. 4ff.

knowledge of Scripture and Mishnah;[122] and those disciples of the wise who lose their children in childhood receive corresponding consolation.[123]

Stern also points out that the use of the parable as an illustrative tool in *Seder Eliyahu* means that the narratives themselves "lose their more symbolic features and simultaneously become less plausible as narratives."[124] The reader of such implausible narratives asks, baffled, "What is this narrative really about?"[125] – as for example, in the first of all the parables in *Seder Eliyahu*, according to which a king is pleased with his servants collecting rubbish and placing it at his door:

> They told a parable: What does the matter resemble? It is like a king of flesh and blood whose servants and household members used to take the refuse and throw it out before the king's doorway. But when he [the king] came out [of the palace] and saw the refuse, he rejoiced with great joy. (ER 4, l. 26–28)

Yet bafflement is not a reaction that arises exclusively when reading the *parables* in *Seder Eliyahu*. *Seder Eliyahu* is a difficult text; the logic with which sentences are concatenated is quite often far from evident, and sometimes it is only after intense reading(s) that the meaning of a passage can be elucidated – or at least the modern reader gets this impression.[126]

---

[122] See ER 69, l. 25ff.
[123] See EZ 191, l. 15ff. Stern, *Parables*, 124, counts consolation in case of the deaths of young children as a recurring theme in *meshalim*: "Sometimes, these *meshalim* attempt to rationalize the death, to explain, almost apologetically, why the tragic loss of a young child or the premature decease of a righteous colleague should not offend their sense of God's justice."
[124] Stern, *Parables*, 215.
[125] Stern, *Parables*, 215.
[126] It is because this chapter attempted to illustrate *Seder Eliyahu*'s arduous textual landscape that parables were quoted not in isolation, but within the lengthy textual units of meaning that frame them.

5 Men with Scripture but No Mishnah

> Einen Punkt hat er [Zunz] jedoch nicht hervorgehoben, der freilich etwas überraschend ist und dem Werke einen besonderen Reiz verleiht. Es ist dies der Umstand, daß an zwei Stellen Elija – d. h. der Verfasser – als Vertheidiger der rabbanitischen Lehre gegen die Karäer auftritt.[1]

Ever since Wilhelm Bacher published his article "Antikaräisches" in 1874 *Seder Eliyahu* has been regarded as a polemical Rabbinic response to Karaism.[2] In Bacher's view, it is not the fact that a late midrash such as *Seder Eliyahu*,[3] contains anti-Karaite polemics that is remarkable, but rather that no other midrash does. He sees an explanation for this special feature in what he assumes to be the work's place of composition – Babylonia.[4]

Some eighty years after Bacher's article, Moshe Zucker would address the issue in more detail.[5] Both Bacher and Zucker were convinced that a number of

---

[1] Bacher, "Antikaräisches," 266–267 ("He [Zunz] failed to emphasise an aspect, admittedly an astonishing one and one which adds particular zest to the work. It is the fact that in two passages Elijah – i.e. the author – appears as defender of the rabbanite doctrine against the Karaites").
[2] See Wilhelm Bacher and Shulim Ochser, "Tanna De-vei Eliyahu," in *The Jewish Encyclopaedia*, ed. Isidor Singer, vol. 12 (New York: Funk / Wagnalis, 1906), 46–49; and Elbaum, "Tanna De-vei Eliyahu."
[3] Which, incidentally, he dates to 970.
[4] In his discussion of late midrashim, Lerner, "Works of Aggadic Midrash," 153, points out in this regard: "The second phenomenon not dealt with by Elbaum ["Between Redaction and Rewriting"] is the anti-Karaite polemics. The Karaite schism begun by Anan b. David during the latter half of the eighth century evoked various forms of response from the leaders of Rabbinic Judaism and it was only natural that anti-Karaite polemics would find their way into contemporary midrashic literature. Surprisingly enough, however, this phenomenon is not too widespread and there is only sporadic evidence for such occurrences in midrashic works dating from the eighth to the tenth centuries. Bacher et al. have argued that certain halakhic passages in *Seder Eliyahu* as well as those stressing the importance of Mishnah study, instead of concentrating exclusively on the Bible, reflect the author's staunch opposition to Karaism. However, this conclusion has been challenged by some scholars, or simply ignored by others. J. N. Epstein and Moshe Zucker have focused on a relatively large number of anti-Karaite polemics in *Mishnat R. Eliezer*, whereas individual attacks are found in *Midrash Tanchuma*, and possibly in *Midrash Mishlei* and *Pesikta Rabbati*. Needless to say, the presence of polemical material against Karaite beliefs and practices in a particular midrash most likely attests to a ninth century or even later origin. However, the somewhat surprising paucity of such material in supposed later midrashic works raises some serious doubts as to the date which scholars have attributed to these works."
[5] Zucker, *Rav Saadya Gaon's Translation*, 116–127, 203–219. On the more general question concerning the evidence of any significant anti-Karaite literature in the period before Seʿadyah, see Yoram Erder, *The Karaite Mourners of Zion and the Qumran Scrolls: On the History of an Alterna-*

passages in *Seder Eliyahu* were based on knowledge of Karaite texts, as evidence of which they refer to texts dated to the late ninth and tenth,[6] but also to the fifteenth centuries.[7] The problem of probable anti-Karaite polemics in *Seder Eliyahu* has been discussed more recently in an article by Lennart Lehmhaus, who provides a reading of the second chapter of *Seder Eliyahu Zuta* in terms of a depiction of the self and a non-Rabbinic other, a semi-learned Jew.[8]

In the following pages, I will discuss the first-person narratives which led Bacher to conclude that *Seder Eliyahu* can be understood as reacting to Karaism. These are texts that give the reader very little information about the historical setting they might represent. The rabbi simply explains that, while travelling from one place to another, he comes upon "a man who has [knowledge of] Scripture but no [knowledge of] Mishnah," a phrase that Bacher and Zucker interpret as an alternative way of referring to a Karaite.[9] In view of the fact that Karaism as a movement appears to have crystallised in several circles only in the second half of the ninth century[10] – that is, after the accepted time of composition of *Seder Eliyahu*, in the first half of the ninth century, I suggest we should speak of allusions to a proto-Karaism in the discussion of passages that appear to hint at the following characteristics of formative Karaism:[11]

---

tive to Rabbinic Judaism, Diaspora: New Perspectives on Jewish History and Culture 3 (Turnhout: Brepols, 2017), 39–49.
6 E.g., Daniel al-Qumisi (ninth century), Salmon b. Yerucham, Yefet b. Eli and Sahl b. Matsliach (tenth century).
7 E.g., Elijah Bashyatsi (fifteenth century).
8 Lehmhaus, "Understanding and Knowledge."
9 Erder, *The Karaite Mourners of Zion*, 6 and 16, argues that the designation "Karaites" (קראים) is derived from the expression "those who call upon God" (קריאי השם) found in the Damascus Covenant and only secondarily acquired the meaning of "champions of Scripture," which is already attested to in the ninth century. Neither the term קראים, nor the expressions "peoples of the Scripture" (בני מקרא) or "masters of the Scripture" (בעלי מקרא), nor the self-designations "returnees from sin" or "mourners of Zion" are ever mentioned in the work. Kadushin, *The Theology*, 5–6, argues that the phrase "who know Scripture but not Mishnah" alludes to "stages of learning," not to any particular type of sectarianism, let alone Karaism. Similarly, Moulie Vidas, *Tradition and the Formation of the Talmud* (Princeton, Oxford: Princeton University Press, 2014), 120, argues that *miqra*, *mishnah*, and *talmud* refer to stages or types of Torah study.
10 See Meira Polliack, "Rethinking Karaism: Between Judaism and Islam," *AJS Review* 30, no. 1 (2006): 70.
11 See Fred Astren, "Islamic Contexts of Medieval Karaism," in *Karaite Judaism: A Guide to its History and Literary Sources*, ed. Meira Polliack (Leiden, Boston: Brill, 2003), 145: "In the Islamic Middle Ages through the late ninth century C.E., the antecedents and origins of medieval Karaism are known from sparse reports in Hebrew and Arabic texts. In this period one can only speak of 'proto-Karaitic phenomena,' that is, those Jewish individuals and movements that would later

1. the recognition of Scripture as the exclusive legal source and the rejection of the Rabbinic concept of the Oral Tradition, including its documents, its tradents, and its authorities in Babylonia;
2. the idea that not only the Torah, but the entire Tanakh can serve as the source of the law;
3. the insistence on the individual study of Scripture, a study that does not rely on "imposed" traditions; and, to a lesser extent,
4. the praise of an asceticism connected with a general inclination towards a "Palestino-centrism" and "messianic nationalism."

5.1 *Seder Eliyahu Zuta*, Chapter 2

The first narrative Bacher adduces as evidence for *Seder Eliyahu*'s anti-Karaism is that transmitted in the second chapter of *Seder Eliyahu Zuta*.[12] It opens as follows:

> I was once travelling (הייתי מהלך בדרך) when I met a man who approached me the way heretics do (בדרך מינות).[13] He had [knowledge of] Scripture, but he had no [knowledge of] Mishnah (ויש בו מקרא ואין בו משנה). He said to me, Scripture was given to us from Mount Sinai. Mishnah was not given to us from Mount Sinai. And I answered him, My son, were not both Scripture and Mishnah uttered by the mouth of the Lord? What is the difference between Scripture and Mishnah? They told a parable. What does the matter resemble? It is like a king of flesh and blood who had two servants, whom he used to love with a complete love. He gave one a measure of wheat and the other a measure of wheat. He gave one a bundle of flax and the other a bundle of flax. The clever one of the two, what did he do? He took the flax and wove it into a linen cloth (מפה). He took the wheat and made a dish of fine flour out of it. He sifted and ground it [the grain], kneaded it [the dough], baked it, set it on the table, and spread the linen cloth over it, but left it [there] until the coming of the king. The foolish one did nothing at all. After some time the king came into his house and spoke to them like this, My sons, bring me what I gave you. One brought out [a loaf of] the dish of fine flour upon the table and the tablecloth spread over it. The other brought out the wheat in a basket and on top of

---

contribute to fully articulated Karaism after the late ninth century. The late ninth through the late tenth centuries witness the emergence of classical medieval Karaism in Palestine with its center at Jerusalem, and is marked by a literature that is specifically Karaite."

12 Unlike the majority of the first-person narratives in the work, in this case the whole chapter consists of a first-person narrative.

13 The Venice print, which Bacher follows for his reading, reads not בדרך מינות, but בדרך מצות, "polemically." Bacher, "Antikaräisches," 267n2, points out that the expression is to be translated with "in polemischer Weise, Absicht." Nissi b. Noach is said to have called arguing Rabbanites מריבי ונצי and הנצים והמלינים. Braude and Kapstein, *Tanna děbe Eliyyahu*, 407, base their translation on both readings: "One time, as I was walking along a road, a man accosted me. He came at me aggressively with the sort of argument that leads to heresy."

it the bundle of flax. Oh, for such a shame! Oh, for such a disgrace! Alas, tell me, which of the two was dear to him? The one who brought out the table with [a loaf of] the dish of fine flour upon it. (EZ 171, l. 16–28)

The first segment or preamble of this narrative, which can be described in Lennart Lehmhaus's terms as "a narrative of 'wandering' and encounter,"[14] consists of what may be inferred as a non-urban spatial setting, the anticipatory characterisation of the rabbi's interlocutor, and the latter's double statement: "Scripture was given to us from Sinai. Mishnah was not given us to from Sinai."[15] The second part of this statement could elsewhere have been an invitation to a disputation. Not so in *Seder Eliyahu*, where the rabbi shows himself as a calm master of the situation, even even in the face of such a provocation.[16] He replies to the challenge rather informally, addressing the man with the words "My son,"[17] thus putting him – of whom we know neither his age, nor anything about his physical appearance, nor anything apart from the words he has just uttered – in the position of one inferior in wisdom, as a son is when compared with his father. Using a rhetorical question to begin his exposition, one that stresses the oral nature of the medium of transmission of *both* Torot, the rabbi goes on to illustrate the nature of the difference between Scripture and Mishnah with a parable. The *mashal* proper suggests that bread and linen can be made out of wheat and flax, provided he who receives them is clever (פיקח) enough. No explicit *nimshal* comes immediately after the *mashal* proper. Instead, the *mashal* is briefly commented upon by means of a question and an answer. In view of the fact that the turns in conversations in *Seder Eliyahu* are generally signalled with inquit formulas, it may be assumed that both question and answer are spoken by the rabbi himself.[18] As far as the preamble is concerned, the matter is settled: Whereas the king loved both servants with a complete love before he gave them wheat and flax, after seeing the transformation of these raw

---

14 Lehmhaus, "Understanding and Knowledge," 236.
15 Friedmann, *Seder Eliahu*, 171n2, points out that MS Parma 2785 provides an answer to the question, "What is [the difference] between Scripture and Mishnah?" – namely, "This [the former] is text, and this [the latter] is interpretation."
16 Lehmhaus, "Between Tradition and Innovation," 222, infers from this characterisation that the rabbi's main agenda is not to demonstrate the superiority of a learned class, but rather to persuade his opponents of the values of his minimal Judaism.
17 For the informal style of address in depicted encounters between Palestinian rabbis and non-rabbis, see Richard Kalmin, "Relationships between Rabbis and Non-rabbis," *Jewish Studies Quarterly* 5 (1998): 161–168; and Lehmhaus, "Understanding and Knowledge," 254.
18 But then, considering that the next segment opens precisely with such an inquit formula, and that it is the rabbi's turn to speak, it may also be the case that the question is actually answered by the man with knowledge of Scripture only.

materials on the part of the industrious servant, that servant becomes the only one he loves. Bacher interprets the *mashal* in the following terms:

> Dieses Gleichnis, welches in überraschender Weise an die neutestamentliche Parabel von den beiden Pfunden erinnert, legt witzig und schlagend den Unterschied dar zwischen dem Stabilismus der einerseits auf den Wortlaut der Schrift pochenden, andererseits in unvermittelter Weise überlieferte Satzungen – סבל ההעתקה – annehmenden Karäern und den, Schrift und Überlieferung einheitlich weiter entwickelnden Rabbaniten.[19]

The next segment in the dialogue consists of a sort of cross-examination, in which the rabbi leads the man to acknowledge that a series of liturgical practices he is evidently familiar with, are not attested in Scripture, and must therefore stem from tradition:

> I said to him, My son, if I test you by the Mishnah (lit. "if I find you in the Mishnah") of the sages, your words will be deemed untrue. He answered, Yes, but ... I said to him, My son, when you go down to the chest on the Sabbath how many [benedictions] do you pray? He answered, Seven. I said to him, And on the rest of the days? [He answered,] The whole Tefillah. [I said to him,] How many men read the Torah on the Sabbath? [He answered,] Seven. [I said to him,] And how many on the afternoon of Sabbath, on the second, and on the fifth [day of the week]? [He answered,] Three [on every one of the] three [occasions]. [I said to him,] And on the seven products [of Palestine] how many [benedictions] do you pray? He answered, Two. A blessing before [eating] them and a blessing after [eating] them. [I said to him,] And on all other sorts of food? [He answered,] Just one benediction. [I said to him,] And [for] the grace after meal [how many benedictions do you pray]? [He answered,] Three, but four with "He who is good and does good." I said to him, My son, do we have all these [prescriptions] from Sinai, or are they not rather in the Mishnah of the sages? When the Holy One, blessed be He, gave Israel the Torah, He did not do it but as wheat from which they were to bring forth a dish of fine flour and as flax from which they were to bring forth a garment. He gave it [the Torah] in [hermeneutical rule of] *kelal u-ferat, ferat-u-khelal* [and, *kelal u-*

---

19 Bacher, "Antikaräisches," 268 ("This parable, which surprisingly enough reminds of the New Testament parable of the talents, is a witty and impressive demonstration of the difference between the stabilism with which Karaites both insisted on the wording of Scripture and accepted the transmitted ordinances just as they were, and the Rabbanites who went on to consistently develop Scripture and tradition"). It could be argued that the similarity of the Rabbinic parable to that of the talents (Matt 25:14–30) is limited to the idea that different people achieve different results with what is given them, be it money or raw materials. Jesus's parable recounts that, before leaving for a journey, a man gives his servants different amounts of money according to their respective abilities. The servants who received five and two talents respectively both double the amount during their master's absence. On the other hand, the one who receives one talent buries it in the earth. On his return, the man is pleased with the way the first two have dealt with his money and very displeased with the behaviour of the third, whom he punishes by having his talent taken away from him and given to the one who already has ten talents.

ferat u-khelal].²⁰ For it is said, *spend the money for whatever you wish* (Deut 14:26): that is a generalization [*kelal*]; *oxen, sheep, wine, strong drink* (Deut 14:26): that is a specification [that follows]; *or whatever you desire* (Deut 14:26): this is yet another generalisation. Here a generalisation needs a specification and a specification needs [in its turn] a generalisation.²¹ (EZ 172, l. 1–13)

The man seems to be well acquainted with the liturgy the rabbi outlines in his questions. This familiarity of the questioner with all the mentioned religious and liturgical practices led Bacher to conclude that the Karaite and Rabbanite rites were not as different at the time of composition of *Seder Eliyahu* – which, as has already been mentioned, he traces back to the end of the tenth century – as they would be later on.²² Scholarship on Karaism, on the other hand, appears to agree on the fact that the development of Karaite liturgy moved in the opposite direction – from the utter rejection of Rabbinic liturgical practices to a relative acceptance of certain aspects in its later stages. Leon Nemoy, for example, argued that it was precisely in its early stages that Karaism rejected central aspects of Rabbanite liturgy, such as the use of non-biblical prayers:

> On one principal point, however, the early Karaites were unanimous, and that was their conviction that formal prayer should consist exclusively of scriptural quotations, mainly the Psalms of David, and that the Rabbanite practice of composing and introducing into the official liturgy new material in the form of prose prayers and versified hymns was unauthorized and unlawful. It was a logical enough line of thought, from the Karaite point of view, and it led them not only to the rejection of such ancient and basic portions of the Rabbanite liturgy as the so-called Eighteen Benedictions …, but also to the adoption of different prophetic lessons …, which are read as appendices to the lessons from the Law.²³

---

20 On the fifth of Hillel's seven hermeneutic rules, *kelal u-ferat u-ferat u-khelal*, a general rule followed by a specification or a specification followed by a generalisation, see Stemberger, *Einleitung*, 31.
21 The same example is given in the *Baraita de R. Ishmael*, which describes the thirteen hermeneutical rules of R. Ishmael in a sort of introduction to the halakhic midrash *Sifra* (later third to fourth century)
22 Bacher, "Antikaräisches," 269, observes, "Aus dieser Stelle läßt sich zugleich schließen, daß der karäische Ritus damals noch keine so durchgreifende Unterschiede von dem rabbanitischen aufzuweisen hatte, als nachher." ("It may also be inferred from this passage that at that point the Karaite and the Rabbanite rites were not as radically different as would later on be the case").
23 Leon Nemoy, *Karaite Anthology: Excerpts from the Early Literature* (New Haven, CT, London: Yale University Press, 1952), 272–273. Jacob Mann, *Karaitica*, vol. 2 of *Texts and Studies in Jewish History and Literature* (New York: Ktav Publishing House, 1972), 51, also mentions the recitation of piyyutim during the Rabbinic synagogue service as a target of Karaite criticism. Another, even more important problem for Karaites – mentioned by Mann and not discussed in this section of *Seder Eliyahu* due to its being, as pointed out to me by Prof. Günter Stemberger, a very late

More recently, Robert Brody has suggested that it was only later that Karaism came to accept post-biblical prayers and other general aspects of Rabbinic liturgy which had been rejected by earlier authorities.[24] In view of this, the dialogue quoted above could therefore be evidence either for a later time of composition of *Seder Eliyahu* than the one now generally accepted or for the fact that the questioner is not consistently depicted as an early-stage Karaite, or at least not as belonging to its better-known circles.[25] In any case, the rabbi's interlocutor is depicted as exhibiting, to quote Lennart Lehmhaus, a "theoretical skepticism towards the divine Oral Torah, paired with practical conformity regarding Rabbinic liturgy."[26]

The list of liturgical practices is of interest not only in relation to the history of Karaite liturgy, but also with respect to the textual and narrative logic of the passage: It constitutes a *nimshal* to the parable of the two servants quoted previously.[27] Given that there is no *nimshal* marker or introductory formula, this *nimshal* is only evident the moment the rabbi explicitly refers back to the two motifs of the *mashal* proper, the wheat and the flax, which the servants handle differently while the king is away: "When the Holy One, blessed be He, gave Israel the Torah, He did not do it but as wheat from which they were to bring forth a dish of fine flour and as flax from which they were to bring forth a garment." In a next step, the rabbi proceeds to interpret the wheat and the flax of the parable not simply as scriptural raw material, but also as hermeneutic rules given to Israel by God together with Scripture – rules that enabled them to infer from the Written Torah the practices mentioned or alluded to in the cross-examination. These practices are therefore identified with the products of wheat and flax in the hands of the clever servant. Whence in Scripture the sages inferred these liturgical practices is not specified in the *nimshal*.[28]

---

development – is the Rabbinic idea that the synagogue was a substitute for the Temple, a concept which the rabbis themselves were generally opposed to.

24 See Brody, *The Geonim of Babylonia*, 95.
25 Erder, *The Karaite Mourners of Zion*, 3, points out, "Because of its initially pluralistic nature the Karaite movement embraced many circles."
26 Lehmhaus, "Understanding and Knowledge," 249.
27 To be sure, it is a less explicit *nimshal* than that found immediately after a *mashal* proper and generally marked by an opening formula such as *le-khakh*.
28 It is worth noting that the rabbi's explanation must have been directed at an audience that was already familiar with what can be achieved through Rabbinic hermeneutics. An interlocutor such as the one of the narrative, who is not familiar with Rabbinic hermeneutics (or with the names of Rabbinic hermeneutic rules), would hardly be able to derive a lesson from the example given by the rabbi, other than the fact that the quotation from Deut 14:26 contains a generalisation (*kelal*) that requires a specification (*perat*), which in its turn asks for another generalisation, all of which is assumed to be valid for other verses.

As Bacher argues, the questions that follow are not specifically characteristic of the representation of anti-Karaite discourse per se, but can be seen as evidence of which topics were typically brought forth in the representation of disputes with non-Rabbinic others at the time of composition of *Seder Eliyahu*. They can be described as variations of one and the same theological question – namely, why there does not seem to be much difference between the ways in which the just and the wicked are rewarded.

The questioner first asks, for example, whether he who carries out a command and he who commits a transgression are both rewarded as they deserve.[29] After claiming that God is an omnipresent king who rules the entire earth He created and the seven heavens as well, the rabbi explains that God takes and distributes his reward among the just and unjust of his world – that is, during their lifetime – only to let people know that whoever suffers privations while living according to the Torah and carrying out its commandments receives his worldly reward, but that the capital (הקרן) of his reward is kept aside for him, as the essence of his reward, in the world to come. Thus the rabbi's answer cannot be said to exclusively represent Rabbinic ideology or to specifically reject Karaism.[30] The text, however, proceeds to connect the notion of the second reward in the world to come with the giving of the Mishnah:

> Because the Holy One, blessed be He, did not find among humanity men who would suffer affliction (בצער) to do the Torah, suffer affliction to carry out commandments, and suffer affliction to build the Second Temple, men who would deny themselves enjoyments (מצערין) for the sake of Torah and for the sake of the commandments, until those men came who suffered affliction to do the Torah and [suffered affliction to] carry out commandments, [and suffered affliction to build the Second Temple] and who endured affliction for the sake of Torah and for the sake of the commandments. Therefore, He gave them the Mishnah, them, and their children, and their children's children until the end of all generations. (EZ 172, l. 22–EZ 173, l. 3)

---

29 See EZ 172, l. 14–15.

30 Louis Ginzberg, as quoted in Kadushin, *Organic Thinking*, 287n383, argues against Friedmann, *Seder Eliahu*, 172n6: "Friedmann put something into the text of which there is not the slightest trace therein. What has the selection of Israel to do with the authority of oral law? Did the Karaites deny the one because they refused to accept the other doctrine? Scripture has in hundreds of passages taught the Selection of Israel. The statement מיום שנברא העולם has nothing to do with the previous argument. The man simply stated that there is justice in this world; and our author agrees, saying that God takes reward (satisfaction) in this world, too. But, adds our author, for the worthy there is a 'double reward', in this world and in the next. It is not a Christian whom our author answers thus, for the former would not have questioned future reward." However, as the text goes on to argue, Friedmann anticipates in this footnote a line of thought that is indeed present in the text of *Seder Eliyahu*.

So this part of the rabbi's answer is more explicit about a Rabbinic agenda, suggesting that the Mishnah's etymon is related to God's double reward of those who sacrifice themselves for the study of Torah. Within this answer and still in a narrative context, the rabbi appears to switch to the homiletical mode of the governing voice itself, addressing the (extratextual) audience of the midrash: In this mode a rhetorical question is posed, pertaining to how God takes his reward from the world He created (EZ 173, l. 3), which opens a thematic segment concerned with the way God proceeds in his awarding certain spaces and people a special status. For this description, the image of the Terumah, the priest's heave offering, is used. First, a parable is told: A king builds a palace and finds it so beautiful that he takes it as his residence. According to the *nimshal*, the parable illustrates how the land of Israel was selected as the place from which God was to create the rest of the lands of the world. In three further steps, God's "selections" are described: From among the peoples of the world, God selected Israel as a heave offering; from among the children of Israel, He selected the tribe of Levi as a heave offering; and from the tribe of Levi, He selected Aaron. The same selections are then explained in a more systematic manner, repeatedly using forms of the root פרש and the expression תרומה to describe God's selections:

> And He brought Israel, who are the heave offering (תרומה) from among all the peoples [of the world], to the land of Israel, which is singled out (פרושה) from among all the lands. Then He brought the tribe of Levi, which He set apart (הפריש) from Israel, to Jerusalem, which is the land of Israel's heave offering (תרומה). And He brought the children of Aaron, whom He singled out (הפריש) from among the tribe of Levi, to the Temple, which He set apart (הפריש) from Jerusalem, to stand and do His will with a whole heart, for it is said, *He stood, and measured the land, He looked and made the nations tremble* (Hab 3:6). And it [Scripture] says, *his ways (הליכות) are everlasting (עולם)* (Hab 3:6). From here they said: Whoever studies (שונה) the laws (הלכות) can be confident that he is a son of the world to come (העולם הבא). Some say that in the place whence the earth for the first man was taken the altar was built, for it is said, *then the Lord God formed man from the dust of the ground* (Gen 2:7). And it [Scripture] says, *You need make for me only an altar of earth* (Exod 20:24). From here they said: As long as the Temple stood, the altar within was [what made] expiation for Israel wherever they dwelt. But outside the Land the sages and the disciples of the sages are [the ones who make] expiation for Israel wherever they dwell. For it is said, *If you bring a grain offering of the first fruits to the Lord* etc. (Lev 1:14). And it [Scripture] says, *A man came from Baal-shalishah, bringing food from the first fruits to the man of God* etc. (2 Kgs 4:42). But was Elishah a priest? There was neither Temple, nor altar, nor High Priesthood there. Elishah was rather a prophet and disciples of the wise would sit before him, either in Dotan or in Samaria. From here they said: Whoever is attached to the sages and to their disciples, Scripture credits him as if he were offering first fruits and doing the will of his Father who is in heaven. (EZ 173, l. 11–26)

The rabbi seizes the opportunity given to him by a rather neutral question to exalt the disciples of the wise for their study of God's ways (הליכות), read as his laws

(הלכות). They are the bearers of that tradition the questioner apparently rejects, and they have ensured Israel's expiation ever since the Temple was destroyed. It is not the priests whom they succeed, but the Temple itself.

In his next question, the third, the man again poses a generally theological topic of discussion – namely, why the peoples of the world are permitted to enjoy the world. With his answer, the rabbi continues the line of argumentation he followed in the previous answer, using the idea that God sets someone or something apart, giving them the status of Terumah.[31]

> They told a parable. What does the matter resemble? It is like a king of flesh and blood who would not find but a single man among a large family who did his will. He sent numerous presents to the members of the family because of this one man who did his will. So too is it with the nations of the world. Their reward is that God set Israel apart from their midst. Therefore they may enjoy this world. (EZ 174, l. 3–6)

The questioner again takes up the problem of the unjust being improperly rewarded in spite of their behaviour, which he already brought up in his second question. It could be argued that not only a theological, but also a semantic problem is at stake here, for the questioner states that both the just and the transgressor are given שכרו ("their reward"). The rabbi's answer shows not only that God discriminates with precision between those who act according to the Torah and those who transgress it by not giving them the same שכר, but also that שכר is a poly-semous term denoting different kinds of reward – both positive and negative reward or punishment:

> He said to me, Rabbi, but then everyone who performs a commandment is given his reward (שכרו), and everyone who commits a transgression is given his reward (שכרו). I answered him, My son, what was the reward of the ancient serpent who proceeded to corrupt the whole world? What was the reward of Adam and Eve who transgressed a command? What was the reward of Cain who slew Abel, his brother? And what was the reward of Lamech who would observe the mourning ceremonies of his father's brother? And what was the reward of Shem, who honoured his father? And what was the reward of Ham who did not honour his father? And what was the reward of Noah who proceeded to forewarn the multitudes during all those hundred and twenty years [of his life], so that it [the punishment] would not befall them? Therefore He [God] caused it to be written about him and announced to the generations, *For I have seen that you alone are righteous before me in this generation* (Gen 7:1). And what was the reward of the great Shem who would prophesy to all the peoples of the world for four hundred years without their heeding him? And what was the reward of our father Abraham who proceeded to destroy all the idols of the world? However, because he said something improper, his children went down to Egypt, for it is said, *But he said, O Lord God, how am I to know that I shall possess it?* (Gen 15:8). Because of that hesitation his children had to go

---

31 Bacher's analysis of this chapter comes to an end at this point.

down to Egypt. And what was the reward of Ishmael who went and buried his father? And what was the reward of Isaac who spoke to his father, Father, bind me well and then put me on the altar, lest I strike and injure you and I am found guilty of two death penalties from heaven; I who am a young man, resistant in my strength, thirty-seven years old? What was the reward of Esau who shed two tears before his father? They gave him Mount Seir where the rains of blessing never cease. And also the sons of Seir, who received the sons of Esau amicably, were given their reward. From here they said: Even if a man has no [knowledge of] Scripture and no [knowledge of] Mishnah, but sits and reads the whole day [the verse], *Lotan's sister was Timna* (Gen 36:22), the reward of Torah is in his hand. And what was the reward of Jacob who acknowledged the truth and spoke the truth in his heart[32] all the days of his life? And what was the reward of the Twelve Tribes who would do the will of Jacob their father, for it is said, *Like grapes in the wilderness, I found Israel. Like the first fruit on the fig tree, in its first season, I saw your ancestors who came* <etc.> (Hos 9:10)? What was the reward of Abraham, Isaac, and Jacob, who conducted themselves with fear in their hearts in the midst of the seventy languages [i.e., all the seventy nations of the world]? [The reward is] theirs, and their children's, and their children's children until the end of the all generations. (EZ 174, l. 6–EZ 175, l. 7)

The rabbi's answer consists of a series of fourteen questions concerning the deeds of single or collective biblical characters and God's reward for them. The scriptural episodes thus alluded to with different levels of specificity are ordered according to the biblical chronology, though in some cases this is altered. Most of the questions follow the same pattern: What was the reward of X who did X? In some, a subordinate clause contains more information than in the rest, including direct speech (Isaac's story) or even scriptural material (on Noah). With the exception of the question concerning Esau, the other questions are not followed by what can be formally recognised as an answer, but rather appear to fulfil their intended allusive function on their own. Another variation of the standard pattern is provided by the question concerning Abraham, which is followed by a short digression. The information contained in the questions and expansions reveals that the understanding of the biblical episodes with which the rabbi presents his challenger relies on *Rabbinic traditions*, and not merely on the biblical text.

With respect to the different types of reward: The first three questions clearly allude to biblical characters who were punished – the ancient serpent, Adam and Eve, and Cain. From the fourth question onwards, most questions are preceded with a *waw*, which seems to have an adversative function, thus marking a contrast with the first group of questions and indicating that these later questions deal with people whom God positively. The fourth question pertains to Lamech's

---

[32] An evident idealisation of Jacob; see Gen 27:24 and 33:13–15.

reward, though it is not clear which Lamech is meant.³³ With the next two questions, dealing with Shem and Ham respectively, the biblical chronology is altered for the first time. The question concerning their differing rewards precedes that dealing with their father, Noah. The latter's story, in its turn, is the first to be expanded with the quotation of a scriptural verse.

After posing a question on Noah's reward, the governing voice again turns to Shem, who is differently contextualised this time. Of Shem it is said, here and also in *Seder Eliyahu Rabbah*, that he prophesied to the peoples of the world for four hundred years.³⁴ With respect to Abraham, the episode concerning the destruction of the idols is mentioned as having earned him a reward. Abraham is the only character whose stories are used to illustrate that one and the same person can earn both a positive reward and a punishment, depending on their deeds. The question concerning his reward is followed by the explanation of why Abraham was also punished for his improper conduct in expressing doubt, in that his children had to go down to Egypt. Ishmael is said to have been rewarded for burying his father. A question dealing with Isaac's reward follows, the first micro-narrative in the series which makes use of direct speech. 37-year-old Isaac, about to be sacrificed by his father, wants to make sure his father succeeds in killing him, thus carrying out God's request.³⁵

The next question deals with the reason why Esau was given Mount Seir and its rains of blessing. Esau's narrative is expanded with another on his sons and those of Seir, as well as with a *mikan amru* statement on the reward of whoever persists in the recitation of Gen 36:22. Following Esau and the narratives associated with him, the governing voice finally turns to Jacob, to the twelve tribes, before closing this series of narratives with a last, vague allusion to the lives of the patriarchs – Abraham, Isaac, and Jacob – with which the dialogue with the man with no Mishnah comes to an end.

---

33 That is, the Lamech of Gen 4 or of Gen 5. As Friedmann, *Pseudo-Seder Eliahu Zuta*, 174n22, points out, no incident with a father's brother (אחי אביו) is known in the biblical text. He suggests that the author relies on Gen 4:19.23, inferring that Lamech killed his father's brother due to the way Lamech compares himself to Cain in Gen 4:24: If Cain killed his brother, then Lamech must have killed his uncle, who can also be called brother, the way a man's grandchildren are called his children. Braude and Kapstein, *Tanna děbe Eliyyahu*, 412n20, follow Ginzberg in reading "father's father" instead of "father's brother." According to Ginzberg, "Cain is meant who was mourned by his grandson (i.e., descendant) Lamech (comp. *Legends*, 1, 116–117); and Lamech's reward was that his daughter Naamah became the mother of mankind by her marriage to Noah; comp. *Legends*, 5, 147n45."
34 See ER 114, l. 14ff.
35 The episode has parallels in BerR 56:8 and PRE 31 among others.

Some of the stories alluded to in these narratives in nuce are comprehensible even without prior knowledge of the Rabbinic traditions on which they are based. Some of these traditions were more popular than others, as attested by the number of parallels. In the context of the present reading of these micro-narratives embedded in polemical dialogue between a rabbi and a challenger of Rabbinic Judaism, it is above all important to note that these are only apparently of scriptural origin. The rabbi's answer primarily demonstrates that he operates using arguments found in a tradition other than a merely scriptural one.

5.2 *Seder Eliyahu Rabbah*, Chapter (14) 15

Bacher describes the dialogue between the rabbi and an unnamed man "who had no Mishnah" contained in chapter (14) 15 as devoid of polemics and dealing with purely aggadic matters. He sees this passage simply in terms of a preamble to the more relevant dialogue depicted in chapter (15) 16. This is the reason Bacher promptly dismisses it after having ascertained that the questioner is a Karaite.[36] For Zucker, conversely, this is a crucial text with respect to *Seder Eliyahu*'s anti-Karaite polemics: According to him, all the questions the man poses in this chapter convey Karaite arguments.[37]

A detailed examination of this dialogue, which is preceded by almost the same narrative frame as the one in *Seder Eliyahu Zuta* that we discussed previously, might reveal the subtlety of its polemic character. The first part reads as follows:

> I was once travelling from one place to another (הייתי עובר ממקום למקום) when I found a man who had [knowledge of] Scripture, but no [knowledge of] Mishnah. He said to me, Rabbi, I would say a thing in your presence, but maybe you will be angry with me and this I fear. I replied, If you ask me something concerning the words of Torah, why would I be angry with you? [He said to me,] Rabbi, why does Scripture say, *[God] gives food to all flesh* (Ps 136:25), but also, *[He] gives to the animals their food* etc. (Ps 147:9)? Does not man prepare it [his food] himself? I replied, My son, is not the way of the world that a man does something with his hands which is afterwards blessed by the Holy One, blessed be He? For it is said, *The Lord your God may bless you in all the work of your hands* (Deut 14:29). One could think that he is to sit and be idle, but then Scripture says, *that you undertake* (Deut 14:29). He said to me, The answer with which you replied to me is the line of thought I first expressed before you, but it

---

36 Bacher, "Antikaräisches," 270, observes: "Die zweite Hälfte des vorangehenden Kapitels besteht zwar ebenfalls aus einem ähnlichen Gespräche, enthält aber Fragen von rein agadischem Charakter ohne polemischen Beigeschmack." ("The second half of the previous chapter is a similar dialogue, but this contains question of purely aggadic character, without any polemics").
37 See Zucker, *Rav Saadya Gaon's Translation*, 205.

is based on tradition (היא מקובלת, lit. "it is received"). I replied to him, My son, it is My father who is in heaven who gave me wisdom, understanding, and discernment to respond to the question you asked me. Go and learn from the fool wandering about in the marketplace. If he is [utterly] deprived of his wisdom, understanding, knowledge, and discernment, he will probably be able to provide for himself for an hour at the most. And so it is with [the rest of the] human beings. Once they are deprived of their wisdom, understanding, knowledge, and discernment they are regarded as cattle, beasts, and fowl, and [the rest of the] breathing beings the Holy One, blessed be He, created on the face of the earth. I call heaven and earth to witness that the Holy One, blessed be He, sits and distributes nourishment among all the inhabitants of the world and all the work of his hands which He created in the world, that is to say, man, cattle, creeping beings, and birds of heaven. (ER 70, l. 7–22)

The narrative frame of this dialogue depicts the anonymous narrator as travelling from one place to another and coming upon (lit. "finding") a man learned in Scripture, but not in Mishnah.[38] Also in this case, the spatial setting for the narrative of wandering and encounter is the road between two urban spaces. The man addresses the rabbi in a very cautious manner: He would ask something but does not dare utter it for fear that his interlocutor might be provoked to anger by his words. The rabbi responds by stating his conditions: Any question pertaining to the Torah he will willingly answer. He reacts as a kind teacher willing to transmit his wisdom, even to someone whose convictions he does not approve of. After this reassuring reply, the man states his first query.

The question addresses a contradiction in Scripture, as implied by parts of verses taken from Ps 136:25 and Ps 147:9. While the second psalm ("gives to the animals their food") is in accordance with the man's understanding that, unlike beasts, human beings provide for themselves, the first ("God gives food to all

---

38 The narrative's preceding co-text is the first half of chapter (14) 15: The opening statement by the governing voice – "Whoever abhors the good life in this world, it is a bad omen for him" – is illustrated by means of two contrasting king parables. The second illustrates the ungrateful attitude of a servant towards his king. The governing voice urges its audience, whom it addresses in an inclusive manner with the first-person plural, to be grateful for what life in this world actually means, which it explains in terms of a foretaste of the world to come and of a time of purification. The choice of the seed of Jacob is further discussed by means of an interpretation of Jer 31:8 – *See, I am going to bring them from the land of the north ... among them the blind and the lame*. The midrash is primarily concerned with the question of who is implied by the last words of the verse quoted here, *the blind and the lame*. It provides a number of alternative answers, all of which identify the *blind* and the *lame* (as well as the *blind* and the *deaf* of Isa 42:16.18) with different types of men, according to their knowledge of Torah and their conduct: Men lacking in knowledge of Torah but who demonstrate proper conduct; sages and their disciples, who possess the whole spectrum of Rabbinic knowledge; men who know Scripture and Mishnah, but who demonstrate terrible behaviour, etc. In this context, therefore, the questioner in the narrative should be viewed as yet another type of "the blind and the lame."

flesh") seems to imply that God gives equally to man and beast. The rabbi explains away the apparent contradiction, suggesting that men are supposed to provide for their own nourishment, which God will then bless – an argument for which he adduces the evidence of Deut 14:29. Even though the rabbi's questioners seldom react to the answers they get, in this case the questioner does object, with words that represent him as a "non-Rabbinic other" – probably a specifically proto-Karaite one. He argues that the rabbi's answer is based on received knowledge or tradition, not on Scripture – even though the rabbi does derive his argument from Scripture – hence it is not convincing. The word he uses to describe the answer is the participle מקובלת ("accepted," "acceptable," but also "received"). The expression is found in fourteen documents in the Maʾagarim database, eight of which are Karaite documents.[39] The rabbi takes up the word again and argues that, in spite of the possible implications of Ps 136:25, God does differentiate between man and beast, providing the former with reason or "wisdom, understanding, knowledge, and discernment" (חכמה ובינה ודיעה והשכל). Nevertheless, even if his generosity is expressed differently to man and beast, he lets every single one of his creatures partake thereof. The rabbi goes on to argue that God does distinguish between his creatures – some of them were given special properties, which are coupled with certain obligations – but despite these differences, all of his creatures are considered worthy. The rabbi continues with his exposition in a second segment, which he opens with a quotation from Scripture:

> Scripture says, *The fear of the Lord is his treasure* (Isa 33:6). It is like a king of flesh and blood who had many sons and servants. He wished to reprimand every one of them personally, but he noticed that they did not accept (מקבלין) his reprimands. So he wrote all his words on paper and hung them in an outer courtyard as an open letter (כאיגרת פתוחה) [addressed] to everyone. The public crier (כרוז) went from the king's presence and announced, Everyone who comes <and reads> this letter will be given bread and different kinds of food from the king. So it is with the house of Israel in this world with respect to words of Torah. When a man comes into the power of Scripture and Mishnah and learns from them the fear of Heaven and good deeds, these nourish, provide for, and sustain him until he enters his eternal abode, <for it is said,> *and he will be the stability of your times [abundance of salvation, wisdom, and knowledge]* etc. (Isa 33:6). (ER 70, l. 23–30)

Thus the rabbi closes his answer with an exegetical *mashal*, which interprets a scriptural quotation to further expound on the notion that God provides for all the inhabitants of His world, although He does so differently. The king of the *mashal*

---

39 These are al-Nahāwandī's *Sefer dinim* (ninth century), Tobias b. Moses ha-Avel's *Otsar nechmad* and *Sefer Machkimat Peti* (both eleventh century), as well as the anonymous *Meshivat nefesh* (eleventh century).

notices that his sons and servants refuse to accept his words of admonition. Therefore, he writes his message down as if in an open letter, not just for his sons and servants, but for everyone to read. It is, however, his public crier – the oral aspect of the message's transmission being thus emphasised – who reminds the king's sons and servants of the reward they are to expect if they care to read the king's admonitions: They will be given food and provisions. Given the *mashal*'s generic characteristics, neither message is given in its entirety: The king's message is summed up in the word "admonitions," and the crier's message is given in indirect speech. The rabbi's application of the *mashal* proper in the *nimshal* interprets it in terms of Israel's relation to the words of Torah. Their reward for learning the fear of Heaven, mentioned in the verse from Isaiah, both from Scripture (*iggeret*) and from Mishnah (*karuz*), is the nourishment that Torah gives them.

The *mashal* is related to the first part of the answer in several ways. The fact that the reward the king offers his subjects is food links the *mashal* proper to the discussion of the apparent contradiction between the two verses from the Psalms, which needs to be rejected. With the word for the notion that the king's subjects were expected to accept his message, מקבלין, the rabbi links the *mashal* with the expression used by the proto-Karaite himself to refer to the rabbi's answer (and perhaps to Rabbinic discourse in general), היא מקובלת. The *nimshal* explains life according to Rabbinic ideals as set down in Scripture and Mishnah – a life lived in fear of Heaven and in which good deeds prevail – as being itself the source of nourishment for man, the prerogative of human beings.[40]

The questioner poses several other questions, which do not seem to address controversial issues between Rabbinic and non-Rabbinic, Karaite Jews. For every question, however, it could be argued that there is a recognisable though very subtle element of anti-Karaite or anti-proto-Karaite polemics – for example, the emphasis on God's love for Israel over against the words of Torah in the second and third questions. The second question[41] is concerned with the words of Torah being more loved by God than anything else He created. According to the rabbi, this is so because they "put Israel on the scale of the balance of merit." God loves the words of Torah, the rabbi explains, more than anything else in this world because they enable Israel's privilege; they educate them in keeping the commandments and lead them to a life in the world to come. A king parable illustrates his argument: A king has many children, who have been educated in proper conduct and the performance of good deeds by one of his servants. When the king is visited daily

---

40 Even the words of Isa 33:6 left unquoted, with which a life according to the Torah is described, as one of "salvation, wisdom, and knowledge (חכמת ודעת)," silently refer back to the gift of "wisdom (חכמה), understanding, knowledge (דיעה), and discernment" in the first part of the answer.
41 See ER 70, l. 31ff.

by the servant and his children, he puts all other matters aside and praises the servant for the education of the children in matters of good conduct and the performance of good deeds. To the third question, of whether Torah or Israel should come first as man's object of love,[42] the rabbi replies that although Torah is generally regarded, according to Prov 8:22 – "The Lord created me at the beginning of his work[, the first of his acts of long ago]" – as coming first, he thinks that it is Israel who come first, and he quotes Jer 2:3 as evidence: "Israel was holy to the Lord, the first fruits of his harvest." Further confirmation follows in the form of another king *mashal*, in which a king with a wife and children in his household writes an edict. Were it not for the queen and the children, who used to act according to his will (so the *mashal*), the edict would not have reached the people. As in the *mashal* of the answer to the first question, the word used to refer to the edict is *iggeret*.[43] Aware that the adduced verses confirm the chronological priority of Torah over Israel – "The Lord created me at the beginning of his work" (Prov 8:22) vs. "Israel was holy to the Lord" (Jer 2:3) – the rabbi backs up his argument by midrashically producing further proof, by quoting yet another verse supporting his position: "The Lord appeared to him from far away[, I have loved you with an everlasting love]" etc. (Jer 31:3). Max Kadushin observes that these two passages are the exception in *Seder Eliyahu* in placing Israel above Torah:

> Taken together, the two passages, following one another, leave no room for doubt that our author, on this occasion, emphasized Israel as against Torah. It is not unlikely that the occasion was one in which our author felt called upon to implant the love for Israel, so outstanding a characteristic of the Rabbis, in a man to whom Rabbinic teaching – the Mishnah – was unknown. But a similar recognition of the rôle of Torah as dependant upon Israel occurs not in any special pedagogic situation.[44]

Finally, the fourth question[45] pertains to the indefinite duration of Israel's exile after the destruction of the Second Temple. Following the first part of his answer, the interpretation of which is rendered especially difficult due to a number of lacunae, the rabbi once again resorts to a king *mashal* in order to illustrate his point, taking up the motif of the "the blind and the lame" (Jer 31:8) from the homiletical context that encompasses the narrative:[46] A king's clever (or lame), mute, deaf, and blind

---

42 See ER 71, l. 9ff.
43 This may be interpreted as another allusion to the right approach to Torah on Israel's part – that is, a Rabbinic approach, in which both the *iggeret* and either a *karuz* or the interpreting queen enable the communication between the king and his subjects.
44 Kadushin, *Organic Thinking*, 21.
45 See ER 71, l. 18ff.
46 See n. 38. This *mashal* was discussed in the previous chapter, p. 156f.

servants, who disappoint the king with their behaviour, only start weeping and following the king once he has left them, to which the king responds that he will return to them in thirty days. In the *nimshal*, these different types of servants are identified with three groups within Israel, depending on their knowledge of only Written Torah alone, of Oral Torah in addition, or their experience in trade. There is a lacuna at the end of God's promise to return to them, so that the duration of the separation is not explicit in the *nimshal*.[47]

The rabbi closes his answer by stating that during the present second banishment, Israel should ask for mercy, just as the servants of the *mashal* and those who were exiled after the destruction of the First Temple did. Israel should also "find another (אחר) doorway in the words of Torah." Friedmann's text has אחר, not אחד as presumed by Braude and Kapstein.[48] If the MS reading is correct, it may be linked to the בית אחרון at the beginning of the segment (ER 71, l. 18–19), but might also be a subtle reference to the second Torah the rabbi's interlocutor has no knowledge of and importance of which the rabbi is keen to emphasise.

In any case, it is the end of the dialogue which surpasses the polemical tone of the beginning:

> He said to me, Rabbi, may your soul be bent [in distress], for my soul is bent [in distress]. I said to him, My son, a Scripture verse says, *Answer the fool according to his folly* (Prov 26:5). But another Scripture verse says, *Answer not a fool* etc. (Prov 26:4). Now it is written in a *mishnah*: "Be alert to study the Law and know how to make answer to an unbeliever (אפיקורוס)" (mAv 2:14).[49] He said to me, Rabbi, there were things I had in my heart I would not have discussed in your presence. I answered, By the [Temple] service! The things you asked me no man had ever asked me before. Were it not for you [asking me about them] I would not have taught them. Blessed be the Omnipresent, blessed be He, who chose the sages and their disciples, who taught us the *mishnah*: "Wander afar to a place of the Law; and say not that it will follow after you or that your companions will establish it in your possession; *and lean not upon thine own understanding* (Prov 3:5)" (mAv 4:14). (ER 71, l. 32–ER 72, l. 8)

The rabbi replies to the dubious words of thanks by quoting two apparently contradictory verses, Prov 26:5 and 26:4, and an anonymised *mishnah*, Av 2:14.[50] He lets these authoritative texts speak for him; they all contain expressions with which the questioner is indirectly criticised: He is called a fool (*kesil*) in both scriptural verses and an unbeliever or Epicurean in the *mishnah*. Both the questioner and the

---

[47] Neither Friedmann, *Seder Eliahu*, 71n22, nor Braude and Kapstein, *Tanna děbe Eliyyahu*, 199, justify the seventy years they suggest or add to the text.
[48] See Braude and Kapstein, *Tanna děbe Eliyyahu*, 200n14.
[49] Braude and Kapstein, *Tanna děbe Eliyyahu*, 200, give the following translation: "Be eager to teach Torah. At the same time [know] how to deal with a confirmed heretic."
[50] Spoken by R. Eleazar in its original context.

rabbi admit that they have not been eager to discuss these matters. If the words of the rabbi, according to which he has never yet been confronted with such questions, are taken at face value – as referring to a contemporary historical reality – this would indicate that the text alludes to a time when tensions with the Karaite movement were only beginning to be felt.

To bring his answer to a close, the rabbi speaks a *berakhah* or benediction,[51] which praises God for choosing the sages and their disciples for the task of teaching their followers another anonymised *mishnah*,[52] which praises the study of Torah in exilic conditions. Bearing in mind that one of the tenets of early Karaism was its so-called Palestino-centrism, the explicit approval of exile in the first part can be understood as a polemic statement directed against the insistence of the Karaite Mourners of Zion on a return to the land of Israel. Likewise, the last part of the quoted *mishnah*, which is actually part of a verse from Prov 3:5, can be seen as containing one last, subtle response to two interrelated aspects of Karaism – namely, the assumption that knowledge can be individually acquired without the aid of tradition, and the theoretical individualism of Karaite exegesis.[53] With this question, but without closing the opening narrative frame, the dialogue with this anonymous proto-Karaite comes to an end and is followed, in the next chapter, by another one.

---

51 Again, it cannot be ruled out that this *berakhah* is actually spoken by the governing voice as a direct address to the audience, having left its narrative mode, after the narrative has been more or less "closed."
52 Also from the tractate *Avot*, where it is spoken by R. Nehorai.
53 Characteristic of this individualism is, for example, the principle of induction or *hekkesh ha-chippus*. On this, see Astren, "Islamic Contexts," 162: "*Chippus*, investigation of scripture on the part of the halakhic researcher, became associated with scripturalism, one of Karaism's primary allegiances." Brody, *The Geonim of Babylonia*, 90, comments in this respect: "Lacking any agreed authority – whether in the form of a body of tradition, an individual author or an institution empowered to issue binding rulings – the early Karaites were extremely individualistic in their approach to legal questions." On the Karaite legitimation of an individualistic interpretation of Scriptures based on the phrase "Rely not on me," allegedly said by ʿAnan, see Erder, *The Karaite Mourners of Zion*, 43n83–84, 46 and 73.

5.3 *Seder Eliyahu Rabbah*, Chapter (15) 16

The rabbi's next conversational partner is, as Bacher points out, more consistently depicted as an opponent.[54] He and the dialogue in which he is involved, a continuation of the one in the previous chapter, represent a clear increase in polemical tone. The dialogue consists of seven sections, each of which deals with a different topic or problem. The first section reads as follows:

> A colleague of his came and sat in front of him (כנגדו). Also this one had [knowledge of] Scripture but no [knowledge of] Mishnah. I said to him, My son, the washing of hands (רחיצת ידים) [comes] from the Torah. He replied, Rabbi, it was not mentioned to us (לנו) from Mount Sinai (מהר סיני). I said to him, My son, we have (יש לנו) many things, many of them of grave import, which Scripture did not deem necessary to mention. Therefore they were imposed (lit. "thrown") on Israel. It [Scripture, or He (God)][55] said, They will set them [Israel] apart, so that they increase their merit. Whence [do we infer this]? You should know that it is so: When Israel were in the wilderness, wandering around, the Holy One, blessed be He, spoke to Moses, *Go to the people and consecrate them* (וקדשתם) *[today and tomorrow. Have them wash* (וכבסו) *their clothes]* etc. (Exod 19:10). And the sages taught in a *mishnah*:[56] "And consecrate them with the ritual bath (וקדשתם בטבילה)." And we learn the washing of hands from the Torah, from Moses, Aaron, and his children, for it is said, *The Lord spoke* etc. *You shall make a bronze basin [with a bronze stand for washing* (לרחצה)*.]* <etc.> *And Moses*[57] *shall wash* (ורחצו) *with it [their hands and their feet]* etc. *When they go into the tent of meeting [or when they come near the altar to minister, to make an offering by fire to the Lord, they shall wash* (ורחצו) *with water, so that they may not die]* etc. (Exod 30:17–20). But of Israel what does it [Scripture] say? *Sanctify yourselves therefore, and be holy* (והתקדשתם והייתם קדושים) (Lev 11:44). Hence Rabban Gamaliel used to eat common food in a state of levitical purity. They said: Not only were the priests given the sanctification, but the priests, the Levites, and all the Israelites, for it is said, *The Lord spoke* etc. *Speak to the congregation*[58] *of the people of Israel and say to them: You shall be holy* etc. (Lev 19:1–2). From here they said: Whoever disregards the washing of hands, it is a bad omen for him. Of him it [Scripture] says, *All who hear the words of this oath* etc. *the Lord will be unwilling to pardon them* etc. (Deut 29:18–19). Here you learn that whoever rebels against the washing of hands, it is a bad omen for him. (ER 72, l. 9–23)

---

54 Bacher, "Antikaräisches," 271, describes the character as follows: "Er bezeugt in den verschiedensten Punkten seinen Unglauben an die traditionelle Auslegung der Schrift." ("He demonstrates in each point his distrust for the traditional interpretation of Scripture").
55 The Hebrew text reads אמר instead of הוא אומר, a phrase that is understood as referring to Scripture and which functions as an introductory formula for scriptural quotations. The verb here could therefore be understood as having God as its subject.
56 Friedmann puts the expression במשנה in brackets to indicate the MS's mistaken reading.
57 MT reads אַהֲרֹן וּבָנָיו.
58 *Seder Eliyahu* reads דבר אל עדת instead of דַּבֵּר אֶל־כָּל־עֲדַת of the MT, i.e., it does not contain the expression "all."

The questioner in this new narrative or narrative section is identified as a colleague of the questioner of the previous dialogue and described in the same terms as the first interlocutor – as one knowledgeable about Scripture, but not about Mishnah.[59] The spatial setting is the same as the previous one. Not only is there no mention of change, we are even told that the new questioner sits in front of his colleague, who remains silent in this second dialogue. The second questioner may be imagined as arriving while the rabbi and the first questioner are still talking, listening to the arguments, and taking up the word in order to assist his colleague and reinforce his line of argumentation. Even if the tone of this dialogue is clearly more polemical than that of the previous one, the courtesy formulas already used and the hierarchical relationship nevertheless remain: The rabbi addresses his questioner repeatedly with the words "my son" and is in turn addressed with "rabbi" or "my master."

The first to speak is the rabbi, who states that the washing of hands is a precept that has its origins in the Torah and is therefore of divine origin.[60] The questioner defines himself as a scripturalist (or a proto-Karaite) by arguing that this precept does not come from Sinai – it is not part of the Torah given to Moses on Mount Sinai.[61] The wording used is interesting with respect to his self-conception: He argues that this command was not said "to us" (לנו), thus implying that he regards the rabbi and himself as belonging to one and the same community. The rabbi himself also uses the first-person plural in the inclusive "we have" (יש לנו). Such an explicit questioning of a command based on the Oral Torah, one that implies that this command is not as binding as those transmitted in the Written Torah, is a challenge for the rabbi, who now proceeds to provide evidence as to the divine origin of the washing of hands. To accomplish this, the governing voice lets

---

59 From among the range of meanings of the term – which, according to Marcus Jastrow, *A Dictionary of the Targumim, Talmud Babli, Talmud Yerushalmi and Midrashic Literature* (Leipzig, London, and New York: W. Druglin / Luzac / Putnam's Sons, 1903), s.v. חָבֵר, include "associate, friend, partner (in sacrifices); colleague, fellow-student; fellow-being; of the same kind" – the idea of sharing the same kind of knowledge appears to be what brings together the two questioners.

60 If we assume that this statement is an answer to a question posed by the rabbi's interlocutor, the fact that the question is missing can be explained as either an ellipsis by the author or an omission by the copyist of the manuscript. In any case, Friedmann does not emend the text by inserting the missing question as Braude and Kapstein, *Tanna děbe Eliyyahu*, 202, do in their translation.

61 Instead of the usual Rabbinic expression נטילת ידים, the rabbi speaks of רחיצת ידים. The Karaite Elijah Bashyatsi (1420–1490) objects in his *Adderet Eliyahu*, the code of Karaite law that came to be regarded as the Karaites' counterpart to the *Shulkhan Arukh*, to the precept of the washing of hands, "which is called the raising of the hands (נטילת ידים)," arguing that it is actually a ruling (מתקנת) of the sages.

him make use not only of Rabbinic sources, but also of a combination of scriptural verses that support his argument and of a micro-narrative which has Scripture as its protagonist: It is the personification Scripture which does not consider it necessary to mention, i.e. in written form, every one of the many important precepts which Israel received. Scripture imposed them on Israel as a means for them to distinguish themselves. This short introductory narrative depicts Oral Torah both as an honour and as a responsibility for Israel, who, by making proper use of it, can increase their reward.

The rabbi then proceeds to expand on this micro-narrative with yet another narrative – in this case, an exegetical one based on three passages of Scripture (Exod 19:10, Exod 30:17–20, and Lev 11:44), with Israel's wandering in the wilderness as the spatio-temporal setting. First, the expression "consecrate them" from Exod 19:10 is interpreted – a verse that, in its second part, contains the words "have them wash." Since this verse would be evidence, as elsewhere in Rabbinic literature,[62] for ritual immersion, but not for the washing of hands, he proceeds to adduce further evidence, which this time consists of another selectively quoted scriptural passage (Exod 30:17–20) that deals with the bronze basin in which Aaron and his sons were to wash their hands and feet. This requirement, the rabbi argues, not only concerns priests – as one who only knows Scripture might assume – but the whole of Israel, evidence of which is an anecdote about the habitual actions of an exemplary rabbi, based on Lev 11:44: Rabban Gamaliel is said to have eaten every kind of food, not just consecrated food, in a state of levitical purity. The governing voice seems to be tacitly using further Rabbinic sources – bBer 53b[63] and bChul 106a[64] – and expanding upon them by again quoting

---

[62] For example, bYev 46b interprets Exod 19:10 as implying ritual immersion. Bacher assumes that it is MekhY *Bachodesh* 3 that *Seder Eliyahu* alludes to in this passage. There we read: "*Have them wash (we-khibesu) their clothes* (Exod 19:10). And whence [do we know] that they were required to perform a ritual immersion? See, [I draw] an analogy. If there, where they are not required to wash their clothes, they are required to perform a ritual immersion, here, where they are required to wash their clothes, is it the proper conclusion that they should be required to perform a ritual immersion? There is no washing of clothes in the Torah that does not also require a ritual immersion."

[63] In bBer 53b, "Sanctify yourselves" (Lev 11:44) is interpreted as referring to the washing of the hands before meals, whereas "and be holy" (Lev 11:44) to the washing of the hands after meals.

[64] In this context, the permissibility of washing the hands with water that has been heated with fire is discussed. Whereas according to R. Hezekiah it is not allowed, R. Jochanan states that it is permitted for, according to Rabban Gamaliel, the great men of Galilee would do it; considering that Rabban Gamaliel would eat (only) consecrated food, his opinion must be authoritative on this issue.

the sages[65] as having stated that not just the priests, but also the Levites and all of the Israelites are expected to sanctify themselves by observing the precept of washing their hands. In the closing statement that condemns those who do not observe the precept, the rabbi also relies upon a Rabbinic source, bShab 62b,[66] and a scriptural one, Deut 29:18–19.

The second section in this dialogue focuses on the precept of ritual slaughter – more precisely, with the question of why this should be performed by slicing the neck. The passage reads as follows:

> He said to me, Rabbi, there is no [precept stating that] the ritual slaughter [is to be performed] at the neck (אין שחיטה מן הצואר). I answered him, My son, how do you reason? Is not the ritual slaughter an integral part of the Torah? For thus taught (שנו) the sages: "If a man slaughtered a bird by [cutting through] either [the windpipe or the gullet], or a beast by cutting through both, what he slaughters is valid; so, too, [if he cut through] the greater part of each" (mChul 2:1). Whoever cuts in a slanting direction (המגרים) the whole [slaughter] is [the product of] selfishness. Blessed be the Omnipresent, blessed be He, who does not favour one over another, for one who slaughters (הטבח) by dragging (מושך) the flesh [away] from the neck by cutting it in a slanting direction renders it disqualified. So his possessions are taken away (מושכין) from him and given to others. For it is said, *One who augments wealth by exorbitant interest gathers [it for another who is kind to the poor]* etc. (Prov 28:8). (ER 72, l. 21–ER 73, l. 4)

Unlike the first section, this one has the questioner himself pose the topic of the dispute. Elliptical though his statement may be, it can be understood as implying that, not being prescribed in the (Written) Torah, ritual slaughter (or rather, one specific aspect of it) is not of divine origin. In reply, the rabbi first quotes a *mishnah* as evidence that שחיטה מן הצואר ("slaughter performed by cutting the animal's neck") is indeed part of the Torah,[67] and then presents the hypothetical case of one who tries to profit illegitimately by cutting in such a way that a minimum of flesh remains near or on the animal's neck.

---

[65] The saying is introduced with "they said" (אמרו), so that it is not Gamaliel himself, as Braude and Kapstein, *Tanna děbe Eliyyahu*, 203, imply with their translation, but the sages' collective interpretation of his conduct that is given in this passage.

[66] According to R. Abbahu, treating the washing of hands with disrespect is one of the three things which bring a man to poverty.

[67] Leon Nemoy (see Braude and Kapstein, *Tanna děbe Eliyyahu*, 203n8) interprets the rabbi's answer as implying that whenever Scripture uses the expression שחט, in those contexts dealing with sacrificial slaughter (e.g., Exod 12:6.21 and 29:11.16; Lev 1:5.11, 3:2, and 4:4.15.24; Num 19:3; Lev 4:24.29.33, 7:2, 9:12, 13:13, and 14:13), the procedure alluded to consisted in cutting the animal's throat with a sharp knife. Therefore שחט is taken to mean "cutting the animal's throat," also in the private sacrificial setting of slaughtering for food.

According to Bacher, the rabbi uses two Rabbinic intertexts in his answer: The first one, bChul 27a,⁶⁸ deals with the same problem posed by the proto-Karaite, but formulates it differently. Rav Kahana is here concerned with the origins of the precept of שחיטה מן הצואר, which he sees in the interpretation of ושחט in Lev 1:5 as implying the cleansing of blood from the neck.⁶⁹ The second, bChul 19a, deals in extenso with the question of the validity of the slaughter depending on where he who slaughters cuts, as prescribed in mChul 1:3. On closer inspection, it is evident that the rabbi of *Seder Eliyahu* relies mainly on the second Rabbinic source, even though the first would help him give a more adequate answer to the question posed. The rabbi does not simply state *where* in the Torah the precept in question is derived from, but concentrates on discussing immoral approaches to its observance. Bacher claims this is due to the fact that, among Karaites, it was customary to explain שחט, the root consonants of שחיטה, as related to those of the verb משך ("to stretch").⁷⁰ The question of the apparent inconsistency in this part of the dialogue might be of interest in discussing the intended audience of the text.⁷¹

---

68 See Bacher, "Antikaräisches," 271.
69 The passage reads: "Whence [do we infer] that the slaughtering [must be performed] at the neck? It was said, *And he shall slaughter (ושחט) the bullock* (Lev 1:5), i.e., he shall cleanse (חטהו) it [from blood] in the place where it bends down (ששח). Whence [do you infer] that חטהו is an expression [that means] "to cleanse" (דכויי)? It is written, *And he shall clean (וחטא) the house* (Lev 14:52) or, if you want to say rather from here [this verse]: *Purge me (תחטאני) with hyssop and I shall be clean (ואטהר)* (Ps 51:9)."
70 See Bacher, "Antikaräisches," 271. The later evidence of *Adderet Eliyahu* (fifteenth century) seems to support this, as seen in the following passage, which presupposes bChul 27a: "[T]he Rabbanites state that the meaning of the expression שחיטה derives from two words, namely 'from the place where it bends down (ששח)' [and] 'he shall cleanse (חטהו),' that is, from the place where his head is humbled from the verse, *People are bowed down, everyone is brought low* (Isa 5:15). Hence they say, 'from the place where it bends down' [and] 'he shall cleanse,' which means from the place where speech comes out, from the verse, *and speak to the earth and it shall teach you* (Job 12:8). And they said that the slaughtering (הזביחה) [derives] from the place where the man with urethral secretion (זב) cleanses himself (חטהו). Truly the sages, peace be upon them, said that the sense of *shechitah* derives the expression 'beaten gold' (זהב שחוט) (1 Kgs 10:16). *Their tongue is a deadly arrow (חץ שחוט)* (Jer 9:8), for they are concerned with the drawing. So the precept of slaughtering (שחיטה) is connected with the drawing of the knife (במשיכת הסכין) with movements to and fro (בהולכתו ובהובאתו)" (*Adderet Eliyahu* 62b). Translated after the Gozleve edition, which is available as Google digitised book. I thank Prof. Daniel Lasker for pointing this out to me.
71 Zucker, *Rav Saadya Gaon's Translation*, 210, addresses this issue, pointing out that even in the text he uses, a version of *Seder Eliyahu* with the commentary of Joshua ben Jacob, the proto-Karaite's answer to the rabbi's question, "How do you reason?" is missing. He argues: "The scripturalist argues that the slaughter (of birds) is not to be performed at the neck but by pinching the bird's head at the nape, as in Anan's view; and when the rabbi asks him, How do you reason?, he answers that the slaughter of profane animals according to the Torah is like in the case of burnt,

One could argue that the elliptical manner in which the rabbi of *Seder Eliyahu* expresses himself in this passage suggests that the text was never intended to be addressed to an audience that was not familiar with Rabbinic tradition. Without the information contained in bChul 27a, such an audience would hardly have been able to understand the passage. The text must therefore be understood as addressed to those who take it for granted that the precept is an integral part of the Torah – that is, a Rabbinic audience – but observe it only superficially, giving their own profit priority in their observance of the precept.

The third topic the proto-Karaite brings forward pertains to the prohibition against eating human blood:

> He said to me, [The eating of] human blood is not prohibited in the Torah. I answered him, My son, how do you reason? He replied, Rabbi, Scripture says, *You must not eat [any blood whatever, either of bird or of animal]* (Lev 7:26). But no human blood is [mentioned] here. I said to him, It is an argument *a minori ad majus*. If in the case of cattle, beasts, and fowl whose nature is that they are edible, it is prohibited, how much more forbidden to us is blood in the case of human beings whose nature is not that they are edible. And it [Scripture] says, *Only be sure that you do not eat the blood* <etc.> (Deut 12:23). And [furthermore] it [Scripture] says, *For the life of every creature [– its blood is its life; therefore I have said to the people of Israel: You shall not eat the blood of any creature]* etc. (Lev 17:14), referring to human blood which is prohibited as food. *You shall not eat the blood of any creature* (Lev 17:14), neither from clean cattle nor from unclean cattle, *for the life of every [creature is its blood; whoever eats it shall be cut off]* etc. (Lev 17:14). By the [Temple] service! Also the blood of a living creature, that which has coagulated or has been drained, collected in its presence, and poured into a vessel, also this [blood] is prohibited, for it is said, *Blood*, wherever it comes from. (ER 73, l. 5–13)

In the case of this question-and-answer passage, the rabbi, whose words up to now have been representative of the usual anti-Karaite position, appears to take sides with the Karaites, who expanded the prohibition against eating blood to that of fish, grasshoppers, and other insects.[72] The proto-Karaite, on the other hand, is the one who expresses the Rabbinic position on the meaning of Lev 7:26, as represented by bKer 20b.[73] What we seem to have here is a "castling" of roles: On

---

sin, and guilt offerings and of all types of sacrifices, therefore, from this perspective the slaughter of a bird not destined to be sacrificed is like the slaughter of a consecrated bird that is to be sacrificed, i.e., by pinching."

72 See *Adderet Eliyahu* 66 c–d.

73 According to this passage, the blood of those who walk on two legs (i.e., of man) is excluded from the prohibition in Lev 7:26. Given that the verse explicitly names fowl and beast, which are subject to both light and weighty uncleanness, the Talmud infers that every creature subject to both types of uncleanness is included in the prohibition. Man is excluded on the grounds of being subject only to weighty uncleanness.

the basis of practically the same scriptural verses, the interlocutors come to contrary conclusions; and, whereas the rabbi speaks what later came to crystallise as a Karaite position – namely, that every kind of blood is prohibited – the purported scripturalist paraphrases the conclusion the Talmud passage arrived at, that human blood is excluded from the prohibition. Such an inconsistency in the construction of characters in this passage is related to the fact that the proto-Karaite and the rest of the non-Rabbinic "others" with whom the rabbi contends, rather than characters, are mouthpieces for ideas.

The fourth question in this dialogue focuses on the possible understanding of Lev 7:25 as permitting the consumption of a specific type of fat – namely, that of animals to be sacrificed:

> He said to me, Rabbi, the fat of an animal which is offered as a sacrifice to the Lord is prohibited. The fat of an animal which is not offered [as a sacrifice to the Lord] is permitted. I answered him, How do you reason? He said, Rabbi, Scripture says, *If any one of you eats the fat [from an animal of which an offering by fire may be made to the Lord, you who eat it shall be cut off from your kin]* etc. (Lev 7:25). I replied, My son, observe how strong the power of Torah is. [In] all its sayings [is] understanding, and each and every word said in her is said in wisdom, understanding, and discernment: Lest a man think (lit. "say to himself") the fat of an animal which is offered as a sacrifice to the Lord is prohibited, but the fat of an animal which is not offered as a sacrifice to the Lord is permitted, Scripture then explicitly states elsewhere, *It shall be a perpetual statute* (Lev 3:17), from now and until the end of the world; *throughout your generations* (Lev 3:17), the word is to be practiced for all generations; *in all your settlements* (Lev 3:17), both in the Land [of Israel] and outside the Land; *[you must not eat] any fat or any blood* (Lev 3:17), just as the eating of blood is prohibited, so is the eating of fat prohibited. And if this is so why then is it said, *you must not eat any fat or any blood* (Lev 3:17)? To bring [both elements of] the commandment in your hand [under the same category by juxtaposing them], for [the eating of] blood is like [the eating of] fat and [the eating of] fat is like [the eating of] blood. And with regard to either you are punishable with death through excision. Therefore it is said, *any fat* etc. (Lev 3:17) And the sages taught in a *mishnah*: "if a man keeps apart from blood – which man's soul abhors – he receives a reward; how much more, if he keeps himself apart from robbery and incest (גזל ועריות) – which a man's soul longs after and covets – shall he gain merit for himself and his generations and the generations of his generations to the end of all generations!" (mMak 3:15). (ER 73, l. 14–28)

The questioner claims that only the fat of consecrated animals is prohibited, and supports this claim with the partial quotation of Lev 7:25, a verse which, in its unquoted wording, explains excision as the punishment for consuming this type of fat.[74] To express his objection to this claim, the rabbi adduces Lev 3:17,[75] arguing that Scripture thus prevents men from saying to themselves what the proto-Karaite has said aloud. The rabbi explains the prohibition against eating the fat of unconsecrated animals first with an atomising interpretation of the verse, which culminates in the analogy between the prohibition against consuming any fat or and that against consuming any blood. Following his interpretation of Lev 3:17, and unlike the way he proceeded in his previous answers, the rabbi poses a rhetorical question at this point – "And if this is so why then is it said" etc. – to prompt the second part of his answer, an expansion of the analogy between "any fat and any blood":[76] He declares fat equal to blood and argues that both the eating of any type of fat and the eating of any type of blood are punishable with excision.[77]

Although for this argument the rabbi could have brought up several scriptural proof-texts,[78] the governing voice chooses to have him speak the last part of a *mishnah* from tractate *Makkot* instead, originally spoken by R. Simon after having quoted "Only be sure that you do not eat the blood; for the blood is the life" (Deut 12:23). It should be noted that this is one of the verses which were previously used in *Seder Eliyahu* in the context of the discussion of the prohibition against eating blood, so that the link between these prohibitions goes back to the Mishnah itself – the founding document of Rabbinic Judaism.

---

74 In his discussion of the development of Karaite sects in the ninth century, Julius Fürst, *Bis 900 der gewöhnlichen Zeitrechnung*, vol. 1 of *Geschichte des Karäerthums: Eine kurze Darstellung seiner Entwicklung, Lehre und Literatur* (Leipzig: Nies'sche Buchdruckerei, 1862), 85, claims that two so-called "sect founders" ("Sektenstifter"), Meswi el-Safarani and Ismael Okbari, were known to have supported in the first half of the century the eating of fat of animals which were not sacrificed.
75 The same two scriptural contexts are used in a talmudic passage which could be seen as an unmentioned source for *Seder Eliyahu* – namely, bKer 4b. It is argued here that two negative commandments, "It shall be a perpetual statute" etc. (Lev 3:17) and "You shall eat not fat of ox or sheep or goat" (Lev 7:23), prohibit the fat of consecrated and unconsecrated animals, respectively.
76 Braude and Kapstein, *Tanna děbe Eliyyahu*, 205, attribute this question to the proto-Karaite: "'But,' asked the questioner, '[if the primary purpose of the words just cited is absolutely to prohibit the eating of fat], why does Scripture here mention blood as well as fat?' 'In order,' [I replied], 'to stress the parallel: the eating of blood is like the eating of fat and the eating of fat is like the eating of blood.'"
77 In Scripture, however, this punishment is expressed only in connection with the eating of the fat of animals that may be consecrated in the context of Lev 7:25: "If any one of you eats the fat from an animal of which an offering by fire may be made to the Lord, you who eat it shall be cut off from your kin," and with respect to the eating of blood in Lev 17:14, which was quoted in the previous question-and-answer segment.
78 E.g., Lev 7:27 and 17:10.14.

The next topic of dispute, robbery, is also anticipated in the previously quoted *Makkot* passage:[79]

> He said to me, Rabbi, maybe the cheating of one's brother (גזל של אח) is permitted? I answered him, How do you reason? He replied, Rabbi, it was not mentioned at Mount Sinai. I said to him, Is this not like the first line of thought, which I presented to you at the beginning? We have many things, many of them of grave import, which Scripture did not deem necessary to mention. Therefore they were imposed on Israel. It [Scripture] said,[80] They will set them [Israel] apart, so that they increase their merit. Scripture says, *Honour your father and your mother; you shall not murder; you shall not commit adultery; you shall not steal* (לא תגנוב); *you shall not bear [false witness against your neighbour* (ברעך)]; *you shall not covet [your neighbour's* (רעך) *house; you shall not covet your neighbour's* (רעך) *wife, or male or female slave, or ox, or donkey, or anything that belongs to your neighbour* (לרעך)] (Exod 20:12–17). Is the oppression of one's brother not [implied] there? I would say that they are chastened by the words of Torah and that they are healed by the words of Torah, for it is said, *My soul yearns for you in the night [my spirit within me earnestly seeks you. For when your judgements are in the earth, the inhabitants of the world learn righteousness]* etc. (Isa 26:9). (ER 73, l. 29–ER 74, l. 6)

The questioner argues that, in view of the fact that it was not explicitly prohibited at Sinai, robbing one's brother (גזל של אח) must be regarded as permitted.[81] Given that he is depicted as familiar with Scripture, it could be argued that his question points to the fact that the wording of the commandments does not explicitly name a syntactical object for the verb תגנוב (Exod 20:15),[82] while the neighbour is the object of the other prohibitions. After repeating an argument given in response to a previous question – namely, that not all the rules Israel must follow are spelt out in Scripture – the rabbi proceeds to quote six commandments from Exod 20:12–17, even though only the last three appear to be relevant to the point in question. The eighth, ninth, and tenth commandments contain expressions which the rabbi interprets as implying a prohibition against robbing one's brother.

What exactly does the questioner mean with the expression "cheating of one's brother"? Braude and Kapstein explain אח in *Seder Eliyahu* as a contraction of אחר ("other" or "non-Jew") and translate גזל של אח accordingly as "cheating a non-

---

[79] As Bacher points out, this is not typically a polemical issue between Rabbanites and Karaites.
[80] See n. 55.
[81] The conduct is condemned elsewhere in Scripture, for example, "As for his father, because he practised extortion, robbed his brother (גזל גזל אח), and did what is not good among his people, he dies for his iniquity" (Ezek 18:18). Lev 19:13 and Prov 28:24 both contain word-forms of the root גזל, but neither is used in the first instance, although they could have worked as a more direct refutation of the questioner's implication. Only after the questioner has told a *maʿaseh* on how he betrayed a Gentile does the rabbi quote the first part of Lev 19:13.
[82] The verb גנב is a synonym of גזל.

Jew."[83] According to the rabbi's answer, the prohibition against robbing one's brother is contained in the commandments, even if this is not written out, and they only mention one's "neighbour." That the transgression itself rather than the identity of the one who is robbed that primarily matters can be inferred from the adduced verse from Isaiah, which identifies the possible victims of robbery with the collective expression "the inhabitants of the world" (יושבי תבל) – that is, Jews and non-Jews alike.[84]

The section does not end with this answer from the rabbi. For the first time, it is the questioner who takes up the dialogue – not to utter a question, but to tell a story, a *ma῾aseh*, in which he himself is involved:

> He said to me, Rabbi, it happened to me [once] that I sold a Gentile (גוי) four *kor* of dates. But I had measured [them] for him in a partially dark house. [He said to me,] You and God in heaven know the measure with which you measure for me. From what I measured for him I left out three *se᾿ah* of dates. Then I took his money and bought with it a jug of oil and placed it where I had sold the dates to the gentile. The jug broke and the oil was poured out and spilt. I replied to him, My son, Scripture says, *You shall not defraud your neighbour[; you shall not steal* (ולא תגזל)*]* (Lev 19:13). You see, your neighbour is like your brother, and your brother is like your neighbour. From here you learn that the cheating of a non-Jew (גזל הגוי)[85] is cheating, and it is not necessary to [further explicitly state] "of a brother" (של אח). But because God saw that men with their transgressions would defraud, steal, and extort each another, he then explicitly stated in the traditional writings through *the priest Ezechiel son of Buzi* (Ezek 1:3), *As for his father, because he practised extortion, robbed his brother (*וגזל גזל

---

83 Later on, however, the questioner refers to a "non-Jew" using the expression גוי.
84 Leon Nemoy (see Braude and Kapstein, *Tanna děbe Eliyyahu*, 206n18), points out: "The verse Isa 26:9 need not be interpreted as referring to the two Torahs, but rather as JV [*The Holy Scriptures according to the Masoretic Text*] interprets it: 'Pursuant to the words of the Torah one is chastised (whether one wrongs an Israelite or a Gentile), and pursuant to them one is healed, as it is said ... The inhabitants of the world (Israelites and Gentiles both).'" A digression follows the quotation of Isa 26:9 which can be described as belonging to the non-narrative mode of the governing voice (see ER 74, l. 6–24). This contains a number of examples – some of which pertain to non-Jewish characters – with which the rabbi (or rather the governing voice) illustrates the notion that, for eight certain (though unnamed) transgressions, the world was (repeatedly) laid waste. The transgressed principles for which these collective and individual characters were allegedly exterminated are, as Leon Nemoy observes, not all of Scriptural formulation. See Braude and Kapstein, *Tanna děbe Eliyyahu*, 206n18. The scriptural quotations adduced to prove that each of these collective or individual characters were rooted out from the world, with the exception of the first example, stem from scriptural contexts dealing with precisely the same characters.
85 A more standard expression in Rabbinic literature appears to be גזל הגר, which is found in *Kallah Rabbati* 5:6, bBQ 109b, bZev 44b, bMen 73a, SifBem 117, BemR *Naso* 8, LeqT *Bemidbar* 84b, LeqT *Naso* 86a, LeqT *Qorach* 117b, YalqShim *Tsav* 492, YalqShim *Naso* 701, and YalqShim *Qorach* 755.

אח)[, *and did what is not good among his people, he dies for his iniquity*] (Ezek 18:18) (ER 74, l. 25–ER 75, l. 7)

What is the purpose of the questioner's telling this *maʿaseh* about how he once cheated a Gentile and was punished for it? It appears as if the answer were contained in the apparently unimportant motif of the cheater placing the oil jug precisely in the same place where he had cheated the Gentile and the jug splitting apart. This motif is a clue as to the reason why the jug broke and he lost his oil, an event which he is not capable of interpreting, and it is the reason why he needs to tell the *maʿaseh* in the first place.

The *maʿaseh* provides the basis on which the rabbi brings his argument to a close. The rabbi begins his answer by quoting the first of three prohibitions contained in Lev 19:13, "You shall not defraud your neighbour." Just as in the commandments of Exod 20, so also in Lev 19:13, "neighbour" implies "brother." The second prohibition, "You shall not steal (תִּגְזֹל)," though left unquoted, contains an expression of the root גזל. In a second step, he proceeds to equate "neighbour" (or Gentile) to "brother" (Jew), so that both prohibitions in the verse can be read as referring to Jews and non-Jews alike. Now that he has clearly explained that robbing a Gentile is equal to the robbery prohibited in the Decalogue and in Lev 19:13, he finally adduces the explicit evidence of Ezek 18:18, which condemns robbing one's brother, to round up his argument that this, like robbing any human being, is prohibited by the Torah. The rabbi therefore suggests that God tolerates no robbery whatsoever, no matter what verb is used to express this prohibition or whether the victim is mentioned (as in Ezek 18:18) or not (as in Exod 20 and Lev 19:13). If robbing a non-Jew is like robbing a brother, then the punishment in the unquoted part of Ezek 18:18 is applicable to the questioner himself.

Bearing in mind that one of the main tenets of Karaism was that not just the Pentateuch, but the entire Tanakh was a source of law,[86] it seems odd that it is the rabbi rather than his antagonist – a character *Seder Eliyahu* purportedly depicts as one who challenges Rabbinic Judaism – who has to eventually argue with the help of a verse from the Writings – Ezek 18:18 – in order to show that גזל של אח is prohibited in the לא תגנוב of Exod 20:15. In Bacher's view, the man's question and

---

[86] Brody, *The Geonim of Babylonia*, 87, observes: "In partial compensation for the unavailability of extrabiblical tradition, the Prophets and Hagiographa are placed on an equal footing with the Pentateuch as legal sources." Yoram Erder, "The Karaites and the Second Temple Sects," in *Karaite Judaism: A Guide to its History and Literary Sources*, ed. Meira Polliack (Leiden, Boston: Brill, 2003), 127, points out: "The Karaites, who discarded the Oral Law as a source of *halakhah*, expanded the basis for their laws by considering, like the 'Zadokites' before them, the entire Bible, not just the Pentateuch, to be a resource for *halakhah*." See also Richard Kalmin, *Jewish Babylonia between Persia and Roman Palestine* (Oxford, New York: Oxford University Press, 2006), 155–156.

anecdote in this context simply illustrate the absurdity of the strict scripturalist approach the questioner seems to represent.[87]

The purpose of the question of whether it is lawful to rob a fellow Jew (or a non-Jew) can therefore be understood as an example in *Seder Eliyahu* of the proper, Rabbinic understanding of the commandments – an understanding that only requires the aid of other parts of the Tanakh (such as Ezek 18:18) as prooftexts, rather than as sources of law, in cases of didactic emergency, such as this dialogue with an obstinate, non-Rabbinic other.

The answer to the sixth question, also anticipated in the quotation of mMak 3:15,[88] according to Bacher, demonstrates the validity of traditional deductive methods, which the Karaites did not reject:[89]

> He said to me, Rabbi, which is [the] graver [offence]? [To have sexual intercourse with] a daughter or [sexual intercourse with] a daughter's daughter? I replied, My son, [sexual intercourse with] a daughter [is] incest and [sexual intercourse with] a daughter's daughter [is] incest. Thus the daughter is like the daughter's daughter. He said to me, But, Rabbi, it is not written in the Torah, You shall not uncover the nakedness of your daughter. I replied, My son, it is an argument *a minori ad majus*. If [sexual intercourse with] a son's daughter and [with] a daughter's daughter is prohibited for a man, how much more so [is sexual intercourse with] his daughter. [With] *You shall not uncover the nakedness of a woman and her daughter[, and you shall not take her son's daughter or her daughter's daughter to uncover her nakedness; they are your flesh; it is depravity]* (Lev 18:17), Scripture teaches [that sexual intercourse] between a woman['s husband] and her daughter by him, a woman['s husband] and her daughter by someone else (lit. "somewhere else"), [between a woman's husband and] her son's daughter, and [between a woman's husband and] her daughter's daughter [is incest]. (ER 75, l. 8–13)

The rabbi's questioner argues that intercourse with a granddaughter is a graver offence than intercourse with a man's own daughter, since the latter is not mentioned in the Torah.[90] On the basis of Lev 18:17, the rabbi argues that it is a case of *qal wa-chomer*, so that if the daughter's daughter is prohibited then the daugh-

---

87 See Bacher, "Antikaräisches," 272. Similarly, Kalmin, *Jewish Babylonia*, 174, observes with respect to Babylonian Rabbinic attitudes towards the Sadducees that these "were responses to literary traditions depicting Sadducees as espousing views they found obnoxious rather than to the existence of actual Sadducee-like groups, such as proto-Karaites, in their midst." This appears to be valid for the depiction of the opponents of Rabbinic Judaism in *Seder Eliyahu*.
88 See p. 200.
89 See Bacher, "Antikaräisches," 272–273.
90 According to Zucker, *Rav Saadya Gaon's Translation*, 212, the scripturalist argues as follows: "Behold, a daughter's daughter is a graver offence than a daughter, for it is mentioned in the Torah, whereas the daughter is not, and in that case it is a matter of *qal wa-chomer*, i.e. it is an inference *a minori ad majus*: If a daughter's daughter is prohibited how much more is the great-

ter is clearly also prohibited. From this verse, he derives three further prohibitions: Sexual intercourse is thus forbidden between father and daughter, stepfather and stepdaughter, and grandfather and granddaughter, whether she be the daughter of a woman's son or of a woman's daughter. In view of the strict regulations of early Karaite family law, this segment also seems to be an inconsistent depiction of a dialogue between a proficient Karaite and a follower of Rabbinic Judaism.[91]

The seventh and last section of the dialogue is also related to sexuality. According to Bacher, it deals with an important subject of controversy between Rabbanites and Karaites:

> He said to me, [What is the] graver [transgression], [sexual intercourse with] a man with an abnormal discharge (זב) or [with] a woman who is menstruating (נידה)? I replied, My son, [sexual intercourse with] a woman who is menstruating is graver than [with] a man with an abnormal discharge. He asked, Have we not learned the ritual immersion of the menstruating woman from that of the man with an abnormal discharge (טבילה לנידה אלא מן הזב)? I replied, My son, it is an argument *a minori ad majus*. If [with regard to] the man with an abnormal discharge, who is not fertile and cannot multiply, ten [times the mention of] uncleanness (טומאות) and seven [times] ritual immersions (טבילות) are required in the Torah<, how much more so with regard to the menstruating woman who is fruitful and can multiply>. Whoever says to his wife and sons and members of his household, Touch the vessels and do as you please, for the ritual immersion for the menstruating woman is not in the Torah, will never find contentment. (ER 75, l. 14–ER 76, l. 2)

As in the previous section, the questioner demands clarification as to which of two offences is graver – this time regarding sexual intercourse with a *zav* or a *niddah*. According to the rabbi, the second transgression is evidently the graver – thus rejecting the Karaite leniency with regard to the *niddah*.[92] As Friedmann explains, this is due to the fact that sexual intercourse with a *niddah* is punishable by ex-

---

granddaughter to be prohibited." I do not find a hint at this type of inference in Friedmann's edition of *Seder Eliyahu*.
91 According to Judith Olszowy-Schlanger, "Early Karaite Family Law," in *Karaite Judaism: A Guide to its History and Literary Sources*, ed. Meira Polliack (Leiden, Boston: Brill, 2003), 280, for example, the categories of prohibited relatives according to Karaite halakhah, as mentioned in Leviticus, include daughter, stepdaughter, and granddaughter, among others. She further observes: "The extension by analogy of these categories is however a particularly distinctive trait of early Karaite halakhah. Unlike the Rabbanites, who limited the use of analogy in matters of incest, the Karaites, prior to the eleventh century, used analogy, and analogy upon analogy to the fourth degree in order to derive further forbidden degrees of kinship." (280)
92 See Zucker, *Rav Saadya Gaon's Translation*, 212–213. Bacher, "Antikaräisches," 273, notes that the Karaites held that intercourse with a *zavah* is a graver offence than intercourse with a woman in her menses. Elijah Bashyatsi claims in *Adderet Eliyahu* 73c, "the defilement [by a] *zavah* is graver than [that by] a *niddah* (זבה טומאתה חמורה מנידה)."

cision – the same punishment mentioned previously for eating fat or blood. The questioner objects that it must be the other way round, for he is certain that the ritual bath for the *niddah* has been learned – inferred – from that prescribed in Leviticus for the *zav*, but he is corrected in this exegetical conviction by the rabbi, who once again makes use of the hermeneutical resource of the *qal wa-chomer*. So far, it is remarkable that neither the questioner nor the rabbi make use of explicit scriptural quotations.

It is otherwise in the subsequent passage. To illustrate his position, the rabbi tells his questioner a *maʿaseh* in which he, the narrator, even if indirectly, is also involved:

> It once happened that a man who read much Scripture and recited much Mishnah, that he went into his eternal abode in the middle of his years. His wife, almost driven to madness, went around the doorways of her husband's colleagues saying to them, My masters, my husband read much Scripture and recited much Mishnah, why did he have to go to his eternal abode in the middle of his years? They would not reply to her. I was once going through the marketplace and walked into the courtyard of her dwelling. She came out, sat down in front of me, and wept. I asked her, My daughter, why are you crying? She answered, My husband read much Scripture and recited much Mishnah, why did he have to go to his eternal abode in the middle of his years? I asked her, My daughter, during the time of your impurity (בשעת נידה), how did he conduct himself with you? She replied, O Rabbi, he would say to me, Set aside all the days [of your period] that you see blood and wait (lit. "sit, be inactive") [still] seven clean days, so that you do not have any doubt [about your ritual purity]. <I said to her,>[93] My daughter, he spoke fairly to you. With regard both to men and women with an abnormal discharge (זבים זבות), [as well as to women] who have menstruated and [women who] have [recently] given birth (נידות ויולדות) the sages taught that only after seven days are such considered ritually pure (טהורין) for their marital duties, for it is said, *If she is cleansed of her discharge, she shall count [seven days, and after that she shall be clean]* etc. (Lev 15:28). During the white days (באותן הימים לבנים), how did he conduct himself with you? Did you perhaps anoint him with oil in your hand? Did he touch <you>[94] even [only] with his little finger? She answered, By your life, I would wash his feet and anoint them with oil. I would sleep with him in a bed but nothing else[95] would enter his head. I said to her, My daughter, blessed be the Omnipresent who does not favour one over another, since it is written in the Torah, *[You shall not approach] a woman to uncover her nakedness while she is in her menstrual uncleanness* <etc.> (Lev 18:19). You might think that he [a man] could embrace her [his wife] and kiss her and talk to her about frivolous matters, but then Scripture teaches, *You shall not approach* (Lev 18:19). You might think that she could sleep with him on the same bed with her clothes on, but then Scripture teaches, *You shall not approach* (Lev 18:19). Lest

---

93 Friedmann emends the MS reading אמרה to אמרתי.
94 Friedmann emends the MS reading ונגע בו to ונגע ביך.
95 According to Friedmann, *Seder Eliahu*, Introduction, 103n1, the expression דבר אחר would be a copyist's interpretation of the acronym ד"א, which also stands for דרך ארץ, a euphemism for sexual intercourse.

> a man think (lit. "say to himself"), [As long as] her flesh is prohibited, so is her bed, [and lest,] when her menstruation has finished, he say (lit. "you say"), Her flesh is <prohibited, but her bed permitted>,[96] Scripture states explicitly in the traditional writings through *the priest Ezechiel son of Buzi* (Ezek 1:3), *he does not eat upon*[97] *the mountains or lift up his eyes [to the idols of the house of Israel, does not defile his neighbour's wife or approach a woman during her menstrual period]* etc. (Ezek 18:6). A *niddah* is comparable to the married woman. <You are warned> with respect to the *niddah* with all the capital punishments mentioned in the Torah. It [Scripture] says, *You only have I known of all the families of the earth* (Amos 3:2), these are Israel among the seventy languages; *therefore I will punish you for all your iniquities* (Amos 3:2), these are the disciples of the wise within the House of Israel. I said to her, My daughter, go and learn from what is written in the Torah: "The reward of a duty [done] is a duty [to be done], and the reward of one transgression is [another] transgression" (mAv 4:2). (ER 76, l. 3–28)

This last passage, the longest in the chapter, addresses a controversial issue of controversy between the Karaites and the Rabbanites – namely, the rejection by the former of the so-called seven clean days.[98]

For my present purposes, it is important to point out that, in the context of a controversial issue between a scripturalist (or proto-Karaite) and a rabbi, the latter replies to his questioner in the first place with the exemplary story (a *maʿaseh*) of a man who dies young because *in spite of* knowing the Written and Oral Torah, he failed to live according to their precepts.[99] Unlike its parallels,[100] this narrative within a narrative in *Seder Eliyahu* depicts the rabbi giving the widow the answer to her plight – the premature death of her husband – thus silencing her repeated questions.

Following this answer, the governing voice takes over – it appears as if the conversation with the widow were over, and what follows is a lengthy monologue on the ethics derived from the *maʿaseh* and the Rabbinic saying from mAv 4:2 that comes at the end.[101] Only in the last section of this speech does the governing voice return to some of the topics of conversation between the rabbi and his opponent:

> Another interpretation, *Who has woe?* Prov 23:29). Those with flattering lips and a tongue that slanders (lit. "speaks great words"), those who are rude to everyone, those who are arrogant with everyone, the householders who do not keep away from robbery (גזל), and the

---

96 Friedmann emends the MS reading מוטר לבשרה ואסור למיטתו to מוטר לבשרה ומותר למיטתה אסור לבשרה.
97 MS reads עַל, MT אֶל.
98 Evidence of which is found, as pointed out by Bacher, in Judah Hadassi's *Eshkol ha-kofer* 111b.
99 I discuss this *maʿaseh* in the following chapter; see section 6.2.
100 These are transmitted in bShab 13a–b and ARN A 2; see section 6.2.
101 Characteristic of these statements of this monologue is the use of conditional structures or casuistic formulations. One cluster of statements stems entirely from another work of Rabbinic literature, *Derekh Erets Rabbah*, a minor tractate of the Babylonian Talmud.

man who is anguished by the [regulations concerning] menstrual uncleanness of his wife. (ER 80, l. 16–18)

The narratological problem of an unclear closure, which has been mentioned previously, in this case has implications for deciding who is being addressed. In the other versions of the *ma‹aseh*, it clearly ends when the dialogue between the rabbi and the woman comes to an end, once the rabbi has realised why the young disciple of the wise has died. Here, the dialogue with the woman is followed by what at first appears to be the rabbi's voice taking his turn in the conversation, but then turns out to be a monologue, a sort of homiletical appendix. This monologue can be understood as a) part of the dialogue with the widow, and therefore also as part of the higher-level dialogue with the proto-Karaite; as b) coming after the closed dialogue with the widow and addressed only to the proto-Karaite and the extradiegetic audience (which is also the intended audience of the Rabbinic document as a whole), but not to the woman anymore; or as c) following a closed first person-narrative and dialogue with both the widow and the proto-Karaite opponent, and only addressed to the audience of the Rabbinic document. In the first two cases, the narrative frame would enclose a homiletical segment; in the third, it would be an example of the usual discursive mode in which the governing voice addresses its audience directly.

An almost identical the same micro-structure is applied seven times in the chapter to discuss the precepts of a) the washing of hands and b) ritual slaughter of an animal by cutting its throat; the prohibitions concerning c) eating human blood or d) the fat of animals, e) robbery, f) incestuous relations and g) intercourse with someone with a genital discharge. With the exception of slaughtering, all the issues pertain to domestic or private life. As has been demonstrated, the rabbi does not deal with every topic to an equal extent or using the same rhetorical, narratological, and hermeneutic resources. The order of the topics seems to respond to a scheme, according to which the last question, in the story of the widow and the rabbi meeting personally, includes a more detailed treatment than the rest of the topics. This would probably have ensured the attention of the intended audience.

5.4 *Seder Eliyahu Rabbah*, Chapter (13) 14

A special case of a first-person narrative dealing with a man who has *neither* knowledge of Scripture nor of Mishnah is that found in chapter (13) 14, as one of a series of *ma‹asim*:

> Furthermore it happened to a man who regretted not having read Scripture nor recited Mishnah that once, as he and I were standing in the synagogue when the reader before the chest reached the Sanctification of the Name, he raised his voice and answered loudly to the Sanctification of the Name. They said to him, Why do you raise your voice [like this]? He answered, Is it not enough that I failed to read Scripture or to recite Mishnah? And now that I am given the chance, should I not raise my voice and let my soul be bent? They said: Not one year went by, not a second, and not a third before that man went up from Babylonia to the land of Israel. They made him deputy of the emperor and he was appointed over all the castles in the land of Israel. They gave him a place and he built for himself a city and dwelt there all of his life and left it to his sons and his children's children till the end of all generations. (ER 66, l. 9–17)

This text does not belong to the group of standard first-person narratives, nor does it deal with a strictly scripturalist antagonist, but it is a good example of *Seder Eliyahu*'s tolerant attitude towards the unlearned but morally upright, towards those ready to accept what Lennart Lehmhaus calls "minimal Judaism."[102] A man unlearned in Scripture and Mishnah seizes the occasion to give his soul relief, compensating for his ignorance by responding loudly to the Kedushah. His intention, rather than his behaviour, is what the narrative rewards by depicting him as prospering socially. This would be an example of that "sympathetic and inclusive attitude" Lehmhaus observes in certain strategies in *Seder Eliyahu Zuta* for dealing with non-Rabbinic others, which "may point to a closer engagement with broader Jewish society."[103] Unlike the *maʿaseh* of the man who dies young, in this case, the first-person narrator does not interact verbally with anyone, but just *witnesses* events worthy of being related as an exemplary narrative. Compared with the other *maʿasim* of the series of which this one is a part, it could be interpreted as more authoritative than the rest precisely because it is told by an eyewitness.[104]

---

102 Kadushin, *Organic Thinking*, 26, also endorses this idea when he suggests that "[s]ingle verses of the Bible or a single *halakah* are designated as Torah" in *Seder Eliyahu*, adducing as an example a passage describing one "who possesses neither Bible nor Mishnah but just reads one verse (Gen 36:22) all day" [EZ 175, l. 1] as having Torah as his reward.
103 Lehmhaus, "Understanding and Knowledge," 237.
104 A parallel is found in BemR 4:20, which also contains the *maʿaseh* preceding this one. Since *Bemidbar Rabbah* is usually dated to a later period than *Seder Eliyahu*, it could be assumed that it used *Seder Eliyahu* as its source for a passage that is not known elsewhere in Rabbinic literature, a fact which is also suggested by both *maʿasim* being introduced with the words "Eliyahu says." Once told, the *maʿaseh* of the unlearned man who is rewarded with honour and prosperity – which in *Bemidbar Rabbah* is incidentally not told in the first, but in the third person – is interpreted with the words: "From here you learn that a man does not behave proudly before the Omnipresent for whoever is proud humiliates himself, and so it [Scripture] says, *for those who honour me I will honour, and those who despise me shall be treated with contempt* etc. (1 Sam 2:30)."

5.5 Conversational Narratives

As has been shown, apart from the narrative frame – which, though short and sparse in content, is relevant insofar as it presents the passages previously discussed in terms of first-person narratives[105] – most of the textual substance of these narratives is made up of dialogue. Moreover, it is not conversations between friends that are depicted, but rather academic disputes on specific matters of law, exegesis, and ethics between unrelated opponents who master a highly specialised (and often elliptical) language. Even though it has been claimed that the scene-like character of the narratives lends them "the dramatic force of living voices"[106] and that they resemble "a dramatic performance on stage,"[107] especially when compared to the monological-homiletical context in which they are embedded, an average modern reader would not necessarily see liveliness and dramatic potential in such schematic and standardised dialogues.

Even if there is no intervention of the first-person narrator in the form of a commentary *on* the narrative in these dialogues, the short narrative preamble in the first-person endows them with a meaning that would not be present were the dialogues presented as "unframed." The fact that the author of *Seder Eliyahu* chooses to let the book's governing voice narrate a debate with a proto-Karaite – introducing it not in the third, but in the first person – lends the whole encompassed dispute the air of a personal testimony to an antagonism, even if the clues as to the possible historical setting are almost completely effaced, and the reader only knows that these conversations took place as the narrating rabbi, explicitly identified as such only by his opponent, was "once travelling from one place to another." These debates tell of a personal encounter that is necessarily "more" powerful as evidence and therefore a more efficient cautionary example for the reader than an anecdote on some similar event in someone else's life.[108] These narratives are told from the perspective of the first-person narrator – that is, the point of view is both external and internal with respect to the narrated world or diegesis,[109] whereby the ideological facet of the perspective clearly predominates.[110]

---

[105] Which would correspond to the Genettian term "autodiegetic narrative," where the narrator is at the same time the protagonist of the narrative.
[106] Braude and Kapstein, *Tanna děbe Eliyyahu*, 21.
[107] Lehmhaus, "Understanding and Knowledge," 237.
[108] According to Lehmhaus, "Understanding and Knowledge," 237, the first-person perspective "lends to the dialogues the effect of a personal, authentic report."
[109] See Fludernik, *Introduction*, 36–37.
[110] See Rimmon-Kenan, *Narrative Fiction*, 82–83. It is worth noting that, in this context, perspective or focalisation has nothing to do with access to a character's consciousness. On the prob-

Some observations on aspects concerning speech representation in these texts need to be made. First of all, it can be ascertained that, although indirect discourse is occasionally present, as a rule *Seder Eliyahu* opts for direct discourse when it comes to the representation of speech and thought in the narratives discussed here. This choice can be viewed as a stylistic option that contributes to the narratives' authenticity and authority.[111] Direct discourse is used for the representation of speech by: a) individual human characters of the first- and second-level narratives (such as the rabbi, the proto-Karaite, and the widow in the *maʿaseh*; the public crier in the *mashal*), as well as for the hypothetical or unspoken thoughts the rabbi attributes to others;[112] b) the character of the sages as a collective body – alleged sages' words or Mishnah quotations are thus introduced with formulas that contain either speech verbs or their equivalents, such as "from here they said" or "the sages taught (lit. "repeated," "recited") in a *mishnah*"; and c) the personification of Scripture and the anthropomorphic representation of God among the super-natural characters. Scriptural quotations are presented as speech and introduced with formulas whose subject is the personified text of Scripture ("and it [Scripture] says"), God ("then He explicitly stated in the traditional writings"), and the impersonal "it" ("for it is said").

The embedded *meshalim*, on the other hand, make use of indirect discourse (for example, "When the king is daily visited by the servant and his children he puts all other matters aside and praises the servant for the education of the children") and of what could be described as "diegetic summary" – that is, "the bare report that a speech act has occurred, without any specification of what was said or how it was said"[113] (for example, in the cases where the communication be-

---

lem of applying the notion of focalisation to the narratives of *Seder Eliyahu*, see pp. 77 and 259. However, as Brownen Thomas, "Dialogue," in *The Cambridge Companion to Narrative*, ed. David Herman (Cambridge: Cambridge University Press, 2007), 82, argues, the explicit naming of the cognitive process – for example, the hermeneutic resource of a *qal wa-chomer* inference – could be said to represent what can be described as a "fluid boundary between speech and thought."
111 See Thomas, "Dialogue," 80.
112 In these narratives, thought is represented less often than speech. However, in the following two cases of casuistic formulations, it is probably thoughts that are represented as speech by the text in italics: "If a man sees an involuntary pollution, he is bound according to the Torah to [immerse himself in] a ritual bath. If he says, *Who sees me? There is nothing to it!*" "If a woman sees [a fleck of] blood like a grain of mustard and says, *Who sees [me]? There is nothing to it!*" Also the expression "lest a man think (lit. "say") to himself" (כדי שלא יאמר אדם לעצמו) might be understood as referring to a non-verbalised thought, as in: "Lest a man think the fat of an animal which is offered as a sacrifice to the Lord is prohibited, but the fat of an animal which is not offered as a sacrifice to the Lord is permitted, Scripture then again elsewhere explicitly states."
113 Rimmon-Kenan, *Narrative Fiction*, 110.

tween a king and his children or servants is referred to as taking place by means of an edict or an open letter, of whose contents or style the reader is not informed).

Concerning the use of so-called "speech tags" in the first-person narratives – that is, of the text generally preceding the direct discourse, which helps the reader identify who is speaking and/or in what manner and/or context – it appears to be the rule that the narratives discussed here consist of simple inquit phrases – that is, a verb-form and a preposition inflected to fulfil an indirect-object function; if literally translated, they would always read "he said to me" or "I said to him." In some cases, though, even these short indications are missing, a stylistic feature which might have been intended.[114] No indication is given as to the manner in which the words are spoken. An exception to this rule might be the readings בדרך מצות ("polemically") of the Venice print and בדרך מינות ("the way heretics do") of the Vatican MS as qualifying the proto-Karaite's general manner of approach.[115] Both expressions would be examples of a collective speech tag – one that describes all of the man's interventions in the dialogue.

Another interesting aspect of these conversations is the occasional instances of explicit self-referentiality they contain. For example, the rabbi refers to his own words in previous sections of a dialogue by reminding his partner that he has already expressed an idea, but repeating it verbatim anyway (e.g., in "I said to him, Is this not like the first line of thought, which I presented to you at the beginning? *We have many things, many of them of grave import, which Scripture did not deem necessary to mention*," where the wording of the internal quotation is set in italics). The opponent also reminds the rabbi of what he has already said when he states, "The answer with which you replied to me is the [same] line of thought I first expressed before you: it is based on tradition" – even though in this case the reference does not make use of an internal quotation.

Apart from the informal forms of address ("rabbi," "my son," "my daughter"), forms which certainly establish hierarchies, the language the interlocutors use in the direct discourse itself is broadly the same – both use the same kind of Hebrew, reminiscent of biblical Hebrew, the narrator (and the governing voice in non-narrative contexts) uses. Both quote Scripture and both tell stories. There are, however, characteristic phrases – so-called catchphrases – with which the reader is made aware of who is talking, and which may result in an emphasis on the au-

---

114 For instance, the passage in chapter 2 of *Seder Eliyahu Zuta* dealing with liturgical practices has explicit speech tags with an introductory verb of speech only for the first questions. The missing speech tags are added between square brackets to facilitate the identification of the dialogue partners by the reader.
115 See EZ 171, l. 16.

thenticity of speech representation.[116] For instance, the rabbi addresses the questioner repeatedly with "my son," the woman of the *maʿaseh* with "my daughter," and several times his reaction to a statement by the proto-Karaite is condensed into the phrase, "How do you reason?" (lit. "what have you seen?," מה ראיתה). While it is only the voice of the questioner that says, "Mishnah was not given to us from Sinai," it is only the rabbi who quotes the Mishnah or an alleged saying of the sages, introduced with the formula *mikan amru*, or who draws an inference, introducing it with the hermeneutic expression *qal wa-chomer*.

The way turn-taking in conversation is distributed in these dialogues emphasises the idea that the author did not aim for a realistic depiction of debates between equals, but that his goal was rather to transmit a didactic message, stylised in the form of dialogues which actually conceal Rabbinic monologues. Rather than engaging in an authentic debate, the proto-Karaite is given the role of a prompter here, who provides the rabbi with cues that enable him to deliver shorter or longer sermons on issues which, from a Rabbinic point of view, were crucial tenets of Judaism, but who never (or very rarely) objects to the answers he gets.[117] As was noted previously, the first-person narratives – not just those with a proto-Karaites, but also those with other non-Rabbinic "others" as interlocutors – aim not at depicting "complete," authentic characters, but rather construct the rabbi and those with whom he interacts as types or mouthpieces for concepts (or ideological frameworks),[118] and it is always the rabbi who seems to have the final say.[119]

That the latter is the wiser and probably older of the two can be inferred from the word with which he is always addressed: "rabbi." Otherwise, little information on the anonymous characters' lives are provided in the narrative frame or the dialogues – no names, details of physical appearance, or situation in life (such as occupation or family) are given. The reader is primarily acquainted with their opinions on the issues they discuss and their corresponding adherence to different (opposing) groups within Judaism. The *maʿasim* are the exception: In the one told by the questioner on how he cheated a Gentile, the reader learns that the for-

---

[116] Thomas, "Dialogue," 80.
[117] In one case, the proto-Karaite replies to the answer he gets from the rabbi to his question pertaining to robbing one's brother, telling a *maʿaseh* himself. This second-level narrative is used by the rabbi in his turn as another prompt, which he interprets as confirming his own argument.
[118] Lehmhaus, "Understanding and Knowledge," 236, suggests that *Seder Eliyahu* constructs "typological figures who serve as a foil to the Rabbinic protagonist."
[119] See Thomas, "Dialogue," 85, who draws attention to the fact that stylistic approaches to the study of dialogue have demonstrated "the value of analyzing verbal interactions as mini social systems rather than individual sentences thrown together."

mer earns his living at least partly from selling oil. The woman in the *maʿaseh* is also an exception, due to the fact that she is questioned regarding her private life. In her case, not only are details given about her life as a married woman, but her emotions in response to her widowhood are also depicted. She is even represented as almost on the brink of insanity in her litany-like utterance of the same question time and again.

An important aspect of the "conversational style" of these narratives should also be addressed. This has to do with the Rabbinic sources the governing voice of *Seder Eliyahu* incorporates into the dialogues. These are generally either not correctly identified or not identified at all. Instead of referring to *Mekhilta* as the source of a certain passage, the rabbi introduces it as a saying of the sages and as having been recorded "in a *mishnah*." The passages of the Babylonian Talmud alluded to are not identified as talmudic traditions – for example, by introducing them with the name of the rabbi in whose name they are transmitted in the Talmud. Concerning this manner in which the governing voice and the rabbi deal with sources, Bacher observes that it is clear evidence of the oral medium in which the work seems to have emerged.[120] Bacher's observation might be correct, but this feature might also have been an intended stylistic choice of the author, who opted for a rather loose manner of citation of Rabbinic sources – on the one hand, by adapting them to the needs of the new context of his work, and on the other, by intentionally representing the lack of precision found in conversations as opposed to written sources.

Finally, the problem of narrative levels can be briefly discussed. As has already been explained, the first-person narratives in *Seder Eliyahu* are always embedded in or framed by a so-called homiletical discourse – although one could object that chapter 2 of *Seder Eliyahu Zuta*, a case in which the whole chapter consists of a first-person narrative, is an exception.[121] A short narrative introduction precedes the cores of these narratives, which consist of direct speech. Embedded within these direct-speech sections, second-level (metadiegetic) narratives, such as *maʿasim* or *meshalim*, are told by characters in the first-level narrative. These metadiegetic narratives themselves may contain dialogue. The complex interplay

---

120 Bacher, "Antikaräisches," 271: [Ü]brigens zeigt sich diese Ungenauigkeit im Citiren im ganzen Werke und beweist, daß dasselbe aus wirklichen an verschiedenen Orten ohne Anwendung literarischer Hilfsmittel gehaltenen Vorträgen entstanden ist, wie es auch in der Sprache viel Rhetorisches bekundet. ("Incidentally the whole work shows this inaccuracy in the quotation praxis, demonstrating that it was composed out of real expositions delivered in several places without the help of literary resources, which fact the rhetorics of the language amply manifests").
121 But then, the entire document *Seder Eliyahu*, or at least *Seder Eliyahu Zuta*, could be said to contain this narrative.

of discursive and narrative levels of which *Seder Eliyahu* makes use could be outlined as follows (L = level of discourse):
- L 1: homiletical discourse = direct speech at L 1; voice: governing voice; addressee: extratextual audience;
- L 2 (embedded in L 1): first-level narrative or diegesis = first-person narratives (consisting of direct speech by the rabbi and dialogue between the rabbi and the proto-Karaite); voice: the extradiegetic narrator; narratee: the extratextual audience;
- L 3 (embedded in L 2): second-level narrative or metadiegesis: e.g., *maʿaseh* (consisting of narrative segment and dialogue between the rabbi and the interlocutor); voice: intradiegetic narrator (the rabbi or a proto-Karaite); addressee: an intradiegetic narratee (the rabbi or a proto-Karaite) and the extratextual audience;
- L 4 (embedded in L 3): third-level narrative or meta-metadiegesis: the widow's recollection of previous life (including dialogue between the widow and the dead husband); voice: intraintradiegetic narrator (widow); addressee: an intraintradiegetic narratee (the rabbi), a proto-Karaite questioner, and the extratextual audience.

The extratextual audience is addressed in all the levels. As we saw above, it is not always clear when the character in an embedded narrative ceases to be the main addressee of a passage.

5.6 Conclusion

According to the typology presented in chapter 3, the passages discussed in this chapter, with the exception of the last one, constitute a sub-group among the characteristic first-person narratives of *Seder Eliyahu*.[122] The main distinctive feature of this sub-group is the presence of an antagonistic interlocutor, who has been identified as a "proto-Karaite."

For every narrative, both those aspects that appear to indicate that the character is constructed as representing Karaite ideas and those that do *not* seem to support this assumption have been discussed. I have also pointed out that even if some of the arguments posed by the rabbi's antagonist do not address typically polemical issues in the later Rabbanite-Karaite debate, they may still be seen as

---

[122] Lehmhaus, "Understanding and Knowledge," 236n18, points out that almost half of the first-person narratives in post-tannaitic literature (18 out of 40) occur in *Seder Eliyahu*.

constituting the subtle response of Rabbinic Judaism to real or potential attacks from anti-Rabbinic positions, including those originating in circles that came to be associated with Karaism.[123]

Even if Karaism is assumed to have crystallised only after[124] the assumed date of composition of *Seder Eliyahu* in the first half of the ninth century, we do get the impression that it is the anti-Rabbinism of early Karaites that this post-talmudic document responds to, which is why the expression "proto-Karaite" appears adequate. An alternative would be to designate these characters as an "unlearned" or "semi-learned others."[125] But then, are they actually depicted as unlearned, or rather as laconic challengers refusing to accept the position the rabbi represents?

Among the central tenets of what scholars regard as constitutive of early Karaism, as evidenced in Karaite sources, it is above all *scripturalism* as an aspect of anti-Rabbinic ideology[126] that is explicitly emphasised in these passages of

---

123 The rabbi's opponent in chapter (15) 16 was also identified as a Christian by Chanokh Albeck in his Additions and Commentaries to Leopold Zunz, *Ha-Derashot be-Yisraʾel: ve-hishtalshelutan ha-historit [Die gottesdienstliechen Vorträge der Juden historisch entwickelt]*, ed. Chanock Albeck (Jerusalem: Bialik, 1974), 56. Against this view, Zucker, *Rav Saadya Gaon's Translation*, 205n798, observed that it is not possible to interpret the passages concerning the eating of the fat of an animal that was not killed to be sacrificed, the oppression of one's brother, sexual intercourse with a daughter, with a daughter's daughter, with a menstruant, or with a man with a pathological discharge in the context of debates between Jews and Christians. Louis Ginzberg, quoted in Kadushin, *Organic Thinking*, 275n121, comments on this: "It is extremely unlikely that it refers to Christians, i.e., Judeo-Christians, who differed not only in questions of law from the rest of Israel. Anti-Pharisaic Sectaries never disappeared completely from among the Jews till they finally crystallized in Karaism."
124 On the context in which Karaism emerged Astren, "Islamic Contexts," 155, argues: "The new Karaite movement emerged at the end of the ninth and tenth centuries as a non-hybrid alternative to both Islam and Rabbinic Judaism. As a revitalization movement within Judaism it offered meaning in a world fractured by the political dissolution of the caliphate, by the economic decline of Iraq and the East and by the demographic decline of Jewry as a consequence of Islamization. By locating itself in opposition to Rabbinic institutionalization and halakhic particularity, Karaism was able to attract remnants from Jewish and other sectarian movements as well as those Judeo-Muslim 'hybrids' who were unwilling to make the final commitment to Islam. However, this successful gathering together of disparate elements of Jewish Middle Eastern society brought with it a great variety of contradictory law and theology." See also Brody, *The Geonim of Babylonia*, 88. Forty years ago Mann, *Karaitica*, 4, still argued for an earlier beginning of Karaism proper: "As against Poznański's conclusion that only in the 10th century the Karaites began to take up their residence in Jerusalem, I have expressed the opinion (*Jews in Egypt*, I, 60) that Karaism had found a foothold there in the first half of the 9th century, an opinion that can now be strengthened by further new evidence."
125 See Lehmhaus, "Understanding and Knowledge," 237.
126 On this, see Astren, "Islamic Contexts," 145. Following Haggai Ben-Shammai, "The Karaite Controversy: Scripture and Tradition in Early Karaism," in *Religionsgespräche im Mittelalter*, ed.

Seder Eliyahu – an aspect which, as Robert Brody explains, remained a "central source of contention" between Karaites and Rabbanites later on.[127]

Other distinctive features of early Karaism are merely alluded to in scattered passages of *Seder Eliyahu*, not just in the first-person narratives: There is reference, for example, to dietary laws prohibiting the consumption of meat in Jerusalem;[128] to the return to Palestine and to Jerusalem in particular;[129] asceticism;[130] to messianism;[131] and to the rejection of anthropomorphism in aggadic literature,[132] as well as of Rabbinic prayers and liturgy.[133]

B. Lewis and F. Niewöhner (Wiesbaden: Harrassowitz, 1992), 22–23; and Ofra Tirosh-Becker, "The Use of Rabbinic Sources in Karaite Writings," in *Karaite Judaism: A Guide to its History and Literary Sources*, ed. Meira Polliack (Leiden, Boston: Brill, 2003), 319–338; Lehmhaus, "Understanding and Knowledge," 247n52, argues that recent scholarship has questioned Karaism's adherence to pure scripturalism and even suggested the use of Rabbinic traditions in Karaite literature. The midrash *Sifre Zuta on Deuteronomy*, for example, is preserved mainly in quotations in the commentary on Deuteronomy by the Karaite Yehoshua b. Yehuda (eleventh century). See Menahem I. Kahana, ed., *Sifre Zuta Devarim [Sifre Zuta on Deuteronomy: Citations from a New Tannaitic Midrash]* (Jerusalem: Magnes Press, 2002).

127 See Brody, *The Geonim of Babylonia*, 92. Ben-Shammai, "The Karaite Controversy," 19, refers to a responsum by Natronai Gaon in which the author distinguishes between heretics who reject both the Written and the Oral Torah and those who reject only the Oral Torah, without identifying the latter with followers of ʿAnan. He concludes that Natronai could have been "referring to scripturalists who were active in the middle of the ninth century and may thus be forerunners of the Karaism of Daniel al-Qūmisī."

128 See Zucker, *Rav Saadya Gaon's Translation*, 216, whose version of ER 133 reads יטול אדם בשר מעט ויין מעט. According to the sources adduced by Mann, *Karaitica*, 65–66, 71–72, Karaites consumed meat in Ramla in the eleventh century and appeared to have permitted it later on (thirteenth century) even in Jerusalem.

129 See Mann, *Karaitica*, 5. As previously pointed out, the rabbi's apparent justification of the present exile of Israel in answer to the fourth question in chapter (14) 15 might indeed be viewed as a reaction to the Karaites' Palestino-centrism and rejection of diaspora Judaism. Astren, "Islamic Contexts," 160, claims that "Palestino-centrism situated the Karaites in diametric opposition to the rabbis, by taking hold of the center while objecting to the diaspora, which was characterized as increasingly corrupt and was led by diasporically-committed Rabbinic leaders." Moreover, he sees scripturalism and Palestino-centrism as related phenomena (see 158). See also Erder, *The Karaite Mourners of Zion*, 4 and 99–102.

130 According to Mann, *Karaitica*, 55, the "joys of life of the Rabbanites" were repudiated by the Karaites. As we observed previously, Moshe Zucker understands the rabbi's reaction to the first question of his interlocutor in chapter (14) 15 as a reaction to the ascetic way of life the Karaites adhered to; see Astren, "Islamic Contexts," 145.

131 See Astren, "Islamic Contexts," 145; and Erder, *The Karaite Mourners of Zion*, 91–102, 309–407.

132 See Mann, *Karaitica*, 5.

133 See Mann, *Karaitica*, 51.

Even if we assume that *Seder Eliyahu* only uses these narratives to allude to the historical phenomenon of Jewish anti-traditionalism or anti-scripturalism in one of the circles which would eventually coalesce into Karaism,[134] and even if we cannot interpret them as authentic depictions of historical encounters with or challenges from heretical movements, we can still read them as fruitful sources of information on the self-perception of their authors, on other cultural agents involved in their production, and on the cultural context in which they emerged. The first-person narratives can be regarded, as Lehmhaus has suggested with respect to those of *Seder Eliyahu Zuta*, as ideal representations (from a Rabbinic point of view) of what such encounters could (or should) look like – that is, how the Rabbinic author of *Seder Eliyahu* wished his readers to conceive of debates with potential non-Rabbinic antagonists.[135] The goal of these textual strategies would be, as Lehmhaus suggests, to address a broader audience within Jewish society by presenting an easygoing version or "condensed form" of Rabbinic Judaism, "a less stringent and more appealing 'minimal' Judaism."[136] Such a *Sitz im Leben* of the document as a dissemination and popularisation of Rabbinic teachings might, however, not be as suitable when it comes to *Seder Eliyahu Rabbah*, whose general style and hermeneutics are not as "minimalist" as appears to be the case with *Seder Eliyahu Zuta*.[137]

---

134 They were criticised in the ninth century by Ben Baboi as "biblicists" or "scripturalists" (בני מקרא). On this, see Astren, "Islamic Contexts," 165–166; Brody, *The Geonim of Babylonia*, 88. What Lehmhaus, "Understanding and Knowledge," 245–246, observes with respect to the terms *minim* and *minut*, the latter used in one of the passages discussed here, the fact that they are umbrella terms the rabbis use "to designate the non-Rabbinic otherness of a specific behavior or idea," rather than particular heresies, could be applied to the entire corpus of first-person narratives, not just to those about men without Mishnah knowledge.
135 See Lehmhaus, "Understanding and Knowledge," 233.
136 Lehmhaus, "Understanding and Knowledge," 235.
137 However, for both parts of *Seder Eliyahu*, it appears to be true, as Lehmhaus argues elsewhere, that their innovative compositional features do not originate in geonic and talmudic halakhic literature, but rather in discourses on the periphery of Rabbinic Judaism, such as those that took shape in "masoretic, (proto-) Karaite or esoteric circles and their Muslim-Christian surroundings." (Lehmhaus, "Between Tradition and Innovation," 241)

6 Late-Midrashic Stories of Women

In her description of the agenda of feminist narratology, the branch of post-structural narratology that "systematically studies story and discourse with an eye to differences of gender," Robyn Warhol stated that, "[d]epending on the approach, the feminist narratologist may focus on the gender of authors, authorial (intended) audiences, actual readers, characters, narrators, and/or narratees."[1] The readings of stories of women in this chapter will not focus on the gender of the author or the intended audience, but primarily on the characters and narrators of a document produced in an androcentric textual system. These readings could be said to be only partially guided by the principles of this theoretical framework, with the aim of "producing gender-conscious readings of individual narrative texts"[2] in *Seder Eliyahu*.

Gendered readings of rabbinic texts have been gaining growing recognition since the 1970s.[3] This chapter does not intend to recover a specific female history or the silenced voices of women from the texts, but rather – in the form of a reflection on the narrative construction of a series of women in short narratives on the textual contexts in which they appear, on their status as characters, on how or whether their speech is represented, and on what their actions are – to reflect not only on what is narrated, but also on how it is narrated.[4]

Women are certainly not one of the main subjects in *Seder Eliyahu*, but time and again they seem to be the focus of its homiletical and narrative discourse. In order to describe part of the narratological gender agenda of *Seder Eliyahu*, I shall

---

1 Robyn Warhol, "Feminist Narratology," in *Routledge Encyclopedia of Narrative Theory*, ed. David Herman, Manfred Jahn, and Marie-Laure Ryan (London, New York: Routledge, 2005), 161.
2 Warhol, "Feminist Narratology," 161. On feminist and gendered narratology, see the seminal article by Susan Lanser, "Toward a Feminist Narratology," *Style* 20, no. 3 (1986): 341–363, as well as Susan Lanser, "Sexing the Narrative: Propriety, Desire, and the Engendering of Narratology," *Narrattive* 3 (1995): 85–94; Monika Fludernik, "The Genderization of Narrative," *Graat* 21 (1999): 153–175; Gaby Allrath and Marion Gymnich, "Gendered Narratology," in *Routledge Encyclopedia of Narrative Theory*, ed. David Herman, Manfred Jahn, and Marie-Laure Ryan (London, New York: Routledge, 2005), 197–198; and Ruth Page, "Gender," in *The Cambridge Companion to Narrative*, ed. David Herman (Cambridge: Cambridge University Press, 2007), 189–191.
3 See the work of Judith Hauptman, Judith Baskin, or Tal Ilan, to name but a few of the most prominent authors in the field. For an overview, see Frederick Greenspahn, ed., *Women and Judaism: New Insights and Scholarship* (New York: New York University Press, 2009), 41–87.
4 Allrath and Gymnich, "Gendered Narratology," 197, observe: "Rejecting a supposedly gender-neutral approach, feminist narratology emphasises that gender is a decisive aspect not only of the story but also of the discourse; that is to say, gender is important not only for the 'what' but also for the 'how' of narration."

discuss narrative passages in which women are either the subject of the main narrator's voice (or other rabbinic male narrative voices) or in which it is women who appear to act and speak for themselves. The result of these readings could be a preliminary typology of the work's women characters as well as subject matters and contexts related to their gender, sexuality, and sex as narratologically meaningful elements.[5]

Before I turn to the readings themselves, we can anticipate that the stories of women in *Seder Eliyahu* fall into two main groups. In the first, we have narratives about biblical subject matter, about named biblical women – exegetical narratives on passages of Scripture in which a woman plays a role (Deborah, Rachel). The second group comprises stories about nameless post-biblical characters acting in rabbinic times. The stories of the first group are, to a certain extent, known to anyone more or less familiar with the stories of Scripture, but those of the second are not necessarily. A further standard distinction in rabbinic literature is that between married and unmarried women; accordingly, the contexts in which they act or are discussed vary.

The expressions "exegetical contexts" and "halakhic contexts" in what follows are simply designations used for descriptive purposes, loosely based on the co-text of the narrative (exegetical co-texts consist of scriptural quotations and their narrativisation in new contexts) or on the non-scriptural subject matter the narrative in question purports to illustrate or expound upon (halakhic contexts). The boundaries between these contexts are often more fluid than this working taxonomy might suggest. All the narratives discussed in the following pages, as in rabbinic literature in general, are told not for their own sake, but to teach or edify, to interpret, or to illustrate. Following the readings of the texts in *Seder Eliyahu*, parallels from rabbinic literature will be discussed in selected cases in order to highlight the specificity of *Seder Eliyahu*'s versions.

6.1 Halakhic Contexts I: The Daughter's Rival

Following Lev 18:6–17, the first chapter of the Mishnah tractate *Yevamot* lists kinship degrees between women and the surviving brother of a man that has died childless which prohibit a Levirate union. Women who fall into these forbidden categories of kinship are not only themselves exempt from the levirate marriage and from the ceremony of the *chalitsah*, but also exempt their co-wives (lit. "ri-

---

5 See Lanser, "Sexing the Narrative," 90.

vals") – the second wives.⁶ Among these is the daughter, legitimate or illegitimate, of the surviving brother, as the following *mishnah* states: "If a man's daughter, or any women within the forbidden degrees, was married to his brother, who had yet another wife, and [this brother] died, then as his daughter is exempt is her co-wife exempt" (mYev 1:2).

The passage below, found in chapter 1 of *Seder Eliyahu Zuta*, reports how, in the days of R. Dosa b. Orkinas the prohibition regarding the daughter's rival came to be lifted, allegedly in his own name:⁷

> In the days of R. Dosa b. Orkinas, the daughter's rival (צרת הבת) <came to be permitted>⁸ to the brothers. The ruling (lit. "the word," "the thing") was [a] very difficult [issue] for the sages because R. Dosa was a great sage and a great scholar, but then his eyes had grown dim, which prevented him from attending the academy. They said, Who will go and inform him? R. Joshua b. Chananiah answered them, I shall go. And who after him? R. Eleazar b. Azariah. And who after him? R. Aqiba. They went and sat before the house entrance. His maid entered [the house] and said to him, Rabbi, the sages of Israel have come to you. He answered her, Let them come in. When they had come in he took hold of R. Joshua b. Chananiah and had him sit on a golden couch. He said to him, Rabbi, if you ask (lit. "speak to") another disciple he will [also] sit. He asked, Who is he? He answered: R. Eleazar b. Azariah. And he said, Does our colleague Azariah have a son? Concerning him he read the following verse, *I have been young, and now am old, yet I have not seen the righteous forsaken [or their children begging bread]* etc. (Ps 37:25). He said to him, Rabbi, if you ask (lit. "speak to") your other disciple he will [also] sit. [He asked,] And who is this? He answered, R. Aqiba. He said to him, Are you Aqiba the interpreter [of Scripture] whose name has gone over the entire world? Sit, my son, sit. Let there be many like you in Israel. Concerning him he read the following verse, *The young lions suffer want and hunger, but those who seek the Lord (ודורשי ה') lack no good thing* (Ps 34:11). They began to consult him with respect to (lit. "surround him with") halakhot until they came to the [issue of the] daughter's rival. When they came to the daughter's rival, they said to him, Our master, what [ruling applies to] the daughter's rival? He said to them, With respect to this issue there is a controversy between the School of Shammai and the School of Hillel. But the Halakhah is according to whose words? [He answered,] According to the School of Hillel. [They replied,] Has it not been said in your name that the daughter's rival is permitted [to marry the brothers]?⁹ He said to them, My teachers, have you heard [this in the name of] "Dosa" or [of] "ben Horkinos"? They answered him, By the life of our

---

6 For an overview on the institution of the levirate marriage in Judaism, see Dvora E. Weisberg, *Levirate Marriage and the Family in Ancient Judaism* (Waltham, MA: Brandeis University Press, 2009), 23–44.

7 The same story is told with minimal variants in bYev 16a.

8 Friedmann emends the MS reading הותרו to הותרה.

9 The parallel in bYev 16a reads at this point: "It has been stated in your name that the halakhah is in accordance with the ruling of the School of Shammai!" Quoted following Isidore Epstein, ed., *Yebamoth*, vol. 1 of *The Babylonian Talmud: Seder Nashim*, trans. Israel W. Slotki (London: Soncino, 1936).

teacher, we heard it anonymously. He said to them, I have a younger brother, first-born of Satan [though], whose name is Jonathan and who is one of the disciples of the School of Shammai. Be careful, or else he will overwhelm you on questions of Halakhah, telling you that the daughter's rival is permitted. But I call heaven and earth to witness that upon this mortar[-shaped seat] the prophet Haggai sat and uttered [the following] three rulings: the daughter's rival is forbidden; Ammon and Moab give the tithe of the poor in the seventh year; and we may accept proselytes from the Cordyenians and the Tadmorites. When they came in they did it through one door. When they went out they did it through three doors. R. Aqiba met him [Jonathan]. He said to him, Are you Aqiba b. Joseph whose name has gone over the entire world? By the [Temple] service, you are not even an oxherd. He replied, I beg of you, not even a shepherd [am I]. (ER 168, l. 13–ER 169, l. 12)

The alleged attribution of a ruling pertaining to the "daughter's rival" to R. Dosa b. Orkinas, a tanna who lived at the end of the first and the beginning of the second century CE,[10] poses a serious problem for the sages; out of their respect for the old master, prevented as he is from attending the academy due to his failing eyes,[11] they see the need to inform him of the situation (or confront him with it). They discuss who is to approach him, R. Joshua b. Chananiah being the first sage to declare his willingness to attempt to tackle such a delicate task. The sages think it necessary for him to have a companion to back him up and name R. Eleazar b. Azariah, who in turn is to be backed by R. Aqiba. The three tannaim go to R. Dosa's house and sit at his door. His maid announces the three sages as "the sages of Israel," and R. Dosa lets them come inside. Once in his presence, the old sage takes hold of R. Joshua and seats him on a golden couch, while the other two are left standing. Joshua suggests that R. Dosa ask another disciple to sit, and the old sage asks who this should be. Joshua names R. Eleazar b. Azariah. R. Dosa comments on the fact that "our colleague Azariah" has a son, quoting Ps 37:25 as referring to father and son. R. Joshua suggests yet again that R. Dosa should invite another disciple to sit, R. Dosa asks after the disciple's name, and R. Aqiba is introduced. With a rhetorical question addressed to him, R. Dosa praises Aqiba as the Aqiba whose name is known throughout the entire world. R. Dosa invites R. Aqiba to sit down, calling him "my son" and praising him, again expressing the wish that there may be plenty like him in Israel. As in the case of Eleazar, so also with R. Aqiba: R. Dosa quotes a scriptural verse as referring to Aqiba (Ps 34:11).

---

10 See Shmuel Safrai, "Dosa ben Harkinas," in *Encyclopaedia Judaica*, ed. Michael Berenbaum and Fred Skolnik, vol. 5 (Detroit: MacMillan Reference, 2007), 760–761.
11 Dosa's blindness could be seen as a metaphor for his presumed misunderstanding of the halakhah, though blindness in rabbis appears to be a recurring motif in rabbinic literature. Prof. Günter Stemberger pointed this out to me in a personal communication.

After this introductory preamble, the three sages are described as "surrounding" R. Dosa with questions of legal practice until they come to the issue that has brought them to the old sage in the first place – the daughter's rival. The question, as posed by the sages – it is not specified who speaks the words – reads simply: "What is [the ruling that applies regarding] the daughter's rival?" R. Dosa replies that it is a matter of dispute between the schools of Shammai and Hillel, but that the halakhah follows the School of Hillel – whose ruling is, however, left unsaid. The younger sages argue that it has been said in R. Dosa's name that a man must marry his widowed daughter's rival or co-wife – even if his daughter herself is prohibited. The dialogue consists of short questions and answers in direct speech, with few introductory formulas. The old sage asks whether the others have heard this ruling quoted in the name of "Dosa" or of the "son of Horkinos," to which the sages emphatically reply that they have heard the law anonymously quoted (סתם ושמענו), a statement that stands in contradiction to their worries. R. Dosa explains that he has a younger brother, whose given name is Jonathan, whom he characterises as the son of Satan, and who is said to be a disciple of the School of Shammai. R. Dosa's language shows him playing with the rhyming words *katán*, *satán*, and *yonatán*; he is nonetheless keen to warn the young sages against being misled by his brother in questions of halakhah. To close his answer authoritatively, R. Dosa states that the prophet Haggai, sitting on the very same mortar-shaped seat they now have in front of them, delivered three rulings, the first of which is that marriage between a man's widow and his brother is prohibited if the latter is the father of the dead man's other wife. Once they have heard this explanation, the sages leave R. Dosa's house – not together, as they had entered it, but separately – and it is R. Aqiba, the last to be addressed by R. Dosa, who happens to meet Jonathan while leaving. Jonathan also identifies Aqiba as *the* famous Aqiba whose name is known all over the world, but then belittles him, saying that he is not even an oxherd, to which Aqiba nonchalantly replies that he does not even identify as a shepherd.

The immediately preceding co-text to the narrative of R. Dosa's brother Jonathan's perpetuation of a ruling that does not accord with the halakhah, but instead with the School of Shammai, is a short first-person narrative in which the anonymous narrator argues that all the troubles that befall Israel are the result of their neglect of the study of Torah. The narrative on R. Dosa's brother, an outsider, appears to illustrate the consequences of such a behaviour. In view of the fact that R. Dosa's brother is mentioned only in this passage and its parallel in bYev 16a, it could be argued that a fiction was created to cleanse the name of R. Dosa – a name that somehow, as this narrative argues, appears to have been brought into disrepute.

Though not quite explicitly, what is discussed in the passage quoted above is the invalidity of a practice "based on" Deut 25:5–10, which obliges a man (*levir*) to marry the wife of his deceased brother (*yevama*) if the latter dies childless, in those cases where the widow is a close relative of the brother and therefore forbidden to him.[12] According to mYev 1:1–2, the co-wives (or "rivals") of women in fifteen types of relationship with their late husband's brother[13] are also exempted from both the levirate marriage and the *chalitsah* ceremony. In *Seder Eliyahu*, this is indeed only alluded to, as the Mishnah is not quoted. The narrative perpetuates a tendency already present in the tractate *Yevamot*, which can be seen with Dvora Weisberg as an attempt to "normalize" levirate marriage and alleviate the situation of the levirate widow, as this is prescribed in Scripture.[14] This narrative has to do with the study of Torah, with renowned rabbis who discuss questions of legal practice and act for the sake of established practices, and with the idea that certain women should be regarded as regular widows (*almanot*, i.e., free to decide whom to marry) instead of as levirate widows (*yevamot*, i.e., bound to their brothers-in-law). Except for R. Dosa's maidservant, women themselves have no voice in the narrative, nor do they play an active role on the diegetic or discursive levels. Women, wives, and co-wives remain silent, powerless, nameless legal subjects.

In a way, the text does reflect on the institution of the levirate marriage, opting for the lenient position found in mYev 1 – the rabbis' intention appears to have been to reduce levirate marriage to a minimum of possible cases – but it does not dwell on the benefits or drawbacks of the institution for man or woman, nor on him or her as a social anomaly,[15] nor on specific cases of exempt widowed rivals.

---

12 See Weisberg, *Levirate Marriage*, 61.
13 These go back to the incest prohibitions in Lev 18 and 20.
14 See Weisberg, *Levirate Marriage*, 123–166. Commenting on this passage, Kadushin, *Organic Thinking*, 103–104, points out that "[w]ith polygamy legitimate under rabbinic law – actually, however, not practiced – laws forbidding a man to marry two sisters and to marry *tsarat ha-bat*, prohibitions perhaps originating in 'taboos,' made for an improvement in the institution of the family."
15 The levirate widow or *yevama* is, in the words of Weisberg, *Levirate Marriage*, 123, "an anomaly, no longer married but not yet independent." She argues further: "This irregular status may explain the anomalous position of the levirate widow, a woman who can be forced into a levirate union against her will but who dominates the ritual of halitza." (125)

6.2 Halakhic Contexts II: The Story of the White Days

In chapter (15) 16, in a first-person narrative, the nameless rabbi of *Seder Eliyahu* tells his questioner a *maʿaseh*, to which I will refer in what follows as "the story of the white days." The rabbi is himself a protagonist in this intradiegetical narrative, in which he finds himself in dialogue with a woman he briefly depicts as almost half-witted due to the early death of her husband, a disciple of the wise.

The narration of the story of the white days is preceded by a series of questions which the questioner poses to the rabbi:

> He said to me, [What is the] graver [transgression], [sexual intercourse with] a man with an abnormal discharge (זב) or [with] a woman who is menstruating (נידה)? I replied, My son, [sexual intercourse with] a woman who is menstruating is graver than [with] a man with an abnormal discharge. He asked, Have we not learned the ritual immersion of the menstruating woman from that of the man with an abnormal discharge (טבילה לנידה אלא מן הזב)? I replied, My son, it is an argument *a minori ad majus*. If [with regard to] the man with an abnormal discharge, who is not fertile and cannot multiply, ten [times the mention of] uncleanness (טומאות) and seven [times] ritual immersions (טבילות) are required in the Torah<, how much more so with regard to the menstruating woman who is fruitful and can multiply>? Whoever says to his wife and sons and members of his household, Touch the vessels and do as you please, for the ritual immersion for the menstruating woman is not in the Torah, will never find contentment. (ER 75, l. 14–ER 76, l. 2)

The elliptical character of this dialogue presupposes a reader familiar with a number of rabbinic concepts: What is the meaning of זב (*zav*)? Of נידה (*niddah*)? By which hermeneutic rule is the ritual bath "learned" – that is, derived from the first and applied to the second?[16] What is meant by the Torah stating ten times that the man is impure and that such impurity requires seven baths? Against what exactly should a man be warned who, convinced that the ritual bath for the *niddah* is not prescribed in the Torah, tells his wife and family that they might do as they please? The rabbi states that sexual intercourse with a *zav* – with a man who has an abnormal, pathological discharge from his member, is less grave an offence than sexual intercourse with a woman during her menstruation. This first answer itself poses further questions. With his next question, the rabbi's opponent argues that the ritual bath for the *niddah* is secondary in nature, stating that this is only a learned ruling – one hermeneutically derived from the ruling pertaining to the *zav*, the only one mentioned in Scripture (Lev 15). Therefore, the questioner

---

[16] See Braude and Kapstein, *Tanna děbe Eliyyahu*, 208n28: "The question, according to Friedmann's n. 21, is whether the requirement that a woman at the end of her menses immerse is based on analogy with a man who suffers discharge from his member, or is based on an argument a fortiori."

argues, the latter must be considered the graver offence. With a *qal wa-chomer*, the rabbi brings his answer to a close: If the word "impure" is used ten times in Lev 15:1–11 to refer to a man who, because of his abnormal discharge, cannot be fruitful and multiply, and seven times we read in Lev 15:5–12 that he should immerse himself to become pure again, the ritual bath for the woman, who after (the impurity of) her menstruation can be fruitful and multiply, is not only logical, but has its origins in the Torah.

To illustrate this point, the rabbi tells his partner the story of the white days. Men with abnormal discharges are not even mentioned; the focus of the narrative is on the punishment to be expected by those who fail to observe the *niddah* laws.

> It once happened that a man who read much Scripture and recited much Mishnah, that he went to his eternal abode in the middle of his years. His wife, almost driven to madness, went around the doorways of her husband's colleagues saying to them, My masters, my husband read much Scripture and recited much Mishnah, why did he have to go to his eternal abode in the middle of his years? They would not reply to her. I was once going through the marketplace and walked into the courtyard of her dwelling. She came out, sat down in front of me, and wept. I asked her, My daughter, why are you crying? She answered, My husband read much Scripture and recited much Mishnah, why did he have to go to his eternal abode in the middle of his years? I asked her, My daughter, during the time of your impurity (בשעת נידה), how did he conduct himself with you? She replied, O Rabbi, he would say to me, Set aside all the days [of your period] that you see blood and wait (lit. "sit, be inactive") [still] seven clean days, so that you do not have any doubt [about your ritual purity]. <I said to her,>[17] My daughter, he spoke fairly to you. With regard both to men and women with an abnormal discharge (בזבים וזבות), [as well as to women] who have menstruated and [women who] have [recently] given birth (נידות ויולדות), the sages taught that only after seven days are such considered ritually pure (טהורין) for their marital duties, for it is said, *If she is cleansed of her discharge, she shall count [seven days, and after that she shall be clean]* etc. (Lev 15:28). During the white days (באותן הימים לבנים), how did he conduct himself with you? Did you perhaps anoint him with oil in your hand? Did he touch <you>[18] even [only] with his little finger? She answered, By your life, I would wash his feet and anoint them with oil. I would sleep with him in a bed but nothing else[19] would enter his head. I said to her, My daughter, blessed be the Omnipresent who does not favour one over another, since it is written in the Torah, *[You shall not approach] a woman to uncover her nakedness while she is in her menstrual uncleanness* <etc.> (Lev 18:19). You might think that he [a man] could embrace her [his wife] and kiss her and talk to her about frivolous matters, but then Scripture teaches, *You shall not approach* (Lev 18:19). You might think that she could sleep with him on the same bed with her clothes on, but then Scripture teaches, *You shall not approach* (Lev 18:19). Lest a man think (lit. "say to himself"), [As long as] her flesh is prohibited, so is her bed, [and lest,] when her menstruation has finished, he say (lit. "you say"), Her flesh is <prohibited,

---

17 Friedmann emends the MS reading אמרה to אמרתי.
18 Friedmann emends the MS reading ונגע בו to ונגע ביך.
19 On the phrase דבר אחר in this context, see p. 207n95.

but her bed permitted>,[20] Scripture states explicitly in the traditional writings through *the priest Ezechiel son of Buzi* (Ezek 1:3), *he does not eat upon*[21] *the mountains or lift up his eyes [to the idols of the house of Israel, does not defile his neighbour's wife or approach a woman during her menstrual period]* etc. (Ezek 18:6). A *niddah* is comparable to the married woman. <You are warned> with respect to the *niddah* with all the capital punishments mentioned in the Torah. (ER 76, l. 3–24)

The story illustrates the dangers of not observing the white days as part of the time of separation between husband and wife, but it fails to prove that the ritual bath for the *niddah* is found in the Torah. The narrative does not even mention the ritual bath, but rather focuses on the concept of the seven additional days of physical distance a couple is to observe after the bleeding has stopped.

6.2.1 Parallel I: bShab 13a–b

The reading of the narrative in *Seder Eliyahu* can be complemented and enhanced from a comparative perspective by considering two parallels transmitted in other rabbinic documents. The following version of the *maʿaseh* of the man who died young is told in the tractate *Shabbat* in the Babylonian Talmud:

> A teaching of the School of Elijah:[22] It once happened that a certain scholar who had studied much Bible and Mishnah and had served scholars much, yet died in middle age. His wife took his tefillin and carried them about in synagogues and complained to them, It is written in the Torah, *for that means life to you and length of days* (Deut 30:20): my husband, who read [Bible], learned [Mishnah], and served scholars much, why did he die in middle age? And no man could answer her. On one occasion I was a guest at her house, and she related the whole story to me. I said to her, My daughter! How was he to you in the days of your menstruation? God forbid! she replied; he did not touch me even with his little finger. And how was he to thee in your days of white [garments]? He ate with me, drank with me and slept with me in bodily contact, and it did not occur to him to do other. I said to her, Blessed be the Omnipresent for slaying him, that He did not condone on account of the Torah! For lo! The Torah has said, *You shall not approach a woman to uncover her nakedness while she is in her menstrual uncleanness* (Lev 18:19). When Rav Dimi came, he said, It was a broad bed. In the West [Palestine] they said, Rav Isaac b. Joseph said: An apron interposed between them. (bShab 13a–b)

---

20 Friedmann emends the MS reading למיטתו ואסור לבשרה מוטר to למיטתה ומותר לבשרה אסור.
21 MS reads עַל, MT אֶל.
22 This quotation follows Epstein, *Shabbath*. While Freedman' English rendering of תנא דבי אליהו appears to suggest that the introductory formula refers to a "work," as I noted above in 2.4.1 with respect to the nine baraitot, also in this case, it is not evident whether the Aramaic expression תנא is to be understood as a verb or a noun.

When compared with the version in *Seder Eliyahu*, several aspects of the narrative in the Gemara stand out.[23] First of all, the woman goes to synagogues and academies, to the central institutions of rabbinic Judaism, to address her deceased husband's colleagues. These spatial settings are not mentioned in *Seder Eliyahu*. Moreover, she describes her husband's exemplarity not just by mentioning that he studied Scripture and Mishnah, but also by relating that he waited on the sages, which elsewhere in *Seder Eliyahu* is very frequently mentioned as an almost constitutive element of the rabbinic curriculum. Her complaint includes another detail not present in *Seder Eliyahu*: She quotes a verse of Deuteronomy which refers to the one hundred and twenty years Moses lived, which are seen as the ideal (today proverbial) age a man can reach. The dialogue itself is comparatively brief. The anonymous first-person narrator, who describes himself as having found himself a guest at the woman's house and is not addressed by her as rabbi,[24] does not mention any examples of forbidden conduct, such as anointing with oil, but lets the woman herself describe the couple's habits during the days in question, whereby eating and drinking are activities "required" by the talmudic context.

In the discussion in the co-text preceding the *ma'aseh* in the tractate *Shabbat*, which discusses the prohibition in mShab 1:3 against a *zav* and a *zavah* eating together on Shabbat, a questioner asks whether a *niddah* may sleep with her husband if both are dressed. The answer consists of a series of statements by Rav Joseph and Rabban Simeon b. Gamaliel, which deal with how impurity can be transmitted through food. In this context, the situation of a couple sleeping in the same bed is compared in several steps to that of diners at a table where a dish of fowl and cheese have been served together:

> They [posed them] a question: May a *niddah* sleep together with her husband, she in her garment and he in his? Said Rav Joseph: Come and hear: A fowl may be served together with cheese at the [same] table, but not eaten [with it]: This is the view of the School of Shammai. The School of Hillel rules: It may neither be served nor eaten [together]! There it is different, because there are no [separate] minds. It is reasonable too that where there are [separate] minds it is different, because the second clause teaches, Rabban Simeon b. Gamaliel said: Two boarders eating at the same table, one may eat meat and the other cheese, and we have no fear. But was it not stated thereon, R. Chanin b. Ammi said in Samuel's name: This was taught only when they do not know each other; but if they do, they are forbidden? And here too they know each other! How can you compare! There we have [separate] minds but no unusual feature; but here there are [separate] minds and an unusual feature. (bShab 13a)

---

23 The *ma'aseh* is told here as part of the exposition on the last sentence of mShab 1:3: "A *zav* must not dine together with a *zavah*, as it may lead to sin" (mShab 1:3).
24 At least according to one MS version, the rabbi is called Abba Eliah.

Further down, we read that to sleep next to a *niddah*, even if both she and the man lying next to her are clothed, is comparable to sleeping with the neighbour's wife, a situation which might lead to sin. In both the Talmud and *Seder Eliyahu* (in a passage following the narrative itself),[25] this comparison makes use of (different parts of) Ezek 18:6 as a proof-text:

> Come and hear: *And he does not eat upon the mountains or lift up his eyes to the idols of the house of Israel, does not defile his neighbour's wife or approach a woman during her menstrual period (niddah)* (Ezek 18:6): Thus a woman who is a *niddah* is assimilated to his neighbour's wife – just as his neighbour's wife, he in his garment and she in hers is forbidden, so if his wife is a *niddah*, he in his garment and she in hers is forbidden. This proves it. (bShab 13a)

Only after this last midrashic unit on Ezek 18:6 does the Talmud turn to the story of the white days. Given its context, the narrative deals with a double transgression of purity laws – that of Lev 18:19, in its extended rabbinic perspective, and that of the *mishnah* commented upon: "A *zav* must not dine together with a *zavah*, as it may lead to sin" (mShab 1:3).

The prohibition against sleeping in the same bed with a *niddah* is valid, according to bShab 13, even in the case of a broad bed or when an object such as an apron is placed between the man and the woman, as suggested by the opinions of the two rabbis, Rav Dimi und Rav Isaac bar Joseph. Such circumstances only apparently mitigate the transgression, which only emphasises the warning.

6.2.2 Parallel II: ARN A, Chapter 2

The second chapter of *Avot de Rabbi Natan* A, an extra-canonical Talmud tractate consisting of a Gemara to the Mishnah tractate *Avot*, applies the story of the white days to part of its interpretation of the dictum "make a fence around the Torah" (mAv 1:1), whereby "fence" is explained in terms of the time of separation to be observed by couples during the days of *niddah*:[26]

---

[25] See ER 76, l. 22–24.
[26] See Jonathan Wyn Schofer, "Rabbinical Ethical Formation and the Formation of Rabbinic Ethical Compilations," in *The Cambridge Companion to the Talmud and Rabbinic Literature*, ed. Charlotte Elisheva Fonrobert and Martin S. Jaffee (Cambridge, New York: Cambridge University Press, 2007), 319–323. Jonathan Wyn Schofer, "Protest or Pedagogy? Trivial Sin and Divine Justice in Rabbinic Narrative," *Hebrew Union College Annual* 74 (2003): 74–81, esp. 76–78, argues that the rabbis interpret "the Torah" in "make a fence about the Torah" as "your words." The first chapters of *Avot de Rabbi Natan* contain a discussion of "make a fence about your words" in which God, Adam, the Torah itself, Moses, Job, the Prophets, the Writings, and finally the rabbis are represented as creators of fences.

There was once a certain man who had studied much Scripture and had studied much Mishnah and attended upon many scholars, who died in middle age. His wife took his tefillin and kept making the rounds of the synagogues and study houses, crying aloud and weeping. Masters, she said to the sages, it is written in the[27] Torah, *for that means life to you and length of days* (Deut 30:20). My husband studied much Scripture and studied much Mishnah and attended upon many scholars. Why did he die in middle age? There was not a person who could answer her. She once encountered Elijah, of blessed memory. My child, he asked her, why are you weeping and crying? Master, she answered him, my husband studied much Scripture and studied much Mishnah and attended upon many scholars, yet he died in middle age. Elijah said to her, During the first three days of your impurity,[28] how did he conduct himself in your company? Master, she replied, he did not touch me, God forbid! even with his little finger. On the contrary, this is how he spoke to me, Touch nothing lest it become of doubtful purity. During the last days [of your impurity], how did he conduct himself in your company? Master, she replied, I ate with him and drank with him and in my clothes slept with him in bed; his flesh touched mine but he had not thought of anything. Blessed be God who killed him, Elijah exclaimed; for thus it is written in the Torah, *You shall not approach a woman to uncover her nakedness while she is in her menstrual uncleanness* (Lev 18:19).[29]

Each of the three versions of the story distinguishes between the first days, during which the woman menstruates, and the last days of rabbinically prescribed separation. *Avot de Rabbi Natan* uses a different, seemingly more explicit wording, stating the number of days of impurity, and it is the prophet Elijah himself who interrogates the widow, distinguishing between "the first *three* days of your impurity" and "the last days."[30] During the first days, her husband used to warn her not to touch anything in order to prevent objects from being rendered potentially impure. During the last days, which are not further qualified, the woman would eat and drink with her husband[31] and even sleep in the same bed, with *his* body touching hers (an explicit detail not present in the other versions). She argues that even if this was the case, her husband would not think of attempting anything more.

This version appears to be closer to the one transmitted in bShab 13a than to the *Seder Eliyahu* narrative, though it contains certain details not present there, while others are left unmentioned.[32] Instead of a nameless rabbi, the woman dis-

---

[27] According to another MS reading: "in your Torah."
[28] MSS readings vary at this point; see Hans-Jürgen Becker, ed., *Avot de-Rabbi Natan: Synoptische Edition beider Versionen* (Tübingen: Mohr Siebeck, 2006), 30–32.
[29] The quotation follows Judah Goldin, trans., *The Fathers According to Rabbi Nathan* (New Haven, CT: Yale University Press, 1956), 16–17, with slight modifications.
[30] A gloss on MS New York Rab. 1305 adds "white days."
[31] Whereas the Talmud passage has the husband as the grammatical subject of these actions, here it is the woman who states, "I ate with him," etc.
[32] Unlike the two other versions, here the setting of this encounter is not mentioned.

cusses her plight with the prophet Elijah.[33] In her description of their marital life, the woman mentions her husband's warning not to touch any object (*keli*), a motif that reminds the reader both of the warning that precedes the narrative in *Seder Eliyahu* and of several verses in Lev 15, which describe the transmission of cultic impurity by means of objects or vessels.

6.2.3 The Scriptural Roots of the Rabbinic *Niddah* Laws

The rabbi of *Seder Eliyahu* supports his argumentation with two scriptural verses from the context of the laws regarding the *niddah* in Leviticus, where the passages in question deal with several aspects of proper conduct with regard to a woman during her menses. The first of these contexts, Leviticus 15, lists the ways in which a man can be rendered impure by coming into contact with a woman whenever she is bleeding, or with objects she touches during this time:

> When a woman has a discharge of blood that is her regular discharge from her body, she shall be in her impurity for seven days, and whoever touches her shall be unclean until the evening. 20 Everything upon which she lies during her impurity shall be unclean; everything also upon which she sits shall be unclean. 21 Whoever touches her bed shall wash his clothes, and bathe in water, and be unclean until the evening. 22 Whoever touches anything upon which she sits shall wash his clothes, and bathe in water, and be unclean until the evening; 23 whether it is the bed or anything upon which she sits, when he touches it he shall be unclean until the evening. 24 If any man lies with her, and her impurity falls on him, he shall be unclean for seven days; and every bed on which he lies shall be unclean. 25 If a woman has a discharge of blood for many days, not at the time of her impurity, or if she has a discharge beyond the time of her impurity, for all the days of the discharge she shall continue in uncleanness; as in the days of her impurity, she shall be unclean. 26 Every bed on which she lies during all the days of her discharge shall be treated as the bed of her impurity; and everything on which she sits shall be unclean, as in the uncleanness of her impurity. 27 Whoever touches these things shall be unclean, and shall wash his clothes, and bathe in water, and be unclean until the evening. 28 If she is cleansed of her discharge, she shall count seven days, and after that she shall be clean. 29 On the eighth day she shall take two turtle-doves or two pigeons and bring them to the priest at the entrance of the tent of meeting. 30 The priest shall offer one for a sin-offering and the other for a burnt-offering; and the priest shall make atonement on her behalf before the Lord for her unclean discharge. (Lev 15:19–30)

As scholars have indicated, this passage does not contain prohibitions, but rather describes how women and men become impure and regain their purity. A clear

---

[33] This identification of the rabbi in *Avot de Rabbi Natan* A is part of the post-biblical traditions on the prophet Elijah, who was believed to appear to people and talk to them.

prohibition, on the other hand, is found in the verse from the second context, Lev 18:19 – "You shall not approach a woman to uncover her nakedness while she is in her menstrual uncleanness" – which is only partially quoted in *Seder Eliyahu*.

In her study on the conception and representation of menstruation in rabbinic and early Christian literature, Charlotte Fonrobert lucidly explains a problem manifest in the text of *Seder Eliyahu*:

> The two *conceptual* contexts for biblical menstruation are, on the one hand, the priestly system of purity and impurity and, on the other, the lists of prohibited sexual relationships. Both contexts are conceptually independent from each other ... Lev. 15 is contingent on a specific social-institutional structure, the existence of the central Sanctuary, whereas Lev. 18 and 20, the lists of sexual taboos, are not.[34]

The *niddah* contexts described by Fonrobert – the laws of ritual purity prescribed for the Temple cult found in Lev 15 and the sexual prohibitions of Lev 18 – are not clearly distinguished in rabbinic literature. Whereas the sexual prohibitions were as valid after the destruction of the Temple as they had been before,[35] the purity laws became partly obsolete,[36] due to the fact that the physical context for their observation was no longer existent,[37] which would not prevent the inclusion in the Mishnah and both Talmudim of a tractate titled *Niddah* in the order of *Toharot* – that is, "purities."[38]

---

34 Charlotte Elisheva Fonrobert, *Menstrual Purity: Rabbinic and Christian Reconstructions of Biblical Gender* (Stanford, CA: Stanford University Press, 2000), 20.
35 See Shaye Cohen, "Menstruants and the Sacred," in *Women's History and Ancient History*, ed. Sarah Pomeroy (Chapel Hill, NC: University of North Carolina Press, 1991), 276, who points out: "The prohibition of 'drawing near' to a menstruant for sexual purposes (Lev. 18:19 and 20:18) is part of a list of prohibited sexual unions and has nothing to do with ritual purity. Even when the purity system would lapse after the destruction of the second temple in 70 C.E., the prohibition of union with a menstruant would not."
36 Some purity laws, e.g., in the context of the consumption of the priestly share, were still observed after the destruction. I thank Prof. Günter Stemberger for this observation.
37 On this, Evyatar Marienberg, *Niddah: Lorsque les Juifs Conceptualisent la Menstruation* (Paris: Belles Lettres, 2003), 132, points out: "Même si les lois directement liées au Temple ou à la terre sont par our la plupart considérées dans le judaisme médiéval comme non applicables pour le moment, elles restent valables et seront, selon les rabbins, réappliquées à l'époque messianique."
38 Michael Satlow, *Tasting the Dish: Rabbinic Rhetorics of Sexuality* (Atlanta, GA: Scholars Press, 1995), 296, argues that the *Niddah* tractate in the Babylonian Talmud paradoxically deals with very specific aspects of the purity laws, but the basic question "Why should anyone follow the laws of menstrual purity?" receives almost no treatment at all. The rest of the tractates dealing with aspects of women's lives are found in the order *Nashim* or "(married) women."

6.2.4 The Allegorization of *Niddah*

Some talmudic passages illustrate the way the language of purity in the first scriptural context wandered towards the second, that of the sexual taboo.[39] The expressions used to designate "pure" (טהור and טהורה) or "impure" (טמא and טמאה) – which belong to the language of cult, of the purity laws, and which have no moral or aesthetic implications[40] – became metaphors for "sexually permitted" or "prohibited," as Charlotte Fonrobert points out: "אני טמאה [i.e., I am impure] comes to mean 'I have my menstrual period.'"[41]

The story of the white days can be seen as a good example of the shift in meaning or the allegorisation of impurity. Returning to the narrative in *Seder Eliyahu*, the nameless woman is asked how her husband conducted himself towards her during the days of her impurity. She answers by reproducing his own words in direct speech: "Set aside all the days [of your period] that you see blood and wait (lit. "sit, be inactive") [still] seven clean days, so that you do not have any doubt [about your ritual purity]." The rabbi is pleased with this answer, which he confirms and expands upon by quoting a tradition of the sages, introduced with the characteristic formula *mikan amru*: "With regard both to men and women with an abnormal discharge, [as well as to women] who have menstruated and [women who] have [recently] given birth, the sages taught that only after seven days are such considered ritually pure for their marital duties."[42] Following this anonymous rabbinic

---

[39] See yKet 2:5 (26c), discussed in Fonrobert, *Menstrual Purity*, 26.
[40] Miriam Berkowitz, "Reshaping the Laws of Family Purity," 2006, 5, www.rabbinicalassembly.org/sites/default/files/public/halakhah/teshuvot/20052010/berkowitz_niddah.pdf, observes in this regard, "Firstly, we should insist that there is nothing inherently horrible or appalling with being טמא – it simply marks a legalistic category with no moral or aesthetic implications. The laws of ritual purity have no real relevance in our days (though they can still be learned – *daresh vekabel schar* or appreciated for their educational or metaphoric significance). These laws were fully consequential only within the domain of the Temple and its hallowed services and priests."
[41] Fonrobert, *Menstrual Purity*, 27. Apart from Fonrobert's study, the subject is also examined in depth in Marienberg, *Niddah*. Both elucidate how the meanings of *niddah* vary contextually. Thus, according to Fonrobert, "The term *niddah* does not have an inherent meaning, in and by itself, of 'the ostracized woman' or 'abhorrence and repulsion,' nor can we reconstruct its original meaning. Rather, it acquires different meanings and connotations in different contexts." (17-18). On the etymology of *niddah*, see Moshe Greenberg, "The Etymology of Niddah: (Menstrual) Impurity," in *Solving Riddles and Untying Knots: Biblical, Epigraphic and Semitic Studies in Honor of Jonas C. Greenfield*, ed. Ziony Zevit, Seymour Gitin, and Michael Sokoloff (Winona Lake, IN: Eisenbrauns, 1995), 69–77 and Jacob Milgrom, "Nidda," in *Theological Dictionary of the Old Testament*, ed. G. Johannes Botterweck and Helmer Ringgren, vol. 9 (Grand Rapids, MI: Eerdsmans, 1998), 232–235.
[42] The narrator is probably alluding in a very general way to the Mishnah tractates *Zavim* and *Niddah*, not to a precise rabbinic authority or tradition. As is often the case in *Seder Eliyahu*, the

tradition, he quotes a proof-text, in which reference is made only to the woman: "If she is cleansed of her discharge, she shall count [seven days, and after that she shall be clean]" etc. (Lev 15:28).

With his next question, the rabbi seeks to find out how the deceased husband behaved during the so-called white days.[43] This time, however, he gives two examples of contact between husband and wife without revealing that both her anointing him with oil and either one touching the other, even if only with the little finger, are prohibited the days in question. The woman first emphatically denies that anything of the sort could ever have happened between her husband and her, though when she describes how they interacted during the white days, she does admit that she would wash his feet and anoint them with oil thereafter, and that they would sleep in the same bed, but that nothing else would enter her late husband's mind. The widow is represented as convinced that her husband did not deserve to die, given that it was she who touched him and not the other way round. It appears that *Seder Eliyahu* seeks to emphasise precisely that it is not just what a disciple of the wise himself does, but also what he allows those around him to do that determines how he is judged. The widow's description of their marital life during the white days are her last words before her story comes to an end. In the rabbi's perception, they are a confession and a clear answer to the woman's repeated question regarding the premature death of her husband. After blessing God's impartiality, for even the disciples of the wise are justly judged, the rabbi explains that whoever does not observe the Torah must die, and quotes a verse whose scriptural context is one of sexual taboos, as a proof-text: "a woman to uncover her nakedness while she is in her menstrual uncleanness [you shall not approach]" etc. (Lev 18:19).

With the death of the disciple of the wise, *Seder Eliyahu* seems to be silently alluding to a third passage in Leviticus, which deals not with these prohibitions, but with the punishment for their transgression: "If a man lies with a woman having her sickness and uncovers her nakedness, he has laid bare her flow and she has laid bare her flow of blood; both of them shall be cut off from their people" (Lev 20:18).[44]

This scriptural passage is not quoted in *Seder Eliyahu* but is transformed into a narrative, an alternative to explicit exegesis. The husband dies, and from this moment onwards, the woman is the widow of an extirpated disciple of the wise,

---

first-person narrator (or in other contexts, the governing voice) refers to traditions of the sages without quoting any *mishnah* or talmudic passage.

43 These are elsewhere designated as "clean days."

44 Extirpation or *karet* is also mentioned in "For whoever commits any of these abominations shall be cut off from their people" (Lev 18:29).

a punishment that reveals a gender distinction. The transgression punished with *karet* or extirpation consists in failing to observe the white or clean days after the menstruation has stopped. It appears that *Seder Eliyahu*, even if it does not exonerate the woman, first punishes the one held responsible – her husband – with premature death, and only secondarily punishes the woman with solitude and incomprehension.

6.2.5 The Emergence of the White Days

With respect to the separation of a menstruant in biblical times, Judith Baskin pointed out:

> The seriousness with which separation from a *niddah* was taken in biblical times is evident in the fact that sexual contact with a *niddah* is also forbidden in Leviticus 18:19 as among those sinful acts punished severely by *karet*, or extirpation from the community.[45]

The story of the white days does not focus on the days of bleeding, but on those (seven) additional days which follow after the bleeding has come to an end – the so called white or clean days. What is the origin of the white days? Not just the phraseology,[46] which does not originate in Scripture,[47] but above all the idea, the very concept of the white days?[48] In Baskin's view, they constitute a stringency of the sexual prohibition in Lev 18, which has its origins in the rabbinic period:

> During the rabbinic era, the prohibition of sexual relations with a menstruating wife was expanded. At some point after the codification of the Mishnah, seven further "white" days of separation were added, following the end of the menstrual period itself. It is impossible to know to what degree these prohibitions were observed at any point during the various eras or in the various locales of rabbinic Judaism. These strictures became normative only in post-talmudic Jewish societies. Still, they probably encountered considerable resistance when

---

45 Baskin, *Midrashic Women*, 24. For the development of the imposition of *niddah* regulations on marital sexuality, see 22–29 and 105–109.
46 Braude and Kapstein, *Tanna děbe Eliyyahu*, 170n32, comment on the white days: "When the discharge of a menstruating woman ceased, she put on white garments and examined herself for seven days in succession, which had to pass without any further discharge of blood before she could be considered ritually clean." Freedman argues similarly in his translation of bShab 13 (53n7).
47 No adjective in Lev 15:28 qualifies the days of waiting after the bleeding. The prohibitions in Lev 18 and 20 pertain to the *niddah* days as the period of actual bleeding.
48 Bernhard Maier, "Reinheit," 474, observes that in ancient Egypt, wearing white clothes was one of the rites which could reinstate or maintain purity.

they were first promulgated, as indicated by the threatening tone of much of the discussion exhorting their observance.[49]

The tone of the *maʿaseh* of the white days in *Seder Eliyahu* is threatening indeed. How do the rabbis explain the emergence of these strictures? The following passage in the Babylonian Gemara to the tractate *Niddah* helps understand how this expansion of the prohibition works, and how it is legitimated by the rabbis:

> Rav Joseph said in the name of Rav Judah who said it in the name of Rav: Rabbi ordained at Sadoth: If a woman observed a discharge on one day she must wait six days in addition to it. If she observed discharges on two days she must wait six days in addition to these. If she observed a discharge on three days she must wait seven clean days. R. Zeira stated: The daughters of Israel have imposed upon themselves the restriction that even if they observe a drop of blood of the size of a mustard seed, they wait on account of it seven clean days. (bNid 66a)[50]

The immediate context of this passage, which is a possible etiological narrative on the white days, is not, however, the discussion of the *niddah*, but of the *zavah* – that is, the woman who has irregular bleeding at times other than that of her regular menstrual bleeding.[51] This distinction is found in the tractate *Niddah*, and therefore it was probably already valid in the tannaitic period. The author of *Seder Eliyahu* appears to be writing his work at a time in which the distinction between *niddah* and *zavah gedolah* (three days of abnormal bleeding) or *zavah qetanah* (one to two days) was no longer valid: After any kind of bleeding, seven additional clean or white days of separation were to be observed.[52] A woman is permitted to have sexual intercourse only after her ritual immersion following these additional days of separation.

Interestingly enough, the Babylonian Talmud attributes this expansion of the prohibition to the daughters of Israel themselves – a legitimation strategy which, read from a gendered perspective, can be described as more invasive of the bodily autonomy of women than the blurring of a distinction between *niddah* and *zavah*, as Evyatar Marienberg observes:

---

49 Baskin, *Midrashic Women*, 25.
50 The quotation follows Epstein, *Niddah*, with slight modifications.
51 As Hauptmann, *Rereading the Rabbis*, 158, points out: "The days that Rebbe requires her to observe are the seven clean days of the *zavah*, not the seven days of menstrual impurity, and certainly not seven clean days after the seven days of menstrual impurity. In fact, the term 'seven clean days,' as it appears in the Talmud, refers in all instances to the days following *zivah*, not *niddah*."
52 See Baskin, *Midrashic Women*, 25.

> Édictées sur la base de l'idée rabbinique qui veut qu'elles constituent une "barrière" supplémentaire, ces restrictions aident, espèrent les rabbins, à réduire le risque que les fidèles transgressent par inadvertance les lois de base. L'exemple le plus représentatif de cette démarche est l'amalgame de deux types d'écoulement mentionnés dans la Bible : les rabbins ou, d'après eux, les femmes elles-mêmes, ont instauré un système selon lequel tout écoulement de sang, même très court, et sans tenir compte du moment où cet écoulement apparaît, est considéré comme un "vrai" sang menstruel et comme un écoulement prolongé, de sorte que les femmes respectent toujours sept jours d'impureté supplémentaires après la fin de tout écoulement. Ainsi, un nouveau concept important, celui des "sept jours propres" (ou "blancs"), est né.[53]

To return to the narrative in *Seder Eliyahu*: What is the point of this story being told at this juncture? The questioner is represented as unfamiliar with the Mishnah but familiar with Scripture; he knows that the regulation regarding ritual immersion for women after their menses is not stated in Lev 15. His implicit question might therefore be paraphrased as follows: How is it possible to justify rabbinically the immersion of the woman after menstruation, if this is not prescribed in Lev 15? Rather than answer this question, the story of the white days appears to give an example of what happens to those like him who question the authority of the ritual bath and regard this institution as not having been prescribed by the Torah: They die. The story is a negative exemplum, a calculated warning, as Judith Baskin suggests:

> Warnings of the dire consequences that will result to men from even the most accidental contact with a *niddah* and to women who do not observe their period of *niddah* strictly, ... reflect rabbinic efforts to enforce by fear a most unpopular series of stipulations.[54]

The story in *Seder Eliyahu* is one of many passages in rabbinic literature which illustrate how two distinct scriptural concepts, such as the purity laws and the sexual taboos were no longer distinguished after the destruction of the Second Temple. The language of purity, in its origins pertaining to the Temple cult, became a way of metaphorically referring to the regulations concerning sexual life. The versions of the story in *Seder Eliyahu*, in the Babylonian Talmud, and in *Avot de Rabbi Natan* A are part of a developing gendered discourse based on male dominated conceptions that seeks to regulate sexuality.[55] It is a discourse that focuses

---

[53] Marienberg, *Niddah*, 31.
[54] Baskin, *Midrashic women*, 105–106. Not only are the transgressors themselves punished with extirpation, but the children they conceive are also punished, for example with leprosy. See Marienberg, *Niddah*, 103–113.
[55] See "Reinheit," 477.

above all, as Marienberg suggests, on ensuring the observation of the basic regulations of family purity.[56]

Depending on the co-text of the narrative – *Seder Eliyahu*, bShab 13a–b, or ARN A 2 – different aspects of the plot are emphasised. All three versions distinguish between the first days (of menstruation) and the last days, which constitute the stringency. Although a special designation, such as "clean" or "white," is used to refer to them in *Seder Eliyahu* and in the Talmud passage, they are understood as belonging to the *niddah* time, the time of impurity, during which sexual contact is prohibited.

With its version of the story, *Seder Eliyahu* attempts to illustrate several points: a) that sexual intercourse with a *niddah* is a graver offence than sexual intercourse with a *zav*;[57] b) that the ritual bath for the *niddah* has its origins in the Torah – although the narrative itself does not mention immersion; and c) that whoever objects to this, as the questioner seems to do and the disciple of the wise in the embedded narrative did, will never find contentment, but rather extirpation as his or her retribution. The agenda of the passage in bShab 13a–b is less comprehensive. Here the story proves d) that on Shabbat, a *zav* should not eat with a *zavah* – a term which, in this context, seems to include both the woman with menstrual bleeding and the woman with irregular bleeding. The prohibition, however, does not apply only on Shabbat. Finally, *Avot de Rabbi Natan* A 2 interprets the fence in mAv 1:1 as a separation between husband and wife during the time of the woman's impurity, thus confirming e) that those who observe the Torah in the everyday life of marriage keep the fence around the Torah upright.

Although Lev 20:18 mentions the punishment of extirpation for both the man and the woman who have intercourse during the *niddah* time, the versions of the story discussed above do make a gender-specific distinction. The man dies young, and his widow is left with questions and no answers. Moreover, *Seder Eliyahu* depicts her as lonely and unable to come to terms with her situation. In all three versions, it could be argued, she remains "impure," since the ritual bath which should have put an end to the *niddah* time never took place.

6.3 Exegetical Contexts I: The Street of the Harlots

Therefore it is said, *Announce to my people their rebellion, to the house of Jacob their sins* (Isa 58:1). Who <are these>? They are the common people [among Israel]. It happened once

---

56 On this expression, see Marienberg, *Niddah*, 40–41.
57 The *zav* is practically of no interest to the narrator, who turns to the *niddah* and does not mention the *zav* again.

that a disciple of R. Aqiba, the head of twenty-four thousand of his disciples, went to the street of the harlots, saw there a prostitute, and fell in love with her. He would send his messenger back and forth between him and her until the evening time. In the evening she went up to the roof and saw him sitting before his disciples like a prince of hosts, Gabriel standing at his right. She said <to herself>, Woe unto that woman to whom all kinds of Gehenna punishments are attached.[58] A man so grandiose as this one, who resembles a king – should such a woman respond to him, when she dies and ceases to exist for this world she shall inherit Gehenna. On the other hand, if he accepts her [refusal], she will save him and herself from the judgement of Gehenna. When he came to her, she spoke to him thus, My son, why do you lose a life in the world to come for the sake of an hour in this world? His mind was not cooled down until she said to him, My son, the place you love is the dirtiest and filthiest of all the parts of the body, <a gourd full of ordure (צואה) and refuse> whose odour no creature can endure smelling. Still, his mind was not cooled down until she took his nose and placed it in that grave. When he smelled the odour, it repelled him so much that he never married a woman. A divine voice went forth proclaiming, Such-and-such a woman and such-and-such a man are destined to life in the world to come. (PsEZ 39, l. 5–PsEZ 40, l. 3)[59]

One of R. Aqiba's disciples falls in love with a woman he sees in an urban area identified by the narrator as a site of prostitution. In this setting, the prostitute and the sage communicate with the aid of a messenger until evening comes and she goes up to the roof, where she reflects on their apparently radically different moral standards. She speaks of herself in the third person as worthy of all the punishments of Gehenna and as a vehicle by which these punishments will be inherited by whoever enjoys her favours. When R. Aqiba's disciple and the prostitute eventually meet, she succeeds in persuading him to give up his intentions. The language she uses – put into her mouth by a male mind and quoted by the male voice of R. Joshua b. Qarcha, to whom the entire passage is attributed[60] – is especially offensive with respect to her own person.[61] The tanna deals in this *maʿaseh* not just with an aspect of women, but rather with a broader idea of woman, as this is

---

58 On the verbal form used, צואת, which has an aleph that is not part of the root of the three verbs that may come into question (צוי, צות, and צבת), see Friedmann, *Pseudo-Seder Eliahu Zuta*, 39n29. Rather than looking for an explanation of this form in similar forms present in *Seder Eliyahu Rabbah* (ER 19), it might be more reasonable to understand the term in its own context, where a few lines later on, the woman herself compares a part of her body to a gourd full of excrement (צואה).

59 The translation is based on Friedmann, *Pseudo-Seder Eliahu Zuta*, the edition of the "spurious" chapters of *Seder Eliyahu Zuta*. For the seven chapters which, in this edition, bear the title *Pirqe deRabbi Eliezer*, the fourth of which contains the translated passage, Friedmann uses the Venice print and MS Parma 3122 (De Rossi 1240) as his textual basis.

60 See PsEZ 38, l. 11ff.

61 A similar way of referring to women in general is found in bShab 152a: "A tanna taught: Though a woman be as a pitcher full of filth and her mouth be full of blood, yet all speed after her (תנא: אשה חמת מלא צואה, ופיה מלא דם - והכל רצין אחריה)."

represented by the prostitute – the passage is one of those attempts in rabbinic literature which Judith Baskin describes as "motivated by a desire to circumscribe, defuse, and control the female not only as potential polluter but also as sexual temptress."[62] Furthermore, according to Friedmann's text, for which he uses the reading of the MS, it is the prostitute who places the sage's nose in her vagina, which is referred to figuratively.[63] On one aspect the narrator chooses not to be explicit – namely, on how the man's "heated mind" manifests itself so that it can be perceived by the prostitute before she proceeds to appease him.

The story of the prostitute is told in an exegetical context, one dealing with Isa 58:1. The governing voice poses a rhetorical question concerning the meaning of the expressions "my people" and "the house of Jacob," respectively, and answers it by suggesting that they are the common people among Israel, the so-called "peoples of the land" (עמי הארץ).

In view of the thematic orientation of the wider co-text of the narrative – the chapter in which this narrative is found deals primarily with repentance[64] – we could claim that it functions as an exemplum of repentance. But then, who is the exemplary character here? The opening of the narrative, a *maʿaseh* formula, seems to imply that it is the sage who mainly functions as an example of repen-

---

62 Baskin, *Midrashic Women*, 30. On the theme of woman as the source of sexual temptation, see 29–36, and the literature cited therein.

63 Braude and Kapstein, *Tanna děbe Eliyyahu*, 471, insert the phrase "the female organ" in the text of their translation without any commentary. The reading of the Venice print, i.e., Friedmann's main textual witness, suggests that the sage himself uses his own nose to prove the harlot's words – the verb forms used are תפשו and הניחו. In this case, Friedmann prefers the readings of the MS, namely תפשתו and הניחתו. In this case it is not only the rabbinic male mind of the copyist at work, but also that of the work's editor in the early twentieth century.

64 I.e., chapter 4 in Friedmann's edition of *Pseudo-Seder Eliyahu Zuta*, which, according to the Venice print where it is transmitted, is chapter 22 of the *Seder Eliyahu Zuta*. In a passage preceding the story of the prostitute, repentance is said to be greater than prayer, since Moses's prayers were not as effective as the harlot Rachab's repentance. See PsEZ 37. According to Jos 2, the prostitute Rachab hid and assisted two men Joshua had sent to spy on Jericho before the city was taken and destroyed. Rachab is depicted as a clever strategist who negotiates her freedom and that of her whole family in return for the assistance she provides to Joshua's men. In *Seder Eliyahu*, her name is interpreted as etymologically related to her ample (רחובה) repentance, for which she was rewarded with progeny that included seven kings and eight prophets: "R. Eliezer b. Jacob said: Why was she called by the name Rahab? Because her merit was ample: due to the repentance she offered, she was rewarded with seven kings and eight prophets going forth from her" (PsEZ 37, l. 19–21). SifBem 78 reads "eight priests and eight prophets," while bMeg 14a has "eight prophets who were also priests." For a discussion of Rachab's gender duality and the manner in which the sages appropriated her story in terms of a conversion narrative, see Inbar Raveh, "Open to Conquest: Prostitution – Temptation and Responses," in *Feminist Rereadings of Rabbinic Literature* (Waltham, MA: Brandeis University Press, 2014), 100–115.

tance. After all, *he* goes to a place where he is not supposed to be, *he* repeatedly needs proof that the woman speaks the truth, and it is *his* "heated mind" that is cooled down after verifying the prostitute's arguments with his own senses. Even though he remains nameless, he is depicted as a renowned disciple of R. Aqiba, judging from the number of disciples among whom he is the first, from the words the prostitute (who compares him with a prince) uses to depict him, and from the fact that the archangel Gabriel appears in a sort of guardian angel role.

Conversely, it could be argued that the protagonist, the main penitent in this narrative told by a heterodiegetic narrator, is the prostitute. She is characterised only in her designation as אשה זונה in the narrator's voice, and indirectly by her own speech and – according the MS Friedmann uses – action. Hence, it could be argued that the narrative expands upon the lemma by showing how a prostitute can behave and speak with the "common sense" wisdom of the illiterate,[65] thus opening the eyes of "the house of Israel."[66]

6.4 Exegetical Contexts II: Deborah

Two consecutive chapters in *Seder Eliyahu* depict the biblical character Deborah as the protagonist of exegetical narratives. Their scriptural point of departure or midrashic lemmata are verses from the book of Judges; their agenda is one of rabbinic concepts.[67]

> *And Deborah, a prophetess[, wife of Lappidoth, was judging Israel]* etc. (Judg 4:4). What was Deborah's nature that she judged Israel and prophesied to them? Was not Phinehas b. Eleazar still serving [in these offices]? I call heaven and earth to witness that the Spirit of Holiness dwells upon everyone – whether they be non-Jew or Israelite, man or woman, manservant or maidservant – according to the deeds they perform. They said: Deborah's husband was illiterate (עם הארץ). His wife spoke to him thus, Go and make wicks and go to the Holy Place in Shiloh, so that your portion may be with the righteous men and you will come to a life in the world to come. And he would make thick wicks (פתילות) so that their light was ample (מרובה). Hence he is called by the name Lappidoth (לפידות). They said: He

---

[65] A recurring motif in *Seder Eliyahu*.
[66] Some questions remain open: Taking for granted that she is the main penitent of the narrative, could she ever have repented and had access to salvation or to a place in a rabbinic story, had she not been desired by a sage? Or is she rather exemplary, in spite of speaking of herself in terms of such self-hatred, only because she leads a man worthy of a better life to the right path of repentance?
[67] As Werblowsky, "A Note," 202, pointed out, the overall theme of this and the following chapter is divine justice. See Kadushin, *The Theology*, who dedicates the last chapter of his book to the justice of God.

has three names: Baraq, Lappidoth, and Michael. Baraq (ברק) because his face resembled a lightning (ברק). Lappidoth because he made wicks and went to the Holy Place in Shiloh. Michael because of [the angel] Michael. The Holy One, blessed be He, who *tests the minds and hearts* (Ps 7:10), said to her, Deborah, you suggested and made⁶⁸ broad wicks so that their light was ample (מרובה). I will enhance (ארבה) you in Israel and Judah and among the twelve tribes of Israel. But who caused Lappidoth to belong to the righteous human beings and come to the world to come? They said: Deborah, his wife. Of her, of those like her and those who resemble her, and those who perform acts like hers, it [Scripture] says, *The wise woman builds her house[, but the foolish tears it down with her own hands]* etc. (Prov 14:1). (ER 48, l. 18–ER 49, l. 2)

The first chapter dealing with Deborah, chapter (9) 10 of *Seder Eliyahu Rabbah*, begins by quoting Judg 4:4 to expound on the exceptional character of Deborah,[69] who was both a prophetess and a judge, as stated in the part of the verse that is left unquoted, although Phinehas was still serving in those offices. Anticipating the exegetical narratives that will follow, and using the recurrent vow formula, "I call heaven and earth to witness,"[70] the governing voice claims that everyone is rewarded according to his or her deeds. The governing voice first refers to an

---

68 The passage presents the following problem: Deborah is addressed, but the masculine pronominal form אתה is used in combination with the verb forms נתכוונתה (which corresponds neither to the masculine nor to the feminine perfect forms, but is closer to the former) and עשית (which can be either masculine or feminine). With the same words, God addresses Aaron in ER 157. One might assume that it is Lappidoth instead of Deborah who is addressed here, and that Deborah is praised for what her husband did.
69 Among the women characters of the book of Judges, Deborah is a special case due to her offices as a religious functionary and a political leader. Susan Ackerman, *Warrior, Dancer, Seductress, Queen: Women in Judges and Biblical Israel* (New York: Doubleday, 1998), 5, observes "[t]hat elsewhere in biblical tradition, these offices are occupied almost exclusively by men." For Ackerman's discussion of the Deborah narrative, especially in Judg 5, see Ackerman, *Warrior, Dancer*, 27–47. Her analysis of women in Judges is based on a history-of-religions approach, which seeks to "describe the place of Judges' 'types' of women characters within the ancient Israelite religious imagination and, even more generally, to discuss the place these 'types' of women occupied within the actual practice of ancient Israelite religion." (9–10) What singles Deborah out, according to Ackerman, is the fact that her depiction defies "Israelite paradigms of gender-appropriate behavior that she can be presented as assuming a leadership role in Israel's military affairs." (28) For a feminist narratological reading of Judg 4, see also Sigrid Eder, *Wie Frauen und Männer Macht ausüben: Eine feministisch-narratologische Analyse von Ri 4* (Freiburg im Breisgau: Herder, 2008), 98–129, especially 200–202, for an analysis of Deborah's characterisation there.
70 This formula, מעיד אני עלי את השמים ואת הארץ, in the words of Werblowsky, "A Note," 203, an "explosive interjection ... of which our author is particularly fond," in his opinion "rather interrupts the plain and smooth course of the exposition, though it anticipates the answer." It can also be argued that this is the governing voice's way of leaving his unequivocal mark even on stories originally authored by others.

anonymous tradition of the sages about Deborah and her husband, introduced by the briefest introductory formula, "they said"(אמרו).⁷¹ Instead of assuming the role of a narrator, in this case the governing voice retells a narrative already told by the sages. According to the latter, Deborah's husband was an ignoramus (עם הארץ). Deborah is said to have commanded her husband to make wicks and take them to the sanctuary at Shiloh. This midrashic expansion on an episode of their scriptural lives, which remains untold in Scripture, has an etymological function: It explains how Deborah's husband came to be called by the name "Lappidoth," a name which can be translated as "bright torches." The midrash thus operates using a pun connecting לפידות and פתילות, two words with a partial overlap of consonants in a different sequence – five out of six consonants are the same.⁷² Deborah's husband – who in the scriptural account has no narrative function whatsoever, apart from being named in a genitive construction as being related to *her* by marriage – is made into a narrative agent in the tradition the governing voice retells, one which depicts him as an obedient, ignorant man whose deeds earn him and the one in charge of him, Deborah, an illustrious reputation.

The governing voice interrupts the narrative flow to adduce yet another tradition of the sages, likewise introduced with "they said," regarding the multiple names of Deborah's husband: He was called by no less than three names – Baraq, Lappidoth, and Michael. The first two go back to his appearance – his face was or shone, as bright as a lightning (ברק) – or to his deeds – making wicks (פתילות) and bringing them to Shiloh. The third was given to him because of his assumed connection with the angel Michael.⁷³

Returning to Deborah's narrative, God, described with wording from Ps 7:10, addresses her in direct speech and promises to enhance (ארבה) her precisely because of *her husband's* making thick wicks that produce ample light (מרובה). As noted previously, the text of this passage might be defective: Even though God addresses Deborah, the pronominal (and verbal) forms used are masculine.⁷⁴ It is interesting, however, that this grammatical "indeterminacy" can be interpreted as constitutive of the narrative of Deborah as a female leader.

---

71 Deborah's marital status in Judg 4 is ambiguous. Even if אשת לפידות is usually translated as "the wife of Lappidoth," it can also be translated, as Ackerman, *Warrior, Dancer*, 38, suggests, as "a fiery woman," which in turn accords with the rabbis' interpretation of the name of her husband and of their righteousness.
72 On this particular midrashic passage, see Werblowsky, "A Note," 202–205. On this type of hermeneutic step, see Samely, *Rabbinic Interpretation*, 378, "Grapheme3."
73 According to YalqShim *Shofetim* 32, Michael is the name given Deborah's husband because he lowered himself (מנמיך) or because he was an angel (מלאך).
74 See n. 68.

The governing voice's claim concerning the just reward for everyone is confirmed in this exegetical narrative that depicts a correspondence between the dimension of Deborah's reward and her deed – having her husband perform an exemplary deed. Her reward is manifest in her genealogy: Deborah's progeny will persist in Israel and Judah – in all of the twelve tribes. This is actually the end of this exegetical narrative on Deborah, but the governing voice appears to be aware of the fact that such an end leaves a question unanswered: If Deborah's reward is enduring progeny, then Lappidoth's reward must be correspondingly emphasised, even if this again takes the form of clear praise of Deborah. The governing voice asks who *caused* Lappidoth to be one of the worthy men and to enter the world to come. To answer this question, the sages are quoted a third time. According to them, it is Deborah, his wife, who made him worthy; she and those who take after her are praised with the verse from Proverbs: "The wise woman builds her house."[75]

A counter-example to Deborah follows, introduced not as a narrative of the sages, but as an expansion by the governing voice itself, which introduces it with a formula addressing the reader:

> Likewise you read (lit. "say") [of] *Jezebel, daughter of Ethbaal, king of the Zidonians* (1 Kgs 16:31), wife of *Ahab, son of Omri* (1 Kgs 16:29.30) [that] she said [to him] from the very first year since she was married, Learn[76] the ways of idolatry! And through her Ahab sold himself to idolatry, for it is said, *Indeed, there was no one like Ahab, who sold himself to do what was evil in the sight of the Lord[, urged on by his wife Jezebel]* (1 Kgs 21:25). And because of her deeds and her husband's deeds they perished from this world and from the world to come, and their children perished with them. A parable: It is like a king of flesh and blood whose servant brought him a present of seven jugs of oil. When he [the servant] spoke too much, he smashed them [the jugs] in front of him. And who caused Ahab to perish from this world

---

[75] This narrative in *Seder Eliyahu* has a parallel in bMeg 14a, which reads: "*Deborah*, as it is written, *Now Deborah, a prophetess, wife of Lappidoth* (Judg 4:4). What is meant by a *woman of flames*? [She was so called] because she used to make wicks for the Sanctuary. *She used to sit under the palm* (Judg 4:5). Why just a palm tree? – R. Simeon b. Abishalom said: [To avoid] privacy. Another explanation is: Just as a palm tree has only one heart, so Israel in that generation had only one heart devoted to their Father in heaven." Werblowsky, who compared the version in *Seder Eliyahu* with those in the *Babylonian Talmud* and in the *Yalqut*, where Deborah herself makes the wicks, suggests that there might have been two versions of the story of the wicks which got conflated in *Seder Eliyahu*. He points out: "The text of SE would then appear to be a conflation of two versions." (204) He argues further: "Friedmann takes it for granted that the passage b. Megillah 14a depends on our SE or a 'similar text.' It seems to me that in the light of the foregoing analysis everything will depend on what we mean by a 'similar' text. The text of SE reveals such a composite and complicated structure that it is hardly possible to regard it as a primary source *tout court*." (206)

[76] Friedmann emends the MS reading למדן to the imperative form למדו.

and from the world to come, so that his sons perish with him? They said: Jezebel his wife. Of her and of those like her, of those who resemble her, and perform deeds such as hers, it [Scripture] says, *but the foolish tears it down with her own hands* (Prov 14:11). Of them it [Scripture] says, *Yet a little while, and the wicked will be no more* etc. (Ps 37:10), *I have seen the wicked oppressing[, and towering like a cedar of Lebanon]* (Ps 37:35). *Again I passed by, and they were no more[; though I sought them, they could not be found.]* etc. (Ps 37:36); *[t]he wicked watch [for the righteous, and seek to kill them.]* etc. (Ps 37:32) And after this [verse] what does it [Scripture] say? *But the Lord laughs at him [the wicked]* etc. (Ps 37:13). (ER 49, l. 3–14)

The narrative has Jezebel, a female villain, as its protagonist. Unlike Deborah, she is defined by her male relations as the daughter of Ethbaal and the wife of Ahab.[77] It was she who brought her husband to idolatry and caused him and their sons to perish in this world and in the world to come. In contrast to the narrative about Deborah, this brief exegetical narrative does not expand upon its scriptural hypotext (the second part of 1 Kgs 21:25) by quoting it. With respect to basic plot, it accords with the scriptural narrative insofar as both depict her as the instigator of the sins of her husband.

The couple's conduct is illustrated with the parable of a mortal king whose servant brought him seventy jars of oil but, in doing so, addressed the king in such a manner that the king smashed the jars in front of the servant. How this parable applies is not explicitly stated; there is no evident *nimshal* to this *mashal* narrative. According to 2 Kgs 10:1, Ahab had seventy sons, who – unlike the descendants of Deborah (and Lappidoth) – did not enhance light, but were killed as oil in broken jars is spilled.[78] The apparently enigmatic *mashal* is thus linked to the figural language of the Deborah narrative. Furthermore, the *mashal* is a material textual counterpart to God's active participation in the text of Deborah's narrative.

Is there a great man behind every great biblical woman? Had both Lappidoth and Ahab been prominent scriptural men, the concluding passages of the narratives about Deborah and Jezebel could be viewed as an illustration in narrative form of the slogan, "Behind every great man, there is a great woman." The narrative parallelism is stressed by a concluding rhetorical question, posed by the governing voice and answered collectively by the sages. Women are thereby classified as either wise or foolish, and Deborah and Jezebel are imagined as corresponding archetypes:

---

[77] Her father is introduced as the king of the Zidonians, her husband as the son of Omri (ER 49, l. 3–4).
[78] See 2 Kgs 10:7.11.17.

And who caused Ahab to perish from this world and from the world to come, and his sons to perish with him? They said: Jezebel, his wife. Of her, of those like her, of those who resemble her, and those who perform deeds like hers Scripture says, *[The wise woman builds her house,] but the foolish tears it down with her own hands* (Prov 14:1). (ER 49, l. 9–12)

The narratives on the Deborah-Jezebel pair are crowned with a series of proof-texts from Psalm 37, reaffirming the notion that the wicked are lost in this world and in the world to come, as are Jezebel, Ahab, and his children.⁷⁹

The governing voice proceeds with its exposition on Deborah based on a second lemmatic verse, Judg 4:5: To return to its starting point – namely, that Deborah illustrates how God rewards everyone according to their deeds, the governing voice speaks a blessing which ends with the joint quotation of both Judg 4:4 and Judg 4:5, summing up his previous exposition and proceeding to the biblical text he aims to interpret:

Blessed be the Omnipresent, blessed be He, for He rewards human beings, [each] man according to his ways, each and every man according to his deeds, and upon them is [the *mishnah*] fulfilled: "With what measure a man metes it shall be measured to him again" (mSotah 1:7). Therefore, it is said, <*And Deborah,*> *a prophetess* <etc.> *She used to sit under the palm of Deborah between Ramah and Bethel [in the hill country of Ephraim; and the Israelites came up to her for judgement]* etc. (Judg 4:4–5). They said: Just as Samuel [sat] in Ramah, so Deborah [sat] in Ramah. Therefore it is said, *She used to sit under the palm* <etc.> They said: There were as few disciples of the wise in Israel as those who fill half the shadow of a palm tree. Hence it is said, *She used to sit under the palm.*⁸⁰ Another interpretation: *She used to sit* <etc.> Since it is not the [proper] way for a woman to meet with others within the house, Deborah would go [outside] and sit under the palm tree and teach Torah to multitudes. Therefore it is said, *She used to sit [under the palm of Deborah] between Ramah and Bethel* <etc.> (ER 50, l. 9–17)

Judg 4:5 is first interpreted by citing a tradition (*amru*) which takes the form of a short analogy: Just as Samuel sat in Ramah, so Deborah sat in Ramah. A second interpretation of the sages (*amru*) follows, this time explicitly projecting rabbinic ideals onto the scriptural narrative: In the days of Deborah, there were so few disciples of the wise in Israel that there was room for all of them under half of the

---

79 Ps 37:10.35.36.32.13. The fact that Jezebel is held responsible at least in part for Ahab's transgression and the fate of his house is implied in the words of the young prophet to Jehu in 2 Kgs 9:7–10. Before returning to Deborah (ER 50), his main thread in this chapter, the governing voice deals with Omri, Ahab's father, making use of a first-person narrative among other literary forms, and with the episode of the sacrifice of Mesha's first-born son (2 Kgs 3:27), as illustrative of God's justice.
80 Friedmann emends the MS reading at this point, placing the sages' statement where it appears in the Venice print.

palm tree. Thus, Deborah appears to be conceived of as the head of an outdoor academy in biblical times, a female forerunner of the rabbis, as it were. A third interpretation, which is not explicitly presented as going back to the sages, is introduced with the formula *davar acher*. Deborah sitting under the palm tree has to do with the fact that it is improper for a woman to be indoors with a man other than her husband or brother. Outdoors, under the palm tree, Deborah could therefore instruct multitudes unhindered. Hence, it could be argued that Deborah's exceptionality is not only manifest in her role as a prophetess, or in her encouraging her husband to be pious, but even more so in her teaching of Torah. This passage of *Seder Eliyahu* achieves a gendering of instruction: The ethical midrash conveys the idea that while men can teach men anywhere, it is the otherness of women that precludes them even from being imagined as teaching men indoors.[81]

After quoting Judg 4:5 as a confirmation of what has been expounded, the midrash proceeds to Judg 4:6, thus bridging exegetical passages which deal with consecutive verses of the scriptural passage in question:

> *She sent and summoned Baraq son of Abinoam from Kedesh in Naphtali, and said to him, Has not [the Lord, the God of Israel,] commanded [you, Go, take position at Mount Tabor, bringing ten thousand from the tribe of Naphtali and the tribe of Zebulun]?* <etc.> (Judg 4:6). What does Scripture teach when it says *has not commanded*? Just that she spoke to him thus, Is it not written in the Torah, *and the judges shall make a thorough inquiry* etc. (Deut 19:18)? And what is the subject matter [of the verse] after this? *When you go out to war* (Deut 20:1). And what is the nature of Deborah['s relation] to Baraq and Baraq['s] to Deborah? Was Deborah not at her place and Baraq at his? However, they said: Baraq ministered to the elders during the lifetime of Joshua and went on ministering to them after his death. Therefore they brought him and placed him near Deborah. At that time Deborah was shown the means by which the Holy One, blessed be He, delivers Israel from among the peoples, [namely] by [the agency of] human beings who go to the synagogue and to the academy early in the morning and <in the evening (משכימין ומעריבין)[82]> and occupy themselves every day without fail with the words of Torah, by them or by [the agency of] those who minister to them. And what distinguished Zebulun and Naphtali among all the tribes that a great deliverance came to Israel through them? They said: Naphtali ministered to our father Jacob and found contentment in doing this; Zebulun ministered to Issachar and showed him hospitality. Because Baraq trusted the

---

81 Contrary to the claim by Dvora E. Weisberg, "Women and Torah Study in Aggadah," in *Women and Judaism: New Insights and Scholarship*, ed. Frederick Greenspahn (New York: New York University Press, 2009), 51, "biblical women, whether praised or criticized, are never portrayed in *aggadah* as students or teachers of Torah," in this passage Deborah is explicitly depicted in the role of a teacher.

82 Friedmann emends the MS reading משחרין (Jastrow, *Dictionary*: "to be early in doing; to get up early") to מעריבין (Jastrow, *Dictionary*: "do late in the evening"), which contrasts with the first verb, משכימין (Jastrow, *Dictionary*: "to rise early, do a thing early"). Also in the following chapter, Friedmann emends the MS reading ומשחיר to ומעריב. See ER 52, l. 22.

God of Israel and believed in the prophecy of Deborah he has a portion with her in her song, for it is said, *Then Deborah and Baraq son of Abinoam sang on that day* (Judg 5:1); *and he said to her, If you will go with me, I will go[; but if you will not go with me, I will not go.]* <etc.> *And she said, I will surely go with you[; nevertheless, the road on which you are going will not lead to your glory, for the Lord will sell Sisera into the hand of a woman. Then Deborah got up and went with Baraq to Kedesh]* etc. (Judg 4:8–9). (ER 50, l. 18–ER 51, l. 5)

The passage deals primarily with the manner in which Deborah persuades Baraq to wage war against Sisera, the commander of the Canaanites, to whom she speaks in Judg 4:6 on God's behalf. The first concern of the midrash, after quoting Judg 4:6, is to interpret the phrase "has not commanded" in Deborah's prophecy. To achieve this interpretive task, the midrash links the quoted verse to two verses from different contexts in Deuteronomy.[83] With the words of her prophecy, the governing voice explains, Deborah implies two partially quoted verses with which she reminds Baraq that God has previously commanded that judges should be in charge of sending others to war. Thus rabbinised, Deborah is presented as a self-confident leader, and this leadership has its legitimation in legal portions of the Torah, with which she herself is familiar.[84]

As we have seen repeatedly above, the reader cannot be certain about who actually speaks the question and the answer that follow the first quoted verse: Deborah or the governing voice on her behalf. In the case of the second verse from Deuteronomy, if the one quoting it is Deborah, she is depicted as familiar not only with Scripture, but also with rabbinic hermeneutics, as the use of the phrase "What is the subject matter of [the verse] after this?," used to to connect scriptural verses, would indicate. The passage would thus suggest that her persuading Baraq to wage war against the Canaanite forces under Sisera is based on the cognitive process by which she contextualises her own situation in the scriptural narrative within the broader context of Scripture by linking her own narrative to these verses from Deuteronomy. The rabbinic text thus reorients the nature of Deborah's military heroism from what is depicted in Scripture towards her performance of hermeneutic tasks.

---

[83] On the one hand, to Deut 19:18, a verse that describes the central role of judges in a scriptural passage concerning witnesses, and which Deborah herself apparently speaks as if the words were her own, i.e., without any introductory formula; on the other, to Deut 20:1, a verse from a scriptural context that pertains to the rules of war.

[84] Ackerman, *Warrior, Dancer*, 1–3, points out that although wartime and battlefield constitute an "arena traditionally reserved for the affairs of men," not only Deborah's story but also those of a number of women in the book of Judges – Achsah (1:11–15), Jael (4:17–22; 5:24–27), Sisera's mother (4:17–22; 5:24–27), the woman of Thebez (9:50–57), and Jephthah's daughter (11:29–40) – have such a setting.

Another aspect of the lemma in the quoted passage which interests the governing voice pertains to the nature of the relationship between Deborah and Baraq, who in rabbinic tradition are assumed to have lived in different places – Deborah on Mount Ephraim and Baraq in Kedeshnaphtali. The answer is provided, once again, by a collective tradition of the sages (*amru*), which projects the rabbinic ideal of ministry to elders back onto the biblical past. Baraq is said to have ministered to the elders during Joshua's lifetime and even after his death. The idea that Baraq was brought to Deborah appears to suggest, in the reading of the sages, that he ministered to Deborah the way he had ministered to the elders. The text does not insinuate a marriage at this point, as Braude and Kapstein suggest with their translation.[85] Marriage might be implied in the selective quotation and combination of verses at the end of the passage. That Baraq and Deborah were husband and wife is, however, implied in the previously mentioned tradition of the sages, according to which Baraq was one of Lappidoth's names. Another rabbinic ideal projected back onto the scriptural narrative is the midrashic claim that during the time when Baraq ministered to her, Deborah came to realise who was responsible for Israel's selection from among the peoples of the world – namely, men who go to the synagogue or the academy in the morning and in the afternoon, who constantly occupy themselves with the words of Torah, as well as those other men who minister to them. These tasks can only be predicated of men, so Deborah only indirectly contributes to Israel's being saved, for as a woman she is excluded from the house of study, from complete participation in the synagogue service, and is not suited to minister to the sages.[86]

The tendency observed above – which consists in depicting Deborah with the traits of a rabbi, such as having disciples or quoting certain passages of Scripture to explain others – is accentuated in this passage, where she is said to have had Baraq as a ministrant, and where the synagogue and the house of study are introduced as spaces linked to the salvation of Israel.

Returning to Baraq, the governing voice argues that his faith in God and in his prophetess was justly rewarded by being named with Deborah in her song, and also by singing it together with her, with a single voice – as suggested by the singular form of ותשר. This is the first verse of the so-called Song of Deborah, a poetic rendition of the war narrative of Judg 4, generally regarded as one of the

---

85 See Braude and Kapstein, *Tanna děbe Eliyyahu*, 156.
86 The motif of ministry leads in its turn to what appears to be a short digression on the reasons for the exceptionality of the tribes of Zebulun and Naphtali. In fact, the midrash just continues its interpretation of the scriptural narrative of Judg 4. There, Deborah's prophetic words single out "ten thousand from the tribe of Naphtali and the tribe of Zebulun," part of the verse that is left unquoted.

oldest texts in the Hebrew Bible. The notion that Deborah and Baraq belong together, even if they are not understood as husband and wife, is reinforced by two further verses quoted from the dialogue between Baraq and Deborah in Judg 4.

In a final text segment, the focus of the governing voice shifts to Jael, asking in its characteristic phraseology what made Jael, who remains unnamed and is defined by her relation to Heber the Kenite,[87] so exceptional that great salvation came through her to Israel:

> And what distinguished Heber the Kenite's wife from the rest of women that deliverance came to Israel through her? They said: She was a righteous woman. And she used to do the will of her husband. From here they said: No woman is righteous unless she does the will of her husband. (ER 51, l. 5–7)

The answer is a tradition of the sages (*amru*), according to which she was eligible due to her being a righteous, worthy, zealous woman (*kesherah*) who did the will of her husband. It could be argued that Jael is left unnamed and identified as Heber's wife because the focus of this passage is a wife's conduct towards her husband.[88] Braude and Kapstein suggest that *Seder Eliyahu* hints at Jael's doing Heber's will "in consenting to leave fertile Jericho and follow him to arid Arad where, together with other Kenites, he was determined to study Torah with Jabez."[89]

Seder Eliyahu does not even hint at Jael's deed in the scriptural hypotext – her killing of Sisera in Judg 4:17–21 – which is discussed elsewhere in rabbinic literature in contexts dealing with the Deborah narrative.[90] Instead, *Seder Eliyahu* focuses on why she was chosen to fulfil this task, thus attempting to give an answer to a question left unanswered in the scriptural narrative. Whereas the exegetical narrative on Deborah departs from scriptural lemmata and the one on Jezebel makes use of proof-texts, the narrative about the unnamed Jael does not make explicit use of scriptural material. The tradition according to which Jael was righteous *and* did the will of her husband the maxim is the basis for the maxim that in order for a woman to be called righteous, she must do the will of her husband.

---

87 A parallel in ER 59 does name her.
88 However, the parallel in ER 59 has the same focus *and* names Jael.
89 Braude and Kapstein, *Tanna děbe Eliyyahu*, 157n14.
90 Focusing on the scriptural narrative, Ackerman, *Warrior, Dancer*, 6, characterises Jael as "a woman who savagely pierces Sisera's head in what Robert Alter ... has called 'a phallic aggressive act'"; see also 93–102. In her reading of Judg 4, Eder, *Wie Frauen und Männer Macht ausüben*, 152, points out that Jael and Judith are the only named women in the Old Testament who kill a person representing Israel's enemy with their own hands. For an analysis of Jael's characterisation in the book of Judges, see 208–210.

The midrashic exposition on Deborah continues beyond the boundaries of chapter (9) 10. Chapter (10) 11, however, focuses on a number of isolated verses in the Song of Deborah (Judg 5), but it is not an exegetical retelling of Deborah's deeds or a radical reinvention of some of them, as was the case in the previous chapter. Instead, the midrashic commentary in this chapter primarily discusses difficult words actually spoken by Deborah in Scripture in an attempt to explain them. It is therefore the poetic language of her song which forms the basis for a number of midrashic expansions.

> *Then Deborah and Baraq [son of Abinoam] sang [on that day, saying]* etc. (Judg 5:1). And what exactly did Deborah prophesy to Israel? She spoke to them thus, Through whom does the Holy One, blessed be He, requite (נפרע) Israel among the peoples of the world? By means of those children of men who go to the synagogue and to the academy early in the morning and in the evening and who answer [saying] "Amen," who bless the Holy One, blessed be He, by [saying] "Amen," for it is said, *when leaders led (בפרוע פרעות) in Israel[, when the people offer themselves willingly – bless the Lord!]* <etc.> (Judg 5:2). (ER 52, l. 17–20)

Judg 5:1, the beginning of Deborah's song, is quoted, followed by the governing voice's question concerning the exact content of Deborah's prophecy to Israel. Her direct speech is then quoted: She asks rhetorically through whose agency God requites Israel (or "collects them from"?) among the peoples of the world, answering herself that it is through pious men who go to the synagogue or the academy in the morning and in the evening, answering "Amen" and praising (מברכין) the Lord with this Amen; they are the reason why Israel is chosen to be a prince or a leader (פרע) among the nations. Deborah uses a variation on a statement brought up in the previous chapter by the governing voice itself – "At that time Deborah was shown (הראוה) the means by which the Holy One, blessed be He, delivers Israel from among the peoples" – that suits her own interpretive task. This consists in deciphering her own scriptural words, "when leaders led in Israel" (Judg 5:2).[91] The verb form מושיע, used previously (ER 50), is supplanted in this context by נפרע, a verb of the same root as בפרוע and פרעות of the scriptural verse, so that the interpretation engages in a paronomastic play with the interpreted verse. This play is based both on the root פרע and on the verb ברך, which is present in the interpretation and in the second part of the quoted verse, "bless (ברכו) the Lord!" Thus, according to Deborah's voice, which again clearly makes use of the tools of male rabbinic hermeneutics, the verse appears to be understood to mean: "Israel is redeemed through those who willingly praise the Lord."

---

91 The verse can be and has been translated in very different ways. See Ackerman, *Warrior, Dancer*, 32–34, who opts for taking פרעות to mean "hair locks."

6.4 Exegetical Contexts II: Deborah — 253

One last segment on Deborah is found in chapter (10) 11 of *Seder Eliyahu Rabbah*:

Deborah said, Since [Torah is] contentment on high and contentment here below, *She is a tree of life to those who lay hold of her* (Prov 3:18). *You who ride on white (צחורות) donkeys* (Judg 5:10): *white* is but an expression for being innocent of theft; *you who sit on rich carpets*: these are the children of men who cause [others] to stand in judgement. Another interpretation: *you who sit on rich carpets (מדין)*: *rich carpets* is simply "judgement" (דין), for it is said, *to turn aside the needy from justice (מדין)* (Isa 10:2) – just as there the expression מדין [means] judgement, so here [מדין means] judgement; *and you who walk by the way<, speak in praise (שיחו)!>* (Judg 5:10): the Sanhedrin is meant by them, for upon them the world leans. Why do you sit? *Sing* about her! Do not ever be idle with regard to her, for it is said, *Hear, O kings[; give ear, O princes; to the Lord I will sing (אשירה), I will make melody to the Lord, the God of Israel]* <etc.> (Judg 5:3). *From the voice that divides (מחצצים מקול)* (Judg 5:11): these are those who determine that the unclean is unclean and that the clean is clean, where the clean should be<, and where the unclean should be>, who <make distinctions with respect to> laws pertaining to the Sabbath, to festive offerings (חגיגות), to the improper use of sacred property (מעילות), and to cases <of dispute> that divide (מחצצים) men. *At the places of drawing water (משאבים)* (Judg 5:11): this is just <but> a [literal] expression for "drawn water," for it is said, *and she drew (ותשאב) for all his camels* (Gen 24:20). And it [Scripture] says, *With joy you will draw water (ושבאתם) from the wells of salvation* (Isa 12:3), <for thence they [the Sanhedrin] teach and draw out words of Torah.> Another interpretation: *At the places of drawing water (משאבים)* (Judg 5:11): out of their disagreements they draw out (שאובים) words of Torah, and out of their indignation with each other the words of Torah increase. Therefore, it is said, *At the places of drawing water, there they repeat the triumphs [of the Lord, the triumphs of his peasantry (פירזונו) in Israel]* <etc.> (Judg 5:11). The Holy One, blessed be He, showed great mercy in dispersing (פיזר) Israel among the peoples of the world. (ER 53, l. 25–ER 54, l. 10)

I shall not attempt to analyse the passage above in detail, but rather to highlight the idea that the whole of it appears to be introduced with the phrase "Deborah said," and that at no point does the governing voice explicitly indicate that it takes up the word again. It is rather as if the exegesis that follows the words of Deborah after the inquit formula is also her own interpretation, indistinguishable in fact from those of the governing voice itself.

If we view the passage as spoken by Deborah, we could claim that she first quotes a verse from Proverbs and provides an interpretation of it.[92] Then she proceeds with an atomising exegesis of Judg 5:10. She explains the first expression, צחורות, which is usually translated as "white," as meaning "the purity of those who do not rob." The expression מדין in the next clause of the verse, usually trans-

---

92 The same verse, Prov 3:18, is quoted by the governing voice in the opening passage of *Seder Eliyahu Rabbah* (ER 3), where he identifies the tree of life with Torah, to which the Proverbs verse is said to refer.

lated as "rich cloth" or "carpets," is interpreted as referring both to "those who cause others to stand in judgement" and to the idea of justice itself.[93] In a second interpretation, introduced with the hermeneutic formula דבר אחר, Deborah draws an analogy between the meaning of the homographs מדין in Judg 5:10 and Isa 10:2, a hermeneutic mechanism that is made explicit by the use of the phrase מה ... האמור להלן ... אף כאן ...[94] Deborah's interpretation of Judg 5:10 in her song culminates with the identification of those "who walk" (והולכי) with the Sanhedrin – the court of law responsible for judging according to rabbinic legislation (הלכה). Her direct address to the Sanhedrin[95] and the extra-textual audience is an admonition to engage in the study of Torah. To close this interpretive passage, Deborah links Judg 5:10 to Judg 5:3, understanding the verb שיחו in the former as meaning not "meditate," but rather "speak in praise," a synonym for אשירה in the latter.

Deborah's exegesis continues with a detailed exegesis of Judg 5:11, reading the expression מחצצים as referring to those who distinguish, חצץ ("cut off, divide"),[96] between ritually pure and impure, those who also take a differentiated approach to matters pertaining to laws and to conflicts between human beings. She continues with the expression משאבים, in "the places of drawing water," interpreting it first literally, as referring to "drawing water," and in a second step metaphorically, as meaning the way in which one gains wisdom from Torah. The verse from Isaiah provides a transition for this second interpretation, since "draw water" is used figuratively there. Deborah claims the conflicts over interpretation among the sages are the source of the words of Torah. It is worth noting that the focus of this second interpretation also includes the preposition בין, not just the word משאבים.

In her interpretation of the last part of Judg 5:11, Deborah connects the form פירזונו ("his peasantry") with the notion that God was merciful even when He "dispersed" (פיזר) Israel, thus demonstrating her familiarity with yet another hermeneutic practice, one that explains a word by adducing another with the same consonants, though in a different sequence – in this case, a word-form of the root פרז is explained by adducing a word-form of the root פזר.[97] The narrative-exegetical segment beginning with "Deborah said" seems to come to a sort of conclusion at this point.[98]

---

[93] This idea is also expressed in bEr 54b by the school of Rav Anan.
[94] This expression is a variation on the much more standard construction: כשם ש ... כך ...
[95] As suggested by the context and by Braude and Kapstein, *Tanna děbe Eliyyahu*, 163.
[96] See Jastrow, *Dictionary*, s.v. חָצַץ II.
[97] A case of metathesis; see Samely, *Rabbinic Interpretation*, 378, "Grapheme1."
[98] The *maʿaseh* which follows this statement may still be considered part of Deborah's speech, unless of course at some point in the exegetical passage the governing voice has silently taken over.

Most of the expressions which the rabbinic Deborah seeks to clarify are of uncertain meaning in their scriptural context. Her interpretation is easily comparable to that provided by famous rabbis elsewhere in rabbinic literature. The fact that the author of *Seder Eliyahu* chooses to put them in Deborah's mouth and to let her, who in the scriptural context was already exceptional because of her offices as judge and prophetess, be the exegete of her own words can be viewed as evidence of a sort of masculinisation or empowerment of the feminine voice (mediated by male textual agents) in late midrash, an important genre of post-talmudic rabbinic literature.[99]

6.5 Exegetical Contexts III: Rachel

Still, it comes as no surprise that most instances of explicit interpretation in *Seder Eliyahu* stem from male voices. The governing voice, specific rabbis, God, or male scriptural characters explain how an expression in a biblical verse is to be understood or retell a passage of Scripture. The cases where this interpretive act is depicted as originating with a woman are rare, as in the last of the passages on Deborah discussed above.

In the text quoted below, found in chapter (30) 28 of *Seder Eliyahu Rabbah*, a midrash of Jer 10:20 is partially handed over to the voice of another biblical woman, the matriarch Rachel:

> *My children have gone from me, and they are no more* (Jer 10:20). Even though Israel was exiled among the peoples of the world, because they engaged in the study of Torah, it was as if they had not been exiled at all. Another interpretation: *My children have gone from me, and they are no more* (Jer 10:20). When Israel were exiled among the peoples of the world, the Holy One, blessed be He, did not intend to return them to their place until the hour in which Rachel stood up in prayer before the Holy One, blessed be He. <She spoke before him, Master of the universe, let it be remembered that I did not mind my rival. Not only that, but even after my husband had worked for my sake seven years,>[100] at the time of my [supposed] entry into the bridal chamber, they substituted (החליפו) Leah, my sister, for me. But I would not speak to Jacob so that he would not tell my voice from my sister's voice. It is an argument *a minori ad majus*: If I, a mortal, did not lose my temper with my rival, will

---

[99] Baskin, *Midrashic Women*, 42, observes that women were known to have undertaken important public roles in the Jewish communities in the Greek-speaking diaspora of the Roman Empire and that their exclusion from participation in worship, study, and leadership was not the only option, but a "deliberate choice" made by men. The Deborah of *Seder Eliyahu* may be seen as evidence of an alternative to that choice in rabbinic Judaism, even if it is only evidence of a textual phenomenon.
[100] Friedmann's addition to the text, not indicated.

You mind the rivalry of idolatry, of them of whom it is said, *They have eyes, but do not see. They have ears, but do not hear* (Ps 115:5–6)? At once His mercies were moved and He swore to Rachel that He would return them to their place, for it is said, *Thus says the Lord: A voice is heard in Ramah, lamentation and bitter weeping. Rachel is weeping for her children[; she refuses to be comforted for her children, because they are no more]* etc. (Jer 31:15). You should not read: *Rachel is weeping for her children*, but rather: "The spirit of God is weeping for its children." *She refuses to be comforted for her children, because they are no more. Thus says the Lord: Keep your voice from weeping[, and your eyes from tears; for there is a reward for your work, says the Lord: they shall come back from the land of the enemy;]* etc. *there is hope for your future, says the Lord: your children shall come back to their own country* (Jer 31:15–17). (ER 148, l. 22–35)[101]

The chapter in which this passage is found opens with the selective quotation of Ps 79:1–2,[102] which is interpreted in the light of Jer 10:20.[103] After discussing the first two clauses of the verse,[104] the governing voice turns to the next part: "My children have gone from me, and they are no more." According to the first interpretation, it is due to their study of Torah during their exile that their exilic experience was not as harsh as it could have been. As a second interpretation of this lemma, we find the narrative about Rachel quoted above.

The governing voice explains the verse as referring to Israel's exile and to the fact that it was Rachel who changed God's intentions with regard to the question of whether Israel should return to their land. The rabbinic Rachel is thus given a powerful voice, with which she addresses God and reminds him of her own predicament on her wedding night, setting an example for God to follow. To do this, she uses a *qal wa-chomer*-argument and quotes a proof-text. The reason why Rachel is chosen from among all the matriarchs to fulfil this narrative and hermeneutic task is made explicit when the governing voice quotes Jer 31:15 to close the passage, revealing the association of the "children" in Jer 10:20 with Rachel's children in Jer 31:15, of whom both verses predicate that "they are no more."

---

101 Friedmann follows the *editio princeps* for this passage.
102 The verses are selectively quoted as follows: "A Psalm of Asaph. O God, the nations have come into your inheritance[; they have defiled your holy temple; they have laid Jerusalem in ruins]" etc. "They have given the bodies of your servants [to the birds of the air for food, the flesh of your faithful to the wild animals of the earth]" etc.
103 This verse, spoken in its original context by God lamenting the destruction, is introduced in *Seder Eliyahu* with a characteristic formula for quotations from the Prophets and the Writings: "Indeed He then explicitly stated in the traditional writings through the prophet Jeremiah."
104 In several interpretive instances, the governing voice focuses on the expressions "my tent" (being) "destroyed" and "my cords" in Jer 10:20.

Whereas no spatial setting is specified in the narrative, the chronological setting is, and – at least judging by the standards of realistic storytelling – in a rather problematic way: Rachel, who clearly belongs to the biblical time of the patriarchs and to a textual context in which idolatry plays no significant role (Gen 29), addresses God during the exile. Does such a story-time suggest a conflation of disparate biblical and post-biblical times, as seems to be implied in Jer 31:15? Or is the governing voice describing a supernatural phenomenon, a sort of incorporeal apparition of Rachel?[105]

In this midrashic story-time, when God does not intend to let Israel return, Rachel addresses God with wording frequently used by the governing voice in *Seder Eliyahu* and retells in the first person, and as a preamble to her hermeneutic argument, her version of the biblical story of Jacob and his two wives. She introduces this story by first pointing out what it should illustrate: that she did not mind Jacob's second wife, her rival, her own sister. Rachel appears to claim that she is worthy of merit because she tolerated the fact that, after her husband had worked for seven years in order to deserve her (Gen 29:18), and as she was supposed to enter the bridal chamber, it was her sister Leah who took her place (Gen 29:23). Rachel argues that she chose not to expose her sister (or her own humiliation). Her contribution to the interpretation of Jer 10:20 consists in having her own story culminate in a *qal wa-chomer*-argument, with which she suggests that if she, as a mere mortal, could put up with the rivalry of her sister, it is expected of God that He should not mind the rivalry of idolatry. Rachel appears to be hinting at the double meaning of *tsarah* – namely, "rival" and "distress." She is familiar with rabbinic hermeneutics, not only making use of rules such as the *qal wa-chomer*-inference, but also demonstrating an ability to adduce proof-texts. Rachel's rhetoric and hermeneutic strategies cause God to change his mind and have compassion for Israel.

After Rachel's *qal wa-chomer*, the governing voice takes over, quoting a later passage from Jeremiah (31:15–17) and proposing "weeping for her children" should be read as referring not to Rachel, but to the spirit of God itself. In the scriptural co-text of this Jeremiah text, as in the exegetical narrative of *Seder Eliyahu*, God addresses Rachel, promising her that her children "shall come back from the land of the enemy."

---

105 Only her speech, not her physical appearance, is represented.

6.5.1 Parallel: *Ekhah Rabbah*, Proem 24

A parallel in Proem 24 of *Ekhah Rabbah* contains a more detailed account of what happened on Rachel's wedding night, which answers some of the questions left open in the version in *Seder Eliyahu*. Rachel's story appears in *Ekhah Rabbah* in a more complex narrative context:[106] As part of an interpretation of Isa 22:12 that consists of an introduction by an anonymous voice and a second part by R. Samuel b. Nachman, Rachel addresses God after Abraham, Isaac, Jacob, and Moses have already pleaded with him to have mercy on Israel. Proem 24 of EkhR attests to a similar hybridisation of biblical and post-biblical times to that of *Seder Eliyahu*. Here, however, both the spatial and the chronological settings of the narrative are spelt out.

The segment in the voice of R. Samuel b. Nachman relates that, after the destruction of the Temple, God requests the prophet Jeremiah to summon the patriarchs Abraham, Isaac, and Jacob, as well as Moses from their sepulchres, and they gather at the gates of the Temple. In the longest of all the dialogue segments, Abraham converses with God, with the Torah, and with its letters, before turning again to God and pleading with him to have mercy on his children. Isaac, Jacob, and Moses proceed similarly, retelling paradigmatically significant moments from their biblical existences before imploring God to have mercy on exiled Israel. The geographic setting changes when Moses asks Jeremiah to lead him to Babylon in order to address the children of Israel and assure them that they will return to their land. When he himself returns to the gates of the Temple, he reports to the patriarchs how Israel is treated in exile. Moses addresses the sun and the Temple in lamentation, and finally addresses the oppressors themselves, imploring them not to kill cruelly death, which he paraphrases as not killing a son in the presence of his father or a daughter in the presence of her mother. The narrator reports that the Chaldeans disregarded his request and made a father kill his son. One last time, Moses reproaches God's silence at the killing of many mothers and sons, in spite of the prohibition in Lev 22:28 against killing a cow or a ewe and its young on the same day.[107] The mention of mothers and daughters appears to be the cue

---

106 This narrative is analysed by Galit Hasan-Rokem, *Web of Life: Folklore and Midrash in Rabbinic Literature* (Stanford, CA: Stanford University Press, 2000), 127–128, and Dvora E. Weisberg, "Men Imagining Women Imagining God: Gender Issues in Classical Midrash," in *Agendas for the Study of Midrash in the Twenty-first Century*, ed. Marc Lee Raphael (Williamsburg, VA: College of William and Mary, 1999), 74–77. A shorter parallel is found in bMeg 13b.
107 The same verse is quoted in another narrative context in *Seder Eliyahu* – that of Miriam and her seven sons, who were killed in her presence. See section 6.6 below.

for the appearance of the matriarch Rachel, who addresses God and retells her biblical story:

> Sovereign of the Universe, it is revealed [and known[108]] before You that Your servant Jacob loved me exceedingly and toiled for my father on my behalf seven years. When those seven years were completed and the time arrived for my marriage with my husband, my father planned to substitute my sister[109] for me to wed my husband for the sake of my sister. It was very hard for me, because the plot was known to me, so I disclosed it to my husband. I gave him a sign whereby he could distinguish between me and my sister, so that my father should not be able to make the substitution. After that I relented, suppressed my desire, and had pity upon my sister that she should not be exposed to shame. In the evening they substituted my sister for me with my husband, and I delivered over to my sister all the signs which I had arranged with my husband so that he should think that she was Rachel. More than that, I went beneath the bed upon which he lay with my sister; and when he spoke to her she remained silent and I made all the replies in order that he should not recognise my sister's voice. I did her a kindness, was not jealous of her, and did not expose her to shame.

This version of Rachel's story clearly contains essential information for the understanding of the plot, which is not available in its concise parallel in *Seder Eliyahu*. *Ekhah Rabbah* follows the scriptural hypotext more closely in depicting Laban as the mastermind of the sisters' swap, and mentioning the fact that both women were in the same room on the wedding night and that only one was heard. The sisters together plan how to deceive Jacob in order to protect Leah. This is not the case in *Seder Eliyahu*: Laban is not mentioned here, nor is the reader informed as to where Rachel is on the wedding night – where it is that she remains silent – or what her intention is in not letting Jacob discern between her and her sister. The change in *Seder Eliyahu* is not minor: Rachel's remaining silent is clearly less humiliating than her replying to her husband from beneath the bed where he lies with her sister. Whereas in *Ekhah Rabbah* the sisters explicitly conspire to keep Jacob in the dark about the situation, in *Seder Eliyahu* he is equally ignorant, but without any secret signs or hidden voice playing any role.

Although the character of Rachel in both versions is empowered by the male rabbinic voice who lets "her" tell her own story in the first person, address God in direct speech, and compare herself to God with a hermeneutic resource which is usually reserved for male voices, to say that Rachel speaks for herself would be an oversimplified view of how these texts operate.

---

108 According to MS Munich 229.
109 The quotation follows Harry Freedman and Maurice Simon, eds., *Lamentations*, vol. 7 of *Midrash Rabbah*, trans. A. Cohen (London: Soncino, 1939). Instead of Cohen's "another," the Hebrew reading אחותי ("my sister") is preferred.

Narratology provides the category of focalisation, which might be helpful not only in a discussion of modernist texts, but also for ancient storytelling.[110] The concept, according to Genette, is said to support the distinction between the questions "who speaks?" (narrator) and "who sees?" (focalizer),[111] but has also to do with how information conveyed by a narrative is selected and restricted – that is, focalisation can also be regarded as "a selection of or a focusing *on* a particular region of the storyworld."[112] Whereas such a distinction between narrator and focaliser might be more evident in heterodiegetic narratives,[113] when it comes to first-person narratives, such as Rachel's retrospective account of her wedding night, it appears especially pertinent to ask how this distinction is to be made. In other words: Is the perspective (point of view or focalisation)[114] in homodiegetic (first-person) narratives necessarily that of the character who is the narrator, or is it possible to distinguish different perceiving subjects – the character of the story-time and the character beyond the story-time, once he or she has assumed the role of narrator? Mieke Bal provides a plausible answer:

> In a so-called "first-person narrative" too an external focalizor, usually the "I" grown older, gives its vision of a fabula in which it participated earlier as an actor, from the outside. At some moments it can present the vision of its younger alter ego, so that a CF [character-bound focalizer] is focalizing on the second level.[115]

---

110 On this concept, see chapter 3, especially p. 77.
111 See Genette, "Discours du Récit," 203.
112 Burkhard Niederhoff, "Focalization," in *the living handbook of narratology*, ed. Peter et al. Hühn (Hamburg University Press, 2009), paragraph 13, http://www.lhn.uni-hamburg.de/article/focalization.
113 In this type of narrative, both internal (character-bound) and external (narrator-bound) focalisation is possible. Bal, *Narratology*, 152, points out: "When focalization lies with one character which participates in the fabula as an actor, we could refer to internal focalization. We can indicate by means of the term external focalization that an anonymous agent, situated outside the fabula, is functioning as focalizor."
114 On the debate concerning the proper methodological use of these terms, see Burkhard Niederhoff, "Fokalisation und Perspektive: Ein Plädoyer für friedliche Koexistenz," *Poetica* 33 (2001): 1–21.
115 See Bal, *Narratology*, 112. William F. Edmiston, "Focalization and the First-Person Narrator: A Revision of the Theory," *Poetics Today* 10 (1989): 729, pointed out that during the first decade of the debate, "[l]ittle attention has been paid to the problem of focalization in texts in which narrator and character are the same individual." Jahn, "Focalization," 100, observes: "Indeed, in many first-person (homodiegetic) texts ... the point of perceptual origin hovers between two co-ordinate systems because first-person narrator and protagonist – also called the 'narrating I' and the 'experiencing I,' respectively – are separated in time and space but linked through a biographical identity relation."

Since we are dealing with a record of what the *biblical* Rachel saw, felt, and (according to Rachel the narrator) allowed to happen, it can be assumed that the narrative conveys her point of view. It could be argued the Rachel of Gen 29 is a focaliser as far as the events and the people involved (the focalised object[116]) are concerned – it is her perspective, not that of Leah, nor that of Jacob, from which their story is told. The texts certainly do not give the point of view of a disappointed young bride (the experiencing I), but rather that of a distant, wise woman (the remembering, narrating I). Furthermore, the language she uses in *Seder Eliyahu* and in *Ekhah Rabbah* is that of a *rabbinic* female narrator, able to use her narrative as a hermeneutic tool.[117] *This* Rachel is given a voice she does not have in the scriptural account and is capable of regarding her own conduct from a distance and using it as the basis for a comparison with God in the speech with which she addresses him. This narrating, remembering self, separated in time (and probably also in space) from the experiencing I, connects her own story with the content and rhetoric of that other, nameless male governing voice in a discourse which encompasses her own narrative. With Bal, we could speak – even in the case of a first-person narrative – of a general external focalisation, since we are dealing with a "narrator-focalizer."[118] As Shlomith Rimmon-Kenan has suggested, the perceptual facet of the Genettean focalisation concept can be complemented with a psychological and an ideological facet. The latter is probably a suitable tool for describing the transformation of scriptural accounts by rabbinic narrative agents, as in the type of exegetical narratives discussed here.[119]

Rachel's brief first-person narrative in *Seder Eliyahu* is framed by an exegetical narrative told by the governing voice. This male rabbinic voice seems to pervade Rachel's vision of the events; it determines where her speech and narrative begins and ends, before taking up Rachel's narrative to link her account with Jer 31:15, which describes Rachel as weeping for her children, and this in turn with Jer 10:20.

---

116 See Bal, *Narratology*, 153–160. Characters and narrators focalise "objects, landscapes, events" and characters, but they also exclude elements in their selection. Laban, the architect of that wedding night, is not even mentioned in Rachel's account in *Seder Eliyahu*.
117 Rachel's familiarity with rabbinic language can be ascertained in her use of expressions found elsewhere in *Seder Eliyahu* and in the rabbinic corpus, e.g., "Master of the universe," ʿal achat kama we-khama, and qal wa-chomer.
118 See Bal, *Narratology*, 152–153. See also Edmiston, "Focalization and the First-Person Narrator," 730, who points out: "Since most theorists define internal focalization as the presentation of events by a character within the fictional world, they all locate personal narration in this category, presumably because an FPN is a fictional character. This definition seems most unsatisfactory because it equates, for purposes of focalization, an FPN with a focal character who perceives but does not narrate."
119 See Rimmon-Kenan, *Narrative Fiction*, 82–83.

To sum up, Rachel is the narrator and external focaliser of her biblical story, as this is seen and cropped out of the more extensive scriptural account by the governing voice, in whose narrative the one told by Rachel is embedded. However, it is to the voice of a midrashic woman, not that of a disappointed bride in the scriptural account, that God responds. The fact that it is a woman who closes the *petichah* is highlighted in the parallel passage in *Ekhah Rabbah*, in which Abraham, Isaac, Jacob, and Moses plead with God to have mercy before Rachel's speech succeeds in convincing God to change his mind.[120]

6.6 Exegetical Contexts IV: Suicidal Women

6.6.1 "The joyous mother of children" (Ps 113:9)

Further on in chapter (30) 28 of *Seder Eliyahu Rabbah*, we find three narratives on how Rome oppressed and killed myriads of Jews, told as midrashim on Ps 79:1. The first two are brief narratives told by R. Eliezer. The third, considerably longer and with a more complex structure, is told in the collective anonymous voice of the sages:[121]

> And the sages said, *A psalm of Asaph* (Ps 79:1). Hadrian Caesar came and seized a widow<, named Miriam daughter of Tanchum>, and her seven sons. He asked her, Who are you? She answered, I am a widow, a mother.[122] <He said,> And these children, whose are they? Yours? Given that they are standing with you? She answered, They are my sons. <He took them and imprisoned them separately.> He brought the first one, the eldest, and said to him, Bow down to this divinity <as your brothers bowed down>. He replied, God forbid <that my brothers should have so bowed down! Neither will I;> I do not bow down to the work of man's hands, for it is written, *So acknowledge today and take to heart [that the Lord is God in heaven above and on the earth beneath; there is no other]* etc. (Deut 4:39). At once they took a sword and cut off his head. He brought the second and said to him, Bow down to this divinity <as

---

120 On the passage in *Ekhah Rabbah* as read by Galit Hasan-Rokem, Weisberg, "Women and Torah Study in Aggadah," 50, remarks: "Rachel's presentation differs on several levels from those of the patriarchs and Moses. They are summoned; she comes of her own accord. They speak of momentous events in the history of the Jewish people; she speaks of her personal struggle. They speak of justice; she speaks of love, loyalty, and empathy. This story highlights a woman speaking with a woman's voice about women's concerns, and it is that voice that impels God, frequently portrayed as an angry, violent father-figure, to relent and show compassion to Israel."
121 The same three stories are told in bGit 57a – the first two anonymously, the third, the one discussed here, by Rav Judah.
122 Friedmann puts the word אם in brackets, the way he usually does whenever he wishes to indicate a deficient reading. Now the fact that the woman sees herself as a widow *and* as a mother does not appear to be a superficial piece of information.

your brothers bowed down>. He replied, God forbid <that my brothers should have so bowed down! Neither will I;> I do not bow down to the work of man's hands, for it is written in the Torah, *For the Lord your God is God of gods and Lord of lords[, the great God, mighty and awesome, who is not partial and takes no bribe]* (Deut 10:17). At once they took a sword and cut off his head. He brought the third and spoke to him, Bow down to this divinity <so [as he had spoken] to the the others>. He replied, God forbid! I do not bow down to the work of man's hands, for it is written in the Torah, *you shall have no other gods besides me* (Exod 20:3). At once they took a sword and cut off his head. He brought the fourth and said to him, Go and bow down to this. He replied, God forbid! I do not bow down to the work of man's hands, for it is written in the Torah, *for you shall worship no other god* (Exod 34:14). At once they took a sword and cut off his head. He brought the fifth. He said to him, Go and bow down to this. He replied, God forbid! I do not bow down to the work of man's hands, for it is written in the Torah, *Whoever sacrifices to any god[, other than the Lord alone,] shall be devoted to destruction* (Exod 22:19). At once they took a sword and cut off his head. He brought the sixth. He said to him, Go and bow down to this. He replied, God forbid! I do not bow down to the work of man's hands, for it is written in the Torah, *The Lord will reign for ever and ever* (Exod 15:18). He brought the seventh, the youngest. He said to him, Go and bow down to this. He replied, God forbid! I do not bow down to the work of man's hands, for we swore to the Holy One, blessed be He, that we would not worship any other god, and the Holy One, blessed be He, swore to us that He would not exchange us for another people, for it is said, *Today you have obtained the Lord's agreement[: to be your God; and for you to walk in his ways, to keep his statutes, his commandments, and his ordinances, and to obey him.]* <etc.> *Today the Lord has obtained your agreement[: to be his treasured people, as He promised you, and to keep His commandments]* <etc.> (Deut 26:17–18). He said to him, If you do not bow down to this divinity, see, I will throw this ring for you and and you will pick[123] it up from in front of it [the divinity], so that everyone standing before it will say, He has listened to Caesar's words and has bowed down to it. He answered, Woe unto you, Caesar, and unto the words you speak to me. Even if you, a carnal being are being put to shame by another carnal being such as me, I will not be put to shame before the King of kings. He asked him, Is there really a God for the world? He answered, Do you think the world is ownerless? [He asked him,] Does your God really have a head? He answered him, It has already been said, *His head is the finest gold* (Song 5:11). He asked him, Does your God really have ears? He answered him, It has already been said, *The Lord took note and listened* (Mal 3:16). He asked him, Does your God really have eyes? He answered him, Has it not already been said, *the eyes of the Lord, which range through [the whole earth]* (Zech 4:10)? He asked him, Does your God really have a nose? He answered, See, it has already been said, *And the Lord smelt the pleasing odour* (Gen 8:21). He asked him, Does your God really have a mouth? He answered, Has it not already been said, *and all their host by the breath of his mouth* (Ps 33:6)? He asked him, Does your God really have a palate (חיך)? He answered, Has it not already been said, *His speech (חכו) is most sweet, and he is altogether desirable* (Song 5:16)? He asked him, Does your God really have hands? He answered, Has it not already been said, *My hand laid the foundation of the earth, and my right hand spread out the heavens* (Isa 48:13)? He asked him, Does your God really have feet? He answered, Has it not already been said, *On that day his feet shall stand on the Mount of Olives* (Zech 14:4)? He asked him, Does your God really have power? He answered, Has it

---

123 Friedmann emends the MS reading ובא to וישא.

not already been said, *See, the Lord's hand is not too short to save* (Isa 59:1)? He said to him, Since your God has power and his eyes see and his ears hear, why has He not revealed himself and rescued you all from my hands? He answered, Fool in the world! You are not worthy of having miracles performed on your account. Given that we are doomed to death, even if you do not kill us, the Omnipresent has many slayers, the Omnipresent has many bears, the Omnipresent has many leopards, many serpents, many scorpions, many lions, who could attack us. At once he ordered that they kill him. At that moment the mother said to him, By your life, Caesar! By your life, Caesar! Give me my son that I might kiss him. He gave him to her. She would embrace him, hug him, and kiss him. She would take her nipple and put it into his mouth, Honey and milk would overflow and fall to the ground, to fulfil what is said, *honey and milk are under your tongue* (Song 4:11). She spoke to him again, By your life, Caesar! By your life, Caesar! Put the sword to my neck and to the neck of my son <at the same time (lit. "together")>. Caesar said to her, God forbid! I shall not do such a thing, for so it is written in the Torah, *[But you shall not slaughter, from] the herd or the flock, an animal [with its young on the same day]* etc. (Lev 22:28). The boy said to him, Fool in the world! Do you [think you] fulfil the whole Torah beyond this verse? At once they took the sword and cut off his head. The sages estimated the boy's age and he was found to be two years, six months, and seven-and-a -half hours old. At that time the peoples of the world tore their hair and beards, and weeping with great lamentation said, What has their Father done that they were thus killed for His sake? Of that time it [Scripture] says, *What is your beloved more than another beloved, O fairest among women?* (Song 5:9). At that time their mother spoke to them, My sons, go and speak to Abraham, your father, Do not be proud because you could say, I built an altar and offered my son upon it. I built seven altars and offered upon them my seven sons. Their mother spoke to them again, Happy are you in that you did the will of your Father in heaven and were in the world only to sanctify His great name <with your hands>, for it is said, *Through those who are near me I will show myself holy* (Lev 10:3). Thereupon she prostrated herself and then went up to the roof, threw herself off and died. A divine voice went forth addressing her, Of you Scripture says, *joyous mother of children* (Ps 113:9). (ER 151, l. 24–ER 153, l. 15)

This passage contains a narrative account of how Hadrian seizes a widow and her seven sons and tries to force the children to worship an idol.[124] Friedmann adds the wording of an interlinear gloss in Codex Vat. ebr. 31, according to which the

---

[124] The are several earlier versions of this story. The earliest is transmitted in 2 Macc 7, in which the historical setting is a different one. The story is told as part of the account of the persecution in the times of Antiochus Epiphanes. On this version, see Paul Volz, *Die Eschatologie der jüdischen Gemeinde* (Tübingen: Mohr, 1934), 237, who considers it as evidence of the inclusion of martyrs of the recent past in the doctrine of resurrection. The story has several rabbinic parallels, including bGit 57b, EkhR 1, PesR 43, YalqShim *Ki Tabo*, and EkhZ 1. Probably in the third century, Christians appropriated this story, stylising the seven sons and their mother as proto-Christian martyrs. By the early fifth century, their martyrdom would be commemorated in the Eastern Church. See Rutgers, "The Importance of Scripture," 26–30. Among the Christianised versions of the story, we may point to Gregory the Great's *Homilia* III on St Felicity's *dies natalis*. As Rutgers points out, this and other stories about the martyrdom of mothers and their seven sons "had nothing to do

woman's name is Miriam, and she is further identified as the daughter of (a certain) Tanchum. When the emperor asks after her identity with the question מה טיביך (lit. "What is your nature?"), she identifies herself first as a widow, then as a mother. Thereupon the emperor inquires whose the children standing next to her are, to which she responds that they are her sons. Hadrian imprisons the children separately and has them brought to him, one after the other, to attempt force them into idolatry. He commands the first three boys to bow down to an idol, which is not further characterised. Friedmann's additions to Hadrian's speech, which are actually interlinear glosses of the manuscript – "as your brothers bowed down" – imply a cunning strategy on the part of the emperor, who tries to persuade the boys by telling each of them that their brothers before him have worshipped an idol. Nonetheless, each of Miriam's sons refuses to obey, assuming that their brothers are not capable of such an action. The wording of the commands to the following four sons is shorter and does not even refer to the divinity with the noun *eloha*, but merely with the deictic *zeh*. After each of the first six sons has refused to worship the idol and quoted a proof-text legitimating his behaviour, he is beheaded without further ado by the emperor's guards.[125] The wording of the dialogues with the first six boys shows little variation; the language each of the boys uses differs from that of his brothers only in the verse he quotes. The boys' characterisation is minimal and consists only of the words they utter, their speech acts. All the boys do is refuse to follow the emperor's order and quote a verse before being beheaded. Rather than fully fledged martyrs, they appear to be mouthpieces for a composite scriptural argument for monotheism. The table below illustrates the schematic character of the first six dialogues between the emperor and the boys.

Table 6.1: Dialogues Between Emperor and the Woman's Sons: Words of Children who Die for God

Emperor's words	Sons' answers
Bow down to this divinity [as your brothers bowed down]	God forbid [that my brothers should have so bowed down! Neither will I:] I do not bow down to the work of man's hands, for it is written, *So acknowledge today and take to heart [that the Lord is God in heaven above and on the earth beneath; there is no other]* etc. (Deut 4:39).

---

at all with historical, real-life persecutions. ... Felicitas and her sons never existed outside the Christian imagination" (30).
125 The plural verb forms suggest this.

Table 6.1: – continued

Emperor's words	Sons' answers
Bow down to this divinity [as your brothers bowed down]	God forbid [that my brothers should have so bowed down! Neither will I:] I do not bow down to the work of man's hands, for it is written in the Torah, *For the Lord your God is God of gods and Lord of lords[, the great God, mighty and awesome, who is not partial and takes no bribe]* (Deut 10:17).
Bow down to this divinity [like this, this way to the rest]	God forbid! I don't bow down to the work of man's hands, for it is written in the Torah, *You shall have no other gods besides me* (Exod 20:3).
Go and bow down to this	God forbid! I do not bow down to the work of man's hands, for it is written in the Torah, *for you shall worship no other god* (Exod 34:14).
Go and bow down to this	God forbid! I do not bow down to the work of man's hands, for it is written in the Torah, *Whoever sacrifices to any god[, other than the Lord alone,] shall be devoted to destruction* (Exod 22:19).
Go and bow down to this	God forbid! I do not bow down to the work of man's hands, for it is written in the Torah, *The Lord will reign for ever and ever* (Exod 15:18).
Come, bow down to this	God forbid! I do not bow down to the work of man's hands, for we swore to the Holy One, blessed be He, that we would not worship any other god, and the Holy One, blessed be He, swore to us that He would not exchange us for another people, for it is said, *Today you have obtained the Lord's agreement[: to be your God; and for you to walk in his ways, to keep his statutes, his commandments, and his ordinances, and to obey him.]* <etc.> *Today the Lord has obtained your agreement[: to be his treasured people, as He promised you, and to keep His commandments]* <etc.> (Deut 26:17–18).

The seventh son, the youngest, is the only one who explains in more detail why he refuses to follow the emperor's order and who repeatedly defies him. Instead of having the boy immediately beheaded, the emperor seems keen on persuading him. He comes up with an idea with which he attempts to trick, not the boy, but rather whoever has witnessed the killing of the children. He explains to the boy that he will throw a ring before the idol, so that when the child bends over to pick it up, he will give the impression that he has actually bowed down to the idol. The child criticises the emperor for stooping to such tricks and putting another mortal to shame, when he himself, a child, would never put God to shame. The next part of the dialogue focuses on God's anthropomorphic attributes. To each question the emperor poses, the child responds with a scriptural quotation confirming an attribute, which the emperor in turn uses to mock the child. He argues that although God has power, eyes, and ears, He has not saved the child and his brothers from the emperor's hands. The child defies the emperor one last time by replying to this question and explaining that the emperor is no more than one of the many tools God can make use of to kill human beings. On this cue, Hadrian orders that the boy should be killed.

Only at this moment does the mother regain her voice in the narrative. The reader can assume that she has silently witnessed the execution of each of her six sons without reacting or being able to make her feelings manifest. In any case, before her seventh son is killed, she begs the emperor to allow her to hold her son and is granted this request. She. embraces, hugs, and kisses her son, after which she breastfeeds the child with spurting "milk and honey" – to depict Miriam's hyperbolic motherliness, the passage chooses a phrase used in Scripture to hyperbolically describe the land of Israel.[126] The woman pleads with Hadrian to kill her together with her son, to which he, a Gentile, argues with the aid of Lev 22:28 that the Torah prohibits killing a cow or a ewe and its young both on the same day. The child calls Hadrian a fool a second time – either for his incompetence with regard to Torah or for his insincerity, since, so the boy argues, fulfilling one verse of Torah does not fulfil the whole Torah. These are his last words before the unnamed guards behead him.

Two digressions interrupt the narrative. First, the governing voice relates how the sages calculated[127] the age of the last child and came to the conclusion that he was two years, six months, and seven-and-a-half hours old.[128] What brings the sages to ask after the age of this last child, while leaving the ages of the rest of his brothers unmentioned? It could be argued that it is for the sake of the contradictory image of a brave, wise child who confronts the emperor while still depending

---

126 The phrase is used in 21 verses, most of them in the Pentateuch, some in the Prophets, and one in Song of Songs. 20 of them are used to refer to the land of Israel, Song 4:11 being the exception, in that it is used to refer to a human being, to describe the lover's mouth.
127 The phrase חכמים שיערו ("the sages estimated, calculated") is very frequent in rabbinic texts. The measure seven-and-a-half is a common one (e.g., bQid 12a etc).
128 Two-and-a-half years, roughly the age of the boy, is the traditional length of the Bar Kochba revolt; see e.g., SOR 30.

on his mother to be breastfed. But the interpretive process by which they arrive at this very precise age is not revealed.

The second short digression relates how, at the time of their death, these children were wept for especially by the peoples of the world, who do not comprehend what is so special about their God that they are willing to die for his sake. The governing voice paraphrases the question of the peoples of the world by quoting Song 5:9.

In the final segment of the narrative, to which the sages return after these digressions, Miriam is the centre of attention. This episode consists of two speeches by Miriam. The first she addresses to her dead children, asking them to deliver in her name another speech in Abraham's presence. In it, she claims that her loss of seven children surpasses the patriarch's attempted sacrifice of his son Isaac. She tells Abraham not to pride himself on building an altar and offering his son upon it, for she herself has built seven altars and offered her seven children. The second speech is a blessing which exalts her children's piety, their willingness to die to sanctify the great name of God. These are her last words before she goes up to the roof, jumps off, and dies as the eighth martyr in her family.[129]

A likewise elaborate version is anonymously transmitted in EkhR 1.[130] Miriam is not introduced as a widow, but her seven children are executed for not obeying the nameless governor's (שלטון) command to bow down to an idol. Unlike the opening of the narrative in *Seder Eliyahu*, the governor identifies the children as belonging to Miriam without questioning her in this regard. As in *Seder Eliyahu*, Miriam is not imprisoned, but only her children, whose executions she witnesses in silence. Her children refuse to revere the idol in front of them, justifying their behaviour with scriptural quotations, which only in three cases are the same as those used in *Seder Eliyahu*.[131] The repetitive character of the questioning of the first six boys is accentuated in that the governor speaks exactly the same words every time: "Bow down to the image as your brothers prostrated themselves" (השתחוה לצלם כשם שהשתחוו אחיך). The seventh child, introduced as the youngest, as in *Seder Eliyahu*, also here refuses to accept the governor's trick and bow down to pick up a ring so that the onlookers think he has given up his resistance. The child refuses to act according to the wishes of the governor, whom he addresses as emperor, due to his fear[132] of the "God of the world." This way of referring to God segues

---

129 Or even ninth, if we assume that she becomes a widow as a consequence of the Romans killing her husband. The parallel in 2 Macc 7 does not even mention the death of the mother.
130 For the following reading, I follow Buber's version of EkhR.
131 See table 6.3, where the verses set in italics appear in EkhR 1, bGit 57a, and *Seder Eliyahu*.
132 Notice that the verb used in this version is אתיירא ("fear"), whereas *Seder Eliyahu* has אתבייש ("humiliate, put to shame").

to a section on the attributes of God, which is structured by the questions of the emperor, as in the parallel version in *Seder Eliyahu*.

Whereas the child in *Seder Eliyahu* only responds with quotations dealing with God, in the *Ekhah Rabbah* version, the child first states that the emperor's idols are referred to as having these attributes but not the functions attached to them, and only then does he reaffirm these attributes as true only of his God: Thus, for each of the emperor's questions, the child responds with two scriptural quotations. The order and number of the attributes, which differ from those in *Seder Eliyahu*, seems to be fixed according to their order in Ps 115, which the child uses for the first part of his answers (as illustrated in table 6.2, where the verses set in italics appear both in EkhR and in *Seder Eliyahu*, even if the scriptural wording actually quoted is not identical).

Table 6.2: Scriptural Verses I: God's Anthropomorphic Attributes

EkhR 1		ER 151–ER 153	
mouth	Ps 115:5; *Ps 33:6*	head	Song 5:11
eyes	Ps 115:5; Deut 11:12	ears	*Mal 3:16*
ears	Ps 115:6; *Mal 3:16*	eyes	Zech 4:10
nose	Ps 115:6; *Gen 8:21*	nose	*Gen 8:21*
hands	Ps 115:7; *Isa 48:13*	mouth	*Ps 33:6*
feet	Ps 115: 7; *Zech 14:4*, Mic 1:3	palate	*Song 5:16*
throat	Ps 115:7; *Song 5:16*	hands	*Isa 48:13*
		feet	*Zech 14:4*
		power	Isa 59:1

Both versions coincide in depicting the emperor arguing against the evidence of Scripture that a God with such attributes should have been expected to rescue the child and his brothers, as He rescued Hananiah, Mishael, and Azariah, in an allusion to Dan 3.[133] The boy replies that these three were righteous men who fell into the hands of a righteous king, worthy of having miracles performed on his account, whereas he and his brothers are sinners and fall therefore into the hands of a wicked and merciless king. The boy argues that God has handed them over to the emperor in order to avenge their deaths on him in the future. The emperor does not reply to the boy, but simply orders his death.

---

133 The emperor alludes to the narrative of Dan 3, where Shadrach, Meshach, and Abednego (i.e., the Chaldean equivalents for the Hebrew names Hananiah, Mishael, and Azariah) were condemned to death in a fiery furnace for refusing to worship the golden image Nebuchadnezzar made, but were rescued by God.

The mother, who this account also suggest has been present during all the questionings, raises her voice at this moment. Her direct speech is introduced with the abbreviated formula א״ל. Her request to hold her child is granted, after which she embraces her son, bares her breast, and suckles the *puer senex* with milk and honey, which calls to mind Song 4:11 as a sort of proof-text. In response to the mother's plea that she be killed together with her son, the emperor in this version also refers to the prohibition in Lev 22:28. At this moment, the narrator qualifies the seventh son as "a wicked child" (תינוק רשע) for the first time. Taken away from her embrace and probably seized by the guards, he is addressed by his mother one last time; she gives him a message to deliver in her name to Abraham: "You built an altar but did not sacrifice your son. I, on the other hand, built seven altars and sacrificed on them my sons. Not only that, yours was a trial, mine were deeds." At the time of the child's death, the sages calculate his age, coming to the conclusion that he was six-and-a-half years and two hours old[134] – a detail which would accentuate Miriam's extraordinary motherliness in being able to breastfeed the child.

The end of the narrative in EkhR 1 differs from that in *Seder Eliyahu* in depicting Miriam as losing her mind (אמרו לאחר ימים נשתטית האשה ההיא). Her death is therefore less of a voluntary act than it is in *Seder Eliyahu*, since her will is no longer in her hands. The narrative comes to an end with the Spirit of Holiness' own words on these events: "For these things I weep" (Lam 1:16). While Miriam has been depicted as particularly resilient, able to endure the deaths of her children, and defy the male biblical paradigm of willingness to sacrifice in the Akedah, this ending allows her to be seen as a more human mother of seven.

The woman is nameless in the version of the story contained in bGit 57b, a less elaborate one than its counterpart in *Seder Eliyahu*.[135] The story is told by the Babylonian Rav Judah, as referring to the verse "Because of you we are being killed all day long, and accounted as sheep for the slaughter" (Ps 44:22). The emperor, who also remains nameless, uses no stratagem, such as imprisoning the brothers separately and trying to persuade each of them to worship an idol by arguing that their brothers have already done so. Moreover, it is not clear that he himself addresses the children. Every child is acted upon and addressed by an impersonal "they": "They brought the first before the emperor and said to him, Serve the idol. He said to them: It is written in the Law ...." The children's answers consist only of an introductory formula and a quotation, with the exception of the last boy's

---

134 According to Buber's reading. The Vilna edition (= MS Munich 229 in Maʾagarim) reads two years, six months, and six-and-a-half hours, as in *Seder Eliyahu*.

135 The story appears in the Gemara to mGit 5:6 (on the Sicaricon), which forms part of a long appendix on the wars against Rome, starting with bGit 55b.

speech. Every child quotes a different scriptural verse (the same as those used in EkhR 1), three of which (in italics in table) are those quoted in *Seder Eliyahu*:

Table 6.3: Scriptural Verses II: A Composite Scriptural Argument for Monotheism

ER 151–ER 153	EkhR 1	bGit 57a
Deut 4:39	Exod 20:2	Exod 20:2
Deut 10:17	*Exod 20:3*	*Exod 20:3*
Exod 20:3	Exod 22:19	Exod 22:19
Exod 34:14	Exod 20:5	Exod 20:5
Exod 22:19	*Deut 4:39*	Deut 6:4
Exod 15:18	Deut 6:4	*Deut 4:39*
Deut 26:17–18	Deut 26:17–18	Deut 26:17–18

As a variation on the versions in *Seder Eliyahu* and *Ekhah Rabbah*, the emperor suggests throwing down a seal engraved with his own image before the boy so that when he bows down to pick it up, he gives the impression of having worshipped the emperor himself. The boy reprimands the emperor, using a *qal wa-chomer* to argue that if the emperor's honour is important, then the honour of the Holy One is that much more important. Here the conversation between the emperor and the boy comes to an end. There is no segment on God's attributes and no further provocation on the part of the emperor. As the boy is led off to be killed, his mother is allowed to kiss her son and compare herself with Abraham, as in the other versions. These are her last words before she goes to the roof and jumps to her death. A *bat qol* praises her, as in *Seder Eliyahu*, quoting Ps 113:9.

An even shorter version is found in the homiletical midrash *Pesiqta Rabbati*, in chapter 43, which deals for the most part with barrenness – not with childlessness as the result of a mother's children being killed. Both forms of childlessness are explained as periods of trial for women such as Hannah, Sarah, and Jochebed, who are eventually rewarded with the birth of central male biblical characters. Miriam's story is told as part of a midrash on Ps 113:9, a verse that R. Tanchuma bar Abba brings up in connection with the *petichah* verse 1 Sam 2:21.[136]

Miriam's narrative is introduced with the quotation of the first part of this verse and a brief, anticipatory interpretation by God himself, who claims to have made Miriam childless in order to enable her to rejoice in her children in the world to come. The narrative itself is told by the sages: Miriam, the daughter of Tanchum, is not arrested herself; rather her seven children are. Who it is that forces every one

---

[136] This verse is quoted as a proof-text in *Seder Eliyahu*, EkhR 1, and bGit 57a by a *bat qol*.

of them to bow before the idol is not explicitly stated, but the chronological setting, in the times of persecution (בימי השמד), allows us to suppose that this version implies the same agents as those in the versions previously discussed.

The short dialogues with the first and second sons are represented in direct speech. To the command to pay reverence to an idol, they both reply that they will not deny their God. The children are not decapitated, but bound to a grid iron (הטיגן) and roasted to death.[137] The trials and deaths of the third through the sixth children are only briefly mentioned as having taken place following the same pattern as the first executions. Only when the narrators, "our masters," come to the seventh boy do they return to a more detailed narrative style, again using direct speech. The boy is threatened with the same torture his brothers endured previously should he refuse to worship the idol. He requests to speak to his mother before giving an answer to his oppressors. Once in front of her, he asks whether he should obey them or not, to which his mother suggests that he should follow the example of his brothers, so as to be with them in Abraham's bosom – a figurative expression which probably meant something close to "the world to come." The child follows his mother's suggestion, suffering the same death his brothers suffered before him. After killing the widow's seventh child, they also kill her – though the narrators do not specify how. God's interpretation of Miriam's story as referring to her childlessness is reiterated at the end of the episode, reminding the reader that she will rejoice in her children in the world to come, fulfilling the words in the psalm, "the joyous mother of children" (Ps 113:9).

6.6.2 "Let me die the death of the upright" (Num 23:10)

Miriam is not the only woman who ends her life in *Seder Eliyahu*, as we see in the following *maʿaseh* about an unmarried woman who would rather die than marry a non-Jew:

> It happened to a maiden (Ar. ברתא) whose father was on very friendly terms with a heathen that [once] while they were eating and drinking, doing their hearts good, the heathen said to her father, Give your daughter to my son for a wife. She remained still before him (החרישה לו) until the time of her wedding came. When the time of her wedding came, she went up to a roof, jumped off, and died. A divine voice (*bat qol*) went forth proclaiming, Of such as her Scripture says, *[Who can] describe Israel's manner of lying down?* (Num 23:10). When Balaam, the son of Beor, prophesied all those comforts and consolations to Israel, he wept in his heart, saying, *Let me die the death of the upright, and let my end be like his!'* (Num 23:10). This teaches that the wicked Balaam wished for the death that Moses and Aaron would have,

---

137 This is also the end of the torture of the first son in 2 Macc 7:5.

saying, If I die on my bed, see, it will be like Moses's and Aaron['s deaths]. If not, it will not be like Moses's and Aaron['s deaths]. (ER 116, l. 15–22)

This *maʿaseh* is told as part of a midrash on Num 23:10 in chapter (21) 19 of *Seder Eliyahu Rabbah*.[138] Contrary to Braude and Kapstein, who translate החרישה לו as "he [the father] said nothing to her,"[139] a literal reading is preferred here, since it is not the father who chooses not to tell the daughter about the marriage arrangements, but rather she who, by remaining silent, only apparently acquiesces. Her decisive answer is given only at the time of the wedding. Although both Miriam and the unnamed unmarried woman in this short narrative decide to take their lives in what could be termed voluntary martyrdom,[140] and their conduct is in both cases praised by a divine voice, the context in which the unmarried woman's story is told is not one of oppression from the outside, but from within her family, which neglects her religious convictions. Unlike Miriam, the young woman remains silent throughout her whole story and only expresses her will regarding her religious ethics and the inadmissibility of intermarriage by killing herself.[141]

The immediately preceding co-text of the *maʿaseh* makes clear that the story is told to exemplify how the young in Israel are masters of their sexual inclinations until they marry. The scriptural confirmation for this notion is found in a reading of the expression רובע in the first part of Num 23:10:[142] "Who can count the dust of Jacob," where עפר ("dust") is read as עופר, as referring to the many "fawns" or "young deer," the young men in Israel who do not occupy themselves with matters related to weapons – that is, they do not fight. In a further hermeneutic operation, the verse is more explicitly interpreted as alluding to the innumerable young boys

---

138 A similar motif is present in the Aggadah of Herod in bBB 3b, in the story of the Hasmonean girl who commits suicide by throwing herself from the roof of her house in order to prevent Herod from marrying her and becoming king. See Yonatan Feintuch, "External Appearance Versus Internal Truth: The Aggadah of Herod in Bavli Bava Batra," *AJS Review* 35 (2011): 85–104.
139 See Braude and Kapstein, *Tanna děbe Eliyyahu*, 293.
140 The story of Miriam is followed by another which depicts Rabban Simeon ben Gamaliel and R. Ishmael as martyrs (ER 153).
141 The Hasmonean girl in a parallel in bBB 3b speaks aloud the reason for her suicide: She wants to prevent Herod from using her to "become" a Hasmonean king. Incidentally, a total of three stories in *Seder Eliyahu* depict a woman going up to the roof, as if we were dealing with gender-specific conduct. See Aptowitzer, "Seder Elia," 9, who discusses this passage as an example of the manner in which *Seder Eliyahu* warns its readers of intermarriage, which has a counterpart in the way the patriarch Jeschu bar Nun polemicises on intermarriage between Jews and Christians.
142 Chapter (21) 19 of *Seder Eliyahu* is a midrash on part of the verse: "Lift your hands to him for the lives of your children, who faint for hunger at the head of every street" (Lam 2:19) and can be seen as an appendix to or a continuation of chapter 18, which deals extensively (ER 89–115) with this verse. The Lamentations verse is read here in the light of the Balaam episode in Num 22–24.

in Israel who sustain their purity until they enter the bridal chamber. And this is true not only of young boys, the midrash goes on to argue, but also of young girls – thus introducing the *maʿaseh* of the suicidal girl.

However, according to the wider context of the chapter, and especially in view of its opening lines, the girl's death is far from exemplary: She belongs among those children who remain silent (ויחריש) when their parents speak superfluous words and whose predicament is that they will not live out their days. Nevertheless, the governing voice sees the girl's behaviour as according with its exegesis of the first part of Num 23:10, thus closing the narrative with the quotation of the second part of the verse.[143] The girl's conduct demonstrates her resolution in refusing to marry a non-Jew as well as her abstinence; her story is a single example of the ideally innumerable, exemplarily chaste lives led by the young in Israel.

6.7 Exegetical Contexts V: *It Is Not Good that the Man Should Be Alone*

> I sat once in the great academy of Jerusalem before the sages. I spoke to them, My masters, May I, who am but dust under the soles of your feet, speak a word in your presence? They answered, Speak. I said, My father who are in heaven, may Your great name be blessed for ever and ever and ever, and may You have contentment in Israel your servants in all the places of their dwellings. For all the comforts and consolations which You spoke to Israel Your servants You uttered only in wisdom and understanding, knowledge, and insight, for it is said, *Then the Lord God said, It is not good that the man should be alone[; I will make him a helper as his partner]* etc. (Gen 2:18). *A helper as his partner* is a helpmate who helps him stand on his feet and helps him open his eyes. They said, Justify your words. I said, I shall. I said to them, My masters, as long as wheat and barley are not prepared and ground in a mill they are nothing but tinder. They answered, True. [I said,] Adam gave them to his wife who prepared them, sifting and grinding them in a mill, and she produced bread from them. What is finer? Bread or fat meat or fat milk or any other kind of good edible things in the world? They said to me, Bread is finer than fat meat or fat milk or any other kind of good edible things in the world. [I said,] Flax is no more than grass. They said <to me>, True. [I said,] Adam gave it to his wife and she wove a garment out of it. <Not only that> but <out of her>[144] he brought increase of mankind in the world; <moreover,> he refrained from going from one place to another committing adultery. These are the four things that a wife does for her husband.[145] <...> And He provides [man] already with food to eat. Does He not provide

---

143 In a footnote to their translation of רובע as "couchings," i.e., sexual couplings, Braude and Kapstein, *Tanna dĕbe Eliyyahu*, 293n9, refer to R. Abbahu's interpretation of the verse in bNid 31a.
144 Friedmann emends the MS reading ממנו to ממנה.
145 This sentence is followed in the MS by the expression והוא and a lacuna. Braude and Kapstein, *Tanna dĕbe Eliyyahu*, 158, include in their translation, the following passage: "She prepares his food, weaves his garments, gives him children, and keeps him from sexual transgression."

food to cattle, beasts, and fowl? <...>[146] [Said the] Master of all the worlds, *I will make him a helper as his partner*, a helpmate who helps him stand on his feet and helps open his eyes. (ER 51, l. 8–26)

In chapter (9) 10 of *Seder Eliyahu Rabbah*, exegetical narratives based on the biblical character of Deborah in Judg 4 are combined with others dealing with Jezebel and Jael,[147] but also with first-person narratives told by the anonymous wandering rabbi. One such narrative is told after Jael, referred to as Heber's wife, has been mentioned as an exemplary wife.[148] The anonymous narrator relates how he once expounded before the sages at the academy in Jerusalem on the expression "a helper as his partner" in Gen 2:18. With the first part of his interpretation of the verse – "would help open (להאיר) his eyes" – the governing voice lets the rabbi take up the metaphorical language used in the first of the exegetical narratives on Deborah, who is said to have caused her husband to prepare thick wicks, the ample "light" (אור) of which made him worthy of the world to come, in spite of being ignorant. The sages request that the rabbi explain his metaphorical language, to provide sound arguments for his statement. The wording of this request, תן טעם לדבריך (here translated as "justify your words") could be a word play[149] alluding to the first part of the explanation that follows: Woman has the merit of transforming wheat and barley into bread (which is judged as better or more savoury than fat meat or milk) and of weaving garments with the fibre of flax. Adam's wife herself is said to have transformed grain into bread. Women thus play a creative role in the household; their creations are of more value than the rest of the edible things available to men in the world. Adam's wife likewise made a garment out

---

146 Another lacuna in the MS.
147 As seen previously in 6.4.
148 The governing voice of *Seder Eliyahu* discusses the role of women in the family context not only in narrative, but also in several non-narrative passages which deal with types rather than characters. In ER 92, l. 1–16, e.g., in an interpretation of Ps 128:3, the qualities of the good wife and the bad wife are contrasted. The brief midrash attempts to explain the comparison of a wife to a fruitful vine in the first part of the verse from the Psalms by arguing that the comparison is valid, i.e., a woman will be fruitful and enable her husband to fulfil the commandment to procreate, if she, like a vine, is rooted to her place, the home. After a counter-example on the bad wife, the governing voice leaves the household sphere to focus on the disciples of the wise, who are to stay within another house, the house of study. At the end of this segment on the wife, it is finally Torah which is now compared to a good wife, a comparison that is seen as confirmed in several scriptural passages quoted as proof-texts (Mal 2:14, Prov 18:22, and Isa 54:6). See Baskin, *Midrashic Women*, ch. 4, "Fruitful Vines and Silent Partners: Women as Wives in Rabbinic Literature," especially the section on "Bad Wives Tales" (112–113), with a parallel of the midrash of *Seder Eliyahu* transmitted in Tan *Vayishlah* 36.
149 See Jastrow, *Dictionary*, s.v. טַעַם. The word can mean "sound reasoning" and also "taste."

flax.[150] Adam's wife stands as a metonymy for wives in general, who ensure that mankind increases, which in turn, the midrash argues, leads men to avoid committing adultery. As a conclusion to his argumentation, the narrator recapitulates that the aforementioned are the four tasks a wife performs for her husband, tasks which define her as a wife: she cooks, weaves his clothes, bears his children, and keeps him from sexual transgression.[151]

Following the passage quoted above, the second part of the rabbi's speech before the sages takes the form of a brief (intradiegetic) eschatological narrative, the spatio-temporal setting of which is the great academy of the future. According to the rabbi, God, presiding over this academy, will address the righteous in praise of their conduct, using a comparison that takes up the subject matter of the preceding passage: Whereas a man takes a beautiful wife but is ready to take another as soon as the first one's beauty has faded, God takes only the righteous and is forever faithful, for their beauty is immutable. This praise of the righteous, uttered by God himself, is supported with two verses from the prophetic books – Hos 3:1 and Jer 3:1 – in both of which God himself is in dialogue with the respective prophet and compares the love between an adulteress and her lovers to the love of the children of Israel for God and for other gods.

In the midrash, God uses an image from the empirical realm, of a wife's fading beauty over time, which the original audience would have been familiar with, to deal with a theological argument, but at the same time to criticise the behaviour of a man who leaves his once-young wife once her physical beauty has left her. The midrash sets up God's "impersonation" of unconditional faithfulness as an example to follow.

6.8 Conclusion

The narratives found in the contexts designated here as halakhic are quite dissimilar. The passage on the sages who discuss with R. Dosa b. Orkinas whether a daughter's co-wife (6.1) is exempt from levirate marriage does not include a specific named or unnamed woman as its theme, but rather discusses hypothetical legal situations in which a woman might find herself. In this narrative, daugh-

---

150 For a parallel of the description of a wife's roles with respect to providing food and clothes, see bYev 63a: "R. Jose met Elijah and asked him: It is written, *I will make him a help* (Gen 2:18); how does a woman help a man? The other replied: If a man brings wheat, does he chew the wheat? If flax, does he put on the flax? Does she not, then, bring light to his eyes and put him on his feet!"
151 The manuscript does not list the four tasks but leaves a gap between "these are the four things" etc. and the next statement.

ters and their co-wives are objectified and silenced as legal personae; they are discussed by named rabbinic authorities who purportedly advocate a lenient position. The story can also be seen as one in which a "legal mystery," one pertaining to the (male) origins of a regulation that affects (primarily) women, is solved by young sages with the aid of an old one. The story of the white days, in its several versions (6.2), does depict a concrete though nameless woman and her plight after the premature death of her husband. Her inability to understand that there are reasons for his death is especially important in her characterisation. She is even granted direct speech, with which she is allowed to tell her story in the first person. In this case, the narrative – framed by someone else's first-person narrative, in which several halakhic issues are discussed – is used as an exemplum of a stringent position pertaining to the *niddah* laws.

The narratives identified as belonging to exegetical contexts cover a wide range of topics. The narrative of the prostitute and R. Aqiba's disciple (6.3) constructs women not simply as sexual temptresses. It depicts the unnamed woman who attracts the sexual attention of a renowned though likewise unnamed sage in relatively positive terms. She is said to belong to the common people and has common sense to share. However, it is worth pointing out that the spiteful language the prostitute uses to depict her own genitals (and metonymically refer to her entire self) not only conveys misogynistic notions, but also expresses, in Judith Baskin's words, the "rabbinic conviction of the potentially dangerous power of women's sexuality."[152]

As part of its expositions, the governing voice also makes use of scriptural narrative material in which biblical women play a central role. The homiletical-exegetical narratives on Deborah (6.4), which interpret selected verses (words and phrases) of passages in Scripture that focus on her, for example, serve to explain that she was an exceptional woman not because she was a prophetess, but rather because, as a wife, she helped her husband obtain the reward of the righteous; because she had disciples of her own, whom she certainly taught out of doors; and also because she was capable of explaining her own prophetic words with the aid of (male) rabbinic hermeneutics. Rachel's narrative (6.5), told to explain a verse from a scriptural context other than her own in the patriarchal narratives in the book of Genesis, depicts her in the role of a midrashic woman narrator who (re-)tells her own biblical story in the first person. Even if her first-person account is set within an exegetical passage narrated by the governing voice, it is nevertheless a case of an empowered feminine voice: According to the parallel version in *Ekhah Rabbah*, her words achieve what a whole pedigree of rabbinic construc-

---

[152] Baskin, *Midrashic Women*, 34.

tions of central male biblical characters does not – namely, she changes God's mind so that He has mercy on Israel and lets them return from exile. The next exegetical narrative deals with a post-biblical character, Miriam, the daughter of Tanchum, who is defined first as a daughter and a widow, but is more clearly characterised as the mother of seven boys who are executed by Hadrian one after the other for refusing to renounce their faith. The narrative is somewhat of a collective hagiography of a family – the proud mother of seven children approves of the death her children die, which she conceptualises as *her own* sacrifice, a sacrifice that surpasses the archetypal sacrifice of Abraham's binding of Isaac. Both Miriam and the unnamed girl who commits suicide to avoid marrying a non-Jew appear to link piety with women's decisions to take their lives. The survey of stories of women[153] comes to a close with a text that focuses on the role par excellence women that assume in rabbinic discourse – that of the wife (6.7). In the context of a scholarly exchange at the house of study, the anonymous rabbi takes "helper" of Gen 2:18 as a lemma for an exposition on the role of woman as the ideal wife.

It comes as no surprise that *Seder Eliyahu* participates in conceptualisations of the feminine usually associated with classical rabbinic Judaism, according to which women constitute a category of creation that must be controlled, regulated, taken care of, and fenced off – at best in the confines of the home. Baskin observes that women in midrash were conceptualised "as fundamentally untrustworthy, they represented constant sources of enticement and societal disorder that had to be maintained under male control in the safety of the domestic realm."[154] This statement holds true for some of the narratives on women in *Seder Eliyahu* discussed above. Not even a biblical heroine such as Jael escapes this fate: She is re-imagined as a righteous woman because she did the will of her husband, not because she killed Sisera with her own hands.

However, even if, as Judith Baskin and Dvora Weisberg remind us, women's voices in rabbinic literature are mediated through male agents[155] and the filter of their "sensibilities and assumptions about women,"[156] in some of the narratives in *Seder Eliyahu* examined previously, we can see that it is not simply "fenced off" voices women are given in certain narratives of this late midrash. In what might

---

153 The corpus of stories of women examined here can be seen as a selection of representative narrative passages, not as covering the entire range of "stories of women" transmitted in *Seder Eliyahu*.
154 Baskin, *Midrashic Women*, 43.
155 Baskin, *Midrashic Women*, 3.
156 Weisberg, "Women and Torah Study in Aggadah," 51.

be described as a counter-hegemonic voice,[157] *Seder Eliyahu* lets certain women characters assume roles traditionally reserved for men. Even if we are not able to recover silenced women's voices when reading their stories in *Seder Eliyahu*, we may ascertain that their voices are instrumentalised and rabbinically tuned, and, through such a masculinisation, empowered to a certain extent.

---

157 Baskin, *Midrashic Women*, 83, quoting Daniel Daniel Boyarin, *Carnal Israel: Reading Sex in Talmudic Culture* (Berkeley, Los Angeles, London: University of California Press, 1993), 183, points out: "These literary constructions may also attest to the existence of 'counter-hegemonic voices that recognize the reality of *some* women's intellectual and spiritual accomplishment.'"

7 Conclusion

This study seeks to participate in an approach to rabbinic literature which reads its ancient texts as historical cultural objects and as sources of a cultural history. Such an approach is more concerned with the ideas, values, and modes of communication which seem to have taken shape in textual form than with a reconstruction of aspects of the empirical, extratextual realities out of which these texts emerged.

An attempt to read a work of a non-narrative character – an ethical midrashic tractate such as *Seder Eliyahu* – *narratologically* appears to be justified due to the pervasive use of narrative that can be ascertained in it. For this purpose, however, the tools of classical narratology must be adapted: The questions posed must be selected according to the types of texts that are under discussion. A crucial aspect of such a reading of the rabbinic document *Seder Eliyahu* pertains to the need to include in the examination particularly the immediate linguistic co-texts within which the narratives are transmitted – generally, texts of a non-narrative character – but also the wider discursive contexts in which they participate.

For my narratologically informed readings of *Seder Eliyahu*, I proceeded in chapter 2 by first discussing the text's calculated anonymity – the anonymity of its governing voice and of the other involved voices, which can be identified both in the text and in some of its paratexts. Another characteristic which was examined in this chapter – which, put briefly, is concerned with the presence of an almost authorial main speaker in different parts of the text, which cannot be ascertained in classical rabbinic documents – and a trait that contributes to the perception of the document as a work is the the conspicuous use of a first-person singular. This rabbinic "I" can be identified throughout the text of *Seder Eliyahu*, in narrative and non-narrative passages alike.

After a preliminary classification of narrative forms or types (chapter 3), I proceeded in the next three chapters to examine selected examples of the most characteristic among them, the *meshalim* and the first-person narratives (chapters 4 and 5), as well as of narrative passages in which women and gender questions appear to play a special role (chapter 6) – in most cases, passages in which a certain level of evident narrativity could be ascertained – and discussing them with regard to their structure, style, characterisation, function, and topical agenda.

These are only some aspects of the work's narrative art. Many remain to be addressed in depth. In a very few cases, for example, I drew on parallels in classical rabbinic literature or in the reception of *Seder Eliyahu* in later medieval documents. My main concern was to study the parts of the document itself and their own intratextual interactions. But it is true that the contrast between both classical and late midrashic and late midrashic and later medieval versions of a story can contribute to shedding light on the cultural differences to which the texts may bear witness. Another narratologically relevant problem in *Seder Eliyahu*, but which could be dealt with in another study, is the fictionality of midrashic and rabbinic narrative – that is, a narrative that is fictional and, at the same time, part of a scholarly (and religious) discourse.[1]

Finally, and probably related to scholarship's enduring concern over the geographical and chronological origins of *Seder Eliyahu*, there remains the unresolved problem related to the uniqueness within the rabbinic corpora of a work with *Seder Eliyahu*'s general characteristics as a closed, authored work. Were it not for its choice of language – that is, the exclusive use of Hebrew – it would be feasible to locate it at least in proximity to the literary system of the Babylonian Geonim – which favoured the traditional diglossia of Hebrew and Aramaic before shifting to that of Judeo-Arabic and Hebrew. It is as part of the literary system of the Geonim – who openly identified as authors, probably under the influence of Islamic culture – that a genre unknown in the history of rabbinic literature up to that point would emerge: the monograph.[2]

Even if it cannot be claimed that *Seder Eliyahu* is a monograph to the same extent as the halakhic monographs of Seʿadyah Gaon, the work can nevertheless be read as a monographic treatise on rabbinic ethics, with a sophisticated organisation of material, a deliberate division into chapters, and a self-conscious governing voice, which repeatedly draws attention to its ubiquitousness in the text – all of which manifests, like the halakhic monographs, a break with the forms of earlier rabbinic documents.[3] Whether this apparent proximity to the genre of the monograph may lead us to assume that *Seder Eliyahu* was composed in the cultural vicinity of the world of the Babylonian Geonim cannot be answered with any certainty.[4] Furthermore, there is sufficient evidence within the work itself that it still preferred to belong to the rabbinic world of the collective voice. It could be argued that, just as the author of a modern novel chooses to write under a pseudonym and this pseudonimity becomes part of her or his work of art, the author of *Seder Eliyahu* may have wanted his readers to imagine him wandering not only between Babylonia, Jerusalem, and other locations, but also between the

---

1 This is an interesting question with regard to many passages of the rabbinic corpus in general.
2 See Brody, *The Geonim of Babylonia*, ch. 16.
3 Of these, Brody, *The Geonim of Babylonia*, 251, points out: "These are the first works of rabbinic literature, certainly in the post-talmudic period, which can be said to have individual authors in something like the modern sense of the word."
4 As demonstrated in section 1.1, much effort has been dedicated to tackle this question with respect to the date and place of origin of *Seder Eliyahu*.

classical world of his rabbinic ancestors and the revolutionalised world of the individual Jewish authorship inaugurated with Seʿadyah Gaon.

Bibliography

Ackerman, Susan. *Warrior, Dancer, Seductress, Queen: Women in Judges and Biblical Israel*. New York: Doubleday, 1998.
Alber, Jan, and Monika Fludernik, eds. *Postclassical Narratology: Approaches and Analyses*. 1–31. Columbus, OH: Ohio University Press, 2010.
Allrath, Gaby, and Marion Gymnich. "Gendered Narratology." In *Routledge Encyclopedia of Narrative Theory*, edited by David Herman, Manfred Jahn, and Marie-Laure Ryan, 197–198. London, New York: Routledge, 2005.
Appelbaum, Alan. *The Rabbis' King-Parables: Midrash from the Third-Century Roman Empire*. Piscataway, NJ: Gorgias Press, 2010.
Aptowitzer, Avigdor. "Seder Elia." In *Jewish Studies: In Memory of George A. Kohut, 1874–1933*, edited by Salo W. Baron and Alexander Marx, 5–39. New York: The Alexander Kohut Memorial Foundation, 1935.
Astren, Fred. "Islamic Contexts of Medieval Karaism." In *Karaite Judaism: A Guide to its History and Literary Sources*, edited by Meira Polliack, 145–177. Leiden, Boston: Brill, 2003.
Azzan-Yadin, Israel. "'On the Basis of This, They Said': Mikan ᾿Amru and the Role of Scripture." Chap. 4 in *Scripture and Tradition: Rabbi Akiva and the Triumph of Midrash*, 73–100. Philadelphia, PA: Pennsylvania University Press, 2014.
Bacher, Wilhelm. "Antikaräisches in einem jüngeren Midrasch." *Monatsschrift für Geschichte und Wissenschaft des Judentums* 23 (1874): 266–274.
———. *Die Bibel- und traditionsexegetische Terminologie der Amoräer*. Vol. 2 of *Die exegetische Terminologie der jüdischen Traditionsliteratur*. Leipzig: J. C. Hinrich'sche Buchhandlung, 1905.
———. *Die bibelexegetische Terminologie der Tannaiten*: vol. 1 of *Die exegetische Terminologie der jüdischen Traditionsliteratur*. Leipzig: J. C. Hinrich'sche Buchhandlung, 1899.
Bacher, Wilhelm, and Shulim Ochser. "Tanna De-vei Eliyahu." In *The Jewish Encyclopaedia*, edited by Isidor Singer, 12:46–49. New York: Funk / Wagnalis, 1906.
Bakhos, Carol, ed. *Current Trends in the Study of Midrash*. Leiden, Boston: Brill, 2006.
———. *Ismael on the Border*. Albany, NY: State University of New York Press, 2006.
Bal, Mieke. *Narratology*. 3rd ed. Toronto: Toronto University Press, 2009.
Baskin, Judith. *Midrashic Women: Formations of the Feminine in Rabbinic Literature*. Hanover, NH: Brandeis University Press, 2002.
Becker, Hans-Jürgen, ed. *Avot de-Rabbi Natan: Synoptische Edition beider Versionen*. Tübingen: Mohr Siebeck, 2006.
Beit-Arié, Malachi, Colette Sirat, and Mordechai Glatzer. *Codices Hebraicis Litteris Exarati Quo Tempore Scripti Fuerint Exhibentes: De 1021 à 1079*. Turnhout: Brepols, 1999.
Ben-Amos, Dan. "Generic Distinctions in the Aggadah." In *Studies in Jewish Folklore*, edited by Frank Talmage, 45–72. Cambridge, MA: The Association for Jewish Studies, 1980.
Ben-Shammai, Haggai. "The Karaite Controversy: Scripture and Tradition in Early Karaism." In *Religionsgespräche im Mittelalter*, edited by B. Lewis and F. Niewöhner, 11–26. Wiesbaden: Harrassowitz, 1992.
Berkowitz, Miriam. "Reshaping the Laws of Family Purity," 2006. www.rabbinicalassembly.org/sites/default/files/public/halakhah/teshuvot/20052010/berkowitz_niddah.pdf.
Berzbach, Ulrich. "The Textual Witnesses of the Midrash Seder Eliyahu Zuta: An Initial Survey." *Frankfurter Judaistische Beiträge* 31 (2004): 63–74.

Berzbach, Ulrich. "The Varieties of Literal Devices in a Medieval Midrash: Seder Eliyahu Rabba, Chapter 18." In *Jewish Studies at the Turn of the Twentieth Century: Proceedings of the 6th EAJS Congress, Toledo, July 1998*, edited by Judit Targarona Borrás and Ángel Sáenz-Badillos, 384–391. Leiden: Leiden, 1999.

Booth, Wayne C. *The Rhetoric of Fiction*. Chicago, IL: University of Chicago Press, 1961.

Boyarin, Daniel. *Carnal Israel: Reading Sex in Talmudic Culture*. Berkeley, Los Angeles, London: University of California Press, 1993.

———. "Interpreting in Ordinary Language: The Mashal as Intertext." Chap. 5 in *Intertextuality and the Reading of Midrash*. Bloomington, IN: Indiana University Press, 1990.

———. *Intertextuality and the Reading of Midrash*. Bloomington, IN: Indiana University Press, 1990.

Braude, William G. "Conjecture and Interpolation in Translating Rabbinic Texts: Illustrated by a Chapter from Tanna Debe Eliyyahu." In *Christianity, Judaism and Other Greco-Roman Cults: Studies for Morton Smith at Sixty*, edited by Jacob Neusner, IV: *Judaism after 70; other Greco-Roman Cults; Bibliography*, 77–92. Leiden: Brill, 1975.

———. "Novellae in Eliyyahu Rabbah's Exegesis." In *Studies in Aggadah, Targum and Jewish Liturgy in Memory of Joseph Heinemann*, edited by Jacob J. Petuchowski and Ezra Fleischer, 11–22. Jerusalem: Magnes Press, 1981.

Braude, William G., and Israel J. Kapstein, eds. and trans. *Tanna děbe Eliyyahu: The Lore of the School of Elijah*. Philadelphia, PA: Jewish Publication Society, 1981.

Bregman, Marc. "Excursus: The Rabbinic Versions of the Blind and the Lame." In *The Apocryphal Ezekiel*, edited by Michael E. Stone, Benjamin G. Wright, and David Satran, 61–68. Atlanta, GA: Society of Biblical Literature, 2000.

———. "Pseudepigraphy in Rabbinic Literature." In *Pseudepigraphic Perspectives: The Apocrypha and Pseudepigrapha in Light of the Dead Sea Scrolls*, edited by Esther Chazon, 27–41. Leiden, Boston: Brill, 1999.

Brody, Robert. *The Geonim of Babylonia and the Shaping of Medieval Jewish Literature*. New Haven, CT: Yale University Press, 1998.

Cassuto, Umberto. *Codices Vaticani Hebraici: Codices 1–115; Bybliothecae Apostolicae Vaticanae Codices Manu Scripti Recensiti Iussu Pii XII Pontificis Maximi*. The Vatican: Biblioteca Apostolica Vaticana, 1956.

Charlesworth, James H. "Pseudepigraphen des Alten Testaments." In *Theologische Realenzyklopädie*, edited by Gerhard Müller, 27:639–645. Berlin: De Gruyter, 1997.

Chatman, Seymour Benjamin. *Story and Discourse: Narrative Structure in Fiction and Film*. Ithaca, NY: Cornell University Press, 1978.

Chihaia, Matei. "Introductions to Narratology: Theory, Practice and the Afterlife of Structuralism." *Diegesis* 1, no. 1 (2012): 15–31.

Cohen, Shaye. "Menstruants and the Sacred." In *Women's History and Ancient History*, edited by Sarah Pomeroy, 273–299. Chapel Hill, NC: University of North Carolina Press, 1991.

Cohn, Dorrit. "Métalepse et Mise en Abyme." In *Métalepses: Entorses au Pacte de la Représentation*, edited by John Pier and Jean-Marie Schaeffer, 121–130. Paris: Éditions de l'École des Hautes Études en Sciences Sociales, 2005.

Cordoni, Constanza. "Biblical Interpretation in Seder Eliyahu." In *"Let the Wise Listen and Add to Their Learning" (Prov 1:5): Festschrift for Günter Stemberger on the Occasion of his 75th Birthday*, edited by Constanza Cordoni and Gerhard Langer, 413–430. Berlin, Boston: De Gruyter, 2016.

———. "Die weißen Tage oder warum die Frau immer noch als 'unrein' gilt, nachdem ihre Unreinheit aufgehört hat." *Protokolle zur Bibel* 21 (2012): 1–17.

———. "The Emergence of the Individual Author(-image) in Late Rabbinic Literature." In *Narratology, Hermeneutics, and Midrash: Jewish, Christian, and Muslim Narratives from the Late Antiquity through to Modern Times*, edited by Constanza Cordoni and Gerhard Langer, 225–250. Göttingen: V&R unipress, 2014.

Cornils, Anja. "La Métalepse dans les Actes des Apôtres: Un Signe de Narration Fictionnelle?" In *Métalepses: Entorses au Pacte de la Représentation*, edited by John Pier and Jean-Marie Schaeffer, 95–107. Paris: Éditions de l'École des Hautes Études en Sciences Sociales, 2005.

Danby, Herbert, trans. *The Mishnah: Translated from the Hebrew with Introduction and Brief Explanatory Notes*. London: Soncino, 1933.

Deeg, Alexander. *Predigt und Derascha: Homiletische Textlektüre im Dialog mit dem Judentum*. Göttingen: Vandenhoeck & Ruprecht, 2006.

Drory, Rina. *Models and Contacts: Arabic Literature and its Impact on Medieval Jewish Culture*. Leiden: Brill, 2000.

Eder, Sigrid. *Wie Frauen und Männer Macht ausüben: Eine feministisch-narratologische Analyse von Ri 4*. Freiburg im Breisgau: Herder, 2008.

Edmiston, William F. "Focalization and the First-Person Narrator: A Revision of the Theory." *Poetics Today* 10 (1989): 729–744.

Elbaum, Jacob. "Bein arikhah le-shikhtuv: le-ofyah shel ha-sifrut ha-midrashit ha-meʾucheret [Between Redaction and Rewriting: On the Character of the Late Midrashic Literature]." In *Proceedings of the Ninth World Congress of Jewish Studies: Division B: The History of the Jewish People (From the Second Temple Period until the Middle Ages)*, 1:57–62. Jerusalem: Magnes Press, 1986.

———. "Tanna deve Eliyahu ve-sifrut ha-sod ha-qedumah [The Midrash Tana Devei Eliyahu and Ancient Esoteric Literature]." *Jerusalem Studies in Jewish Thought* 6, nos. 1–2 (1987): 139–150.

———. "Tanna De-vei Eliyahu." In *Encyclopaedia Judaica*, edited by Michael Berenbaum and Fred Skolnik, 19:508. Detroit: MacMillan Reference, 2007.

———. "Tanna de-Vei Eliyahu: bein midrash le-sefer musar; iyunim bi-ferakim aleph-vav be-Tanna de-Vei Eliyahu [Tanna de-Vei Eliyahu: Between a Midrash and an Ethical Treatise: Analyses of Chapters 1–6 of Tanna de-Vei Eliyahu]." *Jerusalem Studies in Hebrew Literature* 1 (1981): 144–154.

Eppenstein, Simon. *Beiträge zur Geschichte und Literatur im Geonäischen Zeitalter*. Breslau: Koebner, 1908.

———. *Beiträge zur Geschichte und Literatur im Geonäischen Zeitalter*. Breslau: Koebner, 1913.

Epstein, Isidore, ed. ʿ*Abodah Zarah*. Vol. 4 of *The Babylonian Talmud: Seder Nezikin*, translated by A. Mishcon and A. Slotki. London: Soncino, 1935.

———, ed. *Baba Bathra*. Vol. 2 of *The Babylonian Talmud: Seder Nezikin*, translated by Maurice Simon and Israel W. Slotki. London: Soncino, 1935.

———, ed. *Kethuboth*. Vol. 2 of *The Babylonian Talmud: Seder Nashim*, translated by Samuel Daiches and Israel W. Slotki. London: Soncino, 1936.

———, ed. *Ḳiddushin*. Vol. 4 of *The Babylonian Talmud: Seder Nashim*, translated by H. Freedman. London: Soncino, 1936.

———, ed. *Niddah*. In *The Babylonian Talmud: Seder Ṭohoroth*, translated by Israel W. Slotki. London: Soncino, 1948.

——, ed. *Pesaḥim*. Vol. 2 of *The Babylonian Talmud: Seder Mo‹ed*, translated by Harry Freedman. London: Soncino, 1938.
Epstein, Isidore, ed. *Sanhedrin*. Vol. 3 of *The Babylonian Talmud: Seder Nezikin*, translated by Jacob Shachter and H. Freedman. London: Soncino, 1935.
——, ed. *Shabbath*. Vol. 1 of *The Babylonian Talmud: Seder Mo‹ed*, translated by H. Freedman. London: Soncino, 1938.
——, ed. *Tamid*. Vol. 3 of *The Babylonian Talmud: Seder Ḳodashim*, translated by Maurice Simon. London: Soncino, 1948.
——, ed. *Yebamoth*. Vol. 1 of *The Babylonian Talmud: Seder Nashim*, translated by Israel W. Slotki. London: Soncino, 1936.
Epstein, Jacob N. *Mavo le-nusaḥ ha-mishnah [Introduction to the Text of the Mishnah]*. Jerusalem: Magnes Press, 1948.
Erder, Yoram. *The Karaite Mourners of Zion and the Qumran Scrolls: On the History of an Alternative to Rabbinic Judaism*. Diaspora: New Perspectives on Jewish History and Culture 3. Turnhout: Brepols, 2017.
——. "The Karaites and the Second Temple Sects." In *Karaite Judaism: A Guide to its History and Literary Sources*, edited by Meira Polliack, 119–143. Leiden, Boston: Brill, 2003.
Feintuch, Yonatan. "External Appearance Versus Internal Truth: The Aggadah of Herod in Bavli Bava Batra." *AJS Review* 35 (2011): 85–104.
Fishbane, Michael. *The Midrashic Imagination: Jewish Exegesis, Thought, and History*. Albany, NY: SUNY, 1993.
Fleischman, Suzanne. *Tense and Narrativity: From Medieval Performance to Modern Fiction*. London: Routledge, 1990.
Fludernik, Monika. *An Introduction to Narratology*. London, New York: Routledge, 2009.
——. "Changement de Scène et Mode Métaleptique." In *Métalepses: Entorses au Pacte de la Représentation*, edited by John Pier and Jean-Marie Schaeffer, 73–94. Paris: Éditions de l'École des Hautes Études en Sciences Sociales, 2005.
——. *Erzähltheorie: Eine Einführung*. Darmstadt: Wissenschaftliche Buchgesellschaft, 2006.
——. "The Genderization of Narrative." *Graat* 21 (1999): 153–175.
——. *Towards a Natural Narratology*. London, New York: Routledge, 1996.
Fokkelman, Jan P. "Fiktion/Fiktionalität. I. Alttestamentlich." In *Lexikon der Bibelhermeneutik: Begriffe – Methoden – Theorien – Konzepte*, edited by Oda Wischmeyer, 178–179. Berlin, Boston: De Gruyter, 2013.
Fonrobert, Charlotte Elisheva. *Menstrual Purity: Rabbinic and Christian Reconstructions of Biblical Gender*. Stanford, CA: Stanford University Press, 2000.
Fraade, Steven. *Legal Fictions: Studies of Law and Narrative in the Discursive Worlds of Ancient Jewish Sectarians and Sages*. Leiden: Brill, 2011.
——. "Rewritten Bible and Rabbinic Midrash as Commentary." In *Current Trends in the Study of Midrash*, edited by Carol Bakhos, 59–78. Leiden, Boston: Brill, 2006.
Fraenkel, Yonah. *Darkhe ha-agadah veha-midrash [The Hermeneutics of Aggadah and Midrash]*. 2 vols. Givatayim: Yad La-Talmud, 1991.
——. *Sipur ha-agadah, aḥdut shel tokhen ve-tsurah: Kovets mekharim [The Aggadic Narrative: Harmony of Form and Content]*. Tel Aviv: Ha-kibutz Ha-meuchad, 2001.
Freedman, Harry, and Maurice Simon, eds. *Lamentations*. Vol. 7 of *Midrash Rabbah*, translated by A. Cohen. London: Soncino, 1939.

Friedmann, Meir, ed. *Pseudo-Seder Eliahu Zuta (Derech Ereç und Pirkê R. Eliezer nach Editio princeps des Seder Eliahu und einem Manuscripte*. Vienna: Israelitisch-Theologische Lehranstalt, 1904.
——, ed. *Seder Eliahu Rabba and Seder Eliahu Zuta (Tanna D'be Eliahu)*. Vienna: Israelitisch-Theologische Lehranstalt, 1902.
Fürst, Julius. *Bis 900 der gewöhnlichen Zeitrechnung*. Vol. 1 of *Geschichte des Karäerthums: Eine kurze Darstellung seiner Entwicklung, Lehre und Literatur*. Leipzig: Nies'sche Buchdruckerei, 1862.
Genette, Gérard. "Discours du Récit: Essai de Méthode." In *Figures III*, 65–282. Paris: Seuil, 1972.
——. *Métalepse: De la Figure à la Fiction*. Paris: Seuil, 2004.
——. *Palimpsests: Literature on the Second Degree*. Translated by Channa Newman and Claude Doubinsky. Lincoln, NE, London: University of Nebraska Press, 1997.
——. *Paratexts: Thresholds of Interpretation*. Translated by Jane E. Lewin. Cambridge: Cambridge University Press, 1997.
Ginzberg, Louis. *Bible Times and Characters from Joshua to Esther*. Vol. 4 of *The Legends of the Jews*. Philadelphia, PA: Jewish Publication Society, 1913.
——. *Midrash and Haggadah*. Vol. 1 of *Genizah Studies in Memory of Solomon Schechter*. New York: Jewish Theological Seminary, 1928.
——. *Notes to Volumes III and IV: From Moses in the Wilderness to Esther*. Vol. 6 of *The Legends of the Jews*. Philadelphia, PA: Jewish Publication Society, 1928.
Goffman, Ervin. *Frame Analysis: An Essay on the Organization of Experience*. Cambridge, MA: Harvard University Press, 1974.
Goldberg, Arnold. "Das schriftauslegende Gleichnis im Midrasch." In *Rabbinische Texte als Gegenstand der Auslegung*, vol. 2 of *Gesammelte Studien*, edited by Margarete Schlüter and Peter Schäfer, 134–198. Tübingen: Mohr Siebeck, 1999.
——. "Die funktionale Form Midrasch." In *Rabbinische Texte als Gegenstand der Auslegung*, vol. 2 of *Gesammelte Studien*, edited by Margarete Schlüter and Peter Schäfer, 199–229. Tübingen: Mohr Siebeck, 1999.
——. "Form und Funktion des Ma‹ase in der Mischna." In *Rabbinische Texte als Gegenstand der Auslegung*, vol. 2 of *Gesammelte Studien*, edited by Margarete Schlüter and Peter Schäfer, 22–49. Tübingen: Mohr Siebeck, 1999.
Goldin, Judah, trans. *The Fathers According to Rabbi Nathan*. New Haven, CT: Yale University Press, 1956.
Graetz, Heinrich. *Geschichte der Juden vom Abschluss des Talmuds (500) bis zum Aufblühen der jüdisch-spanischen Kultur (1027)*. Vol. 5 of *Geschichte der Juden: Von den ältesten Zeiten bis auf die Gegenwart*, 3rd ed. Leipzig: Leiner, 1895.
Greenberg, Moshe. "The Etymology of Niddah: (Menstrual) Impurity." In *Solving Riddles and Untying Knots: Biblical, Epigraphic and Semitic Studies in Honor of Jonas C. Greenfield*, edited by Ziony Zevit, Seymour Gitin, and Michael Sokoloff, 69–77. Winona Lake, IN: Eisenbrauns, 1995.
Greenspahn, Frederick, ed. *Women and Judaism: New Insights and Scholarship*. New York: New York University Press, 2009.
Güdemann, Moritz. *Geschichte des Erziehungswesens und der Cultur der abendländischen Juden während des Mittelalters und der neueren Zeit*. Vol. 2 of *Geschichte des Erziehungswesens und der Cultur der Juden in Italien während der Mittelalters, nebst bisher ungedruckten Beilagen*. Vienna: Hölder, 1884.

Handelman, Susan A. *The Slayers of Moses: The Emergence of Rabbinic Interpretation in Modern Literary Theory*. New York: State University of New York Press, 1983.
Hartman, Geoffrey H., and Sanford Budick, eds. *Midrash and Literature*. New Haven, CT: Yale University Press, 1986.
Hasan-Rokem, Galit. *Web of Life: Folklore and Midrash in Rabbinic Literature*. Stanford, CA: Stanford University Press, 2000.
Hauptmann, Judith. *Rereading the Rabbis: A Woman's Voice*. Boulder, CO: Westview Press, 1998.
Hedner-Zetterholm, Karin. "Elijah's Different Roles: A Reflection of the Rabbinic Struggle for Authority." *Jewish Studies Quarterly* 16, no. 2 (2009): 163–182.
Heinemann, Joseph. "The Nature of Aggadah." In *Midrash and Literature*, edited by Geoffrey H. Hartman and Sanford Budick, 41–55. New Haven, CT, London: Yale University Press, 1986.
Heinen, Sandra. "Überlegungen zum Begriff des "Impliziten Autors" und seines Potentials zur kulturwissenschaftlichen Beschreibung von inszenierter Autorschaft." *Sprachkunst* 33 (2002): 327–377.
Heinen, Sandra, and Roy Sommer. "Narratology and Interdisciplinarity." In *Narratology in the Age of Cross-Disciplinary Narrative Research*, edited by Sandra Heinen and Roy Sommer, 1–10. Berlin: De Gruyter, 2009.
Herman, David. "Scripts, Sequences, and Stories: Elements of a Postclassical Narratology." *PMLA* 112, no. 5 (1997): 1046–1059.
———. "Toward a Formal Description of Narrative Metalepsis." *Journal of Literary Semantics* 26, no. 2 (1997): 132–152.
Herr, Moshe David. "Midrash." In *Encyclopaedia Judaica*, edited by Michael Berenbaum and Fred Skolnik, 14:182–185. Detroit: Macmillan Reference, 2007.
Jaffee, Martin S. "Rabbinic Authorship as a Collective Enterprise." In *The Cambridge Companion to the Talmud and Rabbinic Literature*, edited by Charlotte Elisheva Fonrobert and Martin S. Jaffee, 17–27. Cambridge, New York: Cambridge University Press, 2007.
Jahn, Manfred. "Focalization." In *Routledge Encyclopedia of Narrative Theory*, edited by David Herman, Manfred Jahn, and Marie-Laure Ryan, 173–177. London, New York: Routledge, 2005.
———. "Focalization." In *The Cambridge Companion to Narrative*, edited by David Herman, 94–108. Cambridge: Cambridge University Press, 2007.
Jastrow, Marcus. *A Dictionary of the Targumim, Talmud Babli, Talmud Yerushalmi and Midrashic Literature*. Leipzig, London, and New York: W. Druglin / Luzac / Putnam's Sons, 1903.
Kadari, Adiel. "Talmud torah be-Seder Eliyahu: ha-mishnah ha-raʿeinit be-heqesherah ha-histori-chevrati [Talmud Torah in Seder Eliyahu: The Ideological Doctrine in its Socio-Historical Context]." *Daat* 50–52 (2003): 35–59.
———. "Talmud torah, mystyqah ve-eskatologiah: ʿal beit ha-midrash shel ha-qadosh barukh hu be-midrash ha-meʾuḥar [Torah Study, Mysticism and Eschatology: 'God's Study Hall' in the Later Midrash]." *Tarbiz* 73, no. 2 (2004): 181–195.
Kadushin, Max. *Organic Thinking: A Study in Rabbinic Thought*. New York: The Jewish Theological Seminary of America, 1938.
———. *The Theology of Seder Eliahu*. New York: Bloch Publishing Company, 1932.
Kahana, Menahem I., ed. *Sifre Zuta Devarim [Sifre Zuta on Deuteronomy: Citations from a New Tannaitic Midrash]*. Jerusalem: Magnes Press, 2002.
Kalmin, Richard. *Jewish Babylonia between Persia and Roman Palestine*. Oxford, New York: Oxford University Press, 2006.

――. "Relationships between Rabbis and Non-rabbis." *Jewish Studies Quarterly* 5 (1998): 156–170.
Kanarek, Jane. *Biblical Narrative and the Formation of Rabbinic Law*. New York: Cambridge University Press, 2014.
Kindt, Tom, and Hans-Harald Müller. "Der 'Implizite Autor': Zur Explikation und Verwendung eines umstrittenen Begriffs." In *Rückkehr des Autors: Zur Erneuerung eines umstrittenen Begriffs*, edited by Fotis Jannidis, Gerhard Lauer, Matías Martínez, and Simone Winko, 273–287. Tübingen: Niemeyer, 1999.
Klein, Gottlieb. *Der älteste christliche Katechismus und die jüdische Propaganda-Literatur*. Berlin: Reimer, 1909.
Kugel, James. "Two Introductions to Midrash." In *Midrash and Literature*, edited by Geoffrey H. Hartman and Sanford Budick, 77–103. New Haven, CT: Yale University Press, 1986. Reprinted from *Prooftexts* 3 (1983): 131–155.
Langer, Gerhard. *Midrasch*. Tübingen: Mohr Siebeck, 2016.
Lanser, Susan. "(Im)Plying the Author." In *Narrative Theory II: Special Topics*, edited by Mieke Bal, 11–18. London, New York: Routledge, 2004.
――. "Sexing the Narrative: Propriety, Desire, and the Engendering of Narratology." *Narrattive* 3 (1995): 85–94.
――. "Toward a Feminist Narratology." *Style* 20, no. 3 (1986): 341–363.
Lausberg, Heinrich. *Handbuch der literarischen Rhetorik: Eine Grundlegung der Literaturwissenschaft*. 2nd ed. Munich: Max Hueber Verlag, 1973.
Lavee, Moshe. "Seder Eliyahu." In *Encyclopedia of Jews in the Islamic World*, edited by Norbert Stillman. Brill Online, 2010.
Lehmhaus, Lennart. "Between Tradition and Innovation: Seder Eliyahu's Strategies in the Context of Late Midrash." In *Approaches to Literary Readings of Ancient Jewish Writings*, edited by Klaas A. D. Smelik and Karolien Vermeulen, 211–242. Leiden: Brill, 2014.
――. "'Blessed be He, who Remembered the Earlier Deeds and Overlooks the Later': Prayer, Benedictions, and Liturgy in the New Rhetoric Garb of Late Midrashic Traditions." In *"It's Better to Hear the Rebuke of the Wise Than the Song of Fools" (Qoh 7:5): Proceedings of the Midrash Section, Society of Biblical Literature*, edited by W. David Nelson and Rivka Ulmer, 95–140. Piscataway, NJ: Gorgias Press, 2015.
――. "Were not Understanding and Knowledge Given to You from Heaven? Minimal Judaism and the Unlearned Other in Seder Eliyahu Zuta." *Jewish Studies Quarterly* 19 (2012): 230–258.
Lerner, Myron B. "The Works of Aggadic Midrash and the Esther Midrashim." In *The Literature of the Sages: Second Part*, edited by Shmuel Safrai, Zeev Safrai, Joshua Schwartz, and Peter J. Tomson, 133–229. Assen, Minneapolis, MN: Van Gorcum, Fortress, 2006.
Levinson, Joshua. "Dialogical Reading in the Rabbinic Exegetical Narrative." *Poetics Today* 25, no. 3 (2004): 498–528.
――. *Ha-sipur she-lo supar: omanut Ha-sipur ha-miqraʾi ha-murchav be-midreshe chazal [The Twice-Told Tale: A Poetics of the Exegetical Narrative in Rabbinic Midrash]*. Jerusalem: Magnes Press, 2005.
Lindbeck, Kristen H. *Elijah and the Rabbis: Story and Theology*. New York: Columbia University Press, 2010.
Lyons, John. "Text and Discourse; Context and Co-text." Chap. 9 in *Linguistic Semantics: An Introduction*. Cambridge University Press, 1995.

Maier, Bernhard, Thomas Podella, Robert Goldenberg, Christian Dietzfelbinger, and Gert Hartmann. "Reinheit." In *Theologische Realenzyklopädie*, edited by Gerhard Müller, 28:473–497. Berlin, New York: De Gruyter, 1997.
Maier, Johann. "Serienbildung und 'numinoser' Eindruckseffekt in den poetischen Stücken der Hekhalot-Literatur." *Semitics* 3 (1973): 36–66.
Mann, Jacob. "Changes in the Divine Service of the Synagogue due to Religious Persecutions." *Hebrew Union College Annual* 4 (1927): 240–310.
———. "Genizah Studies." *The American Journal of Semitic Languages* 46 (1930): 263–283.
———. *Karaitica*. Vol. 2 of *Texts and Studies in Jewish History and Literature*. New York: Ktav Publishing House, 1972.
Margolin, Uri. "Telling in the Plural: From Grammar to Ideology." *Poetics Today* 21 (2000): 591–618.
Margulies, Mordechai. "Li-beayat qadmuto shel sefer Seder Eliyahu [The Problem of the Beginning of the Book Seder Eliyahu]." In *Sefer Asaf*, edited by Umberto Casutto, 370–390. Jerusalem: Mossad ha-Rav Kuk, 1953.
———, ed. *Midrash Wayyikra Rabbah: A Critical Edition based on Manuscripts and Genizah Fragments with Variants and Notes*. 3 vols. Jerusalem: Ministry of Education and Culture of Israel, 1953.
Marienberg, Evyatar. *Niddah: Lorsque les Juifs Conceptualisent la Menstruation*. Paris: Belles Lettres, 2003.
Marnette, Sophie, and Helen Swift. "Introduction: Que veut dire « voix narrative » ?" *Cahiers de Recherches Médiévales et Humanistes* 22 (2011): 1–7.
Martínez, Matías, and Michael Scheffel. *Einführung in die Erzähltheorie*. 9th ed. Munich: Beck, 2012.
McHale, Brian. *Postmodernist Fiction*. New York: Methuen, 1987.
Meir, Ofra. *Ha-sipur darshani be-bereshit rabbah [The Exegetical Narrative in Genesis Rabbah]*. Tel Aviv: Ha-kibutz Ha-meuchad, 1987.
———. "The Narrator in the Stories of the Talmud and the Midrash." *Fabula* 22 (1981): 79–83.
Milgrom, Jacob. "Nidda." In *Theological Dictionary of the Old Testament*, edited by G. Johannes Botterweck and Helmer Ringgren, 9:232–235. Grand Rapids, MI: Eerdsmans, 1998.
Milikowsky, Chaim. "Notions of Exile, Subjugation and Return in Rabbinic Literature." In *Exile: Old Testament, Jewish, and Christian Conceptions*, edited by James M. Scott, 256–296. Supplements to the Journal for the Study of Judaism. Leiden: Brill, 1997.
Natan ben Yechiel. *Aruch completum*. Edited by Alexander Kohut. Vol. 6. Vienna: Brög, 1890.
[Natronai bar Hilai, Gaon]. *Teshuvot Rav Natronai bar Hilai Gaon [The Responsa of Rav Natronai bar Hilai Gaon]*. 2nd ed. Edited by Robert Brody. Jerusalem: Ofeq, 1994.
Nemoy, Leon. *Karaite Anthology: Excerpts from the Early Literature*. New Haven, CT, London: Yale University Press, 1952.
Neusner, Jacob. *The Precedent and the Parable in Diachronic View*. Vol. 4 of *Rabbinic Narrative: A Documentary Perspective*. Leiden, Boston: Brill, 2003.
Niederhoff, Burkhard. "Focalization." In *the living handbook of narratology*, edited by Peter et al. Hühn. Hamburg University Press, 2009. http://www.lhn.uni-hamburg.de/article/focalization.
———. "Fokalisation und Perspektive: Ein Plädoyer für friedliche Koexistenz." *Poetica* 33 (2001): 1–21.
Niehoff, Maren R. "Biographical Sketches in Genesis Rabbah." In *Envisioning Judaism: Studies in Honor of Peter Schäfer on the Occasion of his Seventieth Birthday*, edited by Raᶜanan S.

Boustan, Klaus Herrmann, Reimund Leicht, Annette Yoshiko Reed, and Giuseppe Veltri, 1:265–286. Tübingen: Mohr Siebeck, 2013.
Nikolsky, Ronit. "De functie van parabels (*mesjalim*) in de *Tanchuma*." *Nederlands Theologisch Tijdschrift* 71, no. 2 (2017): 151–168.
Nünning, Ansgar. "Implied Author." In *Routledge Encyclopedia of Narrative Theory*, edited by David Herman, Manfred Jahn, and Marie-Laure Ryan, 239–240. London, New York: Routledge, 2005.
——. "Narratology or Narratologies." In *What is Narratology? Questions and Answers regarding the Status of a Theory*, 239–275. Berlin: De Gruyter, 2003.
Nünning, Ansgar, and Vera Nünning. "Von der strukturalistischen Narratologie zur 'postklassischen' Erzähltheorie: Ein Überblick über neue Ansätze und Entwicklungstendenzen." In *Neue Ansätze in der Erzähltheorie*, 1–33. Trier: WVT, 2002.
Olszowy-Schlanger, Judith. "Early Karaite Family Law." In *Karaite Judaism: A Guide to its History and Literary Sources*, edited by Meira Polliack, 275–290. Leiden, Boston: Brill, 2003.
Ottenheijm, Eric. "De parabels van Jezus en van de Rabbijnen als 'media' van Tora." *Nederlands Theologisch Tijdschrift* 71, no. 2 (2017): 114–130.
Ottenheijm, Eric, Annette Merz, and Marcel Poorthuis, eds. *Parables in Changing Contexts: Interreligious and Cultural Approaches to the Study of Parables*. Leiden: Brill, 2018.
Page, Ruth. "Gender." In *The Cambridge Companion to Narrative*, edited by David Herman, 189–202. Cambridge: Cambridge University Press, 2007.
Pier, John, and Jean-Marie Schaeffer, eds. *Métalepses: Entorses au Pacte de la Représentation*. Paris: Éditions de l'École des Hautes Études en Sciences Sociales, 2005.
Pokorný, Petr, and Günter Stemberger. "Pseudepigraphie." In *Theologische Realenzyklopädie*, edited by Gerhard Müller, 27:645–659. Berlin: De Gruyter, 1997.
Polliack, Meira. "Rethinking Karaism: Between Judaism and Islam." *AJS Review* 30, no. 1 (2006): 67–93.
Porton, Gary. "Defining Midrash." In *The Study of Ancient Judaism*, edited by Jacob Neusner, vol. 1: *Mishnah, Midrash, Siddur*, 55–92. New York: Ktav, 1981.
——. "Definitions of Midrash." In *Encyclopedia of Midrash*, edited by Jacob Neusner, 1:520–534. Leiden, Boston: Brill, 2005.
Prince, Gerald. "Narrative." In *A Dictionary of Narratology*, 58. Lincoln, NE: University of Nebraska Press, 2003.
Rabinowitz, Louis Isaac. "Parable." In *Encyclopaedia Judaica*, edited by Michael Berenbaum and Fred Skolnik, 15:620–623. Detroit: MacMillan Reference, 2007.
Rapoport, Solomon. "*Toledot R. Nathan*." In *Bikkure ha-ʿittim*, 43–44 [Hebr.] 1829.
Raveh, Inbar. *Feminist Rereadings of Rabbinic Literature*. Waltham, MA: Brandeis University Press, 2014.
——. "Open to Conquest: Prostitution – Temptation and Responses." In *Feminist Rereadings of Rabbinic Literature*, 100–115. Waltham, MA: Brandeis University Press, 2014.
Richler, Benjamin, and Malachi Beit-Arié. *Hebrew Manuscripts in the Vatican Library: Catalogue*. The Vatican: Biblioteca Apostolica Vaticana, 2008.
Rimmon-Kenan, Shlomith. *Narrative Fiction: Contemporary Poetics*. 2nd ed. London, New York: Routledge, 2002.
Ringer, Albert. "A Persecution was Decreed: Persecution as a Rhetorical Device in the Literature of the Geʾonim and Rishonim; Part 1." *European Journal of Jewish Studies* 6, no. 2 (2012): 183–206.

Roth, Norman. *Jews, Visigoths and Muslims in Medieval Spain: Cooperation and Conflict.* Leiden: Brill, 1994.
Rubenstein, Jeffrey. *Talmudic Stories: Narrative Art, Composition, and Culture.* Baltimore: The Johns Hopkins University Press, 1999.
Rustow, Marina. "Jews and the Islamic World: Transitions from Rabbinic to Medieval Contexts." In *The Bloomsbury Companion to Jewish Studies*, edited by Dean Phillip Bell, 90–120. London: Bloomsbury Academic, 2013.
Rutgers, Leonard V. "The Importance of Scripture in the Conflict between Jews and Christians: The Example of Antioch's Maccabean Martyrs." Chap. 1 in *Making Myths: Jews in Early Christian Identity Formation*, 19–48. Leuven: Peeters, 2009.
Safrai, Shmuel. "Dosa ben Harkinas." In *Encyclopaedia Judaica*, edited by Michael Berenbaum and Fred Skolnik, 5:760–761. Detroit: MacMillan Reference, 2007.
Samely, Alexander. *Forms of Rabbinic Literature and Thought.* Oxford: Oxford University Press, 2007.
———. *Profiling Jewish Literature in Antiquity: An Inventory, from Second Temple Texts to the Talmuds.* Oxford: Oxford University Press, 2013.
———. *Rabbinic Interpretation of Scripture in the Mishnah.* Oxford: Oxford University Press, 2002.
———. "War Scroll." In *Database for the Analysis of Anonymous and Pseudepigraphic Jewish Texts of Antiquity*, edited by Alexander Samely, Rocco Bernasconi, Philip Alexander, and Robert Hayward. http://literarydatabase.humanities.manchester.ac.uk.
Samely, Alexander, Philip Alexander, Rocco Bernasconi, and Robert Hayward. *Inventory of Structurally Important Literary Features in Ancient Jewish Literature (Version Zero).* Manchester, 2012. http://www.manchester.ac.uk/ancientjewishliterature.
Satlow, Michael. *Tasting the Dish: Rabbinic Rhetorics of Sexuality.* Atlanta, GA: Scholars Press, 1995.
Schmid, Wolf. *Narratology: An Introduction.* Translated by Alexander Starritt. Berlin, New York: De Gruyter, 2010.
Schofer, Jonathan Wyn. "Protest or Pedagogy? Trivial Sin and Divine Justice in Rabbinic Narrative." *Hebrew Union College Annual* 74 (2003): 243–278.
———. "Rabbinical Ethical Formation and the Formation of Rabbinic Ethical Compilations." In *The Cambridge Companion to the Talmud and Rabbinic Literature*, edited by Charlotte Elisheva Fonrobert and Martin S. Jaffee, 313–335. Cambridge, New York: Cambridge University Press, 2007.
Scholem, Gershom. *Jewish Gnosticism, Merkabah Mysticism, and Talmudic Tradition.* New York: Jewish Theological Seminary of America, 1960.
Secunda, Shai. *The Iranian Talmud: Reading the Bavli in its Sasanian Context.* Philadelphia, PA: University of Pennsylvania Press, 2014.
Shemesh, Rivka. "On the Narrative Discourse in Tannaitic Language: An Exploration of the maʿaseh and paʿam ʾachat Discourse Unit." *Hebrew Studies* 49 (2008): 99–125.
Shinan, Avigdor, and Yair Zakovitch. "Midrash on Scripture and Midrash within Scripture." *Scripta Hierosolymitana* 31 (1986): 257–277.
Simon-Shoshan, Moshe. *Stories of the Law: Narrative Discourse and the Construction of Authority in the Mishnah.* Oxford: Oxford University Press, 2012.
Spiegel, Shalom. "Introduction." In *Legends of the Bible*, by Louis Ginzberg. New York: Jewish Publication Society of America, 1956.

Stein, Dina. "Pirqe deRabbi Eliezer ve-Seder Eliyahu: heʿarot maqdimot ʿal poʾetiqa u-mercharv be-midrash ha-meʾuchar [Pirkei deRabbi Eliezer and Seder Eliyahu: Preliminary Notes on Poetics and Imaginary Landscapes]." *Jerusalem Studies in Hebrew Literature* 24 (2011): 73–92.
———. *Textual Mirrors: Reflexivity, Midrash, and the Rabbinic Self*. Philadelphia, PA: University of Pennsylvania Press, 2012.
———. "The Blind Eye of the Beholder: Tall Tales, Travelogues, and Midrash." Chap. 3 in *Textual Mirrors: Reflexivity, Midrash, and the Rabbinic Self*. Philadelphia, PA: University of Pennsylvania Press, 2012.
Stemberger, Günter. *Einleitung in Talmud und Midrasch*. 9th ed. Munich: C. H. Beck, 2011.
———. "Leviticus in Sifra." In *Judaica Minora II: Geschichte und Literatur des rabbinischen Judentums*, 477–497. Tübingen: Mohr Siebeck, 2010.
———. *Midrasch: Vom Umgang der Rabbinen mit der Bibel*. Munich: C. H. Beck, 1989.
———. "Münchhausen und die Apokalyptik: Bavli Bava Batra 73a–75b als literarische Einheit." In *Judaica Minora II: Geschichte und Literatur des rabbinischen Judentums*, 299–316. Tübingen: Mohr Siebeck, 2010.
Stern, David. "Forms of Midrash I: Parables of Interpretation." Chap. 2 in *Midrash and Theory: Ancient Jewish Exegesis and Contemporary Literary Studies*. Evanston, IL: Northwestern University Press, 1996.
———. *Midrash and Theory: Ancient Jewish Exegesis and Contemporary Literary Studies*. Evanston, IL: Northwestern University Press, 1996.
———. *Parables in Midrash: Narrative and Exegesis in Rabbinic Literature*. Cambridge, MA: Harvard University Press, 1991.
Stern, Sacha. "Attribution and Authorship in the Babylonian Talmud." *Journal of Jewish Studies* 45 (1994): 28–51.
———. "The Concept of Authorship in the Babylonian Talmud." *Journal of Jewish Studies* 46 (1995): 183–195.
Stone, Michael E. "Pseudepigraphy Reconsidered." *The Review of Rabbinic Judaism* 9 (2006): 1–15.
Stuckenbruck, Loren T. "Pseudepigraphy and First Person Discourse in the Dead Sea Documents: From the Aramaic Texts to the Writings of the Yahad." In *The Dead Sea Scrolls and Contemporary Culture*, edited by Adolfo Daniel Roitman, Lawrence H. Schiffman, and Shani Tzoref, 293–326. Leiden, Boston: Brill, 2011.
Teugels, Lieve. "Blending the Borders between Literature and Commentary, Interpretation and Self-Reflection: Metalepsis in Rabbinic Midrash." In *Metalepse in Text- und Bildmedien des Altertums*, edited by Ute E. Eisen and Peter von Möllendorff, 405–430. Berlin, Boston: De Gruyter, 2013.
Teugels, Lieve M. "The Contradictory Philosophical Lessons of the Parable of the Lame and the Blind Guards in Various Rabbinic Midrashim." In *From Creation to Redemption: Progressive Approaches to Midrash*, edited by W. David Nelson and Rivka Ulmer, 153–171. Proceedings of the Midrash Section 7. Piscataway, NJ: Gorgias Press, 2017.
The Holy Scriptures according to the Masoretic Text. Philadelphia, PA: Jewish Publication Society, 1917.
Thoma, Clemens, and Simon Lauer, eds. *Die Gleichnisse der Rabbinen*. 4 vols. Bern: Lang, 1986–2000.
———. *Pesiqta de Rav Kahana (PesK) : Einleitung, Übersetzung, Parallelen, Kommentar, Texte*. Vol. 1 of *Die Gleichnisse der Rabbinen*. Bern: Lang, 1986.

Thomas, Brownen. "Dialogue." In *The Cambridge Companion to Narrative*, edited by David Herman. Cambridge: Cambridge University Press, 2007.

Thorion-Vardi, Talia. *Das Kontrastgleichnis in der rabbinischen Literatur*. Frankfurt am Main: Lang, 1986.

Tirosh-Becker, Ofra. "The Use of Rabbinic Sources in Karaite Writings." In *Karaite Judaism: A Guide to its History and Literary Sources*, edited by Meira Polliack, 319–338. Leiden, Boston: Brill, 2003.

Towner, Wayne Sibley. *The Rabbinic "Enumeration of Scriptural Examples:" A Study of a Rabbinic Pattern of Discourse with Special Reference to Mekhilta D'R. Ishmael*. Leiden: Brill, 1973.

Urbach, Ephraim. "Le-sheelat leshono u-meqorotaw shel Sefer Seder Elijahu [On the language and the sources of Seder Eliyahu]." *Leshonenu* 21 (1956–1957): 183–197.

——. "Lesheelat leshono u-meqorotaw shel Sefer Seder Elijahu [On the Language and the Sources of Seder Eliyahu]." In *The World of the Sages*, 418–432. Jerusalem: Magnes Press, 2002.

Vidas, Moulie. *Tradition and the Formation of the Talmud*. Princeton, Oxford: Princeton University Press, 2014.

Volz, Paul. *Die Eschatologie der jüdischen Gemeinde*. Tübingen: Mohr, 1934.

Warhol, Robyn. "Feminist Narratology." In *Routledge Encyclopedia of Narrative Theory*, edited by David Herman, Manfred Jahn, and Marie-Laure Ryan, 161–163. London, New York: Routledge, 2005.

Weisberg, Dvora E. *Levirate Marriage and the Family in Ancient Judaism*. Waltham, MA: Brandeis University Press, 2009.

——. "Men Imagining Women Imagining God: Gender Issues in Classical Midrash." In *Agendas for the Study of Midrash in the Twenty-first Century*, edited by Marc Lee Raphael, 63–83. Williamsburg, VA: College of William and Mary, 1999.

——. "Women and Torah Study in Aggadah." In *Women and Judaism: New Insights and Scholarship*, edited by Frederick Greenspahn, 41–63. New York: New York University Press, 2009.

Werblowsky, R. J. Zvi. "A Note on the Text of Seder Eliyahu." *The Journal of Jewish Studies* 6 (1955): 201–211.

Wimpfheimer, Barry. *Narrating the Law: A Poetics of Talmudic Legal Stories*. Philadelphia, PA: University of Pennsylvania Press, 2011.

Wright, Addison. *The Literary Genre Midrash*. Staten Island, NY: Alba House, 1967.

Ziegler, Ignaz. *Die Königsgleichnisse des Midrash beleuchtet durch die römische Kaiserzeit*. Breslau: Schottlaender, 1903.

Zimmermann, Ruben. "Pseudepigraphie / Pseudonymität." In *Religion in Geschichte und Gegenwart: Handwörterbuch für Theologie und Religionswissenschaft*, edited by Hans D. Betz, Don S. Browning, Bernd Janowski, and Eberhard Jüngel, 1786–1788. Tübingen: UTB Mohr Siebeck, 2008.

Zucker, Moshe. *Al targum Saadya ben Gaon la-Tora: parshanut, halakha, u-polemiqa [Rav Saadya Gaon's Translation of the Torah]*. New York: Feldheim, 1959.

Zunz, Leopold. *Die gottesdienstlichen Vorträge der Juden, historisch entwickelt*. 2nd ed. Frankfurt am Main: J. Kauffmann, 1892.

——. *Ha-Derashot be-Yisraʾel: ve-hishtalshelutan ha-historit [Die gottesdienstliechen Vorträge der Juden historisch entwickelt]*. Edited by Chanock Albeck. Jerusalem: Bialik, 1974.

Zymner, Rüdiger. "Parabel." In *Historisches Wörterbuch der Rhetorik*, edited by Gert Ueding, vol. 6. Tübingen: Max Niemeyer, 2003.

Indices

Index of Subjects

A
actions
– representation of, 75
Adderet Eliyahu, 195, 198, 199
al tiqrey, 113
Alexandria, 93
ᶜ*am ha-arets*, 241, 242
amru chakhamim, 50, 262
amru statement, 130, 244, 245, 247, 248, 250, 251
analogy, 254
anonymity, 49, 50, 54
anti-Karaism, 17
apodictic statement, 62
Aramaic, 281
Arukh, 5, 7, 14, 33
authorship
– collective, 47, 52, 54
– individual, 28, 49, 54
Avot de Rabbi Natan, 230, 239

B
Babylonia, 13, 124
Baraita de R. Ishmael, 180
Baraq, 243, 248, 250, 251
bat qol, 240, 264, 272, 273
Bereshit Rabbah, 17, 33, 96

C
catchphrases, 213
chalitsah, 221
character
– collective body, 74, 185, 212
– God, 74
– individual human being, 74, 212
– scriptural, 255
– supernatural being, 74, 124
characterisation, 75
charity, 127
chronological notes, 7, 8

clean days, *see* white days
Codex Vat. ebr. 31, 4, 31, 50, 63, 264, 265
context, 22
co-text, 22
Ctesiphon, 118

D
David, 53, 66, 71, 93, 149
Deborah, 242–249, 251–255
– *Song of Deborah*, 250
dialogue, 75
direct discourse, 69, 212
direct speech, 34, 35, 75

E
eating blood
– prohibition against, 199
eating fat
– prohibition against, 200
Ekhah Rabbah, 88, 95, 258, 262, 268, 269, 277
Elijah (prophet), 6, 28–31, 33, 37, 43–48, 50
Eli's sons, 99
Elisha (prophet), 44
Enoch, Book of, 27
exegetical narrative, 257

F
Felicitas (Christian saint), 265
fictionality, 73, 281
first fruits, 29
focalisation, 77, 261
fox fables, 132

G
Gabriel (archangel), 242
Gehenna, 58, 59, 240
genre, 2
Geonim, 281

governing voice, 37, 38, 40, 45, 48–50, 52, 66, 70, 71, 75–77, 81, 82, 84, 85, 90, 94, 97, 101, 103, 112–114, 119, 124, 127, 129, 244, 255, 262

H
Hadrian, 94, 264, 265, 267
hagiography, 278
heave offering, 183
– metaphor, 183, 184
Heber, 251
Hebrew, 9, 12, 17, 281
Hechalot literature, 19
hekkesh ha-chippus, 193
homiletical discourse, 38

I
implied author, 50
implied reader, 42, 76
impulse, 59
impurity
– metaphor, 234
indirect discourse, 212
inner life
– representation of, 75
intermarriage, 124, 273
Ishmael's children, 12

J
Jael, 251
Jerusalem, 13
Jezebel, 246, 247
Judeo-Arabic, 281

K
Karaism, 176
– Rabbinic response to, 175–177, 182, 187, 190, 199
Karaite law, 195
Karaite rite, 180
kelal u-ferat, 179

L
land of Israel, 65, 124, 149, 151, 183, 193, 210, 267
Lappidoth, 243–246
Leah, 257, 261

lemma, 77, 83, 95, 111–113
lemmatic chain, 54
levirate marriage, 221, 276

M
maʿaseh, 203, 207, 272
maʿaseh be-, 88
martyrdom, 264, 273
mashal, 78–81, 84, 181, 190, 191, 212
– antithetical, 84
– exegetical, 82, 141–146, 189
– hypothetical, 84, 85
– king parables, 80
– meta-exegetical, 85, 155–161
– narrative-recapitulative, 86, 146–155
– poetology, 131
– question-answering, 87, 164–171
mashlu mashal, 87, 168
Megillat Achimaʿats, 66
Meshivat nefesh, 189
metalepsis, 38–40, 42
metathesis, 254
Midrash Mishlei, 175
midrashic woman, 262
mikan amru statement, 10, 50, 72, 93, 120, 149, 155, 186, 214, 234
Miriam, the daughter of Tanchum, 262, 265, 271–273, 278
Mishnat R. Eliezer, 175
monograph, 281
Mourners of Zion, 193

N
narratee, 76
narrative
– first person, 261
– first-person, 260
– homiletical-exegetical, 95–97, 111, 277
– metadiegetic, 123, 126, 215
– pseudo-historical, 262
– single event, 67–69
narrative level, 76, 122, 215, 216
narrative series, 103
narrativity, 23
narratology
– classical, 23, 260
– feminist, 220, 221

– post-classical, 23, 24
narrator
– autodiegetic, 120
– extradiegetic, 76
– first-person, 38, 120, 259
– heterodiegetic, 34, 120
– homodiegetic, 35
– intradiegetic, 123
– omniscient, 34
niddah, 206, 233, 234, 236, 238, 239, 277
nimshal, 88, 134–136, 139–141, 149, 154, 163, 166, 167, 170, 246

O
Otsar nechmad, 189

P
Pesiqta Rabbati, 9, 175, 271
petichah, 62
phraseology, 52
Pirqe de Rabbi Eliezer, 15, 17, 28
Pirqoi Ben Baboi, 13, 219
poetology, 22, 36
proof-text, 77
prostitute story, 240, 277
pseudepigraphy, 27, 28, 38, 49, 51
pun, 244, 252

Q
qal wa-chomer, 205, 214, 227, 256, 257, 271

R
Rachab, 241
Rachel, 255–262
repentance, 241
ritual immersion, 196

ritual slaughter, 197
Rome, 93
– allegory for, 8

S
Samuel Haida, 6
scripturalism, 219
Sefer dinim, 189
Sefer Machkimat Peti, 189
self-referentiality, 213
Shir ha-Shirim Rabbah, 88
Shulkhan Arukh, 195
Sifra, 5, 31
speech act, 71, 72
speech representation, 212
speech tags, 213
story-time, 75
suicide, 262, 264, 268, 273

T
Tanchuma, 17, 33, 175
tanna debe eliyahu-baraita, 55–58, 228
tetracolon, 53
text-time, 75

W
washing of hands, 194, 197
white days, 235
– story of, 226–228, 230

Y
Yavne, 13

Z
zav, 230, 239
zavah, 230, 237, 239

Index of Persons

A
Appelbaum, Alan, 80, 133, 135, 136, 142
Aptowitzer, Avigdor, 13, 17
Astren, Fred, 176

B
Bacher, Wilhelm, 8, 17, 175–177, 179, 180, 182, 184, 187, 194, 196, 198, 204–206, 215
Bakhtin, Mikhail, 120
Bal, Mieke, 260, 261
Baskin, Judith, 220, 236, 238, 241, 277, 278
Berzbach, Ulrich, 5, 19, 21
Borges, Jorge Luis, 51
Braude, William, 3, 19, 30
Brody, Robert, 181, 218
Budick, Sanford, 22

D
Drory, Rina, 18

E
Elbaum, Jacob, 16, 17
Eppenstein, Simon, 9
Erder, Yoram, 176

F
Fludernik, Monika, 74, 120
Fokkelman, Jan P., 73
Fonrobert, Charlotte E., 233, 234
Friedmann, Meir, 4, 5, 9, 10, 14–16, 21, 55, 242

G
Genette, Gérard, 38, 39, 42
Geula, Amos, 15
Ginzberg, Louis, 5, 14, 15, 37, 43
Goldberg, Arnold, 82, 132, 133, 135, 144, 145, 159, 173
Graetz, Heinrich, 8
Grice, Paul, 66
Güdemann, Moritz, 8

H
Hamburger, Käte, 74
Hartman, Geoffrey, 22
Hauptman, Judith, 220
Heinen, Sandra, 51
Herr, Moshe David, 2

I
Ilan, Tal, 220

J
Jaffee, Martin, 27, 52

K
Kadari, Adiel, 16
Kadushin, Max, 15, 16, 25, 30, 52, 191
Kapstein, Israel, 3, 30
Klein, Gottlieb, 9

L
Lanser, Susan, 220, 221
Lasker, Daniel, 198
Lavee, Moshe, 5
Lehmhaus, Lennart, 19, 176, 178, 210, 219
Lerner, Myron, 1, 27
Levinson, Joshua, 96, 97

M
Mann, Jacob, 10
Margulies, Mordechai, 10
Marienberg, Evyatar, 234
Meir, Ofra, 33–35, 42

N
Nemoy, Leon, 180, 197, 203
Neusner, Jacob, 62, 82, 88, 90, 91, 96

O
Ottenheijm, Eric, 133

R
Rapoport, Solomon, 7, 8
Rimmon-Kenan, Shlomith, 62, 73, 75, 261
Rutgers, Leonard V., 264

S
Samely, Alexander, 4, 37, 51, 54, 60
Scholem, Gershom, 19
Simon-Shoshan, Moshe, 60–62, 66, 69, 73, 113
Stein, Dina, 15, 35
Stemberger, Günter, 19, 35, 52, 180, 223
Stern, David, 3, 21, 22, 76, 79–81, 83, 89, 90, 95–97, 131, 133–135, 140, 152, 154, 155, 163, 169, 172, 174

T
Teugels, Lieve, 38, 158

U
Urbach, Ephraim, 14, 18

V
Voloshinov, Valentin, 120

W
Warhol, Robyn, 220
Werblowsky, Zwi, 2, 20

Z
Zucker, Moshe, 13, 17, 175, 176, 187, 198, 218
Zunz, Leopold, 1, 8, 175

Index of Rabbinic Authorities

A
Anan, 9, 29–31, 50
Aqiba, 49, 57, 222, 240, 242, 277
Ashi, 56

B
Benjamin b. Abraham ʿAnav, 11

C
Chanin b. Ammi, 229
Chanina, 129
Chanina b. Akshi, 49

D
Dimi, 228
Dosa b. Orkinas, 40, 91, 222, 276

E
Eleazar, 192
Eleazar b. Azariah, 49, 222
Eleazar b. Judah of Worms, 33
Eleazar b. Parta, 49
Eliezer (b. Hyrkanos), 28, 49, 94, 262
Eliezer b. Jacob, 49, 241

G
Gamaliel, 49, 194, 196

H
Hillel, school of, 222, 229

I
Isaac b. Joseph, 228
Ishmael, 82, 91, 93
Ishmael b. Eleazar, 49
Ishmael b. Elisha, 49

J
Jochanan, 35, 49, 91, 117, 122
Jochanan b. Bag Bag, 49
Jochanan b. Pinhas, 49
Jochanan b. Zakkai, 49, 68, 90, 117, 118, 122, 128
Jose, 35, 49, 117, 122
Jose the Galilean, 82
Joseph, 229, 237
Joshua, 49
Joshua b. Chananiah, 222, 223
Joshua b. Levi, 49
Joshua b. Qarcha, 91, 240
Judah, 237, 262, 270
Judah b. Tema, 57
Judah the Prince (Rabbi), 49, 129, 237

K
Kahana, 198

N
Nachman, 29
Natan, 49, 57, 90
Natan b. Yechiʾel, 33
Natronai b. Hilai Gaon, 1, 5, 14
Nehemia, 49
Nehorai, 193

O
Oshaia, 129

P
Papa, 57

R
Rav, 237

S
Samuel b. Nachman, 258
Seʿadyah Gaon, 6, 175, 281
Shammai, school of, 222, 229
Sherira Gaon, 7
Simeon, 49, 71, 93
Simeon b. Gamaliel, 49, 91, 229
Simeon b. Judah, 49
Simeon b. Laqish, 49

T
Tanchuma bar Abba, 271

Y
Yannai, 49

Z
Zadoq, 90
Zeira, 237

Index of Karaite Authorities

A
Anan b. David, 17

B
Benjamin al-Nahāwandī, 189

D
Daniel al-Qumisi, 13, 176, 218

E
Elijah Bashyatsi, 176, 195, 206

I
Ismael Okbari, 201

M
Meswi el-Safarani, 201

S
Sahl b. Matsliach, 176
Salmon b. Yerucham, 176

T
Tobias b. Moses ha-Avel, 189

Y
Yefet b. Eli, 176